STATE, MILITANCY AND HUMAN RIGHTS

A Study of Punjab (1980-95)

STATE, MILITANCY AND HUMAN RIGHTS

A Study of Punjab (1980-95)

MALKIT SINGH

REGAL PUBLICATIONS
New Delhi

STATE, MILITANCY AND HUMAN RIGHTS
A Study of Punjab (1980-95)

ISBN 978-81-8484-437-5

Typeset by
RAHUL COMPOSERS
New Highway Apartments, Lakshmi Niwas
760, Pocket-D, Lok Nayak Puram, New Delhi - 110 041

Printed in India at
MAYUR ENTERPRISES
WZ Plot No. 3, Gujjar Market, Tihar Village, New Delhi - 110 018

Published by
REGAL PUBLICATIONS
F-159, Rajouri Garden, New Delhi - 110 027
Phone : 45546396, 25435369
E-mail : regalbookspub@yahoo.com, regaldeepbooks@yahoo.com

Contents

Preface

Respect for human rights of every person is an inherent trait of man. The ethics for the protection of human rights like live and let live others and to create a harmony with the other to live a loveable and peaceful life was imparted to children in every household by way of moral and ethical value from the very beginning of human civilisation. With the development of civilization, new socio-religious norms emerged as the codes of the social stability and protector of peace and harmony among the different social sects. The king and the state were also treated as the part of the socio-religious and political set-ups of the religious order of the every civilization before the renaissance in the west. Although the rights of individuals were protected by some religious norms and ethics. However, the arbitrary use of power by the King and the state machinery was rampant in the name of divine rights of Kings.

The first assertion of the human rights and the example of curbing the dynastic privileges and the divine rights of the Kings can be traced back to the Magna Carta of 1215. Although it could not live longer and failed to deliver the promised rights to the subjects of England because Pope Innocent 3rd and King John again joined hands against this human rights instrument. But it started a journey of thinking of limiting the power of King and to rationalise the theory of the divine privileges of the King and Church in West. The Petition of Rights (1628), English Bill of Rights (1689), American Declaration of Independence (1776) and French Revolution (1789) were the assertions of the democratic rights in Europe and America for limited and responsible governments. The question of social security and the state responsibility towards the citizens welfare are further elaborated under the concepts of the Socialism, Marxism and the Second generation of human rights. The quality life and the clean environment along with the right to development are now becoming a serious concern for the democratic governance of the world.

On the other hand, the reporting on the working of state machinery is adverse to the protection of the human rights in the States are becoming the major violator of human rights. The State objectives or the democratic governance and welfare of the citizens are more or less vanishing these days and State is becoming a necessity for policing and judiciary. With the passing of time under contemporary circumstances the state and its law enforcing agencies became powerful and authoritarian; they consequently started the perpetration of inhuman treatment on the innocent people in the name of maintaining law and order. Police system bureaucracy, armed forces gradually became brutal and corrupt.

No doubt, anti-social elements have been there from very ancient time. Delinquents and criminals are part of every society since corruption has been part and parcel of human behaviour. The contemporary society is infested with criminal activities of all sorts. International conflicts, war, terrorism, illegal trade activities, occupation of weaker States by the powerful militia are the major concern of the human security. Then robberies, murder, crime against women smuggling and trafficking in women and children, etc. become a routine work for the State to control for the greater benefit of the society. It should be ensured that State's machinery works hard and develop the new mechanisms and laws to handle the organised crime successfully. But sometimes State agencies become corrupt and are more brutal than the criminals and use the state force for their personal and professional gains. Particularly in the extraordinary circumstances, like Terrorism, Maoism and armed rebellions for the autonomy can lead to circumstances where State agencies go beyond the legal and constitutional framework of the State. The past experiences have revealed that an illegal detention, arbitrary arrests, torture and inhuman treatment of detainees prisoners, under-trials, custodial deaths, fake encounters become rampant when the state agencies responses to extraordinary circumstance like the one it faced in Punjab recently, in Kashmir, Jharkhand, West Bengal, Odisha, Andhra Pradesh, etc. Earlier people did not have the voice against these. Now with judicial and media activism these cases frequently come to public notice and the concern for the international human rights organisations.

In the present book an attempt is made to collate vital information on human rights violation, various types of inhuman treatment like torture, custodial violence and custodial-deaths, disappearance, and police atrocities, etc. The rights of victims, statutory measures available and response of civil society and other salient issues are elaborately dealt with. The text is supported by facts and figures, case studies, court judgments, etc. The information is gathered under the following headings: Introduction; Torture: A Stigma on Civil Society; Pattern of Torture and Victims; Impunity: Condoning Custodial Violence; Custodial Violence; Causes and Concerns: Police Atrocities and Judicial Measures; Measures for Curbing Torture; Standards and Actions: Disappearances; Appendices; Glossary and Bibliography, etc.

We have drawn upon works of many experts in the field while collating the information. We express our gratefulness to all of them. Though every care is taken to furnish accurate information, there may have crept in some inaccuracies, which we will rectify if brought to our notice by learned readers. We are also grateful to our colleagues and friends for inspiring, guiding and assisting us in different stages of this work. Finally, we are thankful to our publishers for evincing interest in this and publishing it meticulously within shortest possible time.

At the last but not least our argument is that the better and progressive world can be ensured only by securing the human rights and human equality under all circumstances. Human history has been witness to great turmoil and disastrous consequences, as Punjab experiences reveals, whenever the violation of human rights has occurred. This book suggests that the protection and promotion of human rights is imperative for the furtherance of democracy and human security.

DR. MALKIT SINGH

9

Acknowledgements

During my study I have worked with a large number of people whose contribution in assorted ways to my research endeavor and particularly in making of the book deserve special mention. It is a pleasure for me to convey my gratitude to them in a humble way.

In the first place I would like to record my deepest gratitude to my supervisor Prof. Ashutosh Kumar, for his advice and guidance from the initial to the final stage of the study that encouraged me to pursue research on a subject I was always interested in. His constant inspiration and guidance to engage in research on actual problems encircled my growth as a student and as researcher. I am indebted to him more than he knows.

I am thankful to the large number of friends, classmates and the individuals, whom I hardly know, for helping me to enrich my knowledge about the ground realities of the autonomist movement, the resultant violence, state responses to the movement and use of counter-violence, the issue of violation of human rights in Punjab. The ground reality of the human rights violation was different from the social construction of the Khalistan movement by its leaders and academics on the one hand and by the Government of India on the other.

This thesis is not merely an academic exercise for me. As I was born and grew up in Punjab during the turbulent period of militancy, completion of Ph.D. was also a personal journey for exploring certain questions that have bothered me since my childhood days. As a Sikh child I was interacting with other Sikh children while listening often in glowing terms about the heroic acts of the militants in the school and in the village. I carried forward my concerns, regarding militancy and the resultant violation of human rights by both state as well as non-state actors during college days. It was a very crucial period in the political history of Punjab as the Sikh youth were being influenced by the pop-culture and the identity issue was wavering-off as a large number of rural youth particularly from the Jat-Sikh and Mazabhi-Sikh families were becoming clean-shaven and giving up the basic tenets of Sikhism. These were the two communities, which were more associated with the movement and suffered most than any community under the Sikhism. It was very crucial for an understanding of the underlying issues related to the movement and whether human rights were being violated and in which manner during and immediately after the collapse of movement in the Sikh-majority districts and also at the place to which the Sikh-guerillas called the liberated area. The college days were crucial to understand the perspective of the Sikh youths on state politics and religion after much of violence and blood-shed which ruined the state economy and dethroned it from number one state of India. There was also a wounded psyche.

Then came the university days in which I started reading the academic writings and discussing the ideological basis of the ethno-religious autonomist movement. I continued the search for field realities and the government's strategies to counter the movement and the issues regarding human rights during my Post-Graduation in Political Science at the Department of Political Science, Panjab University, Chandigarh. The quest for understanding the movement, Indian state and the issue of human rights as a social scientist took final shape when I decided to work on the violation of human rights in Punjab during the militancy for my M.Phil. and Ph.D. research. The interesting thing which has happened during this period was the joining of my job as lecturer in human rights at D.A.V. College for Girls, Yamunanagar. Yamunanagar is a neighbouring district-town of Punjab in the state of Haryana. It is city with Punjabi-culture and with majority of Punjabi Hindus and Sikh population. More importantly it is like a home to the displaced after Partition of Punjab in 1947 and of the Khalistan Movement, particularly from Amritsar and Gurdaspur districts of Punjab. The discussion on the reasons not only for their displacement and understanding of the movement but also of the stories of their resettlement in the adverse circumstances helped me a lot to understand the human rights movement from multiple angles.

I am also thankful to my friends like Bhagwant Singh, Karam Singh Jahbal, Advocate Simranjeet Singh, and my relatives who have helped me to conduct my field survey.

I am grateful to all my teachers—Professor Pam Rajput, Bhupinder Singh Brar, Prof. Ujjwal Kumar Singh, Prof. Sanjay Chaturvedi, Prof. Ronki Ram, Dr. Anupma Roy, Dr. Deepak K. Singh, Dr. Pampa Mukherji and Dr. Navjot Kaur who have contributed in their own way to the shaping of my research work. I am really thankful to them because they contributed to enrich my knowledge as a Masters Degree student and subsequently as a researcher.

I am also thankful to the other eminent scholars like Dr. Sushma Arya, Principal, D.A.V. College for Girls, Yamuna Nagar, Dr. Anil Dutta Mishra, Deputy Director, Gandhi Memorial Museum, Rajghat, New Delhi, Dr. Vishav Mohini, Director, Women Studies Centre, and Co-ordinator, U.G.C. Studies Centre, D.A.V. College of Girls, Prof. Yoginder Yadav and Sanjay Kumar of Lokniti, C.S.D.S., New Delhi, and Professor Surinder Singh Jodhka, Prof. Ranbir Samaddar, Prof. Pauala Banerjee, Prof. Samir Kumar Das, Prof. Sabyasachi Basu Roychaudhuri, among others in Calcutta Research Group who gave me time for a valid discussion and suggested me the relevant books.

Special thanks are reserved for all friends and family members for the moral support.

MALKIT SINGH

1

Introduction

THINKING ABOUT STATE, MILITANCY AND HUMAN RIGHTS

Human rights refer to "the basic rights and freedoms", to which all humans are entitled, often held to include the right to life and liberty, freedom of thought and expression, and equality before the law. Human rights are concerned with the dignity of human beings. They underline the critical need to ensure that human beings ought to maintain a level of self-esteem that would promote a sense of community among them. In the present post-Soviet world order, they are increasingly being thought to be the grammar of political governance in a polity. This must not be denied by any government irrespective of it being of any form. Articles 1 and 2 of Universal Declaration of Human Rights (UDHR) states in universal terms: "all human beings are born free and equal in dignity and rights" and that "everyone is entitled to all rights set forth in this "Declaration", without distinction of any kind, such as race, colour, sex, language, religion, political or other opinion, nation or social origin, property birth or other status."[1]

The importance and the scope of Human Rights has been increasing day-by-day as they get strengthened through the institutional and constitutional mechanisms which have developed under the auspices of United Nations (UN) especially during the last half of the Twentieth Century. Now they have become the utmost concern of the International Relations. The promotion and the protection of human rights has always remained the focus of the UN. Hence, over the years numerous peace accords have been signed and decisions made on conflict-zones.[2] The burgeoning of literature and the enactment of large number of international Human rights laws have provided them with a global platform. Arguably in the present age of globalization, they are claimed to be a universal entity which is beyond and above of the boundaries of the States.

Although as a subject of international activism and politics Human rights are not an age-old phenomenon and their evolution can be traced back to the rhetoric of Second World War and to Universal Declaration of Human Rights (1948), however, as a concept as an idea, human rights evolved throughout the history of mankind. They were intricately tied to the laws, customs and religion throughout the ages of human civilization.[3] In much of history, people acquired rights and responsibilities through their membership in a family, group, religion, class, community and of state. Most of the human societies and civilizations have had traditions similar to the "golden rule" of "Do unto others as you would have them do unto you." The Hindu Vedas, the Babylonian Code of Hammurabi, the Bible, the quran, and the Analects of Confucius are five of the oldest written sources which address questions of people's duties, rights, and responsibilities. In fact, all societies, whether in oral or written tradition, have had systems of propriety and justice as well as ways of tending to the health and welfare of their members.[4]

It is unfortunate that human life and dignity have been disregarded and subjected to violations throughout the human history. One can substantiate this with the stark examples of slave-trade, racism, caste and gender discrimination, etc. Twentieth century, however, can be contrasted with the previous centuries for its contribution to the development of Human rights. It was only after the Second World War that a systematic mechanism for the promotion and protection of Human rights started to develop at the globe. But it does not mean that there were no rights or no demands upon the rights before the twentieth century. A cursory glace over the history of the Human Civilization can prove that both the individuals and groups used to have with them a written guarantee of rights many centuries before the twentieth century. It is important to note that some of the historians placed the "Magna Carta" of 1215 and the concept of "rule of law", which developed during the Roman Empire as the starting points for the "first generation" of rights.

However, these rights were limited to certain individuals and groups keeping in mind racial, religious, nationality caste and gender, etc. boundaries.[5] Only a hundred years ago more than half of the World was under the colonial rule. Not all citizens had the right to franchise. The state terrorism operated with impunity. Non-interference in the internal affairs of the other countries was the order of the day. The systematic homicide of Jews in Germany and massacre of innocent Japanese civilians by the dropping nuclear bombs were not protested against. There was no profound mechanism and law that could check the "rough states" from committing the inhuman acts of genocide, apartheid and violence against minorities before the establishment of UN.[6]

It was only during the Second World War that the human rights discourse received a considerable space in the mainstream politics. The issue of violation of human rights by the Nazist and Fascist regimes and protection of human rights in future from rouge and apartheid regimes was on the main agenda of Alliance forces. The eight principles of the Atlantic Charter and the address of American President Roosevelt to the American Congress confirmed that the post-World War World was in conformity with certain human rights to ensure the freedom of individual and community against the apartheid and dictatorial governments.[7]

The real and effective development of Human rights at the international level can only be traced back to the establishment of U.N. and the adoption of the UN Charter in 1945. The progressive steps taken by the U.N. to strengthen the human rights at the global level and to secure a valuable space for individual rights against any arbitrary act of the governments can be traced back to the UN General Assembly Declaration of Human Rights on 10 December, 1948.[8] It was followed by a "Bill of Rights" and a large number of Treatises, Covenants and Human Rights Laws, which supplemented the Bill of Rights.[9]

It can be said that the struggle for the protection of human rights which started against the dynastic privileges and arbitrary use of power with the signing of Magna Carta (1215)[10] and containing the dynastic privileges of the King by the passing of the Bill of Rights (1689) by the British Parliament. The new found democratic principles of equality, sovereignty and the individual rights were furthered by the French Revolution (1789), and the resultant Declaration of the Rights of Man and Citizen[11], American Declaration of Independence and the American Bill of Rights.[12] A new dimension and the economic aspect of the individual rights was duly emphasised by the Socialist and Marxists thinkers. A Socialist Charter and the rights of the working class under the Socialist and Marxist society, Declaration of the Rights of the Working and Exploited People was issued by the All-Russian Congress of Soviet after the Bolshevik Revolution.[13] The scope and importance of the human beings has been enlarged to an extent that they have been entered into the third stage and the problem regarding the post-material needs and quality of life has been connected to the human rights in the last decades of the twentieth century.[14]

Thus the last half of twentieth century saw a revolutionary growth in the field of Human rights. More importantly, the developments at regional level like (Inter-American Human Rights System, European human rights system, African Human Rights System and the Arab Human Rights System) with their own regional mechanism of implementing and monitoring of Human Rights proved more effective with the establishment of United Nations Human Rights Commission by the General Assembly of UN. This resulted in the developments like the National Human Rights Commissions.[15] These have been important developments during the last decade of the Twentieth Century. More recently, the long demand of the developing countries for more democratic functioning and to decrease influence of "super-power" on the functioning of Human rights bodies of UN has been fulfilled by the creation of United Nations Human Rights Council in 2006.[16] These remarkable developments in the last half of the twentieth century took place in the history of Human rights. That is why the then Secretary General of UN, Boutros Boutros-Ghali, while making his inaugural remarks at Vienna Conference of Human Rights in 1993 called the Twentieth century as the 'age of rights'.[17]

Cultural relativism and the notion of time and space in different generations and societies regarding the birth and development of Human rights have led to multiple dimensions and multiple definitions of Human rights. This has created a lot of ambiguities and confusions regarding the birth and development of human rights. However, in their historic classification Human rights can be categorized into "three generations" of rights. The First generation of "Red Rights" (Civil and Political rights) is associated with the enlightenment, Magna Carta, English, American and French Revolutions these include the right to life, liberty, property, freedom of speech, religion and worship, etc.[18] The Second generation rights dubbed as "Blue Rights" (socio-cultural and economic rights) is associated with Socialism, Marxism and the Bolshevik Revolution of Russia. This generation of rights includes the right to be employed, right of health care, as well as social-security and unemployment benefit, etc.[19] Finally, the recent world has been witness of the advent of third generation of rights dubbed as "Green Rights" which essentially address the rights of the collective.[20]

Despite the confusion and ambiguities regarding the development of the idea of human rights from the antiquity, the state is viewed as the protector and also as the violator of human rights by the political theorists.[21] The concept of rights or 'human rights', therefore, originates from the voice of protest against oppression perpetrated by the dominant groups in any society, rights are meant to safeguard the individuals from the irresponsible and arbitrary use of power by the ruling class.[22]

Although conflict for the individual rights commences with the birth in one's own family, but the responsibility of protecting the individuals' rights inside as well as outside the home ultimately relies on the state. Simultaneously, the conflict over the protection and violation of individual and community rights is more between the civil society and state rather than any other organisation of the society. The very beginning of the rights of the individual and the other socio-religious organisation started with the defining of their sphere of rights and the sphere of state functioning. The "Magna Carta" of 1215, the first-ever written document in the history of human rights holds the same. Further developments in the human rights took place by delimiting the regal authority with the emergence of the parliamentarian politics in England. Although the Bill of Rights, 1689 was a direct attempt to contain the regal authority from using the inheriting privileges, but in other way it was of limiting the arbitrary powers of the government functionaries. The sphere of the state and the individual rights was further elaborated by the new concept of the Separation of Power and the American Declaration of Independence (1776) that was to be followed by the French Revolution.

At this moment, the established tradition and the state (and its sphere) became the main point of discussion of political philosophers/scholars. The most pertinent questions, which were raised by scholars at that time, were related to the nature of state. How and why the institution of state came into existence? What is the relevance of the state? These questions were followed by the different theories of state dominate the scene of political theory. The three contractualist theorists (Hobbes, Locke and Rousseau) established a link between the social contract and the rights of individuals. However, they projected the different conditions and circumstances of the signing of "social contract". They were agreed that there was a "state of nature" that existed before the social contract and individuals enjoyed some of the "natural rights" even before the social contract or state came into existence. The linking of social utility of state and the rights established that rights are a *priori* to the state and the state must not violate them.[23] Locke argued that the right to life, liberty and property are the absolute and inalienable rights of individual and the state cannot claim upon them. In fact, the "social contract" that led to the formation of state came into existence only for the protection of these rights. So they are prior to the state is not state prior to them.[24]

VIOLATION OF HUMAN RIGHTS AND THE STATE

Violation of human rights occurs when the actions of state or non-state actors abuse, ignore or deny basic human rights (including civil, political, culture, social and economic rights). Furthermore, violations of human rights can occur when any state or non-state actor breaches any part of the UDHR treaty or other international human rights or humanitarian law. With regard to human rights violations of United Nations laws, Article 39 of the United Nations Charter designated the UN Security Council (or an appointed authority) as the only tribunal may determine UN human rights violations. Human rights abuses are reported by United Nations committees, national institutions and government and by many independent non-government organizations, such as Amnesty International, International Federation of Human Rights, Human Rights Watch, World Organisation Against Torture, Free House, International Freedom of Expression Exchange and Anti-Slavery International and many non-governmental and semi-governmental organizations working at the national levels to protect and preserve human rights. These organisations collect evidence and documents of alleged human rights abuses and apply pressure on the state to enforce human rights laws.

HUMAN RIGHTS AND THE INDIAN STATE

The Constitution of India claimed to be one of the most democratic and rights-based constitution in the world. In fact, the democratic porject of realising social justice along with the substantive rights of the citizens was launched by the Indian state through the state-sponsored polity and economy via a model of mixed economy immediately after the Independence.

In the Objective Resolutions, the Constituent Assembly declared its firm resolution to proclaim India as an independent, sovereign Republic. This resolution formed the basis for the incorporation of various Human rights values in various provisions of the Constitution but also in its preamble. Nehru in his concluding remarks said that the objective of the Assembly was not only to free India through a new Constitution, but also to feed starving people and cloth and naked masses and to give every Indians fullest opportunity to develop themselves according to their capacity. Radha Krishna also emphasized that there must be a socio-economic revolution not only to satisfy the fundamental needs of a common man but to bring about a fundamental change in the structure of Indian Society.

When the Indian Constituent Assembly met to draft and adopt the constitution of free India, the UDHR had already been adopted. The impact of the UDHR on the drafting of Indian Constitution was natural. The Constituent Assembly was unanimous in including all Human rights, political, civil, economic, cultural and social and fundamental rights. However, in what shape and what form should they be included was a matter of considerable debate and discussion among the members. Ultimately, a compromise was struck which clearly bore the stamp of UDHR as these rights were divided into two parts: (1) Civil and Political Rights: (2) Social and Economic Rights. The former set of rights termed as Fundamental Rights was enshrined in Part (Three) and the later of rights called Directive Principles of State Policy were enshrined in the Part Four of the Constitution. The basic distinction between the Fundamental Rights and Directive Principles is that the former are justifiable while the latter are not justifiable in the Court of Law. However, Directive Principles are as much part of the Constitution as the Fundamental Rights. The state is duty-bound to give them effect. They are in a sense a command to the state to bring about necessary conditions so that they could become effective. This distinction between the fundamental rights and DP is perfectly in line that went into the preparation and application of the UDHR.

The Preamble of the Constitution of India declares that the people of India have solemnly resolved to constitute India into

Sovereign Secular Democratic Republic and to secure to all its citizens Justice: social, economic and political: Liberty of thought, expression, belief faith and worship; Equality; assuring the dignity of the individual and unity and integrity of nation.

Promulgation of the Constitution of India on January 26, 1950 was a watershed in the history of the concept of Human rights in India. The Preamble, Fundamental Rights and Directive Principles of the State combined together provide the basic of human rights for the people of India. Democratic socialism spelt out in the Preamble and the Directive Principles meant to provide the context in which the fulfillment of Fundamental Rights has to be achieved. While Fundamental Rights stressed on the existing rights, Directive Principles provides the dynamic movement towards the goal of Providing Human rights for all. To enable the Citizens to enjoy human rights, many pieces of social legislation have been enacted over the past 60 years. In addition to these the Supreme Court of India through judicial interpretation, has widen the horizons of Human rights in India.

HUMAN RIGHTS AND FUNDAMENTAL RIGHTS UNDER INDIAN CONSTITUTION

The Fundamental Rights incorporated in the Constitution of India are as under:

(1) Right to equality (Arts. 14-18)
(2) Right to Freedom (Arts. 19-22)
(3) Right against Exploitation (Arts. 23-24)
(4) Right to Freedom of Religion (Arts. 25-28)
(5) Cultural and Education Religion (Arts. 29-30)
(6) Right to Constitutional remedies (Arts. 32-35)

Part 4th: Directive Principles of State Policy (Art. 3)

In contrast to Part III of the constitution, representing Civil and Political Rights i.e., economic, social and cultural rights, the stress of civil and political rights has been on the individual (existing) rights, whereas the Directive Principles are aimed at providing, in a progressive manner, certain economic and social rights for the betterment of the individual as an integral component of the society.

Article 37 of the constitutional dealing with the application of the Directive Principles of the State Policy (DPSP) in this part explicitly makes these principles non-enforceable in any court of law, but 'fundamental in the governance of the country' by making the state duty bound to apply them in making laws. They serve as the guidelines for action on the part of all the three organs of the state. If the state takes any action which is contrary to the DP then the same may be declared as unconstitutional.

Thus like the economic, social and cultural rights contained in International Covenant on Economic, Social and Cultural Rights (ICESCR), the economic and social rights provide in Part 4 of the Constitution do not impose an immediate obligation on the state, as the DRPS are themselves guidelines for future programme of action.

Articles 38 and 39 of the Constitution both have the objectives of securing a 'welfare State'. Article 38 provides that State would be securing a social order for the promotion of welfare of the people.

(1) The state shall strive to promote the welfare of the people by securing and protecting as well as effectively as it may a social order in which Justice; social, economic and political shall inform the institutions of national life.

(2) The state shall, in particular, strive to minimize inequalities in income and endeavour to eliminate inequalities in status facilities and opportunities, not only amongst individuals but also amongst the groups of people residing in deferent areas or engaged national life. [25]

The above article reflects the spirit of Articles 22 and 28 of the UDHR Clause (2) of the Article, which was added by the Constitution (Forty-Four), Amendment Act, 1978, is also in consonance with 2 and 3 of ICESCR.

Article 39 provides certain principles of policy to be followed by the state–The state shall in particular direct to its policy towards securing:

(a) That the citizens, men and women equally, have the right to an adequate means of livelihood;

(b) That the ownership and control of material resources of the community are to be distributed as to sub-serve the common good;

(c) That the operation of the economic system does not result in the concentration of the wealth and means of production to the common detriment;

(d) That there is equal pay for both men and women;

(e) That health and strength of workers, men and women and tender age of children are not forced by economic necessity to enter avocation unsuited to their age or strength; and

(f) Those children are given opportunities and condition of freedom and dignity and that childhood and youth or protected against exploitation and against moral and material abandonment.[26]

Clause 39 (a) added by the constitution 42nd Amendment Act, (1976) Equal justice and free legal aid the state shall secure that the operation of legal system promotes justice, on the basis of equal opportunity, and shall, in particular provided free legal aid, by suitable legislation or schemes or in any other way, to ensure that opportunities for securing justice are not denied too any citizen by reason of economic or other disabilities.

This article is rich enough in terms of its Human rights content. Clause (a) puts obligations on the state to secure to the citizens adequate means of livelihood. The Supreme Court has interpreted this clause as part of article 21 of the constitution. The state may not be compelled to provide adequate means of livelihood. But any person, who is deprived of his right to livelihood except according to just fair and reasonable procedure established by law, can challenge the deprivations offending the right to life confessed by Article 21 of the constitution. In view of this interpretation, the Clause advances the object of article 3 of the UDHR and article 6 of International Covenant on Civil and Political Rights (ICCPR).

Clause (b) and Clause (c) promote the objective of establishing a social welfare state where there is no concentration of wealth in the hands of few are necessary tools for the attainment of equalitarian order and provides socio-economic justice to the people of India.

The corresponding provision regarding "agrarian reforms" and "equal distribution" is found in article 11 'clause 2 (a) and (b)' of the ICESCR.

Clause 39(d) provides for 'equal pay for equal work' for both men and women, the corresponding provision is article 23(2).

Clause 39(e) aims at protecting the health and strength of workers, men and women and tender age of children, is in consonance with the right to life.

Clause 39(f) expects the state to direct its policies in such a manner and in condition of freedom and dignity, which are their basic Human rights.

The right to seek justice is important human right and article 39 A—enables the people to enjoy this right.[27]

Articles 41 to 43 of the Indian Constitution provides as under:

Article 41 provides the important rights like right to work, to education and to public assistance in certain case. The state shall within limits of its economic capacity and development, make effective provision for securing that right to work, to education and to public assistance in cases of unemployment, old age, sickness and disablement, in other cases of undeserved want.

Article 42 provides provision for just and human condition of work and maternity relief—the state shall make provision for securing just and human condition of work and maternity relief.

Article 43 provides for the living wage, etc. for the workers – the state shall endeavour to secure, by suitable legislation or economic organization or in any other way, to all workers: agriculture, industry or otherwise, work ensuring decent standard of life and full enjoyment of leisure and social cultural opportunities and in particular, the state shall endeavor to promote cottage industries an individual or co-operative basis in rural area.

These articles correspond to articles 23 and 25 of the UDHR and articles 6, 7 and 10 (2) of ICESCR.

Article 43-A deals with the participation of workers in management of industries, it was added by the constitution (forty-second) amendment Act. This provision is based on individual democratic principles, in consonance with a conception Man and Human rights.[28]

Article 45 of the constitution provides free and compulsory education for children—the state shall endeavor to provide, within a period of ten years from the commencement of this constitution, for and compulsory education for all children until the age of fourteen year.

This provision corresponds to article 26 of the UDHR and articles 13 and 14 of the ICESCR.

Article 46 of the constitution also says that the state shall promote the educational and economic interest of scheduled castes and weaker section of the people.[29]

Raising the level of nutrition and standard of living and the improvement of public health is considered a primary duty of the state. Article 47 of the constitution provides that it is the duty of the state to raise the nutrition and standard of living and to improve public health. The state shall regard the raisin the level of nutrition and standard of living of its people and improvement of public health as among its primary duties and in particular, the state shall endeavor to bring about probation of the consumption of alcohol except for medicinal purposes, of intoxicating drinks and drugs which are injurious to health.[30]

SOME OTHER CONSTITUTIONAL PROVISIONS

The following provisions of the constitution are also worth noting for their Human rights content.

Article 226 provides that the High Courts are empowered to issue certain writs: notwithstanding anything on Article 32 every High Court shall have power, throughout the Indian territories in relation to which it exercise jurisdiction, to issue any person or authority, including in appropriate cases, and Government within those territories directions, order of writs, including *Mandamus*, Prohibition, *Quo Warranto*, and Certiorari, or any of them, for the enforcement of any of the rights conferred by Part III and for any other purpose.

This Article advances the object of Article 8 of the UDHR providing for the right to effective remedy. In fact, Article 226 together with Article 32 provides effective machinery for the enforcement of fundamental rights.[31]

Article 300A: Persons not to be deprived of his/her property protected by the authority of law.

This Corresponds to the provisions of the Article 17 of the UDHR.

Article 325: No person to be ineligible for inclusion in or to be included in a special electoral role on grounds of religion, race, caste. There shall be one general electoral role for every territorial constituency for elections to either house of Parliament or to the House of Legislature of a State and no persons shall be ineligible for inclusion in any role or claim to be included in any special electoral role for any such constituency on grounds only of religion, caste, sex or any of them.

Articled 326 of the constitution provides with the provisions of the election of the House of the People and the Legislative Assemblies of the States to be on the basis of the adult suffrage.

The elections to the House of the People and to the Legislative Assembly of every State shall be on the basis of adult suffrage, that is to say, every person who is a citizen of India and who is not less than eighteen years of age on such date as may be fixed in that behalf by or under any law made by the appropriate legislature and is not otherwise disqualified under this constitution or any law made by appropriate legislature on the grounds of non-residence, unsoundness of mind crime or corruption or illegal practice, shall be entitled to be registered as a voter at any such election.

Articles 325 and 326 both advance the object of the Article 21 (1) of the UDHR and Article 25 of the ICCPR.[32]

It follows that the Fundamental Rights and the Directive Principles of State Policy and Articles 226, 330-A, 325 and 326 together make elaborate provisions for the International Human rights standard in the original constitution of India.

DEVELOPMENT OF HUMAN RIGHTS LAWS AFTER THE PROCLAMATION OF INDIAN CONSTITUTION

Keeping its commitment towards the promotion and protection of Human rights and taking the new challenges for the human equality and dignified life to all its citizens, the Indian Parliament enacted a number of new laws and established Commissions for the protection of weaker section of the society. It also modified or amended some of provisions of the original Constitution, where it felt that those provisions and laws are becoming hindrance in the social and economic justice, which were proclaimed while adopting the Constitution of independent India. Some of the Constitutional and legal measures are as follows:

(a) Dowry Prohibition Act, 1961.

(b) Commission of Sati (Prevention) Act, 1987.

(c) National Commission for Scheduled Castes and Tribes.
Article 338 of the Constitution requires the constitution of National Commissions for STs and SCs for the better protection of the rights of the two communities.

(d) National Commission for Minorities.
An Act to constitute a National Commission for the Minorities for the better protection of the rights of Minorities was established in 1992.

(e) National Commission for Women Act 1998.
An Act to constitute a National Commission for Women for the better protection of the rights of the Women.

(f) Protection of Civil Liberties Act was enacted in 1995.
Under Article 17 of the Constitution, untouchability is abolished and its practice in any form is forbidden. By this

Act enforcement of any disability arising out of untouchability has been made a punishable offence.

(g) Scheduled Castes and Scheduled Tribes (Prevention of Atrocities) Act 1989.

This Act was enacted to prevent the commission of atrocities against the Members of the Scheduled Castes and Scheduled Tribes and it also provided for the Constitution of Special Court for Trail.

(h) Employment of Manual Scavengers and Construction of Dry Latrines (Prohibition) Act, 1993.[33]

Assuring the dignity of individual and fraternity among the communities are one of the objects proclaimed in the Preamble of Constitution. Article 47 requires the State to raise the standard of living and improve the health of the people. This Act has been enacted to achieve these objectives. It provides for the protection of all manual scavengers as well as the construction or continuation of dry latrines and for the regulation of the construction and maintenance of water-seal latrines.

HUMAN RIGHTS AND INDIAN POLITICS AFTER THE ADOPTION OF CONSTITUTION

After briefly referring to reading the historic and political background of the Human rights development in India anyone can be convinced that "everything is fine" with the state of human rights in India. However, any discernible observer and analyst can note somewhat contradictory provisions to Human rights and civil liberties under the same Constitution. These contradictions and curtailments of civil liberties and fundamental rights have been justified to tackle the emergency conditions threatening the larger interest and the questions of national unity and integrity. Nevertheless, these provisions deprive a citizen of his rights. There are some eminent social scientists and legal luminaries who have thought in other way. They argue that these provisions are against a democratic set-up and made the Indian Constitution an authoritative and undemocratic Constitution. They argue that the absolute powers of the legislature as mandate by the Constitution on which the legislature can deny the basic rights to the people by mere stroke of pen have left no scope for the full enjoyment of Civil Liberties and Fundamental Rights in India.[34]

CONSTITUTION AND HUMAN RIGHTS: A CRITICAL ANALYSIS

The Constitution has clothed almost all the rights in the Part III embodying Fundamental Rights in such phraseology that they are susceptible to diverse and contradictory interpretation. They are capable of being made non-functional in the larger context of arrangement provided to other parts of the Constitution itself. As Upendra Baxi in his celebrated work titled *Crisis of the Indian Legal System*[35] writes that the inclusion of parallel "Preventive Detention System" embodied in the Constitution itself has created a situation where it negates all rights provided in the preamble and Part III and IV of the Constitution. These rights can be curtailed to the extent of extinction by legislature and by the Presidential ordinances as per the provision of constitution itself. The 'rule of law' can be subverted. Right to a judicial scrutiny of the action of the executive can be extinguished. Rule by ordinance can be perpetuated. Elected governments can be overthrown. Emergency can be imposed. Even the right to free election can be negated by provisions of the very constitution by which we swear.[36] The schedule 7, list 3, at Entry 3 will convince a discerning citizen that all for the enjoyment of human rights. It gives power under the Concurrent List to both the Union and the State Governments to legislate for Preventive Detention for reasons connected with the security of State, the maintenance of public order, or the maintenance of supplies and services essential to the community.

To begin with Article 22 of the Fundamental Rights as part of the constitution, it not only allows preventive detention but also find merits in the non-disclosure of ground of detention to the condemned person if detaining authority considers it against the public interest to disclose. Then in Articles 352 to 362, there are "emergency" provisions by which the President by a proclamation can declare "Emergency", when even already 'truncated' Fundamental Rights, as mentioned can be suspended. In addition, under Article 368, the Constitution can be amended by the Parliament and for the benefit of citizens and removal of doubts all pervading powers of Parliament, it is laid down in Article 368 (5); "It is hereby declared that there shall be no limitation whatever on the constitution power of Parliament to amend by any way of addition variation or repeal the provision of the constitution under this Article."[37]

In addition, under Article 371-A, 371-B, 371-C and 371-F of the Constitution of India, special provisions are allowed in respect of states of Nagaland, Assam, Manipur, Hill areas and Sikkim, whereby Governors of respective states are given extraordinary powers and "special responsibilities" with respect to the "law and order". The Governor's "individual judgment" is supreme in respect of law and order in these States and this unbridled power of life and death over the citizen is given to an individual, under our democratic constitution.[38]

The right to Peaceful Assemblies, March and Demonstration can also be denied by the section 141 (of the Indian Penal Code, under chapter entitled of Offence against the Public Tranquility). The control of political assemblies is seen as part of general police function of keeping the peace. The problem posed by political demonstration is regarded as analogous to those posed by a riotous mob, of football fans. The laws applicable are the same for all. It designates that the assembly of five or mere persons is unlawful assembly, if the common object of such person is among other things "to resist the execution of any law, or any legal process". Thus, a protest demonstration against a law, which may be considered unfair by protestors, can be turned into an offence against public tranquility and hence a law and order problem. Again section 129 of the Code of Criminal Procedure, 1979 (which corresponds to section 127 of the code of 1898), empowers any police officer, not below the rank of sub-inspector to disperse any assembly of five or more persons which is likely to cause a disturbance of public peace. "Section 144 of the same Code, is quite frequently restored by the authorities to ban political assemblies. The power of the Delhi Police Commissioner to prohibit any assembly or procession whenever and for such time as he consider such prohibition to be necessary under the section 30 of Delhi Police Act, 1978, is used almost indiscriminately around the Parliament House during Parliament Sessions.[39]

HUMAN RIGHTS AND POLITICAL GOVERNANCE AFTER THE INDEPENDENCE

A number of scholars in their respective works have pointed out that the violation of the Human rights has been perpetuated at the very beginning of Indian Republic.[40] The founder of the Constitution of India denied the basic socio-economic rights when they included these rights into the non-justifiable non-forceable Part IV of the Directive Principles of the State Policy, rather than in the

Part III of the Fundamental rights. It has been facilitating the assault on the democratic rights as a routine in the political governance of independent India. They viewed that colonial practices of divide and rule are adopted by the political elites of India even after the long time of independence. Eminent social scientists like Randhir Singh, Rajni Kothari, Upendra Baxi, A.R. Desai, Bipan Chandra have argued that the decline of Indian politics and the crisis of political governance have been sinisterly designed into the communal politics by the political elite in India. In this context the notion of nation and national identity are hegemonically dependent on the idea of the 'enemy within'. Randhir Singh in his *"Five Lectures in Marxist"* mode wrote that the failure of the Statist model of development, the administrative corruption and the failure of plan and plan holidays plans not only enhanced the distance between the political leadership and people also alienated the masses from the nation-building project or the ideals of the freedom struggle. Further the communalization of politics and chauvinist nationalism of the ruling class has divided the Indian society into different groups. The electoral politics has been dominated by bigotry slogan like "are you for National Unity or Anti-Nationalist, for Nation or ULFA and for Reservation or Anti-Reservation, etc.? He further argues that the decline of politics and the division of people have not only helped the political elite to deny the basic rights to the people but it also strengthens state repression.[41]

The ruling class has been allegedly in alliance with the bourgeoisies for negating the issues of development and welfare issues by converting the development issues into the communal politics. The demand of the people for the democratic social and economic rights, like right to health, education and livelihood has been converted into the divisive politics of caste and religion. The basic demand and the struggle for the basic rights of the people have been dealt as the law and order problem. The vitiation of the social environment and chauvinistic nationalism has always helped political elite to oppress the political opposition and to convert the democratic struggles into law and order problem.[42]

The communalization of state machinery and often alleged connivance of the local administration with the communal forces into the communal violence against the Minorities in India in the last 64 years has further enrooted the crisis to the minority rights. The vitiation of social environment and political use of the "chauvinistic nationalism" and the communal use of the state forces not only threaten the minority rights but it also result into the crisis of political governance. The armed secessionist movements in different parts of India demanding socio-economic and political justice can be seen as the result of the crisis of the political governance in India.[43]

HUMAN RIGHTS AND EXTRAORDINARY LAWS

It has been argued that the rule by the ordinance and the practice of the extraordinary laws to suppress the political opposition, which have been started by the founding fathers of Indian Constitution, has become a permanent feature of the Indian politics. The first Preventive Detention Act was passed by the Congress immediately coming into power after the first election to suppress the political opposition particularly the left. Although this black law was universally condemned but it set a precedent which resulted into the linking of extraordinary laws with the permanent legal system in India. The political crises either internal or external have always been dealt with the help of extraordinary laws. The Preventive Detention Act of 1950 was followed by Defence of India Rules in 1962 in the wake of India and China war was the replica of similar rules enacted during the World War IInd by the British government and sanctioned detention without Trial. The Preventive Detention Act of 1950 was initially meant to be a temporary measure, whose life was extended first every year. Then after every two years and three years till 1969 when it was finally allowed to be lapsed. The year of 1970 was the only year, when the government did not work under the shadow of any extraordinary law in the political history of twenty years of India's independence. It had become possible only because the then Prime Minister lacked the absolute majority in Parliament to introduce such bill and not that the government was not calling to enact.[44]

The Maintenance of Internal Security Act (MISA) was introduced all over India when war broke out between India and Pakistan in 1971. The war was over in about three weeks. MISA, however, remained a fixture in the Statute Book. When Emergency was declared in 1975, it was placed in the Ninth Schedule of the Constitution to escape judicial scrutiny and its provisions were used in most ruthless and arbitrary manner to detain political opponents of the ruling party.

Strangely enough, the very victims of MISA the opposition politicians who came to power after Indira Gandhi's defeat in 1977 moved fast towards the enactment of yet another preventive detention law. Reminiscent of Sardar Patel in 1950, Charan Singh, and Prime Minister of a caretaker government in October, 1979, advised then President to sign an ordinance called 'Preventive of Black Marketing and Maintenance of Supplies of Essential Commodities Ordinance', which provided for Preventive Detention. Earlier as Home Minister in Janata Government in December 1977, Charan Singh had introduced in parliament an amendment to the Code of Criminal Procedure Act incorporating preventive detention in it, but had to withdraw the amendment following widespread protest. National Security Act (NSA) followed soon after Mrs. Gandhi return to power in 1980. Rule by the extraordinary laws became a permanent feature of the Indian politics.[45]

FROM BAD TO WORSE : A JOURNEY OF EXTRAORDINARY LAWS FROM COLONIAL TO POST-COLONIAL INDIA

It should be noted that each successive government, either it was the Congress or the non-Congress whether at the centre or at the state level, there was no respite of these extraordinary laws and misuse of presidential power. Instead, with each successive government the repression of political opposition and democratic struggles has been increasing in terms of the inclusion of the more stringent provision into the new extraordinary laws and interlocking of the extraordinary laws within the Indian Legal system. It has been argued that the Indian democracy and the legal system have experienced a backward journey to colonial laws of British regime. Starting from the British Rowlett Act of 1919 and their upward journey to the TADA (1985) and POTA of (2002), each preventive detention law-starting from the days of British rule attempted to add new provisions that were more rigorous than the earlier.

Thus, while the 1919 Rowlett Act confined itself to arrest without warrant of any person believed to be involved in a scheduled offence in connection with "anarchical or revolutionary movement". The 1932 Bengal Suppression of Terrorist Outrages Act went much beyond the detention of persons suspected to be "acting or about to act in manner prejudicial to public safety or peace", and empowered the authorities to take possession of immoveable property, impose collective fine on inhabitants of turbulent areas.

The Preventive Detention Act (PDA) introduced by the Congress in 1950 authorized detention and imprisonment for one year without Trial of person suspected of being able to cause damage to the country's defence and public order. Unlike earlier Acts which lapsed after a certain period, the PDA was renewed year after year until the end of 1969. The MISA which succeeded PDA by an amendment in 1971 increased the period of detention to two years, and did away with the provision of an opinion from an Advisory Board on such detention (as provided by the earlier PDA). MISA was also periodically renewed year after year until the end of 1969.

Further amendments to MISA in 1975 suspended the release of a detune on bail, permitted the government to refuse an opportunity to the detune to make any representation to the government and provide any reason for his arrest, and to make the Act non-justifiable.

The National Security Act (NSA) went a step further by denying the detune the right to represent his case through a lawyer before the Advisory Board and keeping the proceedings and report of the Board confidential (section 11-4). Section 14 allowed the authorities to make fresh detention order against the detained person on the expiry of detention order. Under Section 16 of NSA , ' No suit or other legal proceeding shall lie against any person, for anything in good faith done or intended to be done in pursuance of this Act". Thus, any redress under the common law of the land was prohibited under NSA.

This onward journey of increasing repression came to zenith with the adoption of TADA and subsequently POTA. Both Acts were claimed to protect the national security from the threats of religious fundamentalism and terrorism in India. POTA and TADA outstripped the old colonial and post-colonial laws to deal with insurgency as well terrorism. The colonial laws enacted by Britain still remain the spiritual home of modern Indian law-makers. More importantly, these laws have been adopted in a political context where the notion of nation and national identity are hegemonically defined and heavily dependent on the idea of the enemy within.[46]

EXTRAORDINARY SITUATIONS/ARMED REBELLION AND HUMAN RIGHTS

The conflicts between the state and ethnic identities, groups for social and economic justice have produced a serious threat to the lives of civilians throughout the world. The homes, town and villages have become the war fields, where the innocent civilian frequently get killed and injured when the parties in conflict exchange the fire, either in a deliberate manner or accidentally. The situation become rampage when the State agencies and the parties in conflict with state target the sympathizers and members of the particular communities.

We witness a series of upsurge of ethnic nationalist movements in British India as well as in recent India. The armed forces in these areas are always provided with the extraordinary power and used their full potential to suppress these movements by hook or crook. The specific thing about them is that they are provided with heavy weapons and latest machine guns which they have to use in their own territory against their own countrymen that turned rebellion against the state. On the other hand, militants were also well armed with the latest weapons which they got from the foreign countries or looted during the attacks on armed forces. In the perpetration of the armed politics by both parties it is the common masses that suffer. The weapons were used in the streets of local strife torn cities, villages and fields. Definitely the people (read innocent civilian) will suffer from these exchanges of firing between the state agencies and so-called ethnic insurgents. The next question is that how the rights of these local people suffer in the hands of both the insurgents as well as the security agencies of the state and how they become the part of armed struggle. The right to freedom of speech or expression even the right to life, right to property and right to representative and democratically elected government is denied by both the parties. How this has occurred we can see from the records where these movements have taken place and brutality suppressed without fulfilling the genuine grievances of the people related to their identity and rights have been going on.[47]

The extraordinary laws like TADA, APSA, which give immense powers to Armed Forces, can result into corruption and arbitrary use of extraordinary powers by the armed forces.[48] Certain non-cognisable offences become cognisable and bailable under the APSA and TADA, the extraordinary laws that automatically invite the maximum penalty for ten years, rigorous imprisonment. Certain offences, not normally warranting the death penalty may, under these Acts can result in punishment. Like any Magistrate or police officer below the rank of sub-inspector may order fire upon or use of force even causing death against any person who is acting in contravention of any law or order for time being in force in such an area prohibiting (a) the assembly of five or more persons, (b) the carrying of weapons or of things capable of being used as weapons. The subjective satisfaction of the sub-inspector, moreover, is the sole criteria for shooting a person to death, and to file a complaint against a policeman, a prior permission of the Home Ministry is required.[49]

The people in such situation live under the shadow of curfew and terror of police surveillance with the pattern of repression. The state forces are always reported to have crossed the constitutional and legal barrier either they were toppling the armed rebellions by the left forces in Andhra Pradesh, West Bengal, Jharkhand, Orissa, Karnataka, Madhya Pradesh, Uttar Pradesh in the mid-1960's and most recently against the Naxalism in the trouble state. The same holds true in the cases of armed ethnic rebellious either it has been Northeast, Jammu and Kashmir or Punjab. The armed upsurges in different parts of India always witnessed the political killings by the religious fundamentalists and the Armed Forces or state sponsored militia as in the case of Punjab.[50]

The innocent civilians in all the troubled states of India are forced to live under horrible circumstances and the civilians are targeted by the Armed Forces as well as by the Armed Guerrillas of the Left and the fundamentalist forces as both want to fetch information and support at crucial hours from the civilians. They are used as human shields both by the armed rebellions and the state forces and also as soft targets by the anti-state forces to pressurize the government. The very pertinent feature of the fundamentalist groups or terrorists is the killing of the members of the other community. The terrorists groups also identify the 'other' as hated enemy, not only the agents of the state but a community or a group of people. The ULFA has targeted Muslim as "foreigners'. Bodos kill Chakmas in particular and Khalistani and Kashmiri terrorists target the people belonging to the Hindu Community. As a result, the people of one community may be forced to migrate to other areas leaving behind their land, homes and jobs.[51]

COMBATING TERRORISM AND THE HUMAN RIGHTS SITUATION IN PUNJAB

The border state of Punjab occupies an extremely important place in India due to its geo-strategic location. The country's largest grain producing state plays a crucial role in defending India against military aggression. In the last century, the state's geographical boundaries have shifted twice, first during the violent partition of India in 1947 and then as result of the administrative division of Punjab state in 1966 into Punjab and the states of Haryana and Himachal Pradesh. In the recent years, the state also faced two periods of internal crisis. There was Naxalism inspired left movement of 1960's and 1970's. The 1980's and 1990,s saw the state plunging into a Sikh militant movement. It is also pertinent to mention that Punjab is the only state where the Indian state is claimed to have ended both the politics of separatism as well as ethnic violence.

The violation of human rights by the Armed forces and terrorists has very long, deep socio-cultural and psychological impacts on any society. Although the conflict between the state and the Sikh armed insurgent is over now but the impact of fundamentalists' violence and the state violence can be felt even after two decades of violence. The children whose parents and the family members were killed or suffered in the hands of terrorists have grown up with a wounded psyche as the gory past of violence continue to haunt them. The impact of the police torture is also telling on the people, especially the youth who were tortured in the police custody during the period. Some of them have lost their mental control and have become insane and others are suffering from mental and physical infirmities due to unbearable torture by the police. The one can also refer to unfortunate parents of those condemned youths who were liquidated by the police from their houses in front of their parents or somewhere from the field, streets of the village and local cities. Their parents are still waiting for them till today because they even don't know whether their loved one were killed by the police in fake encounters or they escaped to other countries. Many cases happened in which their children were falsely declared as dreaded terrorists by the police officers in search of awards and promotion.[52] Arguably the precedent set by the Indian government against the violation of the human rights by the state agencies in Punjab has sent a very wrong message to the protection of human rights and peaceful settlement of conflict in the other states of India like in the case of Jammu and Kashmir.[53]

REVIEW OF LITERATURE

A brief view of the exiting literature provides the significant insights and approaches for understanding questions centered around as to, what, how and why specific phenomenon occurred. A few of these covered the profiles and pattern of thinking of the actors, victims and the state forces and the worldview that determined their assumed roles and actions. What these studies have lacked has been the field views about "terrorism and human rights". The local village context of its internal logic and the perceptions of the villagers: the victims and non-victims and the constant close observation of happenings and the mishappenings.

MILITANCY AND HUMAN RIGHTS IN PUNJAB

Militancy in Punjab and violation of human rights has been the subject of a number of quickly produced journalistic and descriptive studies with semblance of explanation alluding to multiple factors, such as Tully and Jacob, *Amritsar Mrs. Gandhi's Last Battle*, and more analytical, Kuldeep Nayar & Kushwant Singh, 1984, *The Tragedy of Punjab*, Rajinder Kaur, 1992, *Sikh Identity and National Integration*, Vandana Shiva, 1992, *The Violence of Green Revolution*, Ved Marwah, 1995, *Uncivil Wars: Pathology of Terrorism in India*, Joyce Pettigrew, 1995, *The Sikh of the Punjab: Unheard Voices of State and Guerrilla Violence*, D.P. Sharma, 1996, *The Punjab Story: Decade of Turmoil*, V.N. Narayan, 1996, *Tryst with Terror Punjab's: Turbulent Decade*, Ram Naryan Kumar, 1997, *The Sikh Unrest and the Indian State*, Julio Ribeiro, 1998, *Bullet for Bullet; My Life as a Police Officer*, H.K. Puri, *et. al.*, 1999, *Terrorism in Punjab: Understanding the Grassroots Reality*, Harnik Deol, 2000, *Religion and Nationalism in India: A Case Study of Punjab*, Gurpal Singh, 2000, *Ethnic conflicts in India: A Case Study of Punjab*, Inderjit Singh Jaijee, 2002, *Politics of Genocide: Punjab 1984-98*, Ram Narayan Kumar *et. al.*, 2003, *Reduced To Ashes: The Insurgency and Human Rights in Punjab*, Paramjit Singh Judge, 2005, *Religion Identity and Nationhood*, Ram Narayan Kumar, 2008, *Terror in Punjab: Narrative Knowledge and Truth*, and many analytical articles like, Victor D Souza, "Economic Roots of Punjab Communalism", *Economic and Political Weekly*, May 8, 1982, Harji Malik, "A Punjab Report", *Economic and Political Weekly*, September 15, 1984, Amiya Rao, "When Delhi Burnt", *Economic and Political Weekly*, December 8, 1984, Sucha Singh Gill and K.C. Sehghal, "Punjab Problem: Its Historical Roots", *Economic and Political Weekly*, April 7, 1984, PUDR, "Black Laws in Punjab: Report of an Enquiry", *Economic and Political Weekly*, May 11, 1985, Ujjwal Kumar Singh, "TADA: Hard Law for Soft State", *Economic and Political Weekly*, March 25, 2005 and the reports by the International Amnesty, Ensaaf, Committee for Coordination on Disappearance in Punjab, etc. on human rights violations in Punjab, etc.[54] These works have mostly focused on the ground level empirical realities and the legal realities tending to explain what happened and why so happened in the militancy infested Punjab. It may be appropriate, however, to first review the theoretical-oriented explanations by well trained and established social scientist now available in books, chapters and articles in research journals. Whereas most of these studies take note of multiple interrelated factors, the variations in emphasis and framework of explanation are inevitable. These may be discussed broadly under the following categories on the rise and fall of militant movement and the violation of human rights by the state as well as by the militants during the troubled period.

PRIMACY OF CULTURE AND RELIGION

One of the widely held premises relating to the social political dynamics in South Asia is that the contrary to the ideology of secularism, religion is the central point to all the activities in the secular domain. Harnik Deol accordingly argues that the rise of the nationalism has its historical roots in the colonial and post-colonial political set-up of the Indian Union. She has linked the national consciousness with the print-media in India. Deol has argued that the post-green revolution disaffected the Sikh youth and examined the role of popular mass media in the vitalising militancy during the 1970 and 1980's. She has also evaluated the violent responses of the Indian state in fuelling and suppressing the Sikh separatist movement in a tragic sequence of events which included the raiding of Golden Temple at Amritsar and the assassination of Indira Gandhi.[55]

Paramjit Singh Judge, who has been engaged in the study of the social and religious dynamics of the Sikh secessionism since the publication of his book with H.K Puri and Jagroop Singh Sekhon captioned *Terrorism in Punjab: Understanding Grassroots Reality,* also linked the Sikh separatists movement to the construction of singular religious identity by the Singh Sabha in colonial India. Through the analysis of the speeches and messages, leaders of the militant movement argued that the nature and discourse of militant movement can be traced back to the construction of Sikhism in the second half of the nineteenth century. The ideology of the Singh Sabha movement and its attempt at the construction of the singular identity provided the dynamics of the Sikh community. In the process, the religious tradition was invented, which emphasised the singular Sikh identity by paving the way for the dynamics of the Sikh fundamentalism.[56]

Pettigrew, who has also been engaged in the study of the social dynamics of the Sikh community and its politics since the publication of her highly regarded *Robber Noblemen*[57] 30 years ago, also viewed the upsurge as "an idealistic movement". However, the political practice rooted in social dynamics which was completely at odds with the proclaimed idealism was for the author a far more potent determinant of their politics. Whereas the 'guerrilla warfare' was fuelled by a strong reaction to the state terror and violence, the Jat-Sikh values made it only impulsive and was controlled by "village rustic" who had local, small time agenda of 'personal power, vengeance of glamour'. Therefore, as she succinctly observes, "the Sikhs account of their political activities cannot be accorded the status of explanation". The politics of the Sikh community responded more to the individual interests than the community tradition.

Pettigrew took serious note of factionalism as an essential aspect of the patterning of values and tradition among the Jat-Sikh and the Akali politics dominated by the community. That is which determined, according to her, the life as it was lived. "Fetishism of Culture" was therefore not a reliable approach towards an understanding of political activities of the Sikhs. Accordingly, in her study, *Unheard Voices* based on extended interviews with terrorists of the Khalistan Commando Force, she tried to go beyond the "symbolic universe". The character of the movement and its course of action, as she discovered, was determined by thriving individualism, family feuds, vendettas and "interest in guns and popularity". Tending to put all the diverse strata into a cast iron mould she observes that "As a people, Sikh well deserve Locke's caption 'possessive individualists'. Therefore, by their very nature the militant organisations rooted in the political culture of rural areas, were found to have "no basis in political ideology." Further, "their bounding purely personal" as well as linkages had little to do with the act of resistance. Her contention that in order to be successful, "Sikh revolution", had "to free itself of culture and historical constraints" and "to free itself of culture and historical constraints" appeared to conceptualise a fancied history beyond facts.[58]

POLITICAL ECONOMY/MODERNISATION AND RELIGIOUS CULTURAL CONFLICT

More pervasive has been the argument of the social-political costs born of the inherent contradictions of the capitalist agriculture strategy. A rather simplistic and evidently popular version explaining the violence as consequence of large scale unemployment particularly of the educated youth called "the children of green revolution." An awareness of these costs had given the early IMF-World Bank priesthood of the nightmares of "red revolution" following on the heels of the "green revolution", until they were assured by serious scholars and strategies that in country like India, it might rather result in manifestly religious-cultural strife than class war.[59]

The wages of the capitalist agriculture included the accentuation of inequalities as new opportunities only privileged the better endowed section of big farmers. It also led to large scale unemployment spawned by time saving mechanical devices and exclusion of small and marginal farmers. The increasing economic clout of the rich landlords whetted their appetite for greater share in political power. More so, because centralisation of decision-making in a whole range of agriculture operations, trade and pricing of inputs and outputs spelled decreasing returns of the investment in economic terms. It was therefore argued that in their battle against the Indian State, allegedly controlled by the industrial bourgeoisie, the capitalist farmers turned to deploy religious issues for mobilising the poor peasantry around the notion of discrimination.[60]

In a more comprehensive critique of the dynamics and the consequences of the social and political planning underlying the Green Revolution, Vandana Shiva argues that new technology aimed at engineering "not just seeds but social relations as well". The inevitable centralisation of control of all agriculture decisions, trade and prices of goods, according to her, caused both "ecological instability and high vulnerability", leading to unsustainable development. Squeezed by heavy debts and declining returns of investment on the one hand and culture disoriented by the spread of degenerative culture on the other, the farmers felt severely victimized. The violence in Punjab was brought by the "technology fix". According to her, it is therefore 'misleading' to locate its roots in religion.[61]

STATE INTERVENTION: CONTEXTUALISING MILITANT ETHNICITY

The central point of the above framework was the significance of the post-partition choice of the basis of India's unity for explaining the separatist conflict in the country. The historical impulses for the

Sikh militancy have been explained with reference to the denial of "communal safeguards" and centralisation of power. Dipankar Gupta focussed on such intervention made by the Indian State and ruling Congress party as created the context of "special feature" of the occasion. These contributed to the development of what he terms the "Ethnic Imago", leading to widespread violence.

The Punjab agitation according to him pushed into militant violence by the "cynical political manipulation" by Congress. Arguing against "primacy of culture logic", Gupta posits the crucial third dimension of state and ruling Congress, to the 'dyad' of the Sikh ethnic self and "other", advancing what described as "a triadic framework".[62] It was the role of the third dimension which created context in which particular Sikh response could be adequately explained. What happened was not a "structural inevitability"—an argument which appeared to have been advanced and supported by Sangat Singh, Inderjit Singh Jaijee, Kuldeep Nayar and Khushwant Singh[63] on the one hand and Shiva on the other among the political analysts. But as against their arguments central to Gupta's explanation was the context of the state's political prescriptions and pursuit—the failure of three attempts at negotiated settlement; the operations "Blue Star" and "Wood Rose", the massacre of the Sikhs in 1984 and the failure to utilise the opportunity offered by "Operation Black Thunder" in 1988—which determined the particular kind of response. J.S. Grewal, Rajinder Kaur, Puri and Gandhi on the other hand, refers to the presence of two competing tendencies in the Sikh politics of the secular democratic legitimacy of the struggle for economic power in Indian polity and the religious-cultural rhetoric for popular support for confronting the "other". The nature of intervention made by the state is regarded as a crucial factor in frustrating and foreclosing one kind of response and facilitating or provoking the other.[64]

INSTRUMENTAL FRAMEWORK: MANIPULATION BY POLITICAL ELITE

Rejecting both the primacy of culture paradigm and the economic explanation as inadequate basis for explaining the advent of separatist politics, the framework associated with Brass tends to explain the crisis with references to ideologies and strategies devised at the top and the role played by political entrepreneurship in pursuit of their power interest. These include both ruthless, unprincipled intervention by the Centre under Indira Gandhi, opportunism of the Akali and other Sikh political elite.

The instrumentalist view tends to give an impression of over-emphasis on the machinations of the political leader as the mass of followers is always gullible.[65] The crucial question, however, is related to the definition given to the existing situation and the choices which decision-makers at Centre and from within the community made from the option available on particular occasions.[66]

A significant question is raised by Subrata Mitra, "Why does the explanation of the rise of the Sikh militancy have little to do with the causes of its decline"?[67] It seeks an answer. No significant change has been noticed in relation to the variety of reason and causes of its rise highlighted by the ideologues, academics and intellectuals.

A few of the writings based on observation or interviews with the terrorists and the common people points towards the ground reality. One of these is Satyapal Dang's work which points out the dubious role of the Congress and the Akali leadership and the profiles of a number of terrorists, espousing the lie about the idealism of the movement and activists. Dang viewed the movement as the part of Pakistan foreign policy and the American foreign policy which used the criminal elements of Punjab by providing the diplomatic support as well as weapons to disintegrate India unity. According to Dang the violence in Punjab was the problem of law and order which increased due to the political manipulation of the Akali and Congress leadership. He praised the armed forces for their sacrifices which they made while fighting with criminal elements and establish peace in Punjab.[68]

H.K. Puri, Jagroop Sekhon and Parmjit Singh Judge also presented the same view through their extensive survey in the most adversely affected 30 villages of Amritsar and Gurdaspur districts. They argued that the activists of the movement had nothing to do with the ideology of Sikhism and their violence was more of criminal nature and influenced by the social fabrics of village society. The kith and kin relationship and the police oppression against the friends and relatives of the terrorists had contributed to the recruitment of terrorists in Punjab at large, rather than any ideological and religious reason.[69]

V.N. Naryanan, one of the most sensitive observers of the ethnic violence that rocked the state in the eighties concludes that "the violence was more in the genre of criminal and law and order problem rather than the ideology based programme of murder and violent response to the state. It increased due to the lack of the timely responses of the state and the blackmailing of the media by the terrorists which become a mere tool in the hands of terrorists. That contributed to the escalation and fear of violence".[70]

VIOLATION OF HUMAN RIGHTS AND CIVIL SOCIETY RESPONSES: SOME OBSERVATIONS

Violation of human rights both by the militants and state agents has been receiving attention from every nook and corner. Broadly the human rights violation can be divided into the following categories:

As Part of Administrative and Policing Corruption: Militant Movement

In this genre of analysis, *Genesis of Terrorism: An Analytical Study of Punjab* authored by Satyapal Dang can be mentioned at the first place. Through the investigation of the profiles of some terrorists, Dang argued that the terrorists had nothing to do with the ideology. They were essentially criminals who took the advantage of vitiated politics in Punjab. The violent powers of these anti-social elements, however, created a terror among the people due to the diplomatic support and supply of highly sophisticated weapons by Pakistan and sympathic elements based abroad. By narrating his interventionist role in the release of some innocent youths both from Hindus and Sikh communities who were held by the police officers either on suspicion or for extortion purposes, Dang negated any extraordinary situation, power and method under which police violated the human rights at large. In fact, Satyapal Dang praised the police forces for establishing the rule of laws by sacrificing at large.[71] Gurpreet Singh based his study on the basis of a large number of interviews with terrorists and their families in *Terrorism, Punjab's Recurring Nightmare*[72] the book provides a measure of Satyapal Dang version of their actual behaviour and objectives. His study tends to underline the particular feature of the Jat-Sikh society-"natural pride", assertion of the macho image and the motivation of the terrorists. H.K. Puri, Jagroop Sekhon and Parmjit Singh Judge also presented the same view through their extensive survey in the most-affected 30 villages of Amritsar and Gurdaspur districts. Through the scrutiny of the profiles behaviour and the reasoning for the joining of the terrorist ranks by the local youths, they argued that the militants involved in terrorist violence had nothing to do with the ideology of Sikhism or any political ideology seeking temporal homeland for the Sikh nation. Although they recognised the highhandedness and a suppressive policy of the armed forces at some places in their study, but with the help of data on killing and extortion, they ultimately held the terrorist more responsible for violation of human rights than the state forces.[73]

Communalisation of Politics and Crisis in the Governance

Other set of the scholars working on Punjab have been of the view that the Punjab problem and violation of the human rights of the Sikhs in Punjab and outside the state was the part of the communal agenda of the Congress which vitiated the secular politics under which the action of the state forces are motivated by the communal agenda of the ruling power. Some times the state forces were used violence against the minority just to make silent them against the majority violence. Under the vitiated circumstances, state forces were fighting the "enemy within" it.[74] There are still other studies which present the same view on the Punjab politics and violation of the human rights of the Sikhs due to the communalisation of the State Armed forces like Harji Malik in his work titled *A Punjab Report*, has narrated some cases where some army officers abused the villagers because of their Sikh-identity and openly declared them the enemies of the nation. The case of unnecessary harassment of the Sikh Students and a Professor by the Army, which led a large protest in Punjab has also been narrated to established the feeling to which the state armed forces has developed due to the communalisation of politics.[75] Shinder Purewal in his work titled "*Sikh Ethno Nationalism and Political Economy of Punjab*" also holds the same view while narrating the role of the state machinery during the anti-Sikh riots in Delhi and responses of the Centre government to the initiative taken by the Akali leader for the establishment of peace in Punjab after the Operation "Blue Star" and anti-Sikh riots in other parts of the country.[76] The alleged role of the state machinery in the involvement of the mass killing of the Sikhs in Delhi is also questioned by Amiya Rao in her Book *When Delhi Burnt*.[77] The anti-Sikh attitude and inhuman face and the excess which was adopted by the Army during the Operation "Blue Star" and killing of the innocents devotees just because of long Beards and saffron colours of their turbans and the referring of the arrestees as the prisoners of war has also pointed out by the other observers.[78]

Extraordinary Laws and the Colonial Legacies

The arrests of the large number of people under the extraordinary laws particularly under the Terrorist and Discipline Activities (Prevention) Act (TADA) have been taken as the part of colonial legacies by some scholars to suppress the political opposition. They argue that the Indian political elites was denying genuine demands of socio-economic, political and democratic rights like the right to protest, as the democratic protests were taken as the law and order problems. Instead of solving the problems as the political movement, Indian national elite was adopting the policy of silting the people struggle with the help of extraordinary laws and state force. Through their analysis of the provision which involved clauses for arrest, detention and conviction made under the different preventive detention laws from the *Preventive Detention Act, 1950* to TADA, the human rights researchers and activists argued that the journey of extraordinary laws and the political governance of India was going back to the authoritative colonial policies of 'rule by stroke' as for as Punjab was concerned.[79] Through their investigation of some cases, the People's Union for Democratic Rights (PUDR) team revealed that the people of Punjab were denied their constitutional right of equality before the laws and the common people were suffering due to the extraordinary power of the police provided by TADA. The fact finding team of PUDR presented some cases of family feud and the theft cases which were registered under the TADA. Although these cases had nothing to do with the terrorism in Punjab but all that was done by the police was just to escape from the long process of investigation and timely reporting on the case under the ordinary criminal law. The other reason was the intent to extort from the helpless families of the detained by putting ordinary crimes under the extraordinary provisions of TADA.[80]

State in Conflict with its Minorities

This view matched with Rita Manchanda's views on the minorities' rights and position in post-colonial states of South-Asia. According to Manchanda the fluid identities of minorities were politicised under the colonial administration has its long-term effects on the post-colonial political set-up. She argued that during the process of constitutional reforms in the transition to independence, such identities became entrenched. Post-colonial electoral democracy has reinforced the official discourse of majority and minorities, rather than transcending the politics of number.

The early constitutional debates of the state of the region reflected an awareness of the importance of democratising the nation to such an extent that 'minority' as category of powerlessnes disappears and number lose their political value. However, driven by the exigencies of the state power consolidation and paranoia of the Great partition, the founding elite did not anchor minority rights of all people. Instead, state ideology and architecture, increasingly veered towards constituting a majoritianism. For dominant majority-minority rights challenge the state. But for the minorities, it is a common experience of majoritarianism and discrimination and exclusion, resulting in submissive acquiescence or violent revolt. Since India, Pakistan, Sri, Lanka, Bhutan, all have minority problem, it is not the problem of rouge state but a common to the cluster of post-colonial states that have emerged in the region. Political liberalism anchored in equal rights has prove insufficient to deliver equality and justice to minority groups.[81]

Inderjit Singh Jaijee in his book 2002, entitled *Politics of Genocide: Punjab, 1984-98*, deeply argued against centre's politics of discrimination and exclusion under which the Sikh majority state Punjab was deprived from its natural resources, like water, capital city and particularly the scheme of the Indian Prime Minister, Indira Gandhi of limiting the Sikh quota in Indian Army to 2% from the existing 10% and her approval of the SYNL Canal for watering the neighbouring state of Haryana against the principles of the International Riparian Law. Jaijee viewed the violence of the state forces against the Sikh youth in Punjab as part of the anti-minority politics of the Indian State under which the police officers got the consent of the political leadership at both the national and state levels for adopting the extra-constitutional methods while countering the militant movement in Punjab. The impunity to police officers after the alleged charges of the fake encounters and enforced disappearances in Punjab is also viewed as a part of the anti-minority agenda of Indian political class either they were from the Congress or BJP.[82]

Ram Naryan Kumar in his book titled *The Sikh Struggle, Origin, Evolution and Present Phase* and *The Sikh Unrest and the Indian State*, comprehensively analysed the Sikh history from medieval to modern

India and making of separate identity of the Sikhs in colonial India. While writing on the militant movement and violation of the human rights in the 1980 and 1990's Narayan held the anti-minority and Congress politics of delegtimising the Akali Dal as the only political party of Sikhs in India as among the primary cause of the rise of ethno-regional movement. He has viewed the struggle of Sikh militant and the democratic protest by the Sikh leadership as part of their struggle for having autonomy over access and usage to their 'own' natural resources. Analysing the political and legal strategies, which were adopted by the Indian state to protect the armed forces against the charges of the violations of human rights during the counter-insurgency operations in Punjab, Kumar holds the chauvinistic nationalism of majority community responsible for the violation of human rights in Punjab that resulted in the impunity to the police officers who were guilty of killing even under the normal circumstances.[83]

THE SCOPE AND METHOD OF STUDY

The present study was planned following the reports of the violation of human rights in Punjab during the period of militancy and the inadequate response of the state.

It included collection of data based on the responses of the people interview on state's response to terrorism-related violence and violation of human rights. During the interviews conducted, peoples' views about the violation of human rights by the security agencies in the name of combating militancy also came up for discussion. The research universe covered the three border districts of Punjab, which were most adversely affected by militancy. After a comprehensive review of the relevant literature and preliminary investigation, we decided to select Tarn Taran for our case studies which were among the most affected police district in insurgency-prone Punjab. Ten villages as the sites for field study in three districts were selected. Four villages were selected from Tarn Taran district, which was most adversely affected by militancy in terms of violation of human rights (killings, disappearances and police brutality). Rest of the six villages were taken from two other districts (three from each district) namely, Amritsar and Gurdaspur, again being among the worst affected areas in the state during militancy. While selecting the villages, it was kept in mind that the villages were far away from each other in spatial terms. One village selected from all the three districts for case study was to be in the border region neighbouring Pakistan and therefore most disturbed. Other comparable variables linking the villages under study were as under:

(1) The villages covered during the field study were to be a multi-caste village.

(2) The villages selected were representative of an average village of Punjab as per the overall demographic character of the state.

(3) The villages were selected on the basis of the preliminary reports about the occurrences of the violation of human rights there during the militancy period. A pilot survey was conducted for the purpose before sampling the village particularly.

The focus of our investigation was directed towards gaining an initial understanding of the phenomenon. This included a careful scrutiny of the profiles of the victims of both the militants and the state agencies, their motivations and their objectives, their socio-economic background, earlier political association and orientations, if in any political activity they participated in, their behaviour pattern and the perception of others who were directly and indirectly affected by their activities. The activities of the terrorist organizations, their relations with the village members particularly and their behviour towards the village community general was to be analyzed in comparison to the behaviour of the armed forces towards the supporters of terrorists particularly and to the members of the village community general during their anti-insurgency operations.

The present research study followed an inductive method. No hypothesis was considered necessary in view of the explanatory nature of the work played out during the field work after one had sifted through the relevant literature. The responses to the questions raised in one meeting often became the sources for modification or an enlargement of the scope of investigation as the conversational interview method was deployed. It involved extensive open-ended and unstructured interviews with some of settled and unsettled questions with the 52 members of the victims of the terrorist violence and 12 members of the victims of forced disappearance or state oppression. Five respondents were the victims of TADA and brutal torture by the state forces and two were of the victims of Militants torture. More than 10 members of Hindu families which were forced to migrate to the other states were also given interviews. The choice like who should be given interviews followed leads provided in a sequence of interviews through the snow-ball technique.

Persuading the people to talk and discuss and relive the past in a way was a formidable task during the research. More so because of authenticity and on the spot cross-checking and correction, we had decided to discuss the matter in diverse but small gathering of the people in the street or at the common places where they generally gather at afternoon or in the evening. This required winning of contact persons in the selected villages through friends and relatives. The mode of interaction and collection of information involved gathering of a number of people at one place and asking them questions. The size of the group of informants varied from five to seven. The local politics and factionism were also kept in mind while collecting the information and interacting with the informant gathering. In order to check the authenticity of the information provided in the village, another group was interviewed in a separate meeting. Such cross-verification often required another villages and different social settings.

Field Experiences

Generally, field investigations provide rich and varied experiences in meeting different people and encourage social situations hitherto unknown to a researcher even if he or she has the natural advantage of belonging to the area like in the present case. Investigating violation of human rights during terrorism, however, put me in difficult situations where one may sometimes sensed putting one self in some time scary position. Particularly when despite the end of terrorism, certain queries could embarrass different kinds of people and conversely aroused apprehension of the police. Situation has not changed much even after the cessation of militancy long back can be illustrated by referring to the disappearance of Jaswant Singh Khalra, a Human Rights Activist and the killing of former member of police hit-squad Ajit Singh Poohla (head of the Taruna Nihang Sect) inside the Amritsar Central Jail. Jaswant Singh Khalra had challenged the DGP of Punjab Police K.P.S. for open debate on the issue of fake encounters and forced disappearances caused due to the high-handedness on the part of the state agents during the terrorism on the basis of information which he had gathered from the three crematoriums of Amritsar District on the forced disappearance of large number of youths during the terrorism. Khalra's organizations had also filed a petition in High Court and Supreme Court for a comprehensive inquiry into the allegation of disappearance and subsequent, illegal cremations by the police in Punjab.

Ajit Singh Poohla was the head of *Taruna Nihang* sect and was allegedly in charge of a police hit-squad. He was said to have helped the police for killing a number of terrorists with the intelligence as well as active help of his band of Nihangs and was provided with automatic weapons by the police during the terrorism. Poohla was also accused in a number of abduction, murder and rape cases. It was alleged that some police officers used Poohla to set their personal score and it was due to the over-patronizing by the police officers Poohla crossed all the limits. It was after 15 years of the end of terrorism when Phoola was arrested by the Police on the charges of murder, rape and abduction after much embarrassment to the state police caused by the reports filed by the media, human rights organization. Poohla had remained at large at least for two years despite being declared as Proclaimed Offender by the court. Poohla was burnt alive by the co- prisoners in the Central Prison of Amritsar before any comprehensive investigation could take place against his acts.[84]

I was fortunate enough that in spite of the questioning looks and suspicion of the respondents and villagers in common, I was able to explain my objective and also successfully convinced them to give the information to the best of their ability and memory-based knowledge that I needed for my research work. At the first stage my identity as a doctoral candidate of Panjab University has helped to interact with the people on the critical issues and pursue them to converse. Then gradually I would develop a rapport with the people, which helped me a great deal to get the information and stories of the victimization of the villagers at the hands of both the militants and the state forces.

Visiting various villages was a novel enriching experience in another sense also. I noticed that villages were marked by large number of religious places particularly Gurudwaras and Dargahs of the Muslim Peers, in Amritsar and Tarn Taran districts, Mandirs were noticed only in the Gurdaspur District along with the Gurudwaras and Dargahs. Some Gurudwaras which were built in the memories of the militants killed by the police are still there but the majority of monuments and Gurudwaras built in memories of militants in Punjab were erased by the police during the anti-insurgency operations at the last phase of militancy in Punjab in the early nineties.[85] Subsequently, I began to collect information regarding the number of religious places in each village I visited. I found that in the villages there would be Gurudwaras which had historical significance and then there would be Gurudwaras of not so ancient past in each Mohalla/locality. Since population was also segregated along the caste lines/Gotra, it meant that different castes have their own Gurudwaras in recent identity conscious in Punjab. Invariably, the profile of the village was described in terms of number of families and population of each group. Since the most of the respondents were Jats, they were quick to point out the caste background of the non-Jats victims and terrorists, sometimes which we considered odd as they invariably forgot even to mention the names of the victims who belonged to the Mazhabi caste. Whenever I tended to make detailed inquiries about the Mazhabi-Sikh victims of the state and militant's violence, the responses were cryptic, they respond, oh! Lakha?, he was involved in looting cases and was killed by the militants because he was defaming their name, the same is true in the case of other Dalit victims they were either viewed as liquor sellers or butchers or petty criminals disguising themselves as militants by the dominant Jat-Sikh community.[86]

It may be further mentioned that there seem to be defined boundaries drawn by the Sikhs and Hindus over the 'Punjab issue' as they lived together during those turbulent days. While examining the forced migration of Hindus during the terrorism in Punjab, it was found that categories 'we' and 'they' still existed in the villages where the Hindus also had considerable population. All the upper caste Hindus were mentioned as *Bahamans* and *Lala* by our respondents in the districts of Amritsar and Tarn Taran.

Although at the end of the movement, a lot of information appeared on the moral degradation of the terrorists particularly in terms of sexual exploitation and abductions for ransoms. It is to be mentioned that there was unwritten and undocumented information of the sexual exploitation of the women and stealing of gold and some other costly goods by the state armed forces during their anti-incumbency operations in some villages. One such village was Brahmpura in the District of Tarn Taran, although the villagers have reported that they were brutality tortured and even the women were not spared by the CRPF with a sense of great resentment. However, no family and women told me about the alleged sexual abuse due to the social shame. But some persons from the village did tell that they were initially thinking of filing the cases of sexual exploitation, and launching of a campaign against the CRPF for their shameful act. However, they became hesitant due to the social shame. Their protest and campaign against the atrocities committed by then persons of CRPF on the fateful night went through a long way and their protest was supported by the people of Punjab at large. The cases of sexual harassment were apparently not focused upon due to the social stigma. The case of sexual exploitation and killing of the two daughters and the wife of a police Head-Constable was reported by the villagers with a great resentment in the village Tharu. The same kinds of incidents were reported in the village Padhari and Shikar Machhian. Arguably they were not isolated incidents.

I noticed an ambivalent attitude of the people towards both the terrorists and police. In no village we found the sympathizers of terrorists, however, there were some terrorists like Ranjit Singh Rana, Avtar Singh Brahma and Niranjan Singh Mathura who were somewhat also praised by the respondents for defending them against any terrorist attack from rival militant groups. Significantly, I did not find anyone to praise the police for suppressing the terrorists. During the field investigation I even met some former low ranking police officials, i.e. Constables, Head-Constables and Sub-Inspector level who bitterly criticized some of their colleagues for killing of innocents just for rewards and money. The position and the resentments of the villages were expressed in a particular way as evident in the following narratives:

> Like Bha ji eh jo hon Chaudhary bane fer de ne udo dekh de nahi see, sab bhaj gaye see shaher nu. Sade varge mahatar te je police ave tavi juttian khan laye tayer rehande see, je atvadi auande tavi pta nahi kes gal to lambe pa len.

"Brother there was no one to stand against the behaviour of the police and militants. The rich people who become the leaders and boosting now had shifted to the cities to save their skin from the militants as well as from the police. It was we the normal people of the village who faced the tough time and there was no one to speak for us against the atrocities either committed by the police or militants."

Ethe Bahut Mulak marya va dova ne. Police wale ve raat nu jhuthe puls muakble buna de se te Atdvadi ve raat nu mar-mar ke lok sut jande see. Koi darda bahr nikal da sees.

"Both have killed a lot of people. In the nights both the terrorists and the Police took their task of killing the innocents. Police was badly indulged into the practice of fake encounters and militants also killed the innocents in fearful nights. No body dared to get out from the home after the sun-set".

RESEARCH QUESTIONS

- What was the general profile of the victims of the State and Militant Violence perpetrated during the period?
- What were the experiences of the ordinary people residing in the villages during the period of ethnic violence and counter-violence used by the Indian State agents?
- What was the impact of the ensuing violence over the social fabric of village Punjab?
- How did the Indian State look at human rights concerns when it faced existential challenges in terms of its territorial unity and integrity in the form of the ethno-regional armed movement for secession?
- How did Indian state respond to the issue of human rights violation during and after the militancy came to an end and 'peace' was restored?
- To what extent the victims and their family members in Punjab understand the notion of human rights? In what ways do they think that they are victims of human rights violation? Can they identify the state practices which were violative?
- How do the people caught in the violence make sense of the militancy? Do they see the use of violence as a political means to realize their collective claims or consider the violence indulged in by the insurgents as terrorism devoid of any ideology and driven by personal greed and vengeance by the terrorists?
- Do the human rights perspectives of the victims of state violence and the victims of militant violence differ in terms of their perception of the ethno-regional autonomist/separatist movement?

PROFILING THE CASE STUDIES

Tarn Taran (District)
Village Tharu

Socio-Economic Profile of the Respondents/Relatives of the Victims of Militants

Sl. No.	*Name of Victims*	*Respondent*	*Age*	*Sex*	*Relation with the Victim*	*Caste*	*Size of Land-holding in Acres/Business/Service*
(1)	*(2)*	*(3)*	*(4)*	*(5)*	*(6)*	*(7)*	*(8)*
1.	Nirmal Singh	Jagir Kaur	65	F	Mother	Jat-Sikh	3
2.	Mehnga Singh	Harjinder Singh	35	M	Son	Jat-Sikh	80
3.	Dalbir Singh	Daljit Kaur	40	M	Daughter	Jat-Sikh	5
4.	Jaspreet Kaur	Daljit Kaur	40	F	Sister	Jat-Sikh	5
5.	Jagbir Kaur	Daljit Kaur	40	F	Sister	Jat-Sikh	5
	Manjit Kaur	Daljit Kaur	40	F	Daughter	Jat-Sikh	5
6.	Surjan Singh	Ravinder Singh	45	M	Nephew	Jat-Sikh	15
7.	Harbhajan Singh	Kulwant Kaur	58	F	Wife	Jat-Sikh	2

Socio-Economic Profile of the Respondents/Relatives of the Victims Forced Disappearance

Sl. No.	*Name of Victim*	*Name of Respondent*	*Age*	*Caste*	*Relation with Victim*	*Size of Land-holding/ Business? Services*
(1)	*(2)*	*(3)*	*(4)*	*(5)*	*(6)*	*(7)*
1.	Ajit Singh	Roor Singh	35	Jat-Sikh	Son	1/2
2.	Surjit Singh	Inder Singh	25	Jat-Sikh	Uncle	15
3.	Inderpal Singh	Gurdip Singh	70	Jat-Sikh	Village Sarpanch	5
4.	Harpreet Singh (Tishu)	Gurdip Singh	70	Jat-Sikh	Son	5

Village Padhari
Socio-Economic Profile of the Respondents/Relatives of the Victims of Militants

Sl. No	Name of Victim	Name of Respondent	Age	Sex	Caste	Relation with Victim	Size of Land-holding/ Business/Service
(1)	(2)	(3)	(4)	(5)	(6)	(7)	(8)
1.	Harnam Kaur	Joginder Singh	55	M	Jat -Sikh	Grand-Mother	25
2.	Gurcharn Kaur	Joginder Singh	55	—	—	Mother	
3.	Swarn Kaur	Joginder Singh	55	—	—	Sister-in-Law	—
4.	Gurmit Kaur	Joginder Singh	55	—	—	Niece	—
5.	Karmjit Singh	Joginder Singh	55	—	—	Nephew	—
6.	Prabhpreet Singh	Joginder Singh	55	—	—	Nephew	—
7.	Parmjit Kaur	Joginder Singh	55	—	—	Wife	—
8.	Amritbir Kaur	Joginder Singh	55	—	—	Daughter	—
9.	Parmjit Kaur	Joginder Singh	55	—	—	Sister	—
10.	Harbir Singh	Joginder Singh	55	—	—	Nephew	—
11.	Arjan Singh	Bachan Kaur	70	F	Jat-Sikh	Husband	15
12.	Bakhsis Singh	Bachan Kaur	70	—	—	Son	—
13.	Anokh Singh	Bachan Kaur	70	—	—	Son	—
14.	Piar Kaur	Pargat Singh	38	M	Jat- Sikh	Mother	0
15.	Sucha Singh	Kashmir Kaur	40	F	Jat -Sikh	Husband	3
16.	Jagtar Singh	Darshan Kaur	40	F	Mazhabi -Sikh	Husband	0
17.	Lakhbir Singh	Mukhtiar Singh	65	M	Mazhabi- Sikh	Son	—
18.	Bindo	Nirmal Singh	60	M	Mazhabi- Sikh	Daughter	0
19.	Shindo	Mangta Singh	50	M	Mazhabi- Sikh	Wife	0
20.	Bir Kaur	Bachan Kaur	65	F	Mazhabi- Sikh	Daughter	0

Village Brahmpur

Socio-Economic Profile of the Respondents/Relatives of the Victims of Militants

Sl. No	*Name of Victim*	*Name of Respondent*	*Age*	*Sex*	*Relation with the Victim*	*Caste*	*Size of land Holding/ Business/Service*
(1)	*(2)*	*(3)*	*(4)*	*(5)*	*(6)*	*(7)*	*(8)*
1.	Jagjit Singh	Mohinder Kaur	70	F	Husband	Jat-Sikh	12
2.	Hardip Singh	Swinder Kaur	65	F	Son	Jat-Sikh	4
3.	Mukhtiar Singh	Swarn Singh	45	M	Brother	Mazhabi-Sikh	0
4.	Kuldip Singh	Bhajan Kaur	65	F	Son	Jat-Sikh	3
5.	Gurdit Singh	Balbir Singh	65	M	Father	Jat-Sikh	22

Khair-Din–KE

Socio-Economic Profile of the Respondents/Relatives of the Victims of Militants

Sl. No	*Name of Victim*	*Name of Respondent*	*Age*	*Sex*	*Relation with the Victim*	*Caste*	*Size of Land holding/ Business/Service*
(1)	*(2)*	*(3)*	*(4)*	*(5)*	*(6)*	*(7)*	*(8)*
1.	Kulwant Kaur	Kashmir Kaur	35	F	Mother	Jat –Sikh	0
2.	Bir Singh	Rānjit Singh	28	M	Father	Mazhabi-Sikh	0
3.	Harbhajan Singh	Sukhwinder Singh	35	M	Father	Mazhabi-Sikh	0
4.	Sohan Singh	Pheno	80	F	Husband	Mazhabi-Sikh	0

Socio-Economic Profile of the Respondents/Relatives of the forced disappearances

Sl. No	*Name of Victim*	*Name of Respondent*	*Age*	*Sex*	*Relation with the Victim*	*Caste*	*Size of Land holding/ Business/Service*
(1)	*(2)*	*(3)*	*(4)*	*(5)*	*(6)*	*(7)*	*(8)*
1.	Tarshem Singh	Nirmal Kaur	50	F	Son	Mazhabi-Sikh	0
2.	Raju	Joginder Kaur	55	F	Son	Mazhabi-Sikh	0
3.	Manjit Singh (Ladu)	Jaswinder Kaur	60	F	Son	Mazhabi-Sikh	0

Amritsar (District)

Socio-Economic Profile of the Respondents/Relatives of the Victims of Militants

Village Mandiala

Sl. No.	*Name of Victim*	*Name of Respondent*	*Age*	*Sex*	*Relation with the Victim*	*Caste*	*Size of Land holding/ Business/Service*
(1)	*(2)*	*(3)*	*(4)*	*(5)*	*(6)*	*(7)*	*(8)*
1.	Ghulah Singh	Balbir Kaur	47	F	Husband	Mazhabi-Sikh	0
2.	Baldev Singh	Rattan Kaur	90	F	Son	Mazhabi-Sikh	0
3.	Rajpal Singh	Jasbir Kaur	50	F	Husband	Mazhabi-Sikh	0
4.	Baldev Singh	Niranjan Singh	80	F	Son	Mazhabi-Sikh	0
5.	Amar Singh	Sato	60	F	Husband	Mazhabi-Sikh	0
6.	Makhan Singh	Rattan Kaur	90	F	Sister-in-law	Mazhabi-Sikh	0

Socio-Economic Profile of the Respondents/ Relatives of the Victims of Militants

Village Iban Kalan

Sl. No.	*Name of Victim*	*Name of Respondent*	*Age*	*Sex*	*Relation with Victim*	*Caste*	*Size of Land-holding/ Business/Service*
(1)	*(2)*	*(3)*	*(4)*	*(5)*	*(6)*	*(7)*	*(8)*
1.	Balwinder Singh	Jaswant Singh	35	M	Brother	Mazhabi-Sikh	0
2.	Mela Singh	Baldev Singh	65	Male	Father	Mazhabi-Sikh	0
3.	Bitta Singh	Mangal Singh	70	M	Son	Mazhabi-Sikh	0
4.	Bira Singh	Shindo	54	F	Husband	Mazhabi-Sikh	0
5.	Nirmal Singh	Baldev Singh	65	M	Son	Mazhabi-Sikh	0
6.	Shinda Singh	Roshan Singh	34	M	Brother	Mazhabi-Sikh	0

Victim of State Oppression

Sl. No.	*Name of Victim*	*Name of Respondent*	*Age*	*Sex*	*Relation with Victim*	*Caste*	*Size of Land holding/ Business/Service*
(1)	*(2)*	*(3)*	*(4)*	*(5)*	*(6)*	*(7)*	*(8)*
1.	Hardeep Singh	Dalbir Kaur	75	F	Son	Kamboj	3

Socio-Economic Profile of the Respondents/Relatives of the Victims of Militants

Village Mahawa

Sl. No.	Name of Victim	Name of Respondent	Age	Sex	Relation with Victim	Caste	Size of Land holding/ Business/Service
(1)	(2)	(3)	(4)	(5)	(6)	(7)	(8)
1.	Rewail Singh	Gurnam Kaur	70	F	Son	Jat-Sikh	10
2.	Angrej Singh	Satinder Kaur	18	F	Father	Jat-Sikh	5
3.	Lovely Singh	Comrade Charn Singh	70	M	Grand Son	Jat-Sikh	10

Victim of State Oppression

Sl. No.	Name of Victim	Name of Respondent	Age	Sex	Relation with Victim	Caste	Size of Land holding/ Business/Service
1.	Sukhwinder Singh	Dial Singh	70	M	Son	Jat–Sikh	8

Gurdaspur District

Socio-Economic Profile of the Respondents/Relatives of the Victims of Militants

Village Shahpurjazan

Sl. No.	*Name of Victim*	*Name of Respondent*	*Age*	*Sex*	*Relation with Victim*	*Caste*	*Size of Land holding/ Business/Service*
(1)	*(2)*	*(3)*	*(4)*	*(5)*	*(6)*	*(7)*	*(8)*
1.	Parkash Singh	Lakhbir Kaur	59	F	Husband	Jat-Sikh	2
2.	Baldev Singh	Dalbir Kaur	49	F	Husband	Jat-Sikh	7
3.	Swinder Singh	Mohinder Kaur	55	F	Husband	Jat-Sikh	7
4.	Shingara Singh	Dalbir Kaur	49	F	Father–in-Law	Jat-Sikh	7
5.	Parshan Dev	Rajinder Kumar	65	M	Former Sarpanch	Hindu-Khatri	10
6.	Shiv Kumar	Rajinder Kumar	—	—	—	—	—
7.	Thakur Kuldeep	Rajinder Kumar	—	—	—	—	—
8.	Piaralal	Rajinder Kumar	—	—	—	—	—
9.	Ashok Kumar	Rajinder Kumar	—	—	—	—	—

Victims of State Oppression

Sl. No.	*Name of Victim*	*Name of Respondent*	*Age*	*Sex*	*Relation with Victim*	*Caste*	*Size of Land holding*
(1)	*(2)*	*(3)*	*(4)*	*(5)*	*(6)*	*(7)*	*(8)*
1.	Hardip Singh	Baldev Singh	75	M	Son	Jat-Sikh	3
2.	Major Singh	Lakhbir Kaur	59	F	Son	Jat-Sikh	2

Socio-Economic Profile of the Respondents/Relatives of the Victims of Militants

Village Shikar Machhian

Sl. No.	*Name of Victim*	*Name of Respondent*	*Age*	*Sex*	*Relation with Victim*	*Caste*	*Size of Land holding/ Business/Service*
(1)	*(2)*	*(3)*	*(4)*	*(5)*	*(6)*	*(7)*	*(8)*
1.	Tafel Mesiah	Rehmat Mesiah	62	M	Son	Dalit-Charistian	0
2.	Joginder Singh	Charn Kaur	63	F	Husband	Jat-Sikh	5
3.	Parshan Dev	Balwinder Singh	60	M	Village Sarpanch	Jat-Sikh	25
4.	Swarnjit Kaur	—	—	—	Village Sarpanch	Jat-Sikh	25
5.	Balkar Singh	—	—	—	Village Sarpanch	Jat-Sikh	25

Socio-Economic Profile of the Respondents/Relatives of the Victims of Militants

Village Tibbar

Sl. No.	*Name of Victim*	*Name of Respondent*	*Age*	*Sex*	*Relation with Victim*	*Caste*	*Size of Land holding Business/Service*
(1)	*(2)*	*(3)*	*(4)*	*(5)*	*(6)*	*(7)*	*(8)*
1.	Aroma	Veena Prasher	48	F	Daughter	Bhatt, Brahmin	0
2.	Prempal (police Constable)	Sunita	33	F	Husband	Bhatt, Brahmin	0
3.	Sunil Kumar	Dharminder Nath	34	M	Brother	Bhatt, Brahmin	0
4.	Manoharlal	Surjanpal	37	M	Brother	Bhatt, Brahmin	3
5.	Chunilal	Kamla	63	F	Husband	Bhatt, Brahmin	0
6.	Shimla Devi	Janko Devi	60	F	Daughter	Bhatt, Brahmin	0

General Respondents and their Socio-Economic Profile of the Respondents

Tarn Taran District

Village Tharu

Sl. No.	*Name of Respondent*	*Father's Name*	*Age*	*Sex*	*Village Sarpanch/ Member Panchayat/ Numberdar/ Chowkidar etc.*	*Caste*	*Size of Land-holding/ Business/Service*
(1)	*(2)*	*(3)*	*(4)*	*(5)*	*(6)*	*(7)*	*(8)*
1.	Tajinder Singh	Gurbax Singh	52	M	Villager	Jat-Sikh	Driver/ PSEB
2.	Bhanuram	Shantiram	65	M	Villager	Hindu-Khatri	Business
3.	Gurinder Singh	Shakatar Singh	50	M	Villager	Mehra- Sikh	Service
4.	Darshan Singh	Pritam Singh	60	M	Villager	Nai-Sikh	Service
5.	Tajinder Singh	Harkireet Singh	35	M	Sarpanch	Jat-Sikh	20
6.	Lakhwinder Singh	Ajit Singh	55	M	Panchayat Member	Jat-Sikh	5
7.	Ladu Singh	Sulakhan Singh	34	M	Chowkidar	Mazhabi-Sikh	0
8.	Sadhu Singh	Kartar Singh	62	M	Panchayat Member	Mazhabi-Sikh	Paledar (Crop Market)
9.	Rashem Singh	Shingara Singh	45	M	Villager	Mazhabi-Sikh	Paledar (Crop Market)

(Contd.)

(Contd.)

(1)	(2)	(3)	(4)	(5)	(6)	(7)	(8)
10.	Harjeet Singh	Uttam Singh	55	M	Villager	Mazhabi-Sikh	Karyana Shop
11.	Rattan Singh	Bhan Singh	57	M	Villager	Mazhabi-Sikh	Paledar (Crop Market)
12.	Jasbir Singh	Piara Singh	45	M	Villager	Mazhabi-Sikh	Paledar (Crop Market)
13.	Sukha Singh	Mohinder Singh	43	M	Villager	Mazhabi-Sikh	Paledar (Crop Market)
14.	Sanga Singh	Dhirta Singh	50	M	Villager	Mazhabi-Sikh	Retied Constable from Army
15.	Nirmal Singh	Chanchal Singh	50	M	Villager	Mazhabi-Sikh	Paledar (Crop Market)
16.	Shingara Singh	Ram Singh	55	M	Villager	Mazhabi-Sikh	Retied Constable from Army

Village Padhari

Sl. No.	*Name of Respondent*	*Father's Name*	*Age*	*Sex*	*Village Sarpanch/ Member Panchayat/ Numberdar/ Chowkidar etc.*	*Caste*	*Size of Land-holding/ Business/Service*
(1)	*(2)*	*(3)*	*(4)*	*(5)*	*(6)*	*(7)*	*(8)*
1.	Master Sewaram	Meharchand	58	M	Villager	Sansi-Sikh	Retired Teacher
2.	Sukhdev Singh	Ajit Singh	60	M	Villager	Jat-Sikh	20
3.	Jasbir Singh	Laxman Singh	59	M	Villager	Jat-Sikh	10
4.	Balkar Singh	Anoop Singh	59	M	Villager	Jat-Sikh	12
5.	Kala Singh	Sant Singh	62	M	Villager	Jat-Sikh	20
6.	Chanan Singh	Sohan Singh	45	M	Villager	Jat-Sikh	10
7.	Tarlok Singh	Bishan Singh	65	M	Villager	Mazhabi-Sikh	Labour
8.	Balwinder Singh	Pritam Singh	75	M	Villager	Mazhabi-Sikh	Labour
9.	Gurdeep Singh	Kishan Singh	70	M	Chowkidar	Mazhabi-Sikh	Labour
10.	Harbhajan Singh	Jagat Singh	62	M	Villager	Mazhabi-Sikh	Retired Army man
11.	Jaswant Singh	Jagat Singh	65	M	Villager	Mazhabi-Sikh	Labour
12.	Tarlok Singh	Bishan Singh	62	M	Chowkidar	Mazhabi-Sikh	Labour
13.	Kulwant Singh	Chanchal Singh	60	M	Villager	Jat-Sikh	10
14.	Jaswant Singh	Chanchal Singh	65	M	Villager	Jat-Sikh	16
15.	Butaram	Meharchand	40	M	Villager	Sansi-Sikh	J.E, P.S.E.B

Village Brahmpura

Sl. No.	Name of Respondent	Father's Name	Age	Sex	Village Sarpanch/ Member Panchayat/ Numberdar/ Chowkidar etc.	Caste	Size of Land-holding/ Business/Service
(1)	(2)	(3)	(4)	(5)	(6)	(7)	(8)
1.	Mohinder Singh	Daljeet Singh	55	M	Sarpanch	Jat-Sikh	100
2.	Harcharn Singh	Shingara Singh	45	M	Villager	Jat-Sikh	120
3.	Pargat Singh	Baldev Singh	40	M	Villager	Jat-Sikh	10
4.	Gurnishan Singh	Dalbeer Singh	35	M	Villager	Jat-Sikh	6
5.	Harbansh Singh	Gurnam Singh	55	M	Villager	Jat-Sikh	20
6.	Sadha Singh Master	Sohan Singh	65	M	Villager	Jat-Sikh	30
7.	Baldev Singh	Mukhtiar Singh	55	M	Villager	Jat-Sikh	20
8.	Charan Singh	Mehanga Singh	60	M	Villager	Mazhabi- Sikh	Business/ Ex-Chairman Block Samiti
9.	Hira Singh	Mukhtiar Singh	50		Villager	Mazhabi- Sikh	Shop
10.	Sewa Singh	Gurdial Singh	52		Villager	Mazhabi- Sikh	Shop
11.	Tarshem Singh	Mukhtiar Singh	40		Villager	Kumhar-Sikh	5
12.	Balkar Singh	Gura Singh	50		Chowkidar	Mazhabi-Sikh	Labour

Village Khair-Deen-Ke

Sl. No.	*Name of Respondent*	*Father's Name*	*Age*	*Sex*	*Village Sarpanch/ Member Panchayat/ Numberdar/ Chowkidar etc.*	*Caste*	*Size of Land-holding/ Business/Service*
(1)	*(2)*	*(3)*	*(4)*	*(5)*	*(6)*	*(7)*	*(8)*
1.	Karm Singh Jhabal	Panjab Singh	43	M	Human Rights Activist	Mazhabi-Sikh	0
2.	Bakhsish Singh	Panjab Singh	45	M	Panchayat Member	Mazhabi-Sikh	0
3.	Avtar Singh	Inder Singh	52	M	Villager	Ramgarhia-Sikh	Industrialist
4.	Santosh Singh	Anand Singh	76	M	Villager	Ramgarhia-Sikh	Thekedar (Contractor)
5.	Pritam Singh Doda	Mukhtiar Singh	75	M	Villager	Jat-Sikh	5
6.	Mukhtiar Singh	Anand Singh	72	M	Villager	Kamboj	10
7.	Gurmit Singh	Inder Singh	40	M	Villager	Jat-Sikh	15

Amritsar District

General Respondents and their Socio-Economic Profile of the Respondents

Village Mandiala

Sl. No.	Name of Respondent	Father's Name	Age	Sex	Village Sarpanch/ Member Panchayat/ Numberdar/ Chowkidar etc.	Caste	Size of Land -holding/ Business/ Service
(1)	(2)	(3)	(4)	(5)	(6)	(7)	(8)
1.	Gurwinder Singh	Harjit Singh	47	M	Villager	Mazhabi –Sikh	Labour
2.	Dalbir Singh	Jagajit Singh	69	M	Villager	Mazhabi –Sikh	Labour
3.	Gurjit Singh	Gurmukh Singh	50	M	Villager	Mazhabi –Sikh	Labour
4.	Jatinder Singh	Taga Singh	44	M	Panchayat Member	Kamboj- Sikh	7
5.	Jagmit Singh	Bachittar Singh	60	M	Villager	Kamboj	10
6.	Grusewak Singh	Mukhtar Singh	62	M	Villager	Jat-Sikh	12
7.	Shamsher Singh	Gurmukh Singh	47	M	Villager	Jat-Sikh	6
8.	Varinder Singh	Shamsher Singh	50	M	Villager	Jat-Sikh	8
9.	Jaswinder Singh	Dalbeer Singh	55	M	Villager	Jat-Sikh	9
10.	Manjinder Singh	Jaspal Singh	57	M	Villager	Jat-Sikh	10

Village Iban Kalan

Sl. No.	Name of Respondent	Father's Name	Age	Sex	Village Sarpanch/ Member Panchayat/ Numberdar/ Chowkidar etc.	Caste	Size of Land-holding/ Business/ Service
(1)	(2)	(3)	(4)	(5)	(6)	(7)	(8)
1.	Dalbeer Singh	Hari Singh	50	M	Villager	Mazhabi-Sikh	Labour
2.	Joginder Singh	Hari Singh	52	M	Villager	Mazhabi-Sikh	Labour
3.	Mukhtiar Singh	Gurdeep Singh	49	M	Villager	Mazhabi-Sikh	labour
4.	Kuldeep Singh	Sohan Singh	53	M	Panchayat Member	Mazhabi-Sikh	Shop
5.	Gurmukh Singh	Gurbachan Singh	48	M	Villager	Kamboj-Sikh	5
6.	Parmjit Singh	Jaswant Singh	39	M	Villager	Kamboj-Sikh	7
7.	Balwant Singh	Daleep Singh	43	M	Panchayat Member	Jat-Sikh	10
9.	Rajinder Singh	Kulwant Singh	45	M	Villager	Jat-Sikh	15

Village Mohawa

Sl. No.	Name of Respondent	Father's Name	Age	Sex	Village Sarpanch/ Member Panchayat/ Numberdar/ Chowkidar etc.	Caste	Size of Land-holding/ Business/ Service
(1)	(2)	(3)	(4)	(5)	(6)	(7)	(8)
1.	Dharmbir Singh	Gopal Singh	45	M	—	Jat-Sikh	8
2.	Gopal Singh	Ujjagar Singh	80	M	Former Sarpanch	Jat-Sikh	32
3.	Wassan Singh	Assa Singh	50	M	Villager	Jat-Sikh	15
4.	Joga Singh	Dalip Singh	40	M	Villager	Jat-Sikh	15
5.	Virsa Singh	Hakam Singh	65	M	Villager	Jat-Sikh	55
6.	Surjit Singh	Jyota Singh	48	M	Numberdar	Jat-Sikh	25
7.	Gulzar Singh	Tara Singh	49	M	Chowkidar	Mazhabi-Sikh	0
8.	Amar Singh	Mula Singh	70	M	Villager	Mazhabi-Sikh	0
9.	Virsa Singh	Jhimma Singh	40	M	Villagers	Mazhabi-Sikh	0
10.	Tarshem Singh	Taru Singh	50	M	Villagers	Mazhabi-Sikh	0

Gurdaspur District

General Respondents and their Socio-Economic Profile of the Respondents

Village Shahpurjazan

Sl. No.	*Name of Respondent*	*Father's Name*	*Age*	*Sex*	*Village Sarpanch/ Member Panchayat/ Numberdar/ Chowkidar etc.*	*Caste*	*Size of Land Holding/ Business/ Service*
(1)	*(2)*	*(3)*	*(4)*	*(5)*	*(6)*	*(7)*	*(8)*
1.	Baldev Singh	Parkash Singh	59	M	Villager	Jat- Sikh	10
2.	Varyam Singh	Dalbir Singh	49	M	Villager	Jat-Sikh	12
3.	Davinder Singh	Mohinder Singh	55	M	Villager	Jat-Sikh	7
4.	Mukhtiar Singh	Parkash Singh	37	M	Panchayat Member	Jat-Sikh	7
5.	Rajinder Kumar	Parshan Dev	65	M	Former Sarpanch	Brahmin	10
6.	Manguram	Tirathram	60	M	Villager	Brahmin	Shop
7.	Baldevchand	Ravinder Kumar	55	M	Villager	Hindu-Khatri	Shop
8.	Rashem Singh	Balwinder Singh	52	M	Villager	Sunayara-Sikh	Business
9.	Laxmanram	Janakchand	54	M	Villager	Hindu-Khatri	Shop

Village Shikar Machhian

Sl. No.	Name of Respondent	Father's Name	Age	Sex	Village Sarpanch/ Member Panchayat/ Numberdar/ Chowkidar etc.	Caste	Size of Land-holding/ Business/ Service
(1)	(2)	(3)	(4)	(5)	(6)	(7)	(8)
1.	Tarshem Mesiah	Dalbir Singh	62	M	Villager	Dalit-Charistian	Labour
2.	Gurtej Singh	Balwant Singh	49	M	Villager	Jat-Sikh	15
3.	Daljeet Singh	Karm Singh	60	M	Panchayat-Member	Jat-Sikh	25
4.	Rajinder Singh	Swarnjit Singh	52	M	Village Sarpanch	Jat-Sikh	35
5.	Balkar Singh	Rajinder Singh	56	M	Villager	Jat-Sikh	20
6.	Lakhwinder Singh	Balbir Singh	47	M	Chowkidar	Mazhabi-Sikh	

Village Tibbar

Sl. No.	Name of Respondent	Father's Name	Age	Sex	Village Sarpanch/ Member Panchayat/ Numberdar/ Chowkidar etc.	Caste	Size of Land-holding/ Business/ Service
(1)	(2)	(3)	(4)	(5)	(6)	(7)	(8)
1.	Baldev Chand	Veerpal Prasher	50	M	Villager	Bhatt, Brahmin	Business
2.	Surajpal	Gian Chand	49	M	Villager	Bhatt, Brahmin	Business
3.	Balbir Singh	Poran Singh	44	M	Villager	Bhatt, Brahmin	5
4.	Vinodpal	Surjanpal	47	M	Villager	Bhatt, Brahmin	3
5.	Teerthram	Kamla	63	M	Villager	Bhatt, Brahmin	Service
6.	Balbir Chand	Janak Dev	60	M	Villager	Bhatt, Brahmin	Service
7.	Harwinder Singh	Hazoora Singh	65	M	Villager	Jat-Sikh	15
8.	Grursewal Singh	Didar Singh	42	M	Panchayat Member	Jat-Sikh	17
9.	Rajwinder Singh	Avtar Singh	39	M	Villager	Jat-Sikh	10
10.	Jasdev Singh	Sardara Singh	45	M	Villager	Jat-Sikh	12

SCHEME OF WORK

The study has been divided into 6 chapters in all. Chapter 1 is devoted to the evolution of human rights as an idea and a concept. It also refers to the international and national legal-constitutional mechanism to enforce the human rights provisions. The legal burden for the states to implement human rights in their territories and the state responses to armed rebellious and human rights questions against the state action have been analyzed in the chapter. The constitutional and legal provisions for the protection of human rights in India have been duly focused upon along with the issue of political governance. Extra-ordinary laws have also been analyzed. Special focus has been given to the responses of Indian State towards the violence of radical and ethnic secessionists groups; the question of the violence of anti-state forces has also been addressed from the human rights perspective.

Chapter 2 is an attempt to analyze political history of Punjab along with the Sikh history. The chapter focuses upon the factors of socio-religious, political-cultural and economic change and emergence of socio-religious and political movements with their larger implication for the people of Punjab. A comprehensive approach has been adopted while analyzing the changes in the Sikh Movement from Bhakti Movement to the Shakti Movement in the Medieval Punjab. Formation of the *Khalsa Panth* by the Tenth Guru and its larger influence over the established socio-religious structure of Indian society and also the conflict of the Gurus with the dominant powers have been presented with the help of the available academic literature. In addition, the Sikh Struggle after the martyrdom of the tenth guru's against the Mughal invasion and the establishment of Sikh empire at the end of medieval Punjab and in the beginning of modern Punjab has also been focused upon. The Anglo-Sikh alliance and the inclusion of the Sikh soldiers in the British Army after the defeat of the Sikh Empire at the hands of the British have been analyzed with its implication on the socio-religious, economic, and political set-up of Punjab. The anti-colonial struggle and the making of a separate Sikh identity in colonial India along with the emergence of conservative Socio-Religious Reform Movements and deepening of the communal-tension between the different religious communities in Punjab with its larger implication on the identity and electoral politics in post-colonial India has diligently been studied.

The emergence of Sikh consciousness for a separate identity in colonial India and communal disharmony of the Hindu-Sikh relation in the new demographic set-up of Punjab over the demand for a Sikh majority *Punjabi Suba* (Punjabi Speaking state) in post-colonial India, due to the opposition by the Punjabi Hindus under the influence of Jan-Sangh have also been investigated. Simultaneously, the electoral compulsions of the Akali-Dal and the linking of the demand of Punjabi-Suba with Sikh religion have been comprehensively studied.

Chapter 3 revolves around the rise and fall of the Khalistan Movement along with the socio-religious, economic and political circumstances of Punjab. The Akali politics over the river-water distribution between Punjab and Haryana and the issue of some Punjabi-speaking areas and Capital City of Punjab and the responses of the Central ruling party to the Punjab problem and the emergence of Bhindranwale along with failure of green revolution in the state have compressively been examined. Besides, the internal differences of the Congress leadership in Punjab and electoral compulsions of Akali Dal, which resulted in the emergence of fundamental violence and the occupying of the Golden Temple complex by Bhindranwale and his band of terrorists, the state action against Bhindranwale and his men in the Golden Temple complex and the alienation of the Sikh against the alleged action of Indian-Army due to some miscalculation and killing of the civilian who gathered inside the complex to celebrate the martyrdom of the fifth guru are duly focused upon.

The chapter also focuses upon the alienation among the Sikhs from the centre especially after the Operation "Blue Star", anti-Sikh riots in Delhi and other parts of the country after the assassination of Indira Gandhi and the emergence of the Sikh-guerrilla Movement in the country side of Punjab and the state responses to it along with the political calculation of the Congress and Akali Dal.

Apart from this, the failure of the democratic process and political solution of the Punjab problem in the vitiated environment, where both the Akalis and Congress men were trying to discredit each other for electoral gains, the violent suppression of the movement due to the lack of political will and the violation of human rights at the large scale by the government forces and militants have also been scrutinized. The winning over of the militants by the security forces with the help of extra-ordinary laws and allowance of brutal force complemented with the intrusion of State intelligence agencies among the militant organizational ranks, more importantly the losing of faith of the people of Punjab in the militants due to the use of violence against the civilian and indulgence of militants in the local feuds have been extensively studied in this chapter.

Chapter 4 investigates at length into the militants' violence and the state's responses to the violence. The legislative, legal, and security measures of the Indian State to which it adopted for countering the militancy in Punjab have also been the focus of the chapter. Apart from this, a detailed study of the provisions and detentions made under TADA has been made to reveal the draconian nature of the extra-ordinary laws which the Indian government adopted to curb the militancy in Punjab.

A study of the field operation of the state forces and militants has also been done. It is found that the formation of some extra-legal vigilant groups by the security agencies in Punjab resulted in the violation of human rights at large. Also the members of these vigilant groups were reported to have indulged in unethical acts of robbery and murder for their personal gains. The involvement of a large number of security officers especially from Punjab Police in the fake encounter killing has also been brought into limelight. The government of India has been held responsible for the violation of human rights as it had empowered the security forces with extra-ordinary laws like TADA and by adopting the policy of rewards and promotions after the alleged killing of terrorists that consequently resulted in the fake encounter of innocent civilians by the security forces and rampant corruption.

A serious attempt has been made to reveal the unknown facts about the disappearance of the youths by analyzing the reports of news papers. It has been found that they were killed by the Punjab police and for which they received rewards, money, and promotions. A mystery still hovers upon some of the cases of the killings by the security forces and in some cases these militants were 'killed' twice by the police of different districts. The use of mass violence by the militants and violations of human right at large were also reported along with ideological incredibility of the militants.

The legal battle of the families of the victims of human violations in Punjab and the CBI inquiry on the burning the unclaimed dead bodies in two crematorium grounds of Amritsar and in Tarn Taran have comprehensively been studied through the proceeding in the National Human Rights Commission and the responses of the families of the victims and Civil Society in Punjab. The relevant literature has also been surveyed for analytical purposes.

Chapter 5 covers the field experience and the position of the families of the victims of human rights violations in Punjab. To collect the data of the impact of the violence during militancy in

Punjab, a comprehensive plan for the study was designed under which four types of questionnaires, both open ended and close ended, for the victims of different kinds of human rights violation in Punjab were designed. Besides the questionairs for the victims, a village Profile for the selected villages and a plan for the people in general in the selected villages were made for the purpose of the field study.

During my field study, I found that there is hardly a village in the District of Amritsar, Gurdaspur and Tarn Taran, which was not hit by the violence, direct and physical either by the state actors or non-state actors or both during the militancy. The people of these villages were accusing both the militants and the security forces for spreading terror in those black days. After having a close interaction during the interview session with the victims of the militants' violence, I found that majority of the victims had nothing to do with the movement and had no associations with any political ideology and party. In fact, those killings were the outcomes of the local feuds over the issues of land and some other old enmities among the families and individuals. Some youths were killed by militants just because they did not follow their dictates. Regarding the functioning of the state forces, the villagers accused the security for abusing and physical beating and used as human-shield during the routine cordoned off the villages for security check-up. The cases of forced disappearances and fake encounters of the innocent civilians from the villages are also reported. The government's policy of compensation to the victims has also come under the cloud as the victims exposed the facts of corruption and influences of the dominant castes while getting the compensation. There are some Dalit families in these villages which could not get the compensation because either the village Sarpanch or a dominant person from a village did not want it and reported to the police that the victim was killed by the militants because of personal reasons and that they might have had associations with the militants.[87]

Notes and References

1. Universal Declaration of Human rights (Articles 1-2), adopted by General Assembly resolution 217 (III) of December 1948, 1- 4-2005.
2. "Human Rights and Conflict," www.un.org/rights/HRToday/hrconflict.html, 8-7-2007.
3. "Human Rights, the pursuit of an ideal," liberary.thinkquest.org/c0126065/hrhistory.html, 1-6-2007.
4. "Human rights then and now, part 1, a short history of human rights fundamentals," un.edu/humanrts/edumat/hrduseries/hereand now/...history.html, 10-13-2005.

5. The racial discrimination, the concept of Whiteman burden and the disregards of the equal rights of the colonial people by the imperial powers of the west are the stark examples of the violation of the human rights even much after the development of human civilization and the rule of law.
6. The twentieth century was the bloodiest in human history. The sheer statistics numb the mind. Although estimates vary widely, the tale of deaths and destruction is monumental; since 1900 some 115 million persons killed in battles-plus perhaps an equal number of civilian fatalities. The mass killings were not confined to the organized wars between the states but of the savaged their own people by the governments possibly as many as 170 million killed in 'ethnicides' within states, David P. Forsythe, 2000, *Human Rights in International Relations*, Cambridge University Press, pp. 21-24. See also: R.J. Rummel, 1994, *Death by Government : Genocide and Mass Murder Since 1900,* N.J. Transaction Publishers, Brunswick, U.S.A, pp. 51-67, Charles Tilly, 1992, *Coercion, Capital and European States,* Cambridge University Press, Cambridge, p. 67.
7. "Freedoms from want", "Freedom to worship the God". "Freedom of thought and expression" and Freedom from fear, File: Four freedoms human rights. Jpg-Wikipedia, the free encyclopedia, en.wikipedia.org/wiki/File:Four freedoms human rights.jpg, 12-10-2011, four Freedoms-National Archives and Record Administration, www.archives.gov/exhibits/...of.../four freedoms.htm., 12-10-2011, FDR's Four Freedoms-School of Humanities, www.humanities.uci.edu/.../11.7%20FDR%20Freedoms%2..., 12-10-2011
8. On 10 December, 1948 Universal Declaration of Human Rights (UDHR) was adopted by the UN General Assembly without a dissenting vote. The UDHR began with the following statement (whereas) recognition of inherent dignity and equal and inalienable rights of all the members of human family is the foundation of freedom, justice and peace in the world. These words link the world peace and respect for human rights, it was for the first time that rights of the people and peace dominated the scene instead of national security and power in the International politics. The human rights question as an issue of international concern may be said to have started at this point.
9. The provisions like for the human rights and dignity, like freedom from torture or cruel, inhuman degrading treatment or punishment (Art. 5), the right to recognition as a person before law (Art. 6), equality before the law and equal protection of law (Art. 7), right to an effective remedy (Art. 8), freedom from arbitrary arrest, detention or exile (Art. 9), the right to fair trail and public hearing by an independent and impartial tribunal (Art. 10), the right to be presumed innocent until proved guilty(Art. 11), freedom from arbitrary interference with private life, privacy, family, home or correspondence (Art. 12), freedom of movement (Art. 13), right to seek asylum (Art. 14), right to nationality (Art. 15), right to marry and found a family ((Art. 16), right to own property (Art. 17), freedom of thought concise and religion (Art. 18), freedom of opinion and expression (Art. 19), the right to take part in the government

of the country and right to equal access to public services (Art. 21), made under the UDHR was supplemented and enhanced by the other UN Convention and the inter-government treaties at the regional-level, for example, the Covenant on the Civil and Political Rights, 1966, with its two Option Protocols made the provision for the effective implementations of civil and political rights provided under the UDHR. One can also refer to UN Convention against Torture and other Cruel Inhuman Degrading Treatment or Punishment, 1984, International Convention on the Elimination of All Forms of Racial Discrimination, 1965, Convention on the Elimination of All Forms of Discrimination Against Women, 1981, Declaration on the Right to Development, 1986, Convention on the Rights of the Child, 1989, The Vienna Declaration and Programme of Action, 1993. The effective implementation of the human rights has been ensured through there bodies responsible for the functioning of the UN Human rights protection machinery are: General Assembly, ECOSOC, the Council on Human rights and sub-Commission n the Prevention of Discrimination and Protection of Minorities. "Human Rights Treaty Bodies—Petitions," www.2.ohchr.org/english/bodies/petitions/index.htm-, 23-7-2011.

"Inter-State Accountability for Violations of Human Rights," www.upenn.edu/pennpress/book/994.html, 23-7-2011.

Third State Responsibility for Human Rights Violations, www.ejil.org/pdf/21/4/2118.pdf , 25-7-2011.

10. "Magna Carta 1215," www.middle-ages.org.uk/htm, 31-12- 2010. "Magna Carta-Britannia.com," www.britannia/history/magna2.html, 31-12-2010.
11. "Declaration of the Rights of Man and of the Citizen—Wikipedia, en.wikipedia.org/.../.../Declaration of Rights of Man and of the Citizen, 22-12-2010.

    "The Declaration of the Rights of Man," library.thinkquest.org/0006257/.../declaration of rights.html-, 22-12-2010.
12. "Declaration of Independence, U.S. Constitution, Historical..." memory.loc.gov/ammem/help/constRedir.html-, 23-12-2010.
13. Arjun Dev, 1996, *Human Rights: A Source Book*, NCERT, New Delhi, pp. 9-12.
14. Third generation of rights are of those rights that go beyond the mere civil, political and economic rights and they are concerned with the post-material concerns of life. They are expressed in the progressive documents of International law, including the 1972 Stockholm Declaration of United Nations, Conference on Human Environment, the 1992 Rio Declaration on Environment and Development and policies of generally aspirational "soft law." Because of principles of sovereignty and the preponderance of would-be offender nation, these rights have been hard to enact in legally binding documents, three generations of human rights.

    "Wikipedia, the free encyclopedia," en.wikipedia.org.wiki/ three generation of human rights 28k, 31-12-2005.
15. David P. Forsthy, 2000, *op. cit;* No. 6, p. 13. See also: J.K. Chopra, 2010, *Human Rights and The Modern World*, D.P.S Publishing House, New

Delhi, pp 38-68, 69-89. Margot E. Salomon, 2007, *Global Responsibility for "Human Rights: World Poverty and The Development of International Law*, Oxford University Press, New York. The Resource: Part III, The Regional Human Rights System 4/6," www.un.org/socdev/enable/comp303.htm, 23-7-2010.

"African Commission on Human and Peoples' Rights. Commission...," www.achpr.org/, 23-7-2010.THE AFRICAN HUMAN RIGHTS SYSTEM: A CRITICAL EVALUATION..., hdr.undp.org/en/reports/global/hdr2000/papers/MUTUA.pdf, 24-8-2010.

"Regional human rights systems in other parts of the world, OHCR..., Bangkok.ohchr.org, 24-8-210.

"PROTECTION OF MINORITY RIGHTS IN THE INTER-AMERICAN,"www.ohchr.org/Documents/Publications/GuideMinorities5en.pdf , 24-8-2010.

"Inter-American Human Rights System," www1.umn.edu/humanrts/inter-americansystem.htm, 25-8-2010.

"Inter-American Commission on Human Rights—Wikipedia the free ... ," en.wikipedia.org/.../Inter-American Commission on Human Rights, 25-8-2010.

"The Inter-American Human Rights System-HREA," www.hrea.org, 25-8-2010.

"The League of Arab States and the Arab Charter on Human Rights," www.acihl,orgarticles.htm?article id=6, 25-8-2010.

"Human rights in Africa—Wikipedia, the free encyclopedia," en.wikipedia.org/wiki/Human rights in Africa, 25-8-2011.

"Human rights in the Arab world," www.ai-bab.com/arab/human.htm, 26-8-2010.

"Document: The Casablanca Declaration," www.al-bab.com/arab/docs/international/hr/1999.htm, 26-8-2010.

16. "Human Rights Council," www.ohchr.org/english/bodies/hrcouncil, 5-4-2007.
17. No previous century in human history has been privileged to witness such profusion of human rights enunciations on global scale. Never before the language of human rights sought to supplant other ethical languages. No previous century witnessed the proliferation of endless normatively of human rights standard as a core aspect of the inter-governmental desire never before has this discourse been so varied and diverse that it become necessary to regularly publish and updated, through the unique discursive instrumentality of United Nations system, in ever-expounding volumes of fine print, the various texts of instruments relating to the human rights. The Secretary General of United Nations was perhaps, right to observe (at his Inaugural Address at Vienna Conference on Human Rights, 1993) that rights constitute 'common language of humanity'. Indeed it would be true to say that in some ways a human rights discourse merges, in the era of the end of ideology, as the only universal ideology in the making, enabling both the legitimating of power and the praxis of emancipatory politics, Upendra Baxi, 2002, *The Future of Human Rights*, Oxford University Press, New Delhi, pp. 1-2.

18. Arjun Dev, 1996, *op. cit.*, No. 13, pp. 11-15.
19. Nachiketa, 2006, "Human Rights Various Meanings", Tapan Biswal, ed. *Human Rights Gender and Environment,* Viva Books Private Limited, New Delhi, pp. 45-48. See also: O.P. Gauba, 2003, *An Introduction to Political Theory*, Macmillan, New Delhi, 168-79.
20. The term "third generation human rights" remains largely unofficial, and thus houses an extremely broad spectrum of rights including: Group and collective rights, right to self-determination, right to healthy environment, right to natural resources, right to communicate, right to participate in cultural heritage, right to intergenerational equality and sustainability, "three generations of human rights—Wikipedia, the free encyclopedia," en.wikipedia.org.wiki/three generation of human rights 28k, 31-12-2005.
21. The idea of rights for an essential tool of analysis of the relation between individual and the state. The state claims authority over individual, but when the state is viewed as an instrument of society, it is essential that authority of the state is made to depend on the function it performs. In other words, when the state is regarded as a means and individual as the end, the state cannot be armed with absolute authority over individual. If the state claims authority, individual must claim rights. Individual owes allegiance to the state and obey its command because the state serves his interest. Rights essentially belong to the sphere of conflicting claims between individual and state.
22. The Historic declarations on limiting the powers and the dynastic privileges of King and the Royal Families hold the same. One can refer to the Magna Carta (1215); in many clauses John promises to be less harsh in enforcing his feudal rights on the barons and in the Clauses 39 and 40 concerning the legal system; John promises to provide good and fair justice in various ways.

    "To no one will sell, to no on will we deny or delay right of justice". This Clause establishes the principle of equal access to the Courts of all citizens without (exorbitant) fees. In clause 39, the king promises, "No free man shall be taken or imprisoned or diseased or outlawed or exiled in any destroyed, nor will go or send against him, except by the lawful judgment of his peers or by the law of the land." This clause establishes that the King would follow legal procedure before he punished someone. Magna Carta, 1215, *op. cit.*, No. 10. See also: The British Bill of Rights 1689 further curtailed the dynastic privileges and provided the subjects of England with most of the rights which laid foundation of human rights. In the Bill of Rights the British Parliament holds the freedom from royal interference with law (the sovereign was forbidden to establish his own courts to act as judge himself), freedom from taxation by the royal prerogative, with agreement by Parliament freedom of petition to king, freedom to elect the members of parliament without interference from the sovereign, the freedom of speech in parliament, in that proceeding in parliament were not to by questioned in the Court of Law or by anybody outside the parliament itself (the basis of modern parliament privilege), freedom from cruel and unusual punishment, and excessive bail freedom from excessive fines and forfeitures without trail. American Declaration of Independence holds, "we hold these truths to be self-evident, that all men are created equal, that they are endowed by their creator with certain unalienable rights that among these are Life, Liberty and the Pursuit of Happiness. That to secure these rights, governments is instituted among Men, deriving their just powers from the consent of the governed. That whenever any Form of Government becomes destructive of these ends, it is the Right of the people to alter or abolish it and to institute a new Government, laying its foundation on such principles and organizing its powers in such form." French Revolution and the resulted Declaration of the Rights of Man and Citizen, holds "The representative of the French people, constitute as a National Assembly, considering that ignorance, disregard or contempt of the rights of man are the sole causes of public misfortunes and governmental corruption, have resolved to set forth a solemn declaration, by being constantly present to all members of social body, may keep them all times aware of their rights and duties; that the acts of both the legislative and executive power, by being liable at every moment to comparison with the aim of all political institutions, may be the more fully respected; and that demands of the citizens by being founded henceforward on simple and incontestable principles, may always redound to the maintenance of the constitution and general welfare. See, Declaration of the Rights of Man and of the Citizen *op. cit.*, No. 11.

23. Michael Freeman, 2003, *Human Rights: An interdisciplinary approach*, Blackwell Publishers Ltd. USA, pp. 1-26. See also: Michael Freeden, 1998, *Rights*, World View Publications, New Delhi, pp. 1-24.
24. John Dunn, 2003, *Locke: A Very Short Introduction*, Oxford University, Delhi, pp. 35-43.
25. *The Constitution of India*, 2003, Government of India, Ministry of Law and Justice, New Delhi, p. 16.
26. *Ibid.*, p. 16.
27. Dr. J.N. Pandey, 2008, *The Constitution Law of India*, Central Law Agency, Allahbad, pp. 403-04.
28. *Ibid.*, pp. 390-91.
29. Right to education is included in the fundamental rights by the 86th Amendment of the Constitution by the Parliament on 12-12-2002, *Ibid*, p. 224.
30. *The Constitution of India*, 2003, *op. cit.*, No. 25, p. 17.
31. *Ibid.*, p. 78.
32. *Ibid.*, pp. 136-37.
33. Article 17 of the Indian Constitution, legalsutra.org/917/article-17-of-the-indian-constitution, 22-12-2011.
34. Upendra Baxi, 1982, *The Crisis of Indian Legal System*, Vikas Publications, New Delhi. See also: 1995, *Crisis and Change in Contemporary India*, Sage Publications, New Delhi. ", A.R. Desai, (ed.), 1986, *Violation of Democratic Rights in India*, (Vol. I), Popular Parkasan Pvt. Limited, Bombay. A.R. Desai, (ed.), 1991, *Expanding Government Lawlessness and Organized Struggle: Violation of the Democratic Rights of the Minorities*,

Women, Slum Dwellers, Press and Some other Violations, Popular Parkashan, Bombay, Somen Chakraborty, and R.M. Pal, (eds.), 2002, *State and Civil Society: Revisiting Contemporary India,* Indian Social Institute, New Delhi.

35. *Ibid.*
36. P. Padmanabhan, 1986, "Undemocratic Heart of the Indian Constitution", A.R. Desai, (ed.), *op. cit.,* No. 34, p. 74.
37. Durga Das Basu, 1997, *Introduction to the Constitution of India*, Prentice Hall of India, New Delhi, pp. 107-08.
38. Gobind Mukhoty, 1986, "The Indian Constitution and Civil Liberties", A.R. Desai, (ed.) *op. cit,* No. 34, pp. 80-81.
39. Sumanta Bannerjee, 1991, "Colonial laws—Continuity and Innovation", A.R., Desai, (ed.), *op. cit.*, No. 34, pp. 229-30.
40. Upendra Baxi, 1982, *op. cit.*, No. 35. See also: Upendra Baxi, 1995, A.R. Desai, (ed.), 1986, *op. cit.*, No. 34 A.R., Desai, (ed.), 1991, *op. cit.*, No. 35, Somen Chakraborty, and R.M. Pal, (eds.), 2002, *op. cit.*, No. 34.
41. Randhir Singh, 1993, *Five Lectures in Marxist Mode,* Ajanta Publication, New Delhi, pp. 39-40, 61-72.
42. *Ibid.*, p. 27.
43. Asghar Ali Engineer, 2002, "State And Civil Rights", Somen Chakraborty, and R.M. Pal, (eds), *op. cit.*, No. 34, pp. 9-19. See also: Gobind Mukhoty & Rajani Kothari, 1991, "Who are Guilty?," "Punjab, Delhi Riots and Parliamentary Power Politics—Main Culpability of Congress-I", A.R. Desai, *op. cit*, No. 34, pp. 33-59, 60-79.
44. Iqbal A. Ansari, 1991, "Preventive Detention: It's Incompatibility with the Rule of Law", A.R. Desai, *op. cit.*, No. 29, p. 100.
45. Sumanta Banerjee, 1991, "Colonial Law-Continuity and innovations", A.R. Desai, *op. cit.*, No. 34, pp. 232-33.
46. *Ibid.*, pp. 233-35. See also: Ujjwal Kumar Singh, 2004 ,"State and Emerging Interlocking Legal System: Permanence of Temporary", *Economic and Political Weekly*, January 10, pp. 149-59.
47. We can refer to the government response to the left movement in the 1970's and to the ethnic movement in north-east, J&K and Khalistan Movement in Punjab. Ram Narayan Kumar, 2008, *Terror in Punjab: Narrative Knowledge and Truth*, Shipra Publications, New Delhi, See also:, Ram Narayan Kumar, 1997, *The Sikh Unrest and the Indian State,* Ajanata Publications, New Delhi, pp. 275-76, Ram Narayan Kumar, *et al.*, 2003, *Reduced to Ashes: The Insurgency and Human Rights in Punjab,* (Vol. I), South Asia Forum for Human Rights Katmandu, Nepal.
48. Prakash Louis and R. Vashum, 2002, *Extraordinary Laws in India: A Reader for Understanding Legislations endangering Civil Liberties*, Indian Social Institute, New Delhi, pp. 163-64.
49. *Ibid.*, pp. 28-30, 176.
50. Committee for the Protection of Democratic Rights, 1991, "War and Our Civil Liberties", A.R. Desai, *op. cit,* No. 34, pp. 207-11, see also, A.G. Noorani, 1991, "Curfew as Tool of Repression", A.R. Desai, *op. cit.*, No. 29, pp. 212-14, Jagmohan Singh, 1991, "Report on Punjab" A.R. Desai, *op. cit.*, No. 34, pp. 215-24, Kuldeep Nayar, K.G. Kannabiran and

V.M. Tarkunde, 1984 "The Situation in Assam—A PUCL Report", A.R. Desai, *op. cit.*, No. 34, pp. 114-20, Amnesty International Report, 1986, "Political Killings in India", A.R. Desai, *op. cit*, No. 34, pp. 254-57.

51. "Report on Human rights violations," www.india-seminar.com/2000/496%20reort.htm-41k, 31-11-2011. See also: Combating Terrorism While Protecting Human Rights, www. Org/Pubd/2001/issued4/0404p27.html-17k, 30-11-2011.

52. "Human Rights Watch (HRW). "India: Justice Eludes Families of the 'Disappeared' in Punjab: National Human Rights Commission Should Investigate", http://www.hrw.org/press/2003/06/india061003.html, January 23-1-2010. See also:

    "Human Rights Watch (HRW). "India: Justice Eludes Families of the 'Disappeared' in Punjab: National Human Rights Commission Should Investigate" (New York: 10 Jun 2003)," http://www.hrw.org/press/2003/06/india061003.htm, 24-1-2010.

    Ram Narayan Kumar, 2001, *A complex Denial, SFHR Paper Series 10*, Kathmandu 10, Kathmandu: South Asia Forum for Human Rights, pp. 20-25.

53. Kanwar Sandhu, 2007, "Wrong Punjab lessons'', *Hindustan Times*, February 3. See also: TNS, 2006, "570 more victims of mass cremations identified", *The Tribune*, April 4. TNS, 2006, "Mass cremation ; relief orders for kin of 45", *The Tribune* , May 16, Dharminder Rataul, 2006, "Justice cremated, 185 families collect ashes of compensation", *Indian Express*, August 26, PTI, 2006, "Punjab to pay 1.75 lakh to 1,051 families: NHRC names HC ex-judge Bhalla to identify remaining 814 families", *Hindustan Times,* October 11, H.T. News, 2006, "KMO leads protest march", *Hindustan Times*, November 27, Kuldiip Mann, 2006, "Justice Bhalla urged to expand scope ; Rights activists want killing carried out to rehabilitate police cats' probed too", *Hindustan Times*, December 16, Kuldeep Mann, 2007, "Police out with 'doctored' FIRs: Withhold names of official involved in fake encounter", *Hindustan Times*, April 2, Ram Narayan Kumar, 2008, "Human rights: Justice Bhalla Mandate is limited", *The Tribune*, December 31.

54. Please see the bibliography at the end of this work for detailed references.

55. Harnik Deol, 2000, *Religion and Nationalism in India: The Case of Punjab*, Routledge, London.

56. Paramjit S. Judge, 2005, *Religion, Identity and Nationhood*, Rawat Publications, New Delhi.

57. Joyce Pettigrew, 1975, *Robber Noblemen*, Routledge & Kegan Paul, London.

58. Joyce Pettigrew, 1995, *The Sikh of Punjab: Unheard Voices of State and Guerrilla Violence,* Zed Books, London.

59. Harry M. Cleaver, 1972, "The Contradiction of Green Revolution", *The Monthly Review*, Vol. XXIV, No. 2, June.

60. Sucha Singh Gill and K.C. Singhal, 1984, "Punjab Problem: Its Historical Roots", *Economic and Political Weekly,* Vol. XIX, No 14, April 7, pp. 603-606. See also; Nirmal S. Azad, 1976, "Punjab Agricultural Wages", *Economic and Political Weekly*, Vol. XIII, No. 24, June 19, pp. 1107-12,

Master Hari Singh, 1980, *Agriculture Workers Struggle in Punjab*, People Publishing House, New Delhi, Aminderpal Singh, 1979, "Farmer Workers *vs.* Rich Farmers: Class and Caste in the Punjab Villages", *Economic and Political Weekly*, Vol. XIV, No. 42, October 27, pp. 1644-1650, Sucha Singh Gill, 1980, "Land Reforms and Peasant Movement in Punjab", *Mainstream,* June 14, pp. 27-30, Sucha Singh Gill, 1982, "Impact of Economic Development on Rural Artisans in Punjab", *Economic Analyst,* December 14, Victor Disouza, 1982, "Economy, caste, religion and population distribution analysis of communal tension in Punjab", *Economic and Political Weekly,* Vol. 17, No. 19, May 8, pp. 2933, Vinod Kumar, 1981, "Impact of Technology Change on Farm Employment: A case Study of Punjab", Unpublished M.Phil. Dissertation, Department of Economics, Punjabi University, Patiala, pp. 79-83.

61. Vandana Shiva, 1992, *The Violence of Green Revolution,* The Other India Press, Goa.
62. Dipankar Gupta, 1996, *The Context of Ethnicity: Sikh Identity in Comparative Perspective,* OUP, New Delhi.
63. Sangat Singh, 1996, *The Sikh History,* Greater Kailash, New Delhi. See also: Jaijee, Inderjit Singh, 2002, *Politics of Genocide: Punjab 1984-98,* Ajanta Publications, New Delhi, Nayar, Kuldeep & Kushwant Singh, 1984, *The Tragedy of Punjab,* Vision Books, New Delhi.
64. J.S. Grewal, 1998, "Sikh Identity and Khalistan", J.S. Grewal & Indu Banga, (ed.), *Punjab in Prosperity and Violence: Administrative Politics and Social Change 1947 -97,* K.K. Publishers, New Delhi. See also: Rajinder Kaur, 1992, *Sikh Identity and National Integration,* Intellectual Publishing House, New Delhi, Harish K. Puri, 1989, "Religion and Politics in Punjab"; Moin Shakir (ed.), *State, Religion and Politics in India,* Ajanta Publications, New Delhi, J.S. Gandhi, 1988, "System Process and Popular Ethos : A Case Study in Contemporary Politics in Punjab", Paul Wallace and Chopra, *Political Dynamics and the Crisis in Punjab,* Guru Nanak Dev University Press, Amritsar
65. Dipankar Gupta, 1996, *op. cit.,* No. 52.
66. H.K. Puri, 1989, "Religion and Politics in Punjab", Moin Sarkar, (ed.), *State Religion and Politics in India,* Ajanta Publications, New Delhi.
67. Subrata Mitra, 1986 "What is Happening to the Political Science of Ethnic Conflict", *International Journal of Punjab Studies,* Vol. III, No. 1, p. 79.
68. Satya Pal Dang, 1989, *Genesis of Terrorism: An Analytical Study of Punjab,* Patriot Publishers, New Delhi.
69. H.K. Puri, *et al.,* 1999, *Terrorism in Punjab: Understanding the Grassroots Reality,* Haranand Publications, New Delhi.
70. V.N. Narayanan, 1996, *Tryst with Terror: Punjab's Turbulent Decade,* Ajanta Publications, New Delhi.
71. Satya Pal Dang, 1989, *op. cit.,* No. 61.
72. Gurpreet Singh, 1996, *Terrorism: Punjab's Recurring Nightmare,* Sehghal Books, New Delhi,
73. H.K. Puri, *et. al.,* 1999, *op. cit.,* No. 69.
74. Ashgar Ali Engineer, 2002, "State and Civil Society", Somen Chakraborty & R.M. Pal, *op. cit.,* No. 34, pp. 1-18. See also: Ashgar Ali

Engineer, 1991, "Is India for Hindus Only", A.R. Desai, *op. cit.*, No. 34. p. 6., Gobind Mukhoty and Rajni Kothari, 1991, "Who are the Guilty", "Punjab, The Delhi Riots and Parliament Power Politics—Main Culpability of Congress-I", A. R. Desai, *op. cit.*, No. 34, pp. 33-60.

75. Harji Malik, 1984, "A Punjab Report", *Economic and Political Weekly*, Vol. XIX, No. 37 September 15, pp. 609-11.
76. Shinder Purewal, 2000, *Sikh Ethno Nationalism and Political Economy of Punjab*, Oxford University Press, New Delhi. See also: Special Correspondent, 1984, "Who are Guilty", *Economic and Political Weekly*, Vol. XIX, No. 47, November 24, pp. 1979-85, Romesh Thapar, 1984, "The So-called Indira" *Economic and Political Weekly*, Vol. XIX, No. 47, November, 24, p. 1975, Romesh Thapar, 1984, "The Truth is Savage", *Economic and Political Weekly*, Vol. XIX, No. 48, December 1, p. 2017 , Sumantra Banerjee, 1984, "Contradiction with a Purpose", *Economic and Political Weekly*, Vol. XIX, No. 48, December 1, 2028-31, Bharat Dogra, 1984, "Rehabilitation of Riot Victims", *Economic and Political Weekly*, Vol. XIX, No. 50, December 15, pp. 2111-12, Romesh Thapar, 1984, "The Rajiv Party and Hindu", *Economic and Political Weekly*, Vol. XIX, No. 50, December 15, pp. 2105-06, Special Correspondence, 1986, "Delhi, Terror in the Walled City: A Report", *Economic and Political Weekly*, Vol. XXI, No. 17, April 26, pp. 728-32.
77. Amiya Rao, 1984, "When Delhi Burnt", *Economic and Political Weekly*, Vol. XIX, No. 49, December 8, pp. 2066-69.
78. Giani Kirpal Singh, 1999, *Eyewitness Account of Operation Blue Star: Mighty Murderer Our Army Attack on the Golden Temple Complex*, Pub. Bhai Chatter Singh Jiwan Singh, Amritsar.
    Harbir Singh Bhawra, 1985, *Diary de Panhey* (in Punjabi), Hamdard Printers, Jalandhar.
79. Ujjwal Kumar Singh, 2004, *op. cit.*, No. 46. See also: Sumanta Banerjee, "Colonial Law-Continuity and innovations", A.R Desai, 1991, *op. cit.*, No. 29, pp. 232-33.
80. PUDR, 1985, "Black Laws in Punjab: Report of an Enquiry", *Economic and Political Weekly*, Vol. XX, No. 38, May 11, pp. 826-30.
81. Rita Manchanda, 2010, "Ethnic Kin States", Rita Manchanda (ed), *States in Conflict with their Minorities: Challenges to Minority Rights in South Asia*, Sage Publications, New Delhi, pp. 1-12.
82. Inderjit Singh Jaijee, 2002, *op. cit.*, No. 63.
83. Ram Narayan Kumar and George Sieber, 1991, *The Sikh Struggle: Origin, Evolution and Present Phase*, Chanakya Publication, Delhi. See also: Ram Naryan Kumar, 1997, *The Sikh Unrest and the Indian State*, Ajanata Publications, New Delhi, Kumar, Ram Narayan, *et. al.* 2003, *Reduced to Ashes: The Insurgency and Human Rights in Punjab*, (Vol. I), South Asia Forum for Human Rights, Katmandu, Nepal., Ram Narayan Kumar, 2008, *Terror in Punjab: Narrative Knowledge and Truth*, Shipra Publications, New Delhi.
84. Parneet Singh, 2004, "Poohla booked on abduction, murder charges", *The Tribune*, October 18. See also: Varinder Walia 2004, "Tension in Poohla village SGPC threat to 'liberate' gurudwara", *The Tribune*, March 10,

Varinder Sareen, 2006, "Poohla, 8 aides acquitted: Cleared of charges of murder of Nihang in 2002", *Hindustan Times*, October 12, TNS, 2007, "Poohla, six others held", *The Tribune*, April 10, IENS, 2007, "Poohla, six other arrested, sent to judicial remand till April 23", *Indian Express*, April 10, IENS, 2007, "More trouble for Poohla: Ex-servicemen's body says it will expose Poohla links with top police officers, points fingers at former DGP Virk", *Indian Express*, April 12, Varinder Walia, 2008, "Poohla helped police kill 7 in fake encounters, say kin", *The Tribune*, August 4, TNS, 2008, "Poohla shifted to Ludhiana Jail", *The Tribune*, August 8, TNS, 2008, "Controversial Nihang chief, Ajit Singh Poohla: facing trial for rape, murder and other heinous crime burnt alive", *The Tribune*, Aug. 29, Anuja Jaswal, 2008, "Poohla dies", *The Tribune*, August 30, "Neo-Nihang Poohla Burnt to Death. Justice served", www.panthic.org/news,125,ARTICLe/.../2008-08-29.html-, 29-6-2011.

85. We can refer to the Gurdwara of Satwant Singh, (Who killed the Indian Prime Minister) in Village Agwan, Tehsil Dera Baba Nanak in Gurdaspur and the Gurdwara built in the memory of Avtar Singh Brahma (who earned the title of Robinhood, because of his daring encounters with the armed forces during the militancy in Punjab) at village Brahmpura in Tarn Taran. It is to mention that Gurdwaras built in the other villages, like Padhari and Tharu are erased by the Police.
86. Jat-Sikhs may be dubbed as 'dominant caste' on the following three bases. First they are landowning in agrarian Punjab. Second they are numerically strong in all three regions of Punjab namely. Majha, Malwa and Doab and third, they are high in the hierarchical structure in Sikh majority Punjab.
87. Throughout the study references have been given at the end of every chapter in the footnotes with the location citation mentioning the page number at which it can be found in the document referred to, along with the necessary details of the documented concerned. A bibliography has also been added at the end of the book, duly arranged in an alphabetical order on the basis of the names of author or the work as case may be. Work of an author stand differentiated by the year of publication given in parenthesis following the name of the author. Wherever two works of an author, published in a single year have been catalogued, the reference has been distinguished by adding a serial number of the year of publication on the two documents.

2

Making of Sikh Identity: A Historical Narrative

The term Punjab originated from the Persian language/word and is a combination of the two words *Panj* (five) and *ab* (water). The land of Punjab is known as the land of five rivers and five types water also. As a region the state of Punjab has not only been known for long as the sword arm of Indian union but has also lately learned the title of the 'bread basket' of India in the aftermath of Green Revolution. The territorial boundaries of Punjab have their own role and importance in the political history of India as any change in the territorial boundaries of Punjab has its long-term impact on the political set-up at the centre of Indian Union. The territorial boundaries of Punjab had witnessed many changes even before the establishment of British Empire in Punjab in 1849.[1]

The historical memories of expansion and consolidation of the Kingdom of Lahore (Punjab Empire) under Maharaja Ranjit Singh, for example, have played a significant role in the shaping of imagination in the contemporary period. After the annexation, the British Punjab became a big state embracing the plains between Yamuna and Indus rivers but excluded many princely states. In 1947, when India was partitioned, Punjab was divided into two parts, and its western parts included in Pakistan. After the integration of the princely states, the former state of East Punjab was carved out into a separate state, viz., Patiala and East Punjab States Union (PEPSU). In

1956, the PEPSU was merged in Punjab. This was followed by a further intensification of earlier demand for a Punjabi-Suba on the pattern of the linguistic reorganization of other states in India. This led to the separation of the Hindi-speaking areas from Punjab and formation of new state of Punjab in 1966. However, the struggle for inclusion of certain left-out Punjabi-speaking areas is still going on. All these territorial changes were effected by political decisions and occurrences. These were either consequences of or led to the political movements. The movement for Pakistan, Punjabi-Suba and the *Khalistan movement* were three significant movements in this regard.[2] As a region Punjab is straddling the border between India and Pakistan. 'The Five Types Water and the Five Rivers' of Punjab are Beas, Ravi, Sutlej and Jhelum; all these are the tributaries of the Indus River, Jhelum is biggest one. Punjab has a long history and rich cultural heritage. The people of Punjab are called Punjabis and their language is also called Punjabi. The main religions of the Punjab are Sikhism, Hinduism and Islam.

The areas now known as the Greater Punjab in popular parlance once comprised the vast territories of Eastern-Pakistan and northern-western. The bigger section of the Punjab is owned by Pakistan (65% to India's 35%). It comprised, in its original sense, regions extending from Swat/Kabul in the west to Delhi in the east, that are the areas including parts of Afghanistan and the plains up to the Ganges.

Pakistan now comprises the majority of the undivided colonial Punjab province together with Hazara region of the North-West Frontier. The Indian Punjab has been further sub-divided into the modern Indian states Punjab, Haryana and Himachal Pradesh. The Pakistan part of the region that may be called West Punjab covers an area of 205,344 square kilometres, whereas the Indian State of Punjab is 50,362 square kilometres.

The population of the region are similarly divided as 86,084,000 (2005) in West Punjab (Pakistan) and 24,289,296 (2000) in the present-day State of (East) Punjab (India) and a further 30 million in the rest of the region. Punjabi is spoken by (approximately) 65% of population in Pakistani Punjab (another 25% speak Punjabi variants) and 92.2% in Indian Punjab. The capital city of undivided Punjab was Lahore, which now sits close to the partition line as the capital of West Punjab. Indian Punjab has its capital in the city of Chandigarh. After the partition, the capital of the Indian Punjab was Shimla (now is the capital of Himachal Pradesh). Indian Punjab uses the

Gurumukhi script; while Pakistani Punjab uses the Shahmukhi script.

Most of the Punjab land is in nature an alluvial, bounded by Himalayan Mountains to the North. Because of its location in footsteps of Himalaya it is a rich agricultural area due to the extensive irrigation made possible by the great river system traversing it. Punjab region temperature range from -2° to 40°C (Min/Max), but can reach 47°C (117°F) in summers and can touch down to -2°C in winters. The historical region of Punjab is considered to be one of the most fertile regions on the earth. Both the east and west Punjab produce a relatively high portion of India and Pakistan's food output, respectively. The agriculture output of the Punjab region in Pakistan contributes significantly to Pakistan's GDP. The region is important for wheat growing. In addition, rice, cotton, sugarcane, fruits and vegetables are the major crops. Both India and Pakistan are considered to have the best infrastructures of their respective countries. The Indian Punjab has been estimated as first rich state of India for long time. Punjab alone contributes 52% of granary to the Indian food stock, which has led to its naming as the 'Bread Basket of India'.[3]

The land of Punjab has also earned a great place in the history, culture and the literature of the ancient, medieval and modern India. Being a borderland state of India, Punjab has been witness to innumerable wars. The land has also been witness to socio-religious movements. This land is also known as the land of *Shurmas* (Legends) and heroes. A major part of Punjabi folklore and lyrics is devoted to glory of the legends and heroics of Punjabi people. The geographical location of Punjab always forced the native of the land to prepare against any invasion or a threat of from the North-Western boundaries, either it was of ancient, medieval and modern Punjab. A cursory glance over written and oral history of Punjab can prove that martial values have a great place in the Punjabi society. The villages and the cities across the Punjab are full of the monuments and forts which were made by Punjabis to remember the heroism and the sacrifices to which their legends made to save the country and the proud of Punjab particularly. The stories and popularity of the legends of the Punjab has been passing from one generation to another through the traditions of *Melas* (festivals) and the *Vars* (melodies), which are sung on the festivals to remember the martyrs and the heroic traditions Punjab. Although the martial values dominates the whole of Punjab but the Majha region has great importance in the martial values and the history of Sikhs. The first six wars of the Sikhs history against the tyranny of the Muslim King Jahangir under the leadership of sixth guru occurred in the region of Majha. Majority of the coronation ceremonies of the gurus also happened in the holy land of Majha. The concept of two swords of *Piri* (spirituality) and *Miri* (temporal) adopted as tenets in Sikhism after the assassination of the fifth guru at the hand of Muslim King Jahangir at coronation of sixth guru also happened at Majha. Majha is called the 'cradle of Sikhism' due to the presence of the holy shrines of Sikhism in the region.

The militarisation of the Sikh Panth by the sixth guru Shri Guru Hargobind also started from the Majha. After the martyrdom of his father, the fifth guru, Shri Hargobind immediately called for the militarization of Sikhism and made an open call to Sikhs for the contribution of the arms and the military goods to the Sikh-Panth. He also established a centre of *Sikh political power Shri Akal Takhat Sahib* just at the front of *Shri Harimander Sahib*, the supreme spiritual seat of Sikhism. Then the starting of martial art and war exercises, exhibition of the weapons in front of the *Harimandir Sahib* (Golden Temple) by the sixth guru witnessed a radical change in the philosophy of Sikhism. The spiritual leanings took a sharp turn for the socio-religious and political change with new establishment of the Akal Takhat in the complex of Golden Temple, which is playing a dominant role in the Sikh and Punjab history from its very establishment.[4]

In the ancient period Punjab was known as the land of Vedas. Being the land of the Aryans, the Hindu scriptures, the Rig Veda and Upanishads were composed in Punjab. Tradition maintains that the sage Valmiki composed the Ramayana near the present location of Amritsar. In legend, Krishna delivered the divine message of the Bhagwat Gita at Kurukshetra. Eighteen principal Puranas were written in the region. The authors of the Vishnu Purana and the Shiva Puranas belonged to Central Punjab. The epic battles described in the Mahabharata were fought in Punjab. The Gandharas, Kamboj, Trigartas, Andhara, Pauravas, Paurvas, Bahlikas (Bactrian settlers of Punjab), Yaudheyas and other sided with Kaurvas in the greatest battle fought at Kurukshetra. In 326 BC, Alexander the Great invaded Punjab from the north and incorporated it into his empire. His armies entered the region via the Hindu Kush in the north-west Pakistan and his rule extended up to the city of Sagla (modern day Sialkot) in the north-east Pakistan.[5]

The political history of Punjab has always witnessed conflict and chaos and political instability since long time back as the majority of the foreign invaders entered into the territory of India after ruling the land of Punjab. The middle ages especially the Mughal era witnessed conflict, chaos, and political upheaval, except the prosperity and the establishment of relative peace under the Jahangir period.

The above period was also notable for the emergence of Guru Nanak (1469-1539), the founder of Sikhism, which has left a lasting impression on the history and culture of Punjab. Born in the district of Sheikhupura (now in Pakistan), Guru Nanak rejected the division of mankind into rigid compartments of orthodox religions and castes and preached the oneness of humanity, and oneness of God, thus aiming at creating a new order which embraced the all pervasive spirit in man. This new philosophy would serve as foundation for the Sikh faith.

The teaching and the values of first guru were furthered by his nine disciples. Guru Nanak notion of human equality and urge of social change made Sikhism a popular movement for the social, religious and political reforms in Punjab. In due course of time a militarised Sikhism also emerged as challenge to the then politically powerful forces especially after the tragic assassination of the fifth guru Arjun Dev by the Mughal emperor Jahangir on the fake charges of tax theft and organising revolt against the empire.[6]

The assassination of the fifth guru was a watershed event in the history of Sikh Panth as it forced the Sikh-Panth for sharp changes in its philosophy, which witnessed a great change in the earlier socio-political and organisational set-up of Sikh Panth. Successor of the fifth guru was bestowed with two swords. The wearing of two swords by the sixth guru symbolised the combination of *Bhagti* (Spirituality) and *Shakti* (corrective power) for the first time in the Sikh history. After his coronation, the sixth guru started to organise Sikh-Panth as a military force and laid the foundation of *Shri Akal-Takhat Sahib* in front of *Harimandir Sahib* as the symbol of the political power of the Sikh Panth. Newly militarised Sikhs put up a tough challenge to Mughal army that was sent to arrest the Guru. Finally, on his own will, Guru got arrested and was sent to a fort prison in Gwalior by Jahangir, where the Hindu kings were already imprisoned. However, Sikhs and Jahangir came to a compromise and Jahangir agreed to release Guru, but the Guru showing his secular spirit put up a condition that he would come out of Gwalior fort only if the Emperor agreed to release 52 Hindu Kings from the fort along with him. Emperor agreed and obliged the guru. Moreover, for strengthening Mughal ties with the rising military power of Sikh-Panth, Emperor Jahangir also prosecuted the person by name of Chandu, who was the main kingpin in fabricated wrong charges against the fifth guru.[7]

The period of seventh and eighth guru passed peacefully without any turbulence except for the controversy over the succession issue for *guru-gaddi*. Succession to the ninth guru led to confusion and controversies as the eighth guru passed away due to small-pox at a very young age. According to the *Janam Sakhis* the *eighth guru* announced his grand uncle Teg Bahadur, one of the two adopted sons of sixth guru, his successor to the small gathering of Sikhs before he passed away in Delhi. However, the earlier controversies of the seventh and eighth gurus regarding the succession again resurfaced and a large number of fake gurus appeared at Baba Bakala, a place in the Amritsar district now, claimed to be Teg Bahadur and the successor of the Sikhs. According to the Sikh history and Museum of the gurdwara built in memory of guru Teg Bahadur at Baba Bakala, the confusion over the identity of Guru Teg Bahadur as the real guru was revealed by a Muslim businessman Makhan Shah Lubana.

Guru Teg Bahadur moved to Patna in Bihar where his wife gave birth to their only child Gobind Rai who became the tenth guru of Sikhs and the founder of the Khalsa Panth. Guru Teg Bahadur undertook the task of protecting the faith of Kashmiri Pundits, who had approached Guru Teg Bahadur, against their forced conversion to Islam by the Muslim Emperor Aurangzeb.

Guru Teg Bahadur went to Delhi with the Pandits to save their endangered faith. He was captured in Agra and executed in Delhi on the orders of Mughal emperor on 11 November 1675. Guru had been asked to convert to Islam to save himself. Guru sacrificed himself for religious tolerance and for the protection of the Hindu religion against forced conversion of Islam by Aurangzeb.[8]

Guru Teg Bahadur was succeeded by his son Gobind Rai, who was of nine years when he saw his father's severed head cremated at Anandpur Sahib. For reasons of safety he was shifted from Anandpur to a village Paonta Sahile which lies in the region where the Sutlej enters the plains. This section of Shivalik Range between the Sutlej and Yamuna marks today the border of Haryana and adjoining part of Punjab towards Himachal Pradesh. Gobind Rai showed very early that he combined many talents. He quickly learnt Persian and Sanskrit, studied religion and methodological lore, wrote poetry, loved to hunt and engage in military exercise. By the time he was twenty, he had raised an army including Pathan mercenaries and waged his first successful battle against Hindu hill chiefs, who tried to expel him when they saw that Guru was beginning to sap their strength by attracting many of their low castes subjects into casteless society.

Confident of his strength Guru could return to Anandpur, but he hardly established his court there when the hill chiefs together with their overlord, the Raja of Bilaspur came to ask for help. They had so far paid revenues to the Mughals. Another payment was due, and Guru was asked to help them against the then Mughal governor to evade the payment. Guru agreed and led them to victory over the advancing Mughal force. Thereupon Aurangzeb's son Moazzam, the later emperor Bahadur Shah, sent a stronger expedition, which reduced the hill chiefs to submission, but left Guru unscathed.

Within hardly more than a year after his first successful military engagement, the tenth guru had become the brightest light among the leaders of the hills, a Sikh against Hindu Rajput rulers. To uphold his position, he built several fortresses along the low mountains between the Sutlej and Yamuna, among these five were Anandgarh Sahib, Holegarh Sahib, Lohgarh Sahib, Fatehgarh Sahib, Taragarh Sahib were built at Anandpur. Although guru did not want further war but he depended on military strength to work unperturbed on his real project, the reform of the Sikh community, the consolidation of the faith given to them by Guru Nanak.[9]

FOUNDATION OF THE KHALSA PANTH: SAGA OF SACRIFICES AND REFORMS

Guru saw that religious learning was needed; Guru Granth (Holy Book compiled by the fifth guru) was needed to be interpreted correctly, inspiration to the rise of moral courage to fight for the right. Scholarly followers were sent for study to Indian Centres of learning; *bards* flocked in at the Court of Anandpur Sahib to sing of heroes of past. But most important was the unity which was lacking the succession of almost all the earlier Gurus had been disputed by one other faction with their claims to authentic leadership; selection of the child-Gurus after a monarchical pattern was not the idea of Guru Nanak. The system also fostered the continuing inclination among his people to grade even their fellow believer according to their birth. The lack of strong central leadership has also permitted the Masands[10], the heads of Manjis[11] or Preachers to dispose over their collected resources arbitrary and to take sides with whomsoever they liked. Both the tradition of guruship and the autonomy of the Masands had to be finished with, and Guru was determined to have his way.

To test his own authority and sincerity of his followers, Guru sent message to all Sikhs urging that as many as men as possible should attend the spring festival on 13 April, 1699, at Anandpur. On his call thousand of Sikhs assembled before him, he drew his sword and asked for the sacrifice of five heads. After a baffled silence one man named Daya Ram rose, the Guru led him into tent. A thud was heard. The Guru stepped out with his sword dripping with blood. In all five men offered themselves for sacrifice for the panth. Afterwards the people found all the five people were actually unharmed. Guru then proclaimed that for the future the leadership of the community would rest with "*Panj Piaras*" (five dear ones). He stirred sweetend water—"Amrit" (Nectar) in an iron bowl with two-edged dragger to be drunken by the five from the same bowl, and asked them to prepare *Amrit* also for him to drink, thereby symbolising that he had merged his authority into the collective will of the community. The most important to reveal regarding the foundation of The Khalsa-Panth armed at the renunciation of Hindu caste Dharma and Varna system, according to which the work and status of the person was decided by the birth. The absolute majority of the *Panj Piaras* was of low caste among the five, four of low caste and also from out of Punjab. This act was to be sacrament of initiation for all who would forthwith be ready to abandon the caste and pride, and all forms of worship and mannerism concessional to Hinduism against the teaching of Guru Nanak.

Those who joined the panth would express their belonging to the same family by assuming surname Singh, which means "Lion" and belonging to Khalsa "the pure". The famous five *K's* should be worn by them: Kesh, Kirpan, uncut hair, a comb to keep it tidy, a steel bracelet around the wrist of the sword–arm, a short sabre. Several complementary prohibitions were added, relating to temptations a solider might succumb. Having given the new Code of Sikhs, Guru concluded his address with war cry: *Wahe Guru Ji ka khalsa te Wahe Guru ji ke Fateh*, which means "The Khalsa shall rule, distracters shall perish."[12]

The creation of the Khalsa was seen by the hill chiefs not as an inner-Sikh affairs but as a threat to their future. They united and encircled Anandpur to cut the supplies from the villages of the Raja Bilaspur, who called the Mughal for help while Guru shifted to other places. He could repulse the Mughal forces sent from Lahore and Sirhind and foiled another attack of the Raja, who gave in and wanted to come to terms with him. Guru had a breathing space and fortified Anandpur, but the hill chiefs and rajas again went to plead to the emperor. A formidable force of both Muslims and Rajputs encircled Anandpur, the Sikh warriors were starved but Guru could get away with his family and a small band of fiercely loyal Sikh soldiers. What followed in the wake was a tantalising tale of fight, suffering and treachery. His two elder sons along with many of his closest associates got martyrdoms while fighting the enemies of the Khalsa at Anandpur. The Guru left Anandpur and shifted to Malwa. Soon he got the news that his two younger sons and mother got martyrdoms at the hands of the Nawab of Sirhind.

Guru was now in the west region of Sirhind in the land south of Sutlej called Malwa, with the dominant population of Jats who suffered from the ruthless exploitation of Wazir Khan rallying around him. Within no time, a large number of Jats had joined the Khalsa and helped the Guru to throw back the pursuing forces of Wazir Khan. With the enemies put off, Guru could settle in a village called *Dam Dama*, "breathing place", to complete the collection of his own writings known as *Dasham Granth*, the book of tenth Guru.

The crimes of Wazir Khan had not been forgotten, but the Sikhs needed time to prepare for his punishment. The earlier years of the eighteenth century were a time of transition. The war of succession between Aurangzeb's three surviving sons started. Guru sided with Bahadur Shah, who was gentle and generous but weak in decision making. He sent him a detachment of the horsemen who helped Bahadur Shah to defeat one of his two brothers in crucial battle at Jajau south of Agra. In June 1707 Guru was honoured by Bahadur Shah at Agra and was invited to join him on march towards Deccan, where his second brother was to be subdued. When camping in the village Nanded on the bank of Godavari, 150 miles north-west of Hyderabad, Guru was stabbed in his tent by two Pathans, probably hirelings of Wazir Khan, and died from wound on 7 October 1708.[13]

Sikhs after the Tenth Guru

The concept of the living Guru for the Sikhs ended with the

death of Guru Gobind Singh as he made Guru Granth (Holy book of Sikhs) his successors. He asked the Sikhs to follow the teachings of Guru Granth and not to the living Gurus; however, after the demise of tenth guru his disciple Banda Bahadur came to Punjab and routed the Muslim empire. According to the Sikh legend Banda Bahadur, was an ascetic and was called Madho Das in the hills of Nanded. It was at the end stage of his life when guru with small-band of Sikh entered in the Dera of Madho Das suddenly, while fighting with the Mughal forces. The Sikhs soldiers were hungry so they slaughtered some goats of Madho Das, while guru was sitting on the guru-gaddi (spiritual sheet) of Madho Das. Madho was on the river for his morning bath, but his supernatural power made him aware that someone is sitting on his spiritual seat. Madho tried his supernatural power to throw down guru from his spiritual seat but failed. Then Madho ran back to the Dera and found that some of his goats were also slaughtered by the Sikhs. He cried on the slaughter of goats and told the guru that he cannot live in the Dera, because it got impure with blood. Guru replied that how a piece of land or his Dera can remain pure, when the whole land of India was full of the blood of innocents. At this point Madho Das fell at the feet of Guru and cried that I am your Banda (slave); kindly show me the right path.[14]

Banda Bahadur, as his name suggested stood for complete submission to the tenth Guru and his cause. Guru blessed him with extraordinary powers. Guru deputed him to Punjab with the five arrows and a small-band of Sikh army to defeat the Mughal Empire in Punjab. Banda felt about the oppression of the Punjab peasantry. He was deputed to North and raised Sikh army whilst Mughal were still occupied with their campaign in South. Banda was to realize the historical mission of the first head-on confrontation of the Sikhs with central Mughal power. To the army of Sikhs, Banda first planted a banner of the Guru at a village near Delhi, proclaiming that he had come to protect all those who suffered injustice.[15]

His first Army was hardly more than a horde of rustic Sikh peasants armed with lances, knives, hatches, sickles. The army steadily grew into ten of thousands as they marched towards north. They had nothing to lose; petty constables loafing along the villagers ran away and joined the Banda's Army, bringing their own small weapons. First, the state treasury of Sonepat was looted. They seized the muskets from the guards, whosoever tried to resist was killed. Then onwards they marched into Samana, a town of Malwa region, where the executor of the Guru's two sons lived and also many rich

Muslims. Better guarded Samana could resist only for three days. Thousands of attackers were slain, but there was no end of them and they came from all directions. The town was looted, burned. No one was spared. The capture of town was important for the rebel hordes, because they held the granaries, where the fruit of their own sweat were hoarded to feed the rich whilst they starved.

Samana was on way to Sirhind, 80 miles to the Northeast, where Wazir Khan ruled. Peasants groups from Majha on the other side of river Sutlej caught the news and crossed the river to join Banda. The soldiers of Afghan garrison which were deputed by the Mughal ruler of the Sirhind even could not stop the peasants from crossing the river. The united hordes took several towns around the present day Ambala (Haryana), but Sirhind was kept for later for it was well defended. It was in the winters of 1609-10 and Banda postponed further conquest to spruce up training of his military and to collect more weapons. By the end of May 1610 Sirhind was in rubble. Wazir Khan and Sucha Nand, the instigator of the murder of Guru's two sons were killed. The canons and the muskets of the 15,000 of the defenders of Sirhind had proved worthless against the ferocity of the still poorly armed but numerically far superior peasants. Every poor wretch between Sutlej and Yamuna, it was Hindu now wants to be Sikh by growing long hairs and paying at least lip service to the Guru Nanak, also many Muslim peasants became Sikhs. The lands of the conquered landlords were split into small plots for distribution among the actual cultivators.[16]

Banda receded to hills to get more horses and weapons and returned to conquer the towns of east Jamuna. Many of the rich fled in advance towards the Gangetic heartland. He crossed back to Punjab, peasants over ran the region between Sutlej and Ravi and beyond towards North. But the forces of insurrection were too widely fanned out and chaotic to be given a controlled military shape. Instead of rallying them together to capture the fortified core-cities of Lahore and Delhi, Banda Bahadur allowed the emperor to return and win over the important Rajput kings of Rajasthan to ally with them to the emerging forces of peasants. Raja Jai Singh of Ajmer, when he was on his way to Punjab, killed the Sikh messengers sent to him by Banda with appeal to change his mind.

From December 1710 onwards, the united Muslim-Hindu armies under the Imperial flag quickly took back what the peasants believed to have been liberated from Mughals. Advancing to the hills, they captured Banda's fortress of Mukhaligarh, though Banda could escape and penetrate further into hills to vengeance on another enemy of Sikhs, the old Raja Bhim Chand of Bilaspur. The five years left to Banda were marked by a number of ambitious and initially promising attempts to recapture from the hills what he has lost in the plains. But after defeating Muslim army near Jammu and sacking Batala he had again been forced to retreat, the infuriated emperor ordered a massacre of the innocent Sikhs in the region. The fear of the recurring of the revolt was such that all the Hindus in the imperial services were ordered to shave of their beards to prove that they had nothing to do with Sikhs. The government made it policy to win over the influential Hindus to their side. Several Hindu landlords in Batala district, a stronghold of the insurrection, embraced to Islam in return for large grants in land and cash. Many Khatri merchants received benefits for turning to pro-Mughal. Bhagti Mal, an advisor to Government of Delhi, who at the start of insurrection had been imprisoned for his sympathies with the rebels, was released and became Chief Advisor. Muzaffar Alam, a researcher into this period gives a table to show that substantial number of Hindus had risen to high positions in the imperial services and assisted in putting down the insurrection.[17] Thus, sowing the first seeds of distrust between the Hindu elite castes and the Sikh peasant community.

Persecution of the Sikh Community

The reign of Banda came to an end when after a long period of calm the peasants below the hills again became turbulent: 7000 of them made an attempt to capture Ropar, a hill district of the present Punjab, which is near to Himachal Pradesh. Encouraged, Banda left his retreat near Jammu and soon saw himself confronted by a confederate army of Mughals and Rajputs. After a protracted fight near Batala which he lost, he entrenched himself near Gurdaspur, north of Batala after cutting a Canal for the purpose to keep the Mughal Artillery at a distance. But his entrenchment turned into a problem because the besiegers across the water cutting off the supplies. After eight months, the Sikhs were almost starved to death and had to surrender. In December 1715, a ghoulish procession made its way to Delhi arrive there in March.

The plight of the arrested Sikhs was witnessed by the two ambassadors of the East India Company to the Mughal Court. John Surman and Edward Stephan, who wrote about the Sikh arrests in a letter to the Governor of Fort William in Bengal. "Some days ago they entered the city laden with fetters, his whole attendants which were alive being about seven and eight hundred and eighty, all severally mounted on camels which were sent out of the city for that purpose, besides about two thousands heads stuck upon poles. He at present has life prolonged with the hope to get an account of his treasures in several parts of his kingdom, and of those that assisted him, when afterwards he will be executed, for the rest those are hundred in each day beheaded. It is not a little remarkable with what patience they undergo their faith and to last it has not been found that one apostatized from his new formed religion.[18]

In the "Early Annals of the English in Bengal" edited by C.R. William, an eye-witness account is given of the behaviour of the captives. "Life was promised to any, who would renounce his faith, but they would not prove false to their Guru and the place of suffering their consistency was wonderful to look at. 'Me, deliverer, kill me first' was the prayer which constantly rang in the ears of the executioner.[19]

Sikh Outlaws and Mughal Emperors

After the Banda's execution, the emperor issued an order to his officers in Punjab to apprehend and kill Sikhs, conspicuous with their beards and turbans, wherever found. Some of them evaded threat by turning Sahejdhari, other preferred to leave their families lands to turn to the hills and jungles, with plunder as means of their survival. They formed small armed groups called jathas, which became the protective arm of the outlying villages against the harassment of regular revenue collectors. The Jathas evolved the tradition to meet twice a year in larger assembly called *Sarbat Khalsa.* The Governor of Lahore, Zakarya Khan, tried to appease them by legalizing their *de-facto* control over some Jagirs-estates—mainly around Dialpur in the Bari of Majha Doab. The Sarbat Khalsa could meet again at Akal Takhat in Amritsar, where they decided to form an army, the *Dal Khalsa.* But when some armed factions began to control the region not permit to them. The Governor renewed the repression. The head priest of the Harimandir Sahib, Bhai Mani Singh was executed.[20]

The political situation took a new turn when Nadir Shah, the Persian emperor, came to India for the sole purpose to loot and successfully plunder Delhi. But he was not aware of the thing that his strong forces can be attacked by the Sikhs to loot the booty. The returning forces of the Nadir Shah preyed to the attacks of the small groups of Sikhs near the northern hills at the nights; the forces lost a large amount of Delhi plunder to the elusive hit and run tactics of Sikh jathas. Then the Muslim ruler of Punjab Zakarya Khan, promised to annoy Nadir Shah to punish the Sikhs for their daring act, and did so effectively by initiating head-hunting campaign against the Sikhs. Ten rupees for information where they hid; fifty rupees for a Sikh scalp (the long hair was the proof); capital punishment for giving shelter to them. Thousands of Sikhs were beheaded at the horse market in Lahore.

But large number of Sikhs ran to jungles and hills of Shivalik, they not only attacked by state forces but also killed by some of the influential persons of the Mughal Empire. The brother of Lakhpat Rai, a Hindu Minister of Yahaya Khan, who had succeeded his father Zakraya Khan as Governor of Lahore in 1745 was also killed by a Sikh Jatha. The killing of the brother of Lakhpat Rai wrought terrible revenge as around 7000 Sikhs in north of Lahore area were killed, blocked by the hill chiefs when they tried to escape. 3000 were caught alive and executed at horse market in Lahore. The Harmandir Sahib was assaulted, the holy Pond polluted with debris. The event became known as Chhota Ghalughara (small holocaust) of June 1746.[21]

The Big Holocaust

Things changed again when Yahaya Khan was ousted by his brother Shah Nawaz, who tried to appease the Sikhs by jailing Lakhpat Rai, the perpetrator of the "small holocaust". In the meantime, the Persian emperor Nadir Shah had been killed and Ahmad Shah Abdali, a young General of Nadir Shah became ruler of Afghanistan. To finance the confederacy of Afghan tribes, Abdali attacked India nine times between 1747 AD to 1769 AD. His first invasion did not get far and saw the rise of Mir Mannu, brother-in-law of Yahya Khan, who beat the Afghans in a battle near Sirhind and thereupon became the governor of Lahore. Meantime, Sikhs had established themselves all over the region between the Sutlej and the Chenab. Under the leadership of Ahluwalia, the leaders of the *Dal Khalsa* that gave shape to the Army consisting of twelve *Misls* or fighting fraternities and tens of thousands of the cavalry and infantry. Each *Misl* could do as it pleased within its own area, but they were to unite in emergencies when the wealth of the whole community was at stake.

Mir Mannu, who had still troubled relations with Afghans, tried to appease the Sikhs, relying on the good services of his most trusted Minister Kaura Mal, who was a *Sehaj Dhari* Sikh. But after Kaura Mal's death in 1752 during third Afghan invasion, Mir Mannu took his predecessor Zakarya Khan's policy to slaughter the troublesome Sikhs. Khushwant Singh translated a popular poem of Punjabi which has been written to encourage the Sikhs for Martyrdom by giving the references of Sikhs patience against the repression of Manu:

Manu Sadi Datri,
Oh jeve vade sanu,
Asi hor lame hoye.

Mir Manu is our sickle,
We fodder for him to mow,
The more he reaps us more we grow.[22]

After Mir Manu's death in 1754 the Punjab became fully uncontrollable. The Sikhs were engaged in robbing the Afghans as they returned from their looting excursion which had led them beyond Delhi to Agra and Mathura. In 1757, the Afghans took revenge by blowing-off the Harmandir and polluting the sacred pond with entrails of cows. Both Punjab and Sind were under the Afghan rule in 1757, when Ahmad Shah Abdali was granted suzerainty over these provinces.[23]

Last phase of Afghans and the Establishment of Sikh Misls

The Sikhs soon gathered their strength and started taking on the Mughals. Governor of Lahore Taimur Khan was however able to expel the Sikh warriors from Amritsar and also razed a fort of Ram Ṛauni for the defence. But all his efforts soon became meaningless, when the Sikh Misls joined hands to defeat Taimur Khan and his Chief Minister Jalal Khan. The Afghans were forced to retreat and Lahore was occupied by the Sikhs in 1758. Jassa Singh Ahluwalia proclaimed the Sikh's sovereignty and assumed leadership striking coins to commemorate his victory.[24]

While Ahmad Shah was engaged in a campaign against the Marathas at Panipat in 1961, Jassa Singh Ahluwalia plundered Sirhind and Dialpur, seized towns in the Ferozpur, and took possession of Kot Isa Khan on the opposite bank of Sutlej. He captured Hoshiarpur and Naraingarh in Ambala and levied tributes from the Chief of Kapurthala. He then marched towards Jhang. The Sial Chief offered Tarn Taran. Jassa Singh was engaged with his mission to extend his territory, but when in 1762 he crossed the Beas and captured the Sultanpur, Ahmad Shah Abdali again appeared in Punjab. Afghans returned with great preparation with a mission to teach the Sikhs a lesson. A fierce battle between the Sikhs and Afghan took place and 30,000 Sikhs were massacred. A traveller G. Foster in his book "A Journey from Bengal to England" reports: "pyramids were erected and covered with the heads of slaughtered Sikhs, and walls of mosques which the Sikhs had polluted were washed with their blood. The Harmandir was again blown up, however, Jassa Singh who fled to Kangra hills following rout of Sikh forces at the hands of Abdali. Again organised, the Sikhs attacked on Sirhind immediately after the departure of Ahmad Shah. The Governor of Sirhind, Zen Khan was killed in the battle and the fortresses of Sirhind were razed.

Abdali's ninth invasion was nipped in bud. The Afghans were out. Delhi was no longer to be feared. The power of the Afghans declined with the death of Ahmad Shah in June 1773. Taimur Shah ascended the throne at Kabul. By then the Misls were well established in the Punjab. They controlled territory as far as Saharanpur in the east, Attock in the west, Kangra and Jammu in the north and Multan in the south.[25]

Quarrelling Sikh Misls and the Rise of Ranjit Singh

The theocratic confederation of the Sikh Misls, soon came under the clouds. The earlier traditions of *Sarbat Khalsa* and the *Gurmatas* soon became meaningless as there was no common cause or threat from the outside. Misls became paramount. As soon as the Afghans showed their feather, they spread out in all directions to extract Rakhi (protection money) from territories under the Hindu and Muslim chiefs, capturing their towns and losing them again, sometimes falling out among themselves over the spoils. Polier writes in 1780:

> From the spirit of independence so invariably infused amongst them with their mutual jealousy and rapacious roving temper, the Sikhs in this day are seldom seen cooperating in community concert: but actuated by the influence of an individual ambition of private distrust, they pursue such plans only to coincide with these motives.

The mutual jealousy led to serious military confrontations among shifting alliances of the Misls. They reduced themselves to impotence in the Malwa. Instead of taking the remaining Mughal domains they plunder each other, becoming easy prey to their enemies' policy to put them all to fight amongst themselves. Around 1785 they could easily have taken Delhi, but they shrieked from the idea. Their mental courage was as small as their physical courage great and their political vision as dim as they were skilful and alert in dealing with small matters at hand. Disillusioned by their leaders, many Khalsa soldiers became mercenaries with whoever paid best.[26]

The Rise of Ranjit Singh

Chaos and confusion over the leadership of Sikhs prevailed, when Ranjit Singh took control of Sukerchakias Misal. He was born in 1780 to Maha Singh, the chief of Sukerchakia Misal dominant Recha between Ravi and Jhelum. Maha Singh had betrothed the five year old Ranjit to a baby girl from the family of the leader of the powerful Kanhaya Misl, which was dominated by Ranjit Singh's mother-in-law, Sada Kaur. She dreamed of a unified Sikh state and wanted to realise it through her son-in-law. After his father's death in 1892, the twelve year Ranjit Singh became the leader of the Sukerchakia Kanhaya alliance and during the next few years succeeded in improving relations with two more misls, the Nakkiais and the Ahulwalias.[27]

The ambitious Afghans could not forget the ransom and booties, which they had made on the regular basis from their invasions to India before the rise of Sikhs. As soon as the grandson of Ahmad Shah Abdali, Shah Zaman established his rule over Afghan. He dreamed to invade India again and made his first conquest attempt in 1793. He came to Hasan Abdal from where he sent an army of 7000 cavalry under the Shah Shahnachi, but Sikhs routed him. It was a great set back to the strong cavalry of Shah Zaman, but in 1795 he reorganised forces and again attacked Hasan Abdal. This time he snatched Rohtas from the Sukerchakia, whose leader was Ranjit Singh. However, Shah Zaman had to return to Kabul as an invasion of his country from the west was apprehended. When Shah Zaman returned, Ranjit Singh dislodged the Afghans from Rohtas.[28]

The dislodging of the Afghans and the defeats of the forces of Shah Zaman could not stop him to see the dreams to rule over India, instead he thought of taking the revenge of his defeat from the Sikhs. He raised a large Afghan army and in 1796 crossed the Indus for the third time and planned to capture Delhi. His ambition knew no bounds, he was confident that large number of Indians would join him. Nawab of Kasur had already assured him help. Sahib Singh of

Patiala betrayed his countrymen and declared his intentions of helping Shah Zaman. Shah Zaman was also assured of help by the Rohillas, Wazir of Oudh and Tipu Sultan of Mysore. The news of Shah Zaman's invasion spread quickly and people began fleeing to the hills for safety. Heads of Misls, though bound to give protection to the people as they were collecting Rakhi tax from them, were the first to leave the people in lurch. By December Shah Zaman occupied territory up to Jhelum. When he reached Gujarat, Sahib Singh Bhangi panicked and left the place.[29]

Next Shah Zaman marched towards the Sukerchakias Misl. Ranjit Singh was alert and raised an army of 5000 horsemen. However, they were inadequately armed with only spears and muskets. The Afghans were equipped with heavy artillery. Ranjit Singh foresaw a strong, united fight against the invaders as he came to Amritsar. A congregation of *Sarbat Khalsa* was called and many Sikh sardars answered the call. There was general agreement that Shah Zaman's army should be allowed to enter the Punjab and that the Sikhs should retire to the hills.[30]

Forces were reorganised under the command of Ranjit Singh and they marched towards Lahore. They gave the Afghans a crushing defeat in several villages and surrounded the city of Lahore. Sorties were made into the city at night in which they would kill a few Afghan soldiers and then leave under cover of darkness. Following this tactic they were able to dislodge Afghans from several places.[31]

In 1797 Shah Zaman suddenly left for Afghanistan as his brother Mahmud had revolted back home. Shahanchi Khan remained at Lahore with a sizeable army. The Sikhs followed Shah Zaman to Jhelum and snatched many goods from him. In returning, the Sikhs were attacked by the army of Shahnachi Khan near Ram Nagar. The Sikhs routed his army. It was the first major achievement of Ranjit Singh. He became the hero of the land of Five Rivers and his reputation spread far and wide.[32]

Again in 1798 Shah Zaman attacked Punjab to avenge the defeat of 1797. The Sikhs took refuge in the hills. A *Sarbat Khalsa* was again called and Sada Kaur persuaded the Sikhs to fight once again to the last man. This time even Muslims were not spared by Shah Zaman's forces and he won Gujarat easily. Sada Kaur roused the Sikhs sense of national honour. If they were to again leave Amritsar, she would command the forces against the Afghans. She said that an Afghani soldier was no match for a Sikh soldier. In battle they would acquit themselves, and, by the grace of *Sat Guru*, would be successful.[33]

The Afghans plundered the towns and villages as they had vowed and declared that they would defeat the Sikhs. However, it was the Muslims who suffered most as the Hindus and Sikhs had already left for the hills. The Muslims had thought that they would not be touched but their hopes were dashed and their provisions forcibly taken from them by the Afghans.[34]

Shah Zaman requested to Raja Sansar Chand of Kangra to refuse food or shelter to the Sikhs, it was agreed. Shah Zaman attacked Lahore and the Sikhs, surrounded as they were on all sides, had to fight a grim battle. The Afghans occupied Lahore in November 1798 and planned to attack Amritsar. Ranjit Singh collected his men and faced Shah's forces about eight kilometres from Amritsar. They were well-matched and the Afghans were, at last, forced to retire. Humiliated, they fled towards Lahore. Ranjit Singh pursued them and surrounded Lahore. Afghan supply lines were disconnected, crops were burnt and other provisions plundered so that they did not fall into Afghan's hands. It was a humiliating defeat for the Afghans. Nizamuddin of Kasur attacked the Sikhs near Shahdara on the banks of the Ravi, but his forces were no match for the Sikhs. Here too, it was the Muslims who suffered the most. The retreating Afghans and Nizam-ud-din forces plundered the town, antagonising the local people.[35]

The Afghans struggled hard to dislodge the Sikhs but in vain. The Sikh cordon was so strong that it was impossible for the Afghans to break it and proceed towards Delhi. Ranjit Singh terrorised the Afghans. The moment Zaman Shah left, Ranjit Singh pursued his forces and caught them unawares near Gujranwala. They were chased further up to Jhelum. Many Afghans were put to death and their weapons and supplies taken. The rest fled for their lives. Shah Zaman was overthrown by his brother and was blinded. He became a helpless creature, who, twelve years later, came to Punjab to seek refuge in Ranjit Singh's darbar. Singh was now ruler of the land.[36]

Ranjit Singh combined with Sahib Singh of Gujarat (Punjab) and Milkha Singh Pindiwala and a large Sikh force. They fell upon the Afghan garrison while Shah Zaman was still in vicinity of Khyber Pass. The Afghan forces fled north after having been routed by the Sikhs, leaving behind their dead, including the Afghan deputy, at Gujarat.[37]

The choreographed defeat of the Afghans by Ranjit Singh not only established him as the Hero of Punjab, but also of the leader of the Sikh misls, the Maharaja of Punjab and the honour of Sher-E-

Panjab was bestowed upon him also. Sher-E-Panjab succeeded in transforming the turbulent Sikh misls into the sustaining force of flourishing Punjabi nation, where he together with Hindus and Muslims could live in peace and friendly accommodation. Although he chose the title Maharaja in presence of Badshash to signify that he is a native ruler and not a foreigner conquer, it did not mean that he would also take to style of Hindu Maharaja. Seeing himself primary as a peasant leader and preferring to be addressed as Singh Sahib, he refused to wear any sign of royalty and sat on chair instead of a throne. He demonstrated his simplicity by being accessible to everyone and spending several hours a day with his soldiers, competing with them in spirit of sportsmanship in horse riding, tent pegging.[38]

His policy of respectful concern for others was key to his popularity. Ranjit Singh attended Hindu festivals, visited tombs of Muslim saints. He left to Hindus and Muslims to their customary practice of personal laws but also set up alternative courts under the direction of state especially for the criminal acts. Ranjit Singh also allotted the Jagirs and donations in the form of large amount of Land to Hindu and Muslim religious places along with the Sikh Gurdwaras. He not only reduced crime through an affective policing system but was also the only Indian ruler of the day to abolish capital punishment. Although he made no radical change in the revenue collection but the tributes were not too high.[39]

Maharaja Ranjit Singh's Imperial Policy and the Arrival of British

Ranjit Singh's imperial policy had to cope with the Afghans, Marathas and the arrival of British added more to his problems. By 1806 British became the masters of Delhi and clashed with the Maratha Chief Holkar, who was seeking to unite the Indians to drive away the British—if necessary with the help of Afghans. After suffering reverses in skirmish with British troops on east of Sutlej, Holkar entered Ranjit's Punjab to seek shelter. He also flattered the Sikhs by calling the sword-arm of Hindus and implored him to join his mission. As a reply Ranjit Singh signed a treaty of friendship with East India Company, undertaking to expel Holkar along with his army from his territory. The British were those whom Ranjit Singh exalted. In 1809 and more definitely he accepted the suzerainty of the Malwa region whose jealous Sikh chiefs had never fully accepted his authority, should pass on to the British and that had no claim on the land east of the Sutlej. He directed his energies to the north and west to take from the Afghans the Trans-Indus region from Attock to Peshawar, later Kashmir and Multan. In 1815 during the Anglo-Nepal war, an envoy of Hindu King of Nepal approached him for military alliance in the name of common bond of Hindus and Sikhs. He responded by joining Gorkhas. In 1831, he conceded to the British the right to navigate the Indus and other rivers of Punjab. His compliance with them can be seen as a sign of weakness or practical wisdom, depending on one's own bias.[40]

The key to military success of the Ranjit Singh's Empire was of his military professionalism and equipping his soldiers with modern techniques of warfare. He created a standing army under constant drill, with the man having to prove their standard and efficiency in regard to marksmanship, endurance, etc. Sikhs dominated the cavalry; Hindus and Muslim infantry; Muslims the artillery, which easily matched up to that of British. He not only recruited Indians who had deserted the British army but also called many European soldiers, mainly veterans from the Napoleonic wars who hated the British. Ranjit used them as officers and even generals.[41]

Punjab after the Death of Sher-E-Panjab

A rare age clemency and broadmindedness in the land of Punjab was buried along the Sher-E-Panjab on the 27th June, 1839 in Punjab. He left an empire almost ten times the size of the present day Punjab that spread from the north-western frontiers of Afghanistan to the Sutlej and from Kashmir to the deserts of Sind. The sign of political instability and the down fall of the Sikh-Empire to which Ranjit Singh established after a long struggle soon became clear; a war of succession between his sons had been started immediately after his death. Two of his successors Maharaja Kharak Singh and Kanwar Nau Nihal Singh were assassinated by 1843. The Durbar had become a hotbed of treason and conspiracies. The nominal Maharaja Dilip Singh, the youngest son of Ranjit Singh was minor when he was coronated in 1843.[42]

Maharani Jinda, Ranjit Singh's wife and court eunuchs were spoiling the State under their collective misguidance. The Court nobles and the generals of the army were in treasonable communication with the British. The troops were raised and discontented. Yet when the first Anglo-Sikh war broke out in December 1845, the Sikh troops fought with valour. The Chief of the British army, Hugh Gough, wrote about his adversaries. "Policy precluded me from publicly recording my sentiments on the splendid gallantry of our fallen foe, or to record the acts of heroism displayed, not only individually but almost collectively, of the Sikh Sardars and the army: I declare it were not from a deep convection that my country's good required the sacrifice, I could have wept to have witnessed the fearful slaughter of so devoted a body of men."[43]

Although the first Anglo-Sikh war had to be terminated without a conclusive annexation of the Sikh-Kingdom, however, the territory between the Sutlej and Beas was ceded to Great Britain, along with Kashmir, which was sold to the Gulab Singh of Jammu as a British vassal: under the peace treaty to which the Sikh signed with the British to end the war. Some British troops, along with the resident political agents and other officials, were left in Punjab to oversee the regency of Dalip Singh and the size of Sikh army was reduced greatly in size.

The complete annexation of the Punjab to the British came with the second Anglo-Sikh War. When in 1848, out of work the Sikh troops in Multan revolted and killed a British official. Within few months, the unrest had spread throughout the Punjab, and British troops invaded again. The British prevailed in the Second Anglo- Sikh war and under the Treaty of Lahore in 1849, Punjab was annexed by the East India Company and Dalip Singh was pensioned.[44]

Punjab under the Colonial Rule

The Sikhs though conquered did not give themselves to despondency. They who had fought the British foes, did not lose time become loyal subjects when they discovered in the progressive administration that followed, that new rulers were different from the invaders, their country had known. Henry Lawrence, who was against the annexation, was appointed as the President of the Board of Administration with best men in India helping him", as Dalhousie wrote to him.[45] Public works were undertaken at pace. The Grand Trunk Road from Peshawar to Delhi was repaired. The existing canals were extended and new ones built. New varieties of crops were introduced. Education received a new incentive. Presenting a report on its work in first two years of annexation of Punjab, the board stated with pride; "in no part of India had there been more perfect quiet than in the territory lately annexed." The Governor General and director of East India Company congratulated the Board: for prosperous and happy results." They are also accused of giving their support to British during the mutiny of 1857.[46]

In every way, Punjab and the Sikhs were one of Great Britain's most important assets in colonial India to serve the imperial interests. Its political and geographic predominance gave Britain a base from which to project its power over more than 500 princely states that made up India. Lahore was a centre of learning and culture under British rule, and Rawalpindi became an important Army installation. Ninety years of British rule which followed in Punjab represented the most progressive period in the history. The Sikhs received the status of martial race became the backbone of British Indian Army. This not only restored their sense of dignity, impaired after the annexation of Punjab, but also opened up to them an important avenue of employment. The most significant and far reaching of the development which Punjab saw in the sequel was the expansion of modern irrigation, transforming the semi fertile land of the province into the fertile core of the Indian agriculture economy.[47]

INROADS OF CHRISTIANITY: RISE OF COMMUNALISM

Progress was not limited to the material sphere alone. It is also led to the large changes in the socio-religious, political and educational set-up. The rise of the communal sectarian politics in India can be connected to the negative impacts of the movements for socio-religious and education reforms in the early set-up of the British colonial rule. Education got a new touch with the establishment of British rule in India. English became must to earn a job, which provided the Christian Missionaries with the opportunity to open their schools first along with the government schools. The first government school was opened in Amritsar in 1849 and Department of Public Instruction was established in 1856.[48]

Christian Missionary started to prepare their propaganda for the invasion of Christianity in Punjab even before the establishment of British Empire in Punjab. As early as 1836 the Christian literature including the Bible was translated in Punjabi language. By 1851 John Newton published the first comprehensive Punjabi grammar, and in 1854 a Punjabi vocabulary book as well as the first Punjabi dictionary (The latter with Rev. Lev Javier). These works, along with the translation of John Bunyan's Pilgrim's progress marked significant transition from old to modern Punjabi prose. By 1857 Missionaries had established mission stations at Ambala, Amritsar, Jalandhar, Kangra, Kotgarh, Lahore, Ludhiana, Multan, Peshawar, Rawalpindi, Sabtu and Sialkot, in mid-nineties missionaries started the agenda of conversion. Most of the missionaries had a school and hospital with their establishments. Schools were offering western education that included both teaching in English as well the Christian religion. Missionaries provided asylum to orphans, lepers and mentally ill.[49]

Christian evangelism operated at two levels. On the one hand their benevolent acts of providing medical care and education to poor and the underprivileged were great to provide an earlier platform to the Christianity in Punjab. On the other hand, their struggle was for the supremacy of Christianity and the salvation of the man under the Christianity against the indigenous religions. Thus, their major emphasis was on the Christian preaching. Teaching was to convince the people that Christianity offered true way of salvation and that prevailing religions in Punjab were false in that they offered no genuine solution to the human predicament as evangelism had defined it. This particular approach to the evangelism inevitably involved not only challenging the religious assumptions as the audience brought to an unfamiliar message but also making contrasts between the new faith being presented and those with which Punjabis were already familiar with. Christian evangelists brought their message to the people of Punjab first through the direct preaching in the town and city bazaars as well as in the villages by interacting with the peoples. Preaching was supplemented by the distribution of pamphlets appeared in the vernacular press. The efforts of the evangelists had no response and despite of their hard efforts the number of Indian Christians did not exceed few hundreds. However, by the 1870's the number of the Indian Christians increased with a great pace as the lower castes from the Hindus, Sikhs and Muslims responded to the missionaries' call. The conversion movement started in several unconnected villages at about the same time. The kinship network of the individuals who had taken lead in seeking baptism furthered the messages of the evangelism. It spread in the villages of Amritsar, Lahore, Gurdaspur, Gujranwala and Sialkot. The census of 1911 reported 1,63,994 Indian Christians in Punjab, over the forty times of 1881 census.[50]

The growing number of the Indian Christians forced the Indian elite to think about their socio-religious identities under the new circumstances, which were posed by the arrival of Christian Missionaries along with the British. Although the Indian elite has already started to organise as its traditional socio-economic interests were hurtled under the new set-ups of the British. But from 1870s onwards religious awakening and opposition to the missionaries became better organized, as they launched socio-religious reform movements. Dominant among these are *Arya Samaj*, *Singh Sabhas* and *Ahamadiyah Movement*, who trained their preachers and published their own pamphlets to set forth their own truth, claims as well as counter those of their opponents. Emergence of the various social reform movements and religious organizations not only posed a challenge to Christianity, but it also vitiated the communal harmony among the indigenous. The evangelistic practices of conversion of the outcastes of Indian religion were now adopted by the heads of these religious reforms movements.

The growing of religious awakening and the invasion of Christianity in India had also influenced the socio-religious set-ups and the contemporary politics in the Punjab. The religious awakening and the communal formation in the British has been started with formation of three dominant religious and social reform organization. Arya *Samaj, Singh Sabha and Ahamdiyah Movements.* Arya Samaj was founded by Swami Dayanand Saraswati in 1875 at Bombay, within just span of two years, i.e., by 1877, it had captured the imagination of a section of Punjabis and started from Lahore. The first Singh Sabha was founded on 1st of October 1873 by the Sikhs of Amritsar. Five years latter in 1878 a second *Lahore Singh Sabha* was formed and by 1900 there were approximately a hundred similar organizations in Punjab and neighbouring areas. To protect the interests of Muslims in the new imperial set-up Mirza Ghulam Ahmad, who hails from Quadian in Punjab, founded the Ahamadiyah Movement in 1876.[51]

Arya Samaj was one such movement in Punjab, which not only carried on social reforms but also generated many controversies with the Sikhs and Muslims. Although the founder of the Ahamadiyah Movement, Mirza Ghulam Ahmad also instigated a controversy by proclaiming the founder Sikhism (Guru Nanak) was a Muslim *Peer* (saint), however, it could not go longer as the differences between the Sikhs and Muslims were very clear. But the Arya Samaj proclamation and strategy to establish the hegemony of Hinduism and Vedas over the teaching of the Gurus by proclaiming the Sikhism as a part or the sect of Hindu religion had long-term impacts on the Punjab and Sikh-politics. The insecurity and religious separation of the Sikhs to a large extent was the product of the mobilization by the Arya Samaj and the Hindu fundamentalists in the Punjab.

In fact, Hindus and Sikhs in Panjab had worked together for the common cause previous to the Arya Samaj. Some important movements like Kooka Movement, and movement against the cow slaughter had a strong support of both communities. The first branch of the Arya Samaj at Lahore was also opened with the common efforts of the Hindus and Sikhs in 1877, and the founder member of this branch Bhai Ditt Singh and Jawahar Singh were also Sikh. Then the Arya Samaj and Sikhs were considered to be the complementary of each other and both endeavoured to reform Hinduism. However, the ambitious plan of the re-establishment of the supremacy of the Hinduism by giving the slogan of *"Go back to Vedas"* and *Shudhi Movement* (re-conversion of the Hindu out-caste) by the founder of the Arya Samaj Swami Dayanand Saraswati had created insecurity in the minds of the Sikhs. As the Arya Samaj did not hesitate in converting the Sikhs into the Hindu fold along with the converters to Islam and Christians although it enjoyed good terms with the Sikhs.[52]

A well publicized ceremony of August 1878 of Lahore Samaj, under which it reclaimed hundred of out-caste Sikhs to Hindu fold, made the Sikh gentry insecure and they started organizing themselves against the Samaj. Then the politics of countering of each other has been started, the derogatory remarks of the Arya Samaj to the teaching of the Sikhism and Gurus served as a fuel to the smouldering. To claim the supremacy the Samaj proponent Pandit Hans Raj announced that the founder of the Arya Samaj Swami Dayanand is superior to Sikh Gurus, the Sikh founder of the Arya Samaj Bhai Ditt Singh and Jawahar Singh immediately walked-out of the Samaj meeting.[53]

Their responses to the Samaj were very strong and they formed another Singh Sabha in Lahore in 1878. In comparison to the Amritsar Singh Sabha, Sikhs associated with the Lahore Singh Sabha had a very different perspective of Sikhism. The members of the Lahore Sabha came from different classes and castes including aristocrats, lawyers, teachers, publishers, businessmen and minor officials. They joined the movement not of their economic or occupational interests but rather by a shared experience in Anglo-vernacular education and participation in intellectual debate in Lahore, the centre of new school system and an emerging print culture. Aware of western criticism and vulnerability of demarcated boundaries, they sought to present and defend a set of coherent principles and action that would be adopted by most Sikhs.

Their version of a rejuvenated Sikh tradition came to be known as *Tat Khalsa,* that is, a true Sikhism stripped from popular customs and clearly separated from Hinduism. As in the case of Arya Samaj,

Tat Khalsa reinterpreted the Vedic period so as to legitimize its programme. The advocates of *Tat Khalsa* championed a return of real or imagined golden age of Gurus in which Sikhs had a clear identifiable identity. The Lahore Singh Sabha attacked the caste and other social customs that tended to undercut Sikh brotherhood. Similarly the Sikhs were called upon to quit worshipping "living Gurus" such as piris, local saints and families connected with the Ten Gurus. A return to original Sikh values meant also a renewal of attention to the *Adi Granth* as a source of theology and authority, the promulgation of rituals devoid of Brahmanical and Hindu influence, and a cleansing of sacred spaces such as Gurdwaras and shrines. Research and discussion of theology was encouraged in Punjabi, further attempts to de-Sanskrits and de-Hinduism of Sikh history was made by encouraging the use of Punjabi in the writing and translating the Sikh history into Punjabi. The main focus of the activities of the Singh Sabhas was to create a separate identity of the Sikhs.[54]

The new centres of learning and training had a great role to play in the formation of new identities in the new circumstances, which were posed by the colonial set-up. The *Tat Khalsa* created and then dominated the rapidly evolving communication facilities linking Sikhs throughout the world. Secretaries of the Singh Sabha circulated the annual reports and resolutions through the mail and the central body in Lahore helped to publish local proceedings. The correspondent system was completed by circulation of preaching teams and *jathas* (groups) (often with *granthis* and singers) who travelled widely encouraged baptism, adoption of the outward symbols, and the end of *manmat* (unsikh practices), such as worshipping local saints and living gurus. As soon as the railway expanded, preacher visited the dispersed Sikhs and tried to influence their actions. Festivals and meetings also became reutilised. Sabhas sponsored annual diwans, multi-day meetings occasion that brought together local Sikhs as well as zealots from outside. The larger regional and provincial conferences could attract as many as several thousand Sikhs. Moreover, the regular celebration of the various *Gurupurabs* (birth and death anniversaries of the Gurus) and related events in Sikh history were popularized. Such activities provided the chance for discussion, worship, raising funds and in general consolidating the Tat Khalsa position.

Schools and colleges too, played vital role were essential elements in the Singh Sabha programmes. Not only did Khalsa educational institution equiped Sikhs to compete successfully in the new occupations, but they also served to strengthen the Sikh identity. Mixing of western education with the study of Punjabi and religious traditions, teachers were able to influence generations of upwardly mobile students. Sikh philanthropists and activists opened dozens of schools and colleges for boys and girls all over the Punjab; some renounced educational institutions among these were Khalsa College Amritsar, a Medical College in Lahore and a full-fledged university, Punjab University in 1882 at Lahore and finally the establishment of Chief Khalsa Diwan a central committee to coordinate the activities of various Singh Sabhas in 1901.

Sikhs produced an increasing number of small pamphlets and religious books as in the case of Christian missionaries, Arya Samaj and Muslims missionaries. Founded in 1894, the Khalsa Tract Society published didactic and polemical pamphlets regularly. Individuals often specialized in that means of disseminating ideas, such as Ditt Singh and Mohan Singh Vaid who wrote over two hundred books and tracts. One variety of tracts contained religious scripture and sermons, often with emphasis on an issue such as non–Hindu nature of Sikhism. Another related set of pamphlets described incidents and stories that illustrated the victory of Tat Khalsa argument. A third popular type called for support of association or a project. Appeals or *benatis* were accepted elements in the Sikh life and could generate substantial contribution. The polemic provided entertainment and contributed to literary exchanges that can only be described as tract warfare. Finally, the special committees were established to write the authentic version of Sikh history and commentaries on the *Granth*, these committees were even gone to judge the validity of books and tracts published by others.[55]

Also accelerating were confrontations with the Arya Samaj. Both the Singh Sabha and Arya Samaj launched a campaign of Shudhi, especially after 1890 it became more intense. Aryas openly indulged in converting Sikhs to Hindu fold and cut their hair in public. The Sikh Shuddhi Sabha in Lahore countered by having Muslims and low-caste undergoing purification, receiving baptism and then has social relations with Singh Sabha members. The controversies raged, as did the warfare. The titles of the typical pamphlets of the period suggest the strident tone and content. Colloquial Hindi and Punjabi used insulting and derogatory terms and opponents used freely to attack sacred scripture, leaders and position. The administration of British law further fuelled the controversy as the Punjab High Court in 1898, in a case of inheritance ruled that for the purpose of rules of inheritance Sikhs must be treated on par with Hindus, became an occasion to trigger an acrimonious debate as to whether Sikhism is a branch within Hinduism or a separate religion. The ruling of the Punjab High Court has had its own meaning for the Sikhs and Hindu bastion under the designed politics of Panjab. Immediately, leaders from the Arya Samaj, Mahant Thakur Dass and Baba Narayan attacked the separated identity of Sikhs and Singh Sabha, by writing a book *Sikh Hindu Hai* (Sikhs are Hindus). The view of the Arya Samaj was immediately rebutted by the Singh Sabha as the Bhai Kahan in his *Hum Hindu Nahin* (we are not Hindus) clearing the position of the Singh Sabha on the question of the separate identity of Sikhs.[56]

British who were already favouring a separate identity of Sikhs as a Martial race to serve the imperial overseas military of empire further manipulated the situation to help the imperial policies by creating a rift between the two communities. Secondly, the attempts of Arya Samaj to merge the Sikh traditions with Hinduism made the proponents of the Singh Sabha more conscious to not only make the separate the Sikh rituals but also to institutionalize them. Chief Khalsa Diwan became an instrument to institutionalize and create Sikhism as a separate religion with its own rituals, traditions and sense of identity. Generally pursuing policies that would further demarcate boundaries and remove lingering Hindu influence, the Diwan's efforts helped to facilitate the removal of idols from the Golden Temple in 1905 and sparked criticism of Hindu accretion in other local shrines. Another Chief Khalsa Diwan victory, the passage of the Anand Marriage Bill legitimizing a distinct Sikh marriage ceremony devoid of Hindu trappings, marked a highpoint in the campaign to spread Sikh ideology, rituals and daily practices.[57]

RISE OF GURDWARA REFORM MOVEMENT AND THE FORMATION OF SGPC

The Gurdwara Reform Movement began with attempts of the Sikh reformers to liberate their religious places from the control of the Mahants (hereditary priests). It came to be popularly known as the *Akali Movement* because of the large-scale participation of *Akalis-jatha* in the struggle for reform. What began as a purely religious movement in the vitiated politics of Punjab turned out to be major force for India's liberation at the provincial level, because British supported the Mahants to save their vested interests, and nationalist forces supported the *Akali reformers*?

This movement not only provided the opportunity of the national leaders to come close with Sikhs but it also made the Sikhs to realise the hardships of the colonial rule and connected them to the mainstream politics. During their five year peaceful struggle in Punjab, the Akali reformers succeeded not only in wresting control of their historic shrines; they also strengthened the nationalist forces in the country through their high moral of passive suffering. Mahatma Gandhi was so impressed by the Akali reformers' strict adherence to their vows of non-violence that he often quoted their examples to other satyagrahis, such as Munshi Peta and Malegaon, who failed to keep their vow.

Thus far the Akalis had gained control over important Sikh shrines through peaceful means. But it does no mean that Sikhs got back their religious places without shedding blood and suffering. The liberation of Gurdwaras could become success after long struggle sufferings and humiliation for more than five years. The support of the colonial bureaucracy to the *Mahants made* hard for the non-violent *Akali-Jathas (*Religious Groups) to fought against the enemy who was not only using the violence but also have a state to defend it. Some of the tragedies to which the Sikhs faced during the Gurdwara reformers became the noted history of patient suffering for the cause in the world. Some of the important are *Nankana Tragedy* where 130 peaceful Akalis were brutally murdered by the mercenaries of Mahant Narain Das. The struggles on key affairs, Guru Ka Bagh Morcha, Jaito Morcha are of worth-noting. Before the government recognised Akalis demand for passing of the Sikh Gurdwaras and Shrines Bill, thousands of Sikhs were arrested and heavy fines were imposed upon them, near about 4000 Sikhs lost their lives and thousands were also brutally tortured. Open instigation of the Mahants by the colonial bureaucracy also resulted in the formation of Babbar Akalis, (a violent organisation of Sikh Youth), which adopted violent means to pressurize the government for the acceptance of Sikh demands. In, fact Babbar Akalis became an instrument to eliminate some of the government stooges not only during the Gurdwaras Reform Movement but also during the freedom struggle.[58]

Finally, the management of the Gurdwaras fully came into the Akalis hands with the passage of *Sikh Gurudwaras Act, 1925*. The Act recognised that an elected body of Sikhs alone would qualify as the repository of genuine Sikh tradition. The legislation not only invested the SGPC with authority to impose liturgical standards at the Sikh Shrines, but also control their management. The establishment of the SGPC as the first elected democratic body to manage the religious affairs of the Sikhs has its own meaning in the national as well as on the provincial politics of Punjab. It not only provided a platform to Sikh politics in Punjab, however, it strengthen the national struggle by giving the concept self ruling through the democratic elected government in India. Since then SGPC is supposed to be the religious body to save the interest of Sikhs in the colonial as well as the post-colonial political set-up in India.[59]

The Gurdwaras Reform Movement, though itself was a product of the general awakening and growing political consciousness in the country. It greatly strengthened the nationalist forces by rejecting the Mahants, the landed aristocracy and other pro-British elements in the Sikh community, who had been declared the natural leaders of the Sikh by the British. The movement provided the Sikh community with a new type of middle–class nationalist leadership, consisting of barristers, school and college teachers and retired military officers. This new leadership, instead of playing into the hands of British officials as the previous leadership of the Chief Khalsa Diwan, they preferred to join the mainstream of nationalism in the country. It was not surprising, therefore, to find a majority of Akali leaders turning from the original Akali programme of Gurdwaras reform and linking it with non-cooperation launched by Mahatma Gandhi and larger programme of the country's struggle for freedom. It was mainly due to the Indian National Congress (INC) and other nationalist forces in the country to give moral support to the Akalis in their struggle against the government, the Congress leadership passed formal resolutions supporting them in whatever they did. An attack on the SGPC and Shiromani Akali Dal was described by the Congress as direct challenge to the right to freedom of association of the Indians and below aimed at all movements for freedom. Dr. Kitchlew, the convener of Satyagraha Committee, emphasized that "the Akali's struggle is now national struggle and defeat of the Akalis will be the defeat of Congress." The Akalis were also eulogised as "the only living wing of the national movement" and the strongest community in India because of the triumph of satyagrah, of which they had given full proof.[60]

THE RISE OF COMMUNALISM AND THE DEMAND OF AUTONOMY/SELF-RULE BY THE AKALIS IN LATE COLONIAL INDIA

The Gurdwara's Reform Movement was not only successful in freeing the Gurudwaras, but it also had important role in the process of institutionalising of the Sikh identity. In the process of gaining liberation of the Gurdwaras, the latter turned into a campaign against government in which political feelings became as strong as the religious feelings. The general awakening brought about by the Akalis campaign strengthened the National Movement in India.[61]

As the dream of freedom was coming close, the future socio-political set-up of the India dominated the minds of the political elites of the different religious and caste communities in India. As an ethno- religious minority Akalis also got worried to save the interests of the Sikhs in the political set-up of free India. Secondly they were afraid of their rights in the Muslim dominated Punjab. Akalis decided to bargain with the British and Congress (a dominant national political party) as the Dalits and other religious Minorities were doing at national level, although they had a very close relation with the Hindus and Congress at the time.

Once considered the sword-arm of the British Empire in the world, the Akali Sikhs were now in the same tone with the empire as the Congress and Muslim League were. They were not only opposing the empire but also wanted to negotiate for the protection of their interests in the colonial as well post-colonial India. The strong opposition of the Sikhs at large to Simon Commission during it's twice visits to Lahore in the months of March and October in 1928, was the direct result resentment to the empire and their closeness to the Congress, which they got during the Gurdwara Reform Struggle.

Sikhs all over Punjab followed the boycott calls of the Congress session of Madras, All India Muslim League and Hindu Maha Sabha. The Working Committee of Akali Dal met on 16 January 1928 under Sardar Udham Singh Nagoke who has announced its decision to boycott the Commission. This was followed by the All Sikh Parties Conference at Amritsar on 29 January 1928.[62] On the other hand, some moderate Sikh leaders formed Central Sikh Association. The Central Sikh Association met the Commission and demanded for increased representation for the Sikhs in Punjab and Central Legislatures.[63] The Khalsa Biradari, an organisation of Mazhabi Sikhs which was considered as the representative of the interest of the depressed classes among the Sikhs met the Commission and *inter alia* demanded adult suffrage.[64] A deputation headed by Sardar Sunder Singh Majithia met the commission and submitted a memorandum. In order to save the Sikhs from government nurtured majority of the Muslims, they (Sikhs) demanded a complete abolition of communal representation, but if it was to be retained the Muslims could be given only 40 seats and the rest of the Hindus and Sikhs were to each.[65] But the government went its own way and recommended the composition of the 134 seats of the house as following. In terms of percentage, Muslims were given 66, Hindus 40 and Sikhs 24 against the Sikhs demand of 30 per cent representation. Barely 18 per cent representation was given to the Sikhs, which deeply hurt the feelings of Sikhs who had a long alliance with the empire serving its imperial interests not only within India but at global level.[66]

Along the nationalists parties Sikhs disapproved of the Simon Commission recommendations and participated in an All Parties Conference on the call of nationalists at Delhi in 1928. The conference appointed a committee led by Moti Lal Nehru to evolve an agreed formula on the representation. To represent Sikh view Mangal Singh was appointed as a Sikh member to the Nehru Committee. The Sikhs suggested that the communal electorate should be abolished and the joint electorates system should be introduced all over the country. The report recommended separate electorates for the Muslims in provinces other than Punjab and Bengal. Mangal Singh, the lone Sikh representative to the committee, expressed his strong dissent. He proposed proportional representation, but he was ultimately persuaded to sign the report in the interest of country. For this act he was accused by his fellow Akalis of having acted contrary to the instructions given to him by the party. Master Tara Singh, Gyani Sher Singh and other Akali leaders strongly opposed the Nehru Report. They claimed that their demand was for the complete abolition of communal representation not only in Punjab but all over the country. They argued that if the communal representation is to be given to any minority in any other province, the same concession should be given to the Sikh minority in the Punjab.[67]

Moreover, they alleged that by accepting universal adult suffrage on the communal basis Nehru Report would establish Muslim rule in Punjab because Muslims had a numerical majority in the Province. The prominent leaders of the Sikhs were deadly against the Nehru Report. While addressing a Central Sikh League at

Gujranwala Akali leader Kharak Singh condemned the Nehru Report as unjust and highly prejudicial to Sikhs interests and asked them to throw it into the basket of waste papers. Their protest to the Nehru Report was continuing and again an All Party Conference in Calcutta in December 1928 Master Tara Singh along with a Sikh deputation met Mahatma Gandhi, however, they could not arrive to any compromise. On this occasion Mehtab Singh tried to move a resolution saying that communalism in any form would not be the basis of any future constitution. But Dr. Ansari (President of the Conference) ruled his suggestion to be out of order. As the result Central Sikh League declared its withdrawal of the support to the Nehru Report and quit the conference. It was felt that Mahatma Gandhi was convinced that Sikh objections to the report were justified. The Sikh threat to boycott the Lahore Session perturbed the Congress.[68]

Before the Congress Session began at Lahore, Dr. Ansari, Mahatma Gandhi and Pandit Motilal Nehru met Master Tara Singh, Baba Kharak Singh and other Sikh leaders to listen their grievances. They assured them that in future no proposal or decision would be acceptable to the Congress which would not satisfy Sikh and Muslim minorities. A resolution to this effect was passed by Congress in its Lahore Session. It states "the Congress believing that in an independent India communal question can only be solved on national lines; but as the Sikhs in particularly and the Muslim and other minorities in general have expressed dissatisfaction over the solution of communal question, proposed in the Nehru Report, the Congress assure the Sikhs, the Muslims and other minorities that no solution thereof in any future constitution will be acceptable to the Congress that does not give full satisfaction to the parties concerned. This resolution according to Gandhi was adopted primarily to satisfy Sikh minority in Punjab[69].

The Nehru Committee failed to produce any agreed document that could serve as the future constitution of India. The British Government called Round Table Conference of Indian leaders at London in November 1930 to discuss the basis of a new constitution for Indians and the quantum of power to be transformed to Indians. The Congress and Central Sikh League, however, decided to boycott the First Round Table Conference. The government, however, prevailed upon some moderate Sikh leaders such as Sampurn Singh and Sardar Ujjal Singh to represent the Sikhs in the Round Table Conference.[70]

The Sikh representatives presented a memorandum for the rights of their community. According to this memorandum, the Sikhs wanted the same treatment as the Muslim minorities had received in other province, i.e. 30% representation in Punjab. The Muslims strongly opposed this demand of the Sikhs and described it as an attempt to rob the Muslims of their majority. The conference was unsuccessful. But still it was considered advisable to proceed with the work of the final form of future constitution of India in the absence of Congress and Central Sikh League; it was decided to call a Second Round Table Conference on 5 March 1931, the Gandhi-Irwin Pact was signed and Congress agreed to participate in Second Round Table Conference. Similarly, the Central Sikh League also decided to participate. A deputation led by Master Tara Singh met Gandhi and presented him a Charter of 17 demands. The main classes were:

1. 30% share for the Sikhs in Punjab legislative Council and Administration.
2. One-third share in the Punjab Cabinet and Public Service Commission.
3. In case these demands are not acceptable, Muslim majority districts of Punjab should be merged with N.W.F.P. so that the residue Punjab may have communal balance.
4. In case even this was not acceptable, Punjab should be kept under Central rule till an agreement was hammered out.
5. Punjabi should be the official language of Punjab with option to write it in any other script also.
6. 5% representation of Sikhs in the Legislative Assembly in centre.
7. Central Cabinet should always have at least one Sikh Minister.[71]

These demands of the Sikhs were probably a reaction to Dr. Mohammed Iqbal's scheme of separate state compromising Punjab, North West Frontier Province, Sind and Balochistan. Gandhi disagreed with the Sikh deputation and described these demands as communal, Master Tara Singh replied, "the only way to fight communalism is by counter demand of the same nature. The Congress at this point evolved a new formula to solve the communal issue but it was not accepted by the Sikhs, the Muslim and other minorities. The formula was: "For the Hindus in Sind, the Muslims in Assam and Sikhs in Punjab and NWEP and Hindus and Muslims in any province where they are less than 25% of population, seats shall be reserved in the federal and provincial legislature on the basis of population with right to contest additional seats. The Congress formula had only turned down the Sikh demand of 30% representation to 13% (in proportion to their population) in Punjab, whereas under the Montague-Chelmsford scheme they had 19.1% seats. Therefore, an All Sikh parties meeting rejected the Congress proposal and reiterated their charter of 17 demands.[72]

The Second Round Table Conference opened in London on September 1931. Gandhi was sole representative of Congress, Sardar Ujjal Singh and Sampuran Singh were representative of the Sikhs. Like the first Round Conference a Minority Committee was again appointed. They demanded for the Sikhs 30% representation in Punjab and 5% at the Centre, with at least one Sikh member in the Central Cabinet. Sardar Ujjal Singh presented an alternative that the Rawalpindi and Multan divisions (excluding the Layallpur and Montgomery districts) from the Punjab should be attached to the North West Frontier Province, which makes the communal proportion in Punjab 43.3% for Muslims, 42.3% for Hindus and 14% for Sikhs. In Punjab the Sikhs would not ask any weightage in Punjab and if they would ask for it that would be in the North West Frontier Province and Sindh as the Muslim would be receiving it in other provinces. This proposal of Sikhs received a scant consideration from the Conference and was rejected along with a similar but from the Sikh point of view less satisfactory, proposal by L.W.G. Corbett to detach Ambala Division from the Punjab and join it to the United Provinces. The Conference arrived at no agreement and Gandhi returned empty handed to the Country. Gandhi addressed a Conference at London in which he said that he was sorry that he had not been able to solve the communal problem.[73]

As the Indian could not arrive at any settlement Ramsay MacDonald (Prime Minister of England) gave his famous award as the Communal Award on 16 August 1932. The distribution of seats in Punjab as awarded was:

Total	:	175	
Muslims	:	86	49.14%
Hindus	:	43	24.5%
Sikhs	:	32	18.29%

The Sikh leaders' reaction to the Award was sharp and bitter. It had not only reduced the Sikhs representation to 18.29% as against their demand of 30%. The Muslims were given 33.1% weightage in the Cèntre and 86 out of 175 seats in Punjab. The Sikhs were also given weightage but not in the same measure as the Muslims, their position was as follow: 33 out of 175 in Punjab Assembly and 3 out of 150 in North West Frontier Province (NWFP): 6 out of 250 in the federal Legislative Assembly and 4 out of 150 in the Council of States.[74]

The Sikhs got nothing in the United Provinces and Sindh where they had then reasonably sizeable population Sampurn Singh and Sardar Ujjal Singh marked their protest by resigning from the Consultative Committee of Round Table Conference. In July 1932 a Sikh Conference was called at Lahore representing the Akali Dal and Central Sikh League. An Akali *Shahidi Dal* of one Lakh Sikhs was raised for agitation against the award. The Akali asked the Congress to support them against the Communal Award. But the Congress instead of helping them adopted a neutral attitude. The Congress neither accepted nor rejected it, but a section of Punjab Provincial Congress opposed it. The main object of the Sikhs was to get rid of the Communal Award and to protect the interest of own community. The only party that found the award satisfactory was the Union Party.

The third Round Table Conference was convened on 24 December 1932 at London. As the leading Sikhs for Punjab refused to participate, the Government nominated Tara Singh, an ex-member of Punjab Legislative Council to represent the Sikhs. He protested against the idea of Provincial autonomy for Punjab under a permanent Muslim majority. He demanded safeguards to ensure that measures affecting the minorities would not be enacted without the consent of third-fifth of the community concerned and would be subjected to the Governor veto. He pleaded for weightage in services, five percent representation in federal legislature and Sikh representation in Sindh. Despite the opposition by the Sikh representatives no change was made. Finally, the Communal award was included in the white papers embodying the proposal of British Government for institutional reforms.

The first election to the provincial councils under the proposed new constitution in 1935 which incorporated Communal Award was held in 1937. The most successful were the Unionists who won 95 out of 175 seats. Among the other parties, the Khalsa Nationalist Party secured 14; the Akalis got 10 and the Congress got 5. Muslim

League could got 2 seats. One or two each were won by the Congress Nationalists, the Socialists, the Majilis-Ahrar and the Itihad-I-Milliat and there nineteen independent legislators. With the absolute majority the Unionist Party in Punjab Legislative Assembly, under the leadership of Sikander Hayat Khan formed the formed the ministry with the help of Nationalist Progress Party and Khalsa Nationalist Party. Sunder Singh Majitha the leader of Khalsa party joined the new Ministry. But within short span the Unionist leader preyed to the Muslim League and Sir Sikandar Hayat Khan was invited to the Luckhnow Session of the All India Muslim League, where Jinnah and Punjab Premier signed the Sikandar-Jinnah Pact. The Pact changed the scenario or the communal harmony into communalism, as the Gokal Chand Narang a Hindu legislature of the Unionist left the party, however, Sunder Singh Majitha remained in the Ministry on the assurance of Sir Sikandar Khan that the pact would not make any difference to the policies of party. However, the promises of the Sikandar Khan could not go longer in suspicious environment; secondly, the ground for the secularism was already eroded by the *Shahid Ganj* agitation and the campaign against the Muslim league in Punjab. The Panthic forces and Akalis appealed to the Sikhs and passed resolutions requesting Sikhs to join hands against the Muslim Communalism. The pact brought the Akalis and the Congress formally closer to one another. In November 1938, when the All India Akali Conference was held at Rawalpindi the Akali and Congress flags were hoisted together.[75]

The beginning of the Second World War increased the bargaining position of the Sikhs, as the British needed more Sikh for its Army. Simultaneously, the prestige and power of the Congress as it had formed its ministries in 8 out of 11 provinces too was in better position to pressurize the British to satisfy Indian aspirations. However, it took a down-turn as its leadership committed the blunder by asking its ministers to resign from the government. Congress fell to the British policy of divide and rule as the British began to boost the Muslim League.

Support of the British Empire to the Muslim League resulted in the passage of first Resolution demanding the formation of Pakistan at its Annual Session in March 1940 at Lahore. Although the idea of a Muslim majority state called 'Pakistan' had been in air since 1930. The idea of the physical division of the country was underlined by the Muslim League throughout 1939. The Sikh leadership rejected the idea out rightly and made a common cause with the nationalists to it tooth and nails to end. To counter the first resolution of the Muslim League the Sikh leaders called an Akali Conference just a day after the conclusion of the League Session at Anandpur Sahib, the birth place of Khalsa Panth. The Sikh leaders like Giani Dhanwant Singh and Master Ajit Singh condemned Jinnah 'two-nation theory'. Master Tara Singh at Uttar Pradesh Sikhs Conference on 15 April 1940 in Lucknow warned that "if the Muslim League wants to establish Pakistan, they will have to pass through the ocean of Sikh blood."[76]

Determined to stop Muslim League from demanding Pakistan, Sikhs came out with the counter demand of *Khalistan* (a separate sovereign state for the Sikhs as the Pakistan for the Muslims. V.S. Bhatti[77] of Ludhiana issued pamphlets demanding Khalistan soon after the League Pakistan resolution. Khalistan according to Dr. Bhatti was meant to serve as a buffer state between India and Pakistan. With the Maharaja of Patiala as its head, Khalistan was to be a theocratic state consisting of several federating units. A corridor was to link it with the Arabian Sea. Master Tara Singh, who was President of the Shiromani Akali Dal, then denounced the pamphlet for confounding the confusion already created by the Muslim league. Two Conferences to popularize the idea of Sikh state were organized by Baba Gurdit Singh Kamagata-Maru, a known supporter of Congress. The League leadership out rightly rejected the idea of Khalistan by stating that some Akalis were using the Congress platform to propagate the idea of *Sikh Raj* to scuttle the idea of Pakistan.[78]

As the prospects of freedom were coming closer, the Sikhs' concern for future became greater. In March-April 1942 Stafford Cripps conceded in principle that it was not obligatory for a province to join the Indian federation. This concession appeared to carry the implication that the Punjab could become an autonomous political unit outside the Indian state. The Akali leaders did not like to be subordinated permanently to Muslim majority in the proposed state of Punjab which they feared would be an Islamic state based on two nation theory. The All-parties Committee submitted to Cripps proposal of a province with different proportion of three major Communities of the Punjab. The name given to the province of their conception was *Azad Punjab*. It gave an impression as if it was meant to be an independent state. Keen to sell their idea to Hindus also, the Akali leaders explained subsequently that this province was meant to be a part of Indian federation. The term *Azad* was meant to suggest that each community of this province would be free of the fear of domination by another community. It stood for autonomy. The Muslims and Hindus of this province would account for the bulk of its population 40 percent each Hindu and Muslim Sikhs would form 20 percent. Rooted in the fear of the creation of Pakistan that can place the Sikhs under the domination of the Muslims for ever Sikhs campaigned for the Azad Punjab. Azad Punjab was essentially a defensive strategy adopted in response to the recognition of the idea of Pakistan by British government through the Cripps proposal and by the Congress through its resolution of 2 April 1942. In their opposition to the idea of Pakistan, the Sikh leaders did not hesitate to share platforms with Hindu Mahasabha who stood for India as a single political unit. Unlike Khalistan, the Azad Punjab was to be part of India: it was also to have a democratic constitution. All that the Sikhs could hope to gain was possibly an effective collaborative role in the affairs of Azad Punjab.[79]

Azad Punjab remained on the political agenda of Akalis leaders for about two years. After C.R. Formula and Gandhi-Jinnah talks, the Azad Punjab scheme was theoretically modified in two ways. Its name was dropped to bring in the idea of a Sikh state; and this proposed Sikh state was meant to be sovereign. But in the religious composition there was no change. Furthermore, its creation was conditional. Sovereign Sikh state was claimed not only by the Akalis but also by other Sikh organizations. This view was spelt out in the early 1945 by Sikh leaders who represented nearly the entire community. In their memorandum to the British government, Sikh leaders underlined the fact that accounting of four million persons in British India, the Sikhs are numerically next to the Hindus and Muslims. Their political, historical and economic importance is much greater than their numbers. Their contribution to defence and economy of the country is unique. Punjab is their holy and as well as their home land. Nonetheless, the Constitutional Reforms of 1935 had reduced them to a state of political subjection. The Hindus as well as Muslims disowned their mother tongue in favour of Hindi and Urdu. Discrimination against the Sikhs is exercised even in matters of religion. The Sikhs are against any partition of India on communal basis. If the demand of Pakistan is to be accepted they would insist on the creation of a separate Sikh state. The basic demand of the memorandum was united and strong India and the weightage for the Sikhs in a reorganized Punjab.[80]

At this point both Congress and Jinnah were trying to assure an autonomous status to the Sikhs if they are willing to go with Pakistan after the Independence. Jinnah promised to concede a semi-autonomous Sikh state within the political boundaries of Pakistan also. Akalis, however, stuck to the demand of a self-determined status of the Sikh state to which Jinnah was not ready to accept. At that time Akalis had two factions Jathedar Udham Singh and other prominent Sikhs led by Giani Kartar Singh; both were somehow ready to accept the Jinnah proposal. But Master Tara Singh was not prepared to trust the Muslim League unless there was a foollproof guarantee for the independent status of the Sikhs. There were some other proposals too but none guaranteed political freedom to the community.[81]

The Congress party at that time was fully assured by the Sikh leadership (read Akali leadership) that partition would not take place. If at all it would take place the Sikhs would be provided with special privileges in the north-west provinces of India. It was at this stage that Jawaharlal Nehru, while briefing the Press after the meeting of Congress working committee at Calcutta said,

"The brave Sikhs of Punjab are entitled to special consideration. I see nothing wrong in an area and a special set-up in north where in the Sikhs could also experience the glow of freedom."[82] Gandhi supplemented this assurance by saying "I ask you to accept my words and resolution of Congress that it will not betray a single individual much less a community. If it does so, Congress would not seal its down but that of the country too, moreover, the Sikhs are brave people and they know how to safeguard their rights. At that time Congress party was opposed to the division of India". Mahatma Gandhi assured that partition would take place over his dead body.[83]

The Congress assured that it will not accept the demand of the formation of Pakistan or the division of country on communal basis. Akali leadership trusted the Congress promises and made an alliance with the Congress and Hindu leadership against any communal division of India. Even at the last stage of the freedom struggle on 2 of March 1947, when the coalition government of Sir Khizar Hyat Khan collapsed. Master Tara Singh along with the Akali MLAs raised slogan of 'Pakistan Murdabad' (death of Pakistan) before the Muslim mob which was raising pro-Pakistan Slogans in front of the Assembly of Lahore. This demonstrates the determination of the Akali to oppose the creation of Pakistan.

The vibrant opposition of the Akalis soon put the community against the ire of Muslim fundamentalism. Then the League Leaders decided to crush the Sikh opposition. In the vitiated environment of Punjab, anti-Sikh riots were engineered to frighten the Akalis in general and Master Tara Singh in particular about the impending danger, if they persisted in their opposition towards the formation of Pakistan. The move behind the riots was clear from the words of then Governor of Punjab: "These riots were necessary to set right the brain of Master Tara Singh." These remarks were also conveyed to Master Tara Singh. Consequently the fury of March 1947 riots was more intense in Rawalpindi, the home district of Master Tara Singh, than anywhere else. After the riots the Governor again tried to persuade Master Tara Singh to opt for Pakistan but he reported that "My brain has yet been set right."[84]

It was on 20 February 1947, when Prime Minister Atlee announced his government decision to hand over power to Indians by June 1948. The new Viceroy Mountbatten took over on 24 March to effect the transfer of power. Within a month of his arrival it became clear to all the concerned that the division of the country could not be averted. The Congress which was a major party to oppose the division of country, itself passed a resolution to the partition of Punjab. Pandit G.B. Pant, said this was the only way to achieve freedom and liberty of the country. It would assure an India with strong Centre. This cleared the road for the formation of Pakistan. Even at the end of the movement, Akalis their tried best to keep the Sikh population together. The Sikhs were spread all over the Punjab without being a majority in a single district of the province. The Akali revived the idea of *Sikhistan* between river Yamuna and Chenab on the basis of Sikhs having landed property and sacred shrines in this area. Mountbatten made it clear that Sikhistan was not possible and that whatsoever the dividing line, nearly half of the Sikh population should fall in Pakistan.[85]

But all the efforts of Akalis to avert the division of Punjab failed and Mountbatten finally prevailed upon Jinnah to agree to the partition of the Punjab and also of Bengal by conceding the right of self-determination to the non-Muslims minorities in these provinces. The Mountbatten Plan of 3 June provided for the division of India into two sovereign countries. According to 3 June Plan, Pakistan was conceded on the principle of contiguous majority areas and Sikhs were no where in majority in any district of Punjab. In order to secure majority the Shiromani Akalis had been demanding not only the partition of Punjab, but also exchange of population as it is clear from Shiromani Akali Dal resolution of April 16, 1947.

Shiromani Akali Dal demanded that before transfer of power to the Indian hands in June 1948, the Punjab should be divided into two provinces... The Shiromani Akali Dal further demanded that facilities be provided for exchange of population and property and that special arrangements be made for protection, honour, integrity, and sanctity of historical religious places. In fact, some British officers were also suggesting the same to Viceroy after his June Plan, even the Governor of Punjab after receiving the circulation of June Plan pointed out to Viceroy that the 3 June plan would adversely affects the Sikhs as it would divide the Sikhs into India and Pakistan. The Viceroy's reply was that the Sikhs could improve their position through negotiations. Consequently, the meeting between the Jinnah and Liaquat Ali Khan and the Maharaj of Patiala and Baldev Singh then the Defence Minister of the Interim Government was arranged. Since the Sikhs had already put forth the demand of a Sikh State the talks naturally centered on that issue. Jinnah and Liaquat Ali Khan agreed to the formation of a Sikh State with its separate military establishment within the Pakistan. But the Sikh leaders demanded the right of opting out of Pakistan for the Sikh State to which the Muslim League did not agree. According to Master Tara Singh, if Jinnah had agreed they would have negotiation with the Congress for better terms.[86]

After the announcement of 3 June 1947 of the Mountbatten Plan for the division of country into India and Pakistan on the basis mainly of religious persuasion (though "other factors" were considered) and the appointment of the Boundary Commission under Sir Cyril Radcliff to demarcate the areas into Muslim and non-Muslim. The League therefore accepted the plan first. Thereafter, Congress passed a resolution on 15 June 1947 accepting the proposal embodied in the announcement of 3 June. Now there was no alternative before the Sikhs except to leave the historic Sikh shrines (besides 700 crore worth of property) and half of the Sikh population in Pakistan. Master Tara Singh immediately rejected it as also the Akali Dal and Panthic Board, but Baldev Singh then the Sikh Defence Minister announced on All India Radio, "It does not please everybody not the Sikhs, not the Sikhs anyway, but it certainly is something worthwhile. It is not compromise but a settlement, let take it as that".

The Sikh leadership thought that the division had compromised their stand against the creation of Pakistan but they left with no option as things changed very fast because the communalization of the Punjab led to the communal riots in Lahore in the month of June, which were followed in Gujranwala, Wazirabad, Seikhupura,

Sialkot and Lyallpur. The Hindu and Sikhs in the dominant Muslims region of the West Punjab were forced to leaves their homes, property and lands due to chaos, which has been emerged because of the division of the India on the religious lines.[87]

PUNJAB AFTER THE INDEPENDENCE

The independence of India in 1947 and the partition of British Punjab between India and Pakistan on the basis of Hindu and Muslim majority areas not only altered the demographic composition of Indian Punjab, but it has also had long-term implications on the socio-political set-up of Punjab. As the social fabrics of Punjabi society were communalized beyond the political solution and the communal riots of the partition left the people with bitter psyche of religious carnage. Millions of lives were broken-down because of communal carnage, the entire Hindu and Sikh population of the western district of Pakistan Punjab fled to India. Similarly, Muslims from the East Punjab fled to Pakistan.

Although Hindus and Muslims both beared the burnt of partition, but as a community, Sikhs were the worst victims of the partition, because they were of a distinct small/unrecognised minority. Unfortunately, they were considered to be the sword arm of the Hindus. Moreover, their geographic position also added to their worst as the province of Punjab was to be divided between India and Pakistan. According to the demographic logic of the Hindus and Muslims population. However, the Sikhs were again at the worst end as the population of this small religious minority was happen to be equal in size on the both sides of Radcliff line, which was to be drawn between the two countries. Each side of it made up to 2 million of Sikh people, of their total of 4 millions. They even donot have a single district to be claim as the majority, except Moga and Tarn Taran Sikh majority teshil before the Partition of India.[88]

The most important for their misfortune in the Muslim dominated region of the north-west Punjab was their strong opposition to the creation of Pakistan as the Muslim League wanted. So they have bear the burns of communal violence most. The partition of India not only forced them to leave their inherited lands of the Canal rich colonies of Sialkot and their business in Lahore once the capital of Sikh Empire. In fact, the day of freedom became with the message of destitute and misery. Their sense of honour and respect were badly ruined during the communal carnage.

The division of Punjab between India and Pakistan at the time of Independence resulted in the loss of 2.5% of the total Sikh population with the burns of shame due to rapes and abduction of their women-folk at mass though the Sikh community was also not the above board as for the similar acts of atrocities against the Muslims were concerned. Irrespective of the loss of the honour and members of the families they suffer economically also. Their social and economic statutes have been also lost in the agrarian economy of India as they were forced to leave the canal-rich colonies and their inherited lands in Pakistan. (Figures published in the statesman on September 25, 1969, show that 78 percent of the fertile, irrigated and rich lands of the community were left in the West Punjab. Prosperous colonies developed by the industrious and capable peasantry had to be abandoned. As against the area of 60 lakh acres (equivalent to 39,35,131 standard acres abandoned in west Punjab, only 47 lakh acres equivalent the 2,44,830 standard acres were available in the East Punjab and East Punjab States Union (PEPSU). Their holy shrines including the Nankana Sahib the birth place of Sikhs first guru and the Capital of the Sikh empire were left in the Pakistan.[89]

LANGUAGE AND IDENTITY POLITICS: AFTER THE PARTITION OF PUNJAB

After the partition, there began a new phase of history in truncated Indian Punjab. The lack of resources and the destitution of the refugees of partition from the Western Punjab to Eastern Punjab had its own implication for the age old relations of Hindus and Sikhs in the new demographic set-up of Punjab. The displacement of the Muslims from the Eastern Punjab and the mass migration of the Hindus and Sikhs from the western Punjab to eastern Punjab changed the demography of Punjab radically. In the united Punjab the Hindus were of 30% and the Sikhs were 14%. Both were in minority and constituted a united power against the 56% Muslim majority. After the division of Punjab between India and Pakistan, the Hindus became the dominant majority with of 62.3% and the Sikhs who were of 14% now constituted a recognizable minority of 35%, the erstwhile population majority community the Muslims were reduced to non-political entity now.[90] The displacement of the Muslims also meant that Urdu had lost its importance in the Indian Punjab now. The old alliance of the Hindus and Sikhs against the Muslim majority had no relevance in the new demographic set-up.

The integration of the princely states into PEPSU and rehabilitation of the people from the north-western districts of Rawalpindi, Gujranwala, Sheikhpura, Lyalpur, Jalandhar and Ludhiana, etc. and those from the south-west districts Multan, Jhang and Dera-Gazi Khan in Hissar, Rohtak and Gurgaon districts further consolidated the Sikhs in central Punjab and the Hindus in the eastern districts.[91] In fact, in the Sikhs princely states and the districts of Gurdaspur, Amritsar, Jullundhar, Hoshiarpur, and Ludhiyana and Ferozpur, the Sikh came to represent more than half of the total population. The Sikhs in these districts eliminated the major block to the earlier territorial demand of the Akali Dal especially that of sovereign Sikh state in absence of a geographically compact Sikh majority area. For the first time in their history they found themselves concentrated in a large contiguous territory.

The Akali leadership was actually aware of the logic of changed ratio. They felt that there would be no escape from the political domination of majority. It was under these circumstances that some Akali leaders rejected to accept the relegation of the Sikh community to the position of a permanent minority. The leadership realized in good time that it was going to be an uphill task to achieve a smaller province in which the Sikhs could hold their own. Master Tara Singh saw the Sikhs constituting a majority in a strategic province, the possibility of the Akali becoming the exclusive repository of power independently of Congress. In August 1948, Master Tara Singh addressed a Press Conference in Delhi and demanded the creation of Punjabi-speaking State. He said that he wrote to Dr. Rajendra Prasad, the President of Constituent Assembly, that the Punjabi Suba should be demarcated on the basis of linguistic principles.[92]

A high level committee of Congress including Jawaharlal Nehru, Vallabhabhai Patel and Dr. Pattabhi Sitaramayya had already cleared the Congress stand on the reorganisation of the Provinces on the Linguistic basis. While taking back its commitment to the formation of linguistic Provinces dates back to 1920-21 the Committee held. When the Congress had given a seal of its approval to the general principles of linguistic provinces, it was not faced with the practical application of the principle and hence, it had not considered all the consequences that arose from this practical application; the primary consideration must be the security, unity and economic prosperity of India and every separatist and disruptive tendency should be rigorously discouraged; language was not only binding force, but also a separating one and the old Congress policy of having linguistic provinces could only be applied after careful thought had been to each separate case and without creating serious administrative dislocation or mutual conflicts which would jeopardise the political and economic stability of the country.[93]

While the drafting of constitution was under consideration of the Constituent Assembly the Akali Dal in a resolution on 8 October 1948 observed that:

> "It has become a fashion in the politics of the day to condemn the separate electorate system. But in the composite state that India undoubtedly is, the right to choose one's own representative is the most effective and prized safeguard for a minority. Separate electorates are the only age-old democratic maxim.....It would be open to the majority party and other political parties to set-up their own candidates to contest and secure Sikh seats by winning the confidence and support of the Sikhs. It will promote confidence and concord between the different communities but eliminating causes and chances of friction".[94]

The demand received impetus when minorities' rights were being discussed in the Constituent Assembly. The question relating to a committee of the Constituent Assembly which included Jawaharlal Nehru, Vallabbhai Patel, Rajendra Prasad and Bhimrao Ambedkar. This committee appointed a ten-member sub-committee to evolve an agreed formula in respect of all communal questions affecting the East Punjab. A memorandum was submitted by Akali Dal to the Sub-committee on Minorities of the Constituent Assembly demanding among other things 50% seats for the Sikhs in Punjab Assembly and 5% in the Central Legislature and communal representation for Sikhs.[95] In November 1948, all the Sikh members of the East Punjab Assembly had drawn a list of 13 demands. The important among them were:

1. Representation be given to the Sikhs on the basis of 1941 Census without excluding Sikhs who have migrated to the other provinces.
2. They should be given five percent representation in the Centre and reservation of seats in other provinces.
3. One Sikh Minister and one Deputy Minister be taken in

Central Cabinet.

4. Posts of Governor and Premier of East Punjab should go alternately to a Hindu or a Sikh.
5. Fifty per cent of representation in the Provincial Cabinet and Assembly was to be reserved for them.
6. Gurgaon district and Loharu State should be separated from the East Punjab.
7. Forty per cent seats should be reserved for Sikhs.
8. If the above demands were rejected, Sikhs should be allowed to form a new province of seven districts, i.e. Hoshiarpur, Jullundhar, Ludhiana, Ferozpur, Amritsar, Gurdaspur and Ambala.[96]

When the Minorities Sub-committee rejected the demand of Akalis for statutory safeguards they fell back on Punjabi Suba as the sole means of attaining their objective of dominant position for the Sikhs in Punjabi -speaking areas of the province. "The rejection of the demand for the retention of the existing safeguards had left them with no other weapon in their armoury.[97]

The Working Committee of the Shiromani Akali Dal announced holding of a conference at Delhi on 20 February 1949, to voice the grievances such as the alleged discriminatory treatment of Sikhs in services, denial of constitutional safeguard and denial of Punjabi language its rightful place in the education and administration of East Punjab. The central authorities tried to pursued Akali Dal not to hold this conference but of no avail. The Delhi administration clamped a ban on the meeting in the whole of Delhi. Master Tara Singh and other leaders were arrested.

The Shiromani Akali observed a protest day throughout Punjab on 2 March, 1949 and 4th April 1949 a Conference of Sikh intellectuals were called in Amritsar where from the first time the resolution for Punjabi Suba was passed.[98] The Constituent Assembly had been eager to consider the issue the statutory reservation for religious minorities before August 1947, but after the creation of Pakistan it favoured the abolition of all such reservations. In May 1949, the Advisory Committee of the Constituent Assembly was clearly of the view that there was no room for weightage to be given to the religious minorities in a federal republic with parliamentary democracy based on adult suffrage, and with the fundamental rights of all citizens enshrined in a written constitution. In any case, the Sikhs as a 'highly educated and virile community needed no weightage'.[99] Some events at this time gave a handle to Akalis to spread Punjabi Suba Movement further. In February 1949, the Jalandhar Municipal Committee unanimously decided that it would have Hindi as medium of education in schools instead of Punjabi. On 9 June 1949 Panjab University rejected the proposal for Punjabi as medium of education.[100] This was strongly resented by the Akali Dal. It appeared that the seeds of Punjabi Suba were being simultaneously sown elsewhere with these decisions of the government. As a consequences of the independence, a new political state called PEPSU came into being in 1948. It consisted of Patiala and other Princely states in East Punjab. All these states with the exception of Malerkotla had Sikh rulers. PEPSU had Sikh Maharaja Yadvendra Singh as its Rajparmukh, a Sikh aristocrat Gian Singh Rarewala as Chief Minster and majority of its population was Sikhs. The formation of PEPSU was therefore a step forward towards the formation of Punjabi Suba. Sardar Patel while performing its inaugural ceremony characterised it as "Homeland of the Sikhs" and it was utilised by the Akalis as an argument in favour of its merger into the Sikh majority areas of Punjab and the formation of Punjabi-speaking state.[101]

Although Akali Dal was trying its best to mobilise the masses on the Punjabi Suba issue, however, all its efforts were going vain as in the changed political and demographic situation the rural peasantry was more inclined towards the Congress. In fact, all over India Congress was trying to forge an alliance with the landed classes. Under these circumstances, the post-partition Akali politics followed nearly the pre-partition pattern, i.e., it broke into two factions, one pro-government (Congress) consisting primarily rural Jat Sikhs, and other anti-government led by urban leadership. Unfortunately after the partition the leaders of anti-government group Master Tara Singh and Giani Kartar Singh had also lost control over the Sikh Stage as most of their following had been dislocated and scattered, the pro-government group had a greater say. On 15 March a well knit group of the Akali legislators joined the Congress. Consequently, the Akali Dal got itself merged with the Congress in 1948.[102] Subsequently, president of the Akali Dal, Giani Kartar Singh had a resolution passed by the Executive Committee, stating that the Akali Dal would not engage in political activity henceforth.[103] The Akali members inside the Congress party functioned as a separate group under the leadership of Giani Kartar Singh and Gopi Chand Bhargava became increasingly dependent on the support of this group to maintain his position as Chief Minister. Bhargava's opponents led by Bhim Sen Sachar severely criticized him for a secret deal with the Akali Dal and for succumbing to Akali Dal pressure. But Sachar himself carried on secret negotiation with the Akali Dal with a view to wrest political power. Akali Dal extended its support to Sachar who became Chief Minister on 6 April 1949.[104]

After the rejection of the demand for separate electorates and reservation of seats in the legislature for the Sikhs by the Constituent Assembly, the Akalis put up after the demand of implementation of Punjabi in the Gurmukhi script as the official language and as the medium of instruction in Punjab at the school level. The Chief Minister of Punjab Bhim Sen Sachar evolved a formula then. This formula provided a division of the province into two zones, a Punjabi speaking zone and a Hindi zone. In the Punjabi zone, the medium of instruction was to be Punjabi written in Hindi script. In order to retain the bilingual character of the province, it provided for a compulsory learning of both languages in each zone. Sachar formula, however, was not acceptable to a section of Hindus living in the Punjabi Zones, and was not implemented in the schools of Arya Samaj. The Sachar lost support within the Congress and Gopi Chand Bhargava regained power.

Akalis soon separated from the Bhargava government and the Congress as they were annoyed with Congress over the rejection of their demands for the special safeguards of the Sikh interests in the Constitution of Independent India and the delaying of the implementation of the Bhim Sen Sachar formula on the Punjabi language. It was in July 1950 when Master Tara Singh on behalf of Dal issued a call to all its MLAs for the returning back to their fold. The call could not impress its legislators as only 1 MLA from the 23 of Akalis had responded to the Dal call. Disappointed over a close alliance of the Sikh peasantry and Congress, Master Tara Singh then decided to start a campaign for demarcation of Punjab on the language base. He saw that in the post-partition demography of Punjab, the Sikhs are consolidating majority in a strategic zone and the demand of Punjabi-Suba can bear the fruits in this zone.

Harcharan Singh Bajwa, a member of Akali Dal Working Committee (1931-60) in his book *Fifty Years of Punjab Politics* has pointed out the political aspects of demand. "Now what mattered was the vote, the history making potency, chivalry, ambition and sacrifices remained no more as criteria of sovereignty. On bewilderment, I took along with me Bhupinder Singh Mann and Gyani Kartar Singh and the trio of us knocked at the door of Dr. Ambedkar. We solicited guidance from him and quick he was in presenting the recipe of our peril. He told us; "If you had cast lots with Pakistan you would have been a minority there. In joint Punjab you were a minority except in two tehsils, which too were not contiguous. In Eastern Punjab, too, you are a minority. If you clamour for Sikh State, it will cry in the wilderness. Why don't you ask for a Punjabi-speaking state? Congress is committed to linguistic basis for the reorganisation of the states. They can defer satisfaction of this demand but they cannot oppose it for long. I have told you the way. You can have a Sikh state in the cloak of 'Punjabi Suba'."[105]

On hearing this suggestion of Dr. Ambedkar, Bajwa writes, "Our faces brightened. We knew that narrow mindedness of Patel had left little scope for our carving a *de jure* Sikh state. But there was way to get *de facto* Sikh state. We launched struggle for Punjabi Suba".[106]

AKALIS RESOLUTION ON PUNJABI SUBA

Although the Akalis were clear that any demand for the Sikh majority state was to be strongly opposed by the nationalist leadership and were equally clear that the opposition of the Punjabi Hindu who were residing in the province would also oppose it. Hence religious fanaticism and religion-based demands had no place in the post-colonial India as it was in the colonial India and before the creation of Pakistan. Looking into their electoral basis Akalis linked the Demand of Punjabi Suba with the identity politics. In the first resolution on Punjab Suba Akalis accused centre for discriminating against the Sikhs.

"The callous and unsympathetic treatment of the government had made respectable life impossible for them, they (Sikhs), therefore strongly felt the utter necessity of the creation of a Punjabi-speaking province for the protection and preservation of their culture, language and self-respect, particularly when this solution is universally recognised as a democratic and which even the Indian National Congress stand pledged."[107] As such there was no doubt that the demand for a Punjabi Suba was essentially for a state with clear Sikh majority. Although in the course of the time the emphasis shifted from the plan of Sikh majority to that of Punjabi-speaking majority having Punjabi Gurmukhi script as the sole official language but the achievement of the Punjabi Suba and the fulfilment of the Sikh aspirations remained always linked. The Hindu opposition to the creation of Punjabi Suba along with the communal lines and electoral politics gave further imputes to this movement.[108]

THE PUNJABI SUBA MOVEMENT AND THE ELECTRO POLITICS

Whereas at the time of last elections in the pre-independence Punjab the main contending parties were Congress, Muslim League, the Unionist and the Akali Dal, after the partition the Muslim League and the Unionist Party ceased to be in East Punjab. Their place, however, was taken by many new entrants this time. Apart from the Communists, who were there in 1946 also, there were socialist splinters from the Congress, Scheduled Caste Federation and newly founded Jana Sangh. People of the erstwhile princely states, now grouped in the province of PEPSU, also participated in the elections of independent India.[109] By the time of First General Elections in 1952 both the Akali Dal and the Hindu Organisation such as Jan Sangh and Arya Samaj had become distrustful to each other and appealed to the religious and linguistic sentiments of voters. At the time of 1951 Census, the Hindu press launched a big propaganda as a result of which majority of Punjabi Hindus and Harijans mentioned their mother tongue as Hindi.[110] As a consequence, the Akalis met in Patiala in September 1951 in which about 4 to 5 lakh Sikhs took part. A great prominence was given to the Punjabi Suba demand in this conference.[111] Meanwhile a debate on Hindu Code Bill was going on in the Parliament. In section two of this bill like the Buddhists and Jains, the Sikhs were also taken as Hindus. The Akalis legislators protested against this.

The Shiromani Akali Dal also chose to fight the elections held between November 1951 and January 1952 both in Punjab and PEPSU on Punjabi Suba issue. The Akali Dal manifesto of 1952 elections elaborated the reasons for demanding a Punjabi-speaking State: "The true test of democracy in the opinion of Shiromani Akali Dal is that the minorities should feel that they are really free and equal partner in the destiny of their country: (a) To bring this sense of freedom to the Sikhs, it is vital that there should be a Punjabi-speaking language and culture. This will not only be in the fulfilment of the pre-partition programme and pledges, but also in the entire conformity with the universally recognised principles governing formation of provinces; (b) The Shiromani Akali Dal is in favour of formation of provinces on a linguistic and cultural basis throughout India, but it hold that it is the question of life and death for the Sikhs for a new Punjab to be created immediately: (c) The Shiromani Akali Dal has reason to believe that a Punjabi-speaking province may give

Sikhs needful security. It believed in Punjabi-speaking province is an autonomous unit of India".[112]

There is no doubt that the elections of 1952 were fought on the basis of Punjabi Suba. But the Akali Dal was badly mauled by the Congress both in Punjab and PEPS. In the house of 186 (126 in Punjab and 60 in PEPSU) the Akalis were only able to win 33 seats and just 14% of votes, the Congress won 122 seats with 34.8 per cent votes. The Communist Party of India and the Jana Sangh also received 5.3 and 5 per cent of votes respectively.[113] It is found that in the Punjabi speaking region, the Congress polled 31.3 percent votes as against Akali Dal 24 per cent votes (See table). The Akalis won a majority seats in Sikh majority areas. But none of them got more than 33 per cent votes. On the other, hand Congress percentage in no Sikh areas went below 21.7 per cent (even in Bathinda with Sikh population as high as 72.3 per cent). It even got more votes than the Akalis in two Sikh majority Districts Amritsar and Patiala(See table). Moreover, the Congress party won seats in all the districts whereas the Akali Dal could not get even a single seat in many districts with considerable Sikh population for instance Jullundhar and Gurdaspur with 44.8 and 42.9 per cent Sikhs.[114]

Percentage of Seats and Votes polled by Political Parties in 1952 in Punjab and PEPSU (Combined)

Political Party	*Total Seats in Vidhan Sabha*	*Percentage of Votes*	*Seats in Punjabi-speaking Region*	*Percentage of Votes in Punjabi-speaking Region*
Congress	122	34.8	60	31.3
Akali Dal	33	14.7	31	24.0
Communist Party	6	5.3	6	6.1
Jan Sangh	2	5.0	—	4.0
Other and Independent	21	40.2	13	34.6

Source : Compiled from India Election Commission Report on the First General Election in India, 1951-52, Volume II, New Delhi, Manager of Publication, 1956.[115]

The Congress in Punjab with 31.3 percent votes, no doubt emerged as the weakest Congress organization in any of the major Indian states. Its proportion of popular vote was the lowest in any of the 15 major states. *(The Spokesman Weekly,* July 22, 1963) In PEPSU it was not able to win a clear majority. In PEPSU, however, Akalis succeeded in forming a United Front Ministry headed by Sardar Gian Singh Rarewala. United Front had strength of 27 in the House of 49 (there were 2 vacancies in the House of 51). It was the first and the only non-Congress ministry since Independence.

Party Performance in District with Hindu and Sikh Majorities, 1951-52

District	*Religious composition*		*Akali Dal*		*Congress*	
	Hindu	*Sikh*	*Seats*	*Percentage votes*	*Seats*	*Percentage votes*
Hissar	89.2	9.9	1	31.1	8	34.5
Rohtak	98.5	0.5	—	—	9	36.5
Gurgaon	81.6	0.7	—	—	9	49.5
Karnal	86.8	11.8	—	—	11	43.9
Ambala	71.4	24.8	0	1.8	5	40.4
Rupar	67.7	31.0	1	28.0	1	21.5
Hoshiarpur	67.7	31.0	1	8.2	7	37.2
Jullundhar	54.0	44.8	0	20.7	11	37.1
Ludhiana	35.7	63.0	5	34.1	2	22.1
Ferozepur	40.6	57.9	5	22.5	3	22.5
Amritsar	33.0	64.5	1	20.6	11	36.8
Gurdaspur	50.1	42.9	0	.23.3	8	41.5
Patiala	45.8	52.8	4	24.5	7	35.7
Bhatinda	27.1	72.3	8	32.8	3	26.3
Kapurthala	41.0	58.2	8	28.3	3	26.8
Sangrur	51.9	43.7	6	33.3	4	24.5
Mohindergarh	99.2	0.4	—	—	4	31.4
Himachal District	96.8	1.2	—	—	10	44.1

Source : Manorma Kohli, 1985, "Protest Movements in Punjab: A Case Study of Punjabi Suba Agitation", *Punjab Past and Present*, Vol. XVII, No. II, August, pp. 390-91.

In PEPSU, however, Akalis succeeded in forming a United Front Ministry headed by their Chief Minister Gian Singh Rarewala.

United Front had strength of 27 in the house of 49 (there were 2 posts vacant in the house of 51). It was for the first and only non-Congress ministry since independence.

The Congress success in 1952 elections did not fundamentally alter the Punjab political system. Although the Dal had failed to engender the support, it expected and also to substantiate its claim as the sole representative of the Sikhs despite a campaign conducted on the Punjabi Suba issue, it did not give up the demand. Rather it realised that it needed the support of Sikh masses and to win their support it become necessary to stir the emotions by using cultural symbols upon which the claims for group rights could be based. The necessity to control over the supreme religious body SGPC was also dawned upon the Akalis immediately after the First General Election. In October 1952, Akalis wrested the office of President of SGPC from Udham Singh Nagoke who was a pro-Congress Akali. With the administration of Gurdwaras now on its side, the Akali Dal was in better position to fight the battle for Punjabi Suba. Significantly the control over SGPC became a major source of financial help for the Akalis.[116]

At this stage, Akalis began demanding the amalgamation of the Punjabi region of the exiting Punjab with PEPSU. In October 1952, Hukam Singh opposed the Punjabi region of the East Punjab. It was to be merged with PEPSU and Punjabi speaking region of Rajasthan to create portion of Punjab and PEPSU in forming them into one administrative unit. While asking for the amalgamation of PEPSU and Punjabi-speaking region to constitute a Punjabi Suba they could at this stage feel sure that it was bound to be the Sikh majority state. The Akali Dal Working Committee in a resolution in 1953 said:

> "Shiromani Akali Dal notes with extreme regret and sorrow that the independence of the country has brought no relief to the Sikhs. Their lot has worsened. They have been suppressed, slandered and maligned, and have practically become untouchable in their own land. They have been particularly chosen to be discriminated against in all walks of life. They sought solution of difficulties by all peaceful and constitutional methods but they have not been given hearing."[117]

Similarly, a resolution on Punjabi-speaking state passed at the 9th All India Akali Conference at Moga in April 1953 read:

> "Freedom of the country has so far connoted to the Sikhs their

ceaseless misrepresentations, vilification, discrimination and suppression and naturally there is a great anguish and ferment in their souls over this treatment. Degrading and demoralising conditions in which they find themselves are serious menace to the vital principles of the "Guru Panth" existence of Sikhs as self-respecting community and the preservation of Punjabi language. The Conference call upon the Congress government to honour without any further loss of time its pledge made to the people at large and which also perfect accord with the national and democratic principles and creates a Punjabi-speaking state forthwith. Sikhs urge this solution also for reason of their protection against aggressive communalism".[118]

The identity based politics was further crystallised by alleging the Centre for discriminatory treatment against the Sikhs and demands the same benefits for the Sikh SCs and STs Castes across India as the Hindus SCs and STs and taking. In the matter of Defence and Civil Services Akalis allege that Sikhs were discriminated against in matters of promotion and posting, so far as public services in Punjab as well as in the Centre were concerned. It was alleged by the representation of Akalis that the Sikhs representation in almost civil departments of the East Punjab Government was very low. So much so that higher grades and key posts they were hardly ten per-cent. Similarly, the ratio of the Sikhs in the armed forces was being drastically reduced. They also complained that the government did not continue the British practice of enforcing the requirement of standard Sikh religious discipline among the Sikh personnel in defence forces.[119]

After the first election, the Akali leadership not only started to present the demand for Punjabi Suba as necessity to get rid of discriminatory treatment and to protect the Sikhs culture but they also impressed upon the Sikhs. According to the Sikh religion, it was obligatory on their part to participate in politics as a group. This approach of the Akali Dal bore fruits and helped the Dal to retain its rural support during the agitation at the time of pleading its case before the States Reorganisation Commission (SRC).[120] In the beginning of 1953, two things happened that spurred the Akali Dal for greater tempo in demanding Punjabi Suba. One of them was in distant South. In the beginning Potti Sriramula died on fast for creation of Andhra Pradesh. Four days later the Prime Minister announced the separation of Andhra from Madras as Telgu-speaking state. Incidentally this spurted the Punjabi Suba movement. Then the President of PEPSU Akali Dal Sampuran Singh Raman stated fast unto death for the formation of Punjabi Suba. He stated that the government must concede the principles of the reorganization of Punjab on linguistic and cultural basis. He was not allowed to die but his health was deteriorated badly.[121] The second was the political crisis in PEPSU and the imposition of President Rule in March 1953. The Shiromani Akali Dal now got extremely keen on demanding the amalgamation of Punjabi speaking region of PEPSU and Punjab. The Akali Dal Working Committee in a resolution said: "The haste and hurry with the government was suspended in the PEPSU State, where Sikhs alone constitute majority, and the administration taken over by the President proves that how the Congress Government went to suppress the opposition (Akalis). And then the methods and long term measures for beyond the scope of his authority and appointment that are being adopted by the present advisor to eliminate effectiveness of the Sikhs and their homeland are well known."[122] Congress high command was strongly against the formation of Punjabi Suba. Even during the mid-term elections in PEPSU, Nehru openly opposed the Akalis resolution on the demand of Punjabi in a rally at Fatehgarh Sahib. He also accused Master Tara Singh for the misuse of Sikh religion. Master Tara Singh who was present in the congregation protested against Nehru for misusing the religious stage which was organised on the anniversary of martyrdom of the two sons of tenth guru. Meanwhile, the supporters of the Akali Dal created disturbance and Nehru was not allowed to speak.

The issue of reorganisation of the provinces in India acquired urgency due to the regional resentments against the Centre. To address the issue of the reorganisation of the states, the Union Parliament appointed the States Reorganisation Commission on 29 December 1953.[123] The Commission was given the task to investigate the conditions of the present demand of the reorganization, the historical background, the existing situation and the bearing of all relevant important factors thereon.[124] The appointment of the commission was welcomed by the Sikhs as it was opportunity for them to represent their case of Punjabi Suba and get adjudication thereon. The Working Committee of Shiromani Akali Dal drew up its memorandum. The Akali Dal demanded the following areas in its memorandum to the Commission.

1. Punjab; District of Gurdaspur, Amritsar, Ferozpur,

Ludhiana, Jullundhar, Hoshiarpur, Ambala, Karnal (Except Panipat tehshil) and Hissar (except Sirsa, Fatehabad and Thana Tohana).

2. District of Patiala, Barnala, Bathinda, Kapurthala, Fathehgarh Sahib and Sangrur (except Jind and Nirwana tehshils).
3. District of Ganganagar.
4. These areas would give Punjabi Suba territory of 35,185 square miles. While providing evidences before the Commission the General Secretary of Akali Dal waived claim to an area of Karnal District and Ganganagar district (except Hanumangarh tehsils).[125]

These areas would give the Punjabi Suba a territory of 35,185 square miles. While providing evidences before the Commission the General Secretary of Akali Dal waived claim to any area of Karnal district and Ganganagar district (except Hanumangarh and Ganganagar tehshils).[126]

Akali Dal further argued that the demand for Punjabi Suba was in line with demands in the other parts of India for the linguistic reorganization of States. It further said that Punjabi was a distinct language, and had been so recognized in the Indian constitution. It is also endowed with special script known as Gurmukhi which is not derived from "Devanagri" script of Hindi but from Brahmi.

Akali Dal denied the allegation that the Sikhs had asked for Punjabi Suba out of communal motives. "The Sikhs have been the greatest of patriots and they are Indians first and last". It further said that in any case Punjabi Suba was not going to be an independent country; it would be subject to Central control always. In conclusion, the Akali Dal said that the formation of Punjabi Suba would lead to the following beneficial results among others:

1. The creation of a geographically compact, economically sound and financially viable state;
2. The eradication of the causes of the present unrest in Punjab and the restoration of communal harmony which is essential in a border state;
3. The elimination of the language controversy, and the provision of education through the mother tongue in single language state, thus assuring further progress in the state. and

4. The securing of a contended Sikh community for the country.[127]

The Akalis memorandum was, however, countered by the Hindu Political parties and organization like Arya Samaj, Jana Sangh the Hindu Maha Sabaha and the All Parties Maha Punjab Front Samiti in their joint memorandum, condemned the Akali Dal demand for Punjabi Suba on the ground that the Akalis were communalists and their intentions were suspect. Their demands it was asserted was basically communal in nature camouflaged as a demand for Maha Punjab comprising of the Punjab, PEPSU, Himachal Pradesh, Delhi and few western districts of the United Province. They held this was more suitable in the changed political situation of this border state after the partition; consideration of unity and security of India must outweigh all other considerations they urged. The strategically important location of Punjab demanded that the state should be strong enough "to face the aggressive and hostile challenges of Pakistan."[128]

Aim for the creation of Punjabi-speaking State was alleged to bring into being a State where the Sikhs would be either numerically a majority or such a substantial minority as "to make them the real power in the State." The Maha Punjab Samiti held that for various administrative purposes greater Punjab was already functioning and therefore in order to attain financial stability and solvency reamalgamation of Punjab, PEPSU and Himachal Pradesh into Maha Punjab was an imperative necessity.[129] Punjab Pradesh Congress and Punjab Government under Partap Singh Kairon supported the proposal for integration of the three states—Punjab, PEPSU and Himachal Pradesh, a proposal identical the demand of Maha Punjab minus Delhi. The memorandum of the government of Punjab also supported the demand of Maha Punjab.[130]

The Akali Dal contested the 1954 PEPSU election primarily on the Punjabi Suba issue. Its economic programme remained vague. Akali Dal in this mid-term election succeeded in securing 10 seats with 27.6 per cent votes. Congress won 22 seats with 40.4 per cent votes. The Congress assumed power in PEPSU with Colonel Raghbir Singh as premier and Brish Bhan as his deputy.[131]

The Congress which was the ruling party in PEPSU did not enunciate a clear policy of the party. Most of PEPSU Congressmen wanted to be merged into Punjab. But in November 1954, Chief Minister Ranbir Singh strongly pleaded for the retention PEPSU as a separate State.[132] The picture was radically changed after the death of

Performance of Political Parties in 1954 PEPSU Election

Political Party	*Seats contested*	*Seats won*	*Percentage of Votes*
Congress	43	22	40.4
Akali Dal	33	20	27.6
Akali Dal Rarewala	—	—	—
CPI	—	—	—
Jan Sangh	07	—	0.6
PSP	03	—	0.1
Independent	37	05	13.3

Source : A.S. Narang, 1986, *Punjab Politics in National Perspective*, Gitanjali Publishing House, New Delhi, 1986, p. 32.

Ranbir Singh. Soon after Brish Bhan Singh's taking over as Chief Minister of PEPSU a piquant situation arose because he was known to have pro-merger view which ran counter to the stand taken by the PEPSU Government in the memorandum submitted to the State Reorganisation Commission.[133]

During this period the demand for a Punjabi-speaking State had gathered momentum. The Akali Dal in PEPSU was willing to surrender the Hindi-speaking areas of Narnaul and Kandaghat if the Ganagnagar district in Rajasthan could be transferred to PEPSU. Gian Singh Rarewala has also supported the demand of Punjabi - speaking state in the form of modified PEPSU. He recommended that the historical background and tradition of this region would help to retain the PEPSU in the modified form. He stated that, if, however for any political exigencies PEPSU and Punjab could be merged into each other, a Punjabi-speaking state out of this merged area should be formed.[134]

The right wing of Akali Dal favoured the retention of PEPSU and was opposed to its merger with Punjab. The party felt that the merger of PEPSU would be against the interest of Sikhs. The Sikh majority in PEPSU was only marginal, as they constituted only little more than 49% and exceeded the Hindus by only 20,000. The left wing of Riasti Akali Dal (Raman Group) on the other hand, stood for the merger of Punjabi-speaking areas of PEPSU with Punjab, it emphatically argued, "The Punjabi and no-Punjabi areas of Punjab are quite distinct. The Hindi-speaking people of Haryana areas of Punjab and PEPSU should be free to join their contiguous Hindi-speaking area..... The new Punjabi speaking State will surely stimulate the Punjabi consciousness of Punjabis irrespective of their caste creed and will ensure to the people their social and political solidarity. The formation of Punjabi-speaking State, would do away with the undemocratic and unwanted institutions of the Rajparmukh".[135]

Deputations of almost all the political parties and other organisations again met the State Reorganisation Commission on 18 April 1955 at Patiala. The diversity in their position and opinion on the issue was significant. The delegation of the Akali Dal and the Communist Party, the deputation of the Ganganagar Citizens, the Bathinda District Citizen's Committee and the Barnala Citizen Committee demanded the creation of Punjabi–speaking state.[136] The Akalis in PEPSU pleaded against the main Akali Dal for the retention of PEPSU preferable in its expanded or modified form. In the second half of 1954, Punjab was full of excitement generated by almost a public debated on respective merits of Punjabi Suba and the Maha Punjab. While State Reorganisation Commission (SRC) was touring the rest of country, the Punjab Congress was holding public meeting against the demand for Punjabi Suba and was mobilising support for what it called Maha Punjab.

The climax was reached on the eve of the elections for the SGPC to be held in January 1955. The Akali Dal entered this electoral contest on the issue of Punjabi Suba, in alliance with Desh Bhagat Board of the Communist. The Akali Dal won an overwhelming majority of the seats. The Congress sponsored Khalsa Dal contested 132 seats and could win only 3 seats.[137] After winning the Shiromani Gurdwara Parbandhak Committee election on the issue of Punjabi Suba, the Akali Dal intensified its struggle with renewed vigour. It was the first time when the Akali Dal got a clear memorandum on the issue of Punjabi Suba. Taking the advantage of its hold over the Sikh religious shrines, Dal strongly launched a campaign against the government interference in Gurdwaras. Master Tara Singh in a meeting with Bhim Sen Sachar, the Chief Minister of Punjab, pin-pointed the instances of interferences by the government in the Sikh Gurdwaras. The Akalis control over the SGPC also provided them with opportunity to mobilise the Sikh masses from the religious shrines and Gurdwaras. Master Tara Singh strongly condemned the government intervention in the Sikh religious matters and asserted that the Sikh wanted an honourable existence.[138] The Sikh public opinion was being mobilized in favour of Punjabi Suba.

To curb the Akalis from popularising the demand of Punjabi Suba, the Sachar ministry imposed a ban on the Punjabi Suba slogan, on the plea that it was endangering communal harmony in the State. At this stage master Tara Singh issued an ultimatum to the Punjab Government to withdraw the ban by a specific date or face Akali Morchas. In consultation with the Union Government, the Punjab government announced that it was not ready to bow to the Akali threats. The Morchas were launched on 10 May 1955 and Master Tara Singh was first to offer himself for arrest.[139] Addressing a huge congregation inside the Golden Temple at Amritsar, he said: "O Singho! We ask for freedom and they want to ensure us deeper into slavery. We are not satisfied with the present situation and ask for Punjabi Suba, but they stop us even to propagating the demand of Punjabi Suba. They have imposed a ban on raising slogans for the demand. Khalsa ji! Understand this that all this is to finish our honour. In the present time we should offer our heads peacefully like Guru Tegh Bahadur. The rivals are haughty rulers, but we have faith in the Guru".[140] The Akali Dal Started sending the Jathas who offered themselves for arrest by defying the ban. The movement reached its peak in the first week of July 1955 when a large number of volunteers poured into the premises of Akal Takht, not only from different parts of the Punjab, but from other provinces also. The organisers had to increase the number of *Satyagrahis* from 50 to 100 daily. Although, Amritsar was the focal point of the Morcha, yet Akali workers violated the law in other towns and courted arrested. As the Morcha continued for nearly two months and volunteers kept coming forward for arrest, the government took a strong step of allowing the police to enter the premises of Golden Temple on July 4 1955 to arrest the Akali leaders and volunteers that had gathered in the Parikarma (Compound) of Golden Temple. This incident created a greater resentment among the Sikh community and Morcha came to be considered as conflict not only between the Akali and government, rather between the government and the Sikhs at large".[141]

Finding no let-up in the agitation against the government the Chief Minister announced the lifting of the ban on Punjabi on the shouting of the slogan on 12 July 1955 and stated, "Unfortunately, while our leaders had been busy with the great problem of the world peace, we at home, particularly in Punjab find ourselves in a situation of increasing tension between the communities and parties. It 'behoves' each one of us to utilize the occasion of the hoe-coming of apostle of peace to do all we can bring about condition of peace in the State."[142]

The government stated that the ban was lifted to mark the occasion of Nehru's from peace mission abroad. The Chief Minister went to the Golden Temple to tender an unconditional apology on the behalf of his Government for whatever acts of sacrilege his police might have committed inadvertently. The Punjab Government announced that it would release the Akalis by instalments. To begin with, Master Tara Singh was released on 8 September followed by others as the agitation came to an end.

The State Reorganisation Commission's Report was published in October 1955. Despite the show of wide-spread Sikh support by the Akalis which came in the midst of deliberations of the SRC, the recommendation of the Commission rejected the Punjabi Suba Demand observing: "The case of Punjabi-speaking State falls firstly, because it lacks the general support of the people inhabiting the area, and secondly, because it will not eliminate any of the cause of friction from which the demand for a Punjabi-speaking State emanates. The proposed State will solve neither the language problem nor communal problem and far from relieving internal which exists between communal and not linguistic groups, it might further exacerbate the existing feelings".[143] On the other hand SRC recommended the integration of Punjab, PEPSU and Himachal Pradesh into an administrative unit. The Akalis opposed the recommendations of the SRC and alleged that it was a conspiracy to destroy the Sikh Nation and that the Commission had delivered the "Sikhs bound hand and foot to the slavery of an aggressive communal group." On 11 October 1955, Master Tara Singh declared at Gurdwara Manji Sahib that they had already announced their non-confidence in the Commission and therefore, they were not bound by its recommendations.[144]

Following the above development Master Tara Singh gave a 'Do or Die' call to the Sikhs, in an appeal he said: "Dear Sikh brothers today we are faced with a calamity that bound to finish us. The present stage is do or die. Set a side all pondering, and let there be no wavering of indecision. It is the time for immolation to death, the symbol of sacrifice that has been picked. This is the time when all resources shall have to be exhausted, all efforts made and sacrifice undergone."[145] Giani Kartar Singh said that out of 14 languages in the Indian Constitution, 13 States had been formed on linguistic basis. Only Punjabi Suba had not been formed because Sikh loyalty was suspected. Hukam Singh, another senior leader of the Akali Dal referred to it "as another deadly blow to the Sikhs and threaten that the Akalis would launch an agitation if peaceful negotiation failed.[146] Akalis called a convention of all parties and reorganization of the Sikhs on 16 October and underlined the secular and democratic character of the demand. They opined that the recommendation of the Commission appeared to be partisan as the most rabid could wish. Even the Sachar Formula, which the Commission recognised was not implemented, was whittled down. The convention authorised Master Tara Singh to approach the government of India on behalf of Sikh community.[147] Master Tara Singh met Jawaharlal Nehru on 24 October in the presence of Abdul Kalam Azad and G.B. Pant. He was accompanied by Giani Kartar Singh, Hukam Singh and Gian Singh Rarewala. Their talks were inconclusive. Another deputation met the Prime Minister to suggest that the PEPSU formula could be extended to the Punjab for solving the language problem and Punjabi language could be promoted in the whole state.[148] Akali also launched popular demonstration to appeal the democratic instinct of Jawaharlal Nehru. A tenth All India Akali Conference was held near the venue of Annual All India Congress at Amritsar on 7 February 1956. In the Conference Akali proved the mass support of the Punjabi Suba to Nehru as they gathered a huge crowd. Brecher, the author of *Nehru: A Political Biography* writes that thus procession had impressed Prime Minister Nehru: "Nehru was sympathetic to the Sikh fear, but was reported by the friends to be under strong pressure from communal minded Hindu Congressmen who were not prepared to place the Punjabi Hindus in an inferior political position".[149] In his speech to the Sikh masses Master Tara Singh said: I must say that we cannot be satisfied unless we get rid of the communal domination of Punjabi Hindus, led by the Arya Samajists, who in their efforts to destroy our religion went so far as to even deny their mother tongue. We have demanded a Punjabi-speaking state as the only permanent solution of Punjab problem. It solves both the question of communal domination and of language. Some modified forms of our proposal are suggested by some well wishing gentlemen, but to me all these solutions appear to be temporary and not conducive to permanent peace and settlement.[150] This popular demonstration appealed to the democratic instinct of Jawaharlal Nehru. He was now prepared to accommodate the Akalis as much as he could in the face of contending pressures.

Hukam Singh had formulated a scheme which essentially met some of Akalis demands without actually creating a Punjabi-speaking

State.[151] This became the basis of discussion in January 1956, the General body meeting of the Akali Dal was held. Gian Singh Rarewala presented the Regional Formula and Giani Kartar Singh succeeded in overpowering the opponents of the Regional formula. Some critics of this move were of the opinion that Hukam Singh and Kartar Singh were impatient to get office from the Congress Government. Hukam Singh got the Deputy Speaker of Lok Sabha and Kartar Singh becomes a Minister in Punjab. Master Tara Singh made his position clear through the short speech that he made at the meeting. He said, "Our objective is not to create trouble. The proposal offered by the Government does not constitute the Punjabi Suba, but under the present circumstances, I do not want to fight".[152] In this meeting, majority of the leaders were in favour of accepting the scheme finalised afterward. The scheme came to be known as the Regional Formula. The main provision of the agreement which represented a compromise between the Hindu demand for the Union of all three states in greater Punjab and the Sikhs demand for a separate Punjabi-speaking state, were as follows:

- Punjab and PEPSU should be merged in a single bilingual state with a common Governor, Ministry, Legislature, Public Service Commission and High Court. The predominately Hindu State of Himachal Pradesh would be provisionally become a Union Territory.
- For the transaction of government business with regard to certain specified matter the State would be divided into two regions-one Hindi-speaking and the other Punjabi-speaking.
- For each there would be a regional committee of the Punjab State Assembly consisting of members of the Assembly, including the ministers belonging to the region but excluding the Chief Minister.
- Legislation regarding specific matters would be reoffered to the regional committees, which could also make legislative proposal to the State Government. Advice tendered by the regional committees would normally be accepted by the government and the State Legislature, but in the event of difference of opinion the matter would be referred to the Governor, whose decision would be final and binding.
- The regional committee would be *inter-alia* with the

development of economic planning (with framework) of General Development Public Health, Fisheries, Cooperatives Societies and Charitable and Religious Institutions.

- The demarcation of the Hindi and Punjabi regions would be carried out in consultation with the State Government and other interest concerned.
- Both Punjabi and Hindi would be recognised as official language of the State. At district level and below the official language of each region would be the regional language. The State Government would set-up two separate departments for promoting the Punjabi and Hindi languages. The proposals contained in the State Reorganisation Bill were unanimously approved by the PEPSU Legislative Assembly.[153]

After the agreement on the Regional Formula and the political compromise between the government and the Akali Dal the Sikh grievances as the Akali leaders were themselves admitted, were readdressed. But the compromise left the Akali Dal in a political wilderness and it had to decide upon the course to be adopted in future. The parties were in a situation of political drift and Gian Singh Rarewala, even said in a statement that under the changed circumstances, the Akali Dal should leave the political field and confine itself only to the social, cultural, religious and educational activities of the Sikhs and allow its members and support to join the national and progressive forces.[154]

In fact, he even started discussion with the Congress leaders in order to facilitate the entry of his group into the Congress. An acrimonious debate followed among the Akali leaders, Master Tara Singh immediately branded Rarewala's move as a "treachery" and made it clear that the Akali Dal would maintain its independent political entity of the Sikhs. Hukam Singh characterised Rarewala's advice to join the Congress party as virtually an act of sabotage and betrayal of trust. The Working Committee even expelled Rarewala's and his five associates for their advocacy. However, the Akali Dal in view of increasing tilt towards Congress among rural Sikhs started negotiating with Congress about political cooperation. Eventually the convention of the Akali Dal held at Amritsar on 2 October 1956 under the Chairmanship of Master Tara Singh unanimously decided that it was "desirable that Dal should again repose confidence in

Congress and its leader's so far political programme is concerned." It further resolved that the Dal would concentrate on and confine itself to the religious, education, culture, social and economic fields for the betterment of Sikhs."[155]

Thus on 24 November 1956, the General body meeting of the Akali Dal decided to delete from the Akali Dal's constitution those clauses which related to the national aspiration of a separate political entity. It was further resolved that in regard to political activities the members of Akali Dal should join the Congress.[156]

An area of close and cordial relations began between the Congress and the Akali Dal. Master Tara Singh declared that he would never forsake Jawaharlal Nehru on his turn praised Master Tara Singh for his courage and honesty of purpose.[157]

The government, however, kept the content of Regional Formula guarded secret Balramji Dass Tandon had to resort to hunger strike in Amritsar just to get the copy of the scheme for the Regional Standing Committee. Under the pressure of the Hindu organizations the government was finally forced to publish the Regional Formula Scheme.[158] The Hindu Maha Samiti outrightly rejected the content of Regional Formula and called a Conference at Karnal on 25 June 1956. The Maha Punjab Samiti also supported the Hindu Maha Samiti and both accused the Government of India yielding to the pressure of Akalis by relegating Hindi as second language in the Punjabi-speaking region. The Samitis aroused the sentiments of the people of Haryana region, who had hitherto supported the demand of Punjabi-speaking state against the advocates of the Punjabi-speaking region.

Those by the scheme of the Regional Formula areas with considerable resources and potentialities were targeted to put in the Punjabi-speaking region while the areas with poor resources were incorporated in the Hindi-speaking region leaving no possibility of its future growth and development. Similarly, all the important professional and technical institutions like the medical, law and agriculture colleges and industrial training institutions were located in the Jalandhar division and Haryana had been left to hold the baby.

The Punjabi was neither the regional nor the national language of Haryana and, therefore, the study of the Punjabi and Gurumukhi script as a compulsory second language for the students of this region from the 5th class in accordance with the Sachar Formula was to be abrogated the Samiti held.[159] The Maha Samiti further threatened 'direct action' if a mutually satisfactory solution of the Punjab tangle was not immediately found. The Congress government did not yield to the pressure of the Samiti and the Samiti launched a movement known as 'Hindi Satyagraha.' The 'Hindi Satyagraha' was supported by the Arya Samaj and Jana Sangh and slogan of 'Save Hindi' and 'Hindi in danger'. The leader of the Arya Samaj, Swami Atmanand Saraswati, said "The Regional Formula means Sikhstan of Punjab and Sikhstan means Khalistan. It being a border state; this conspiracy will not be allowed to succeed."[160] Even the Hindu leaders of Congress in Punjab openly wrote against the Regional Formula and under the leadership of Jagat Narain more than fifty members of Congress in Punjab submitted a memorandum to the Prime Minister.[161]

The failure of the regional plan once again made the Akali leadership to launch a movement in support of Punjabi Suba. Under the leadership of Master Tara Singh Akali Dal held a big rally in Delhi. This rally was followed by the Master Tara Singh giving a call of by his own fast unto his death or until the fulfilment of the demand of Punjabi Suba and unto death. To avoid any unwanted incident, the Government decided to put him under the preventive detention on 15 March 1959. On the intervention by the central government, Master Tara Singh was released on 21 March 1959.[162]

In the meantime, the elections of the Shiromani Gurdwara Parbandhak Committee became due and were held in January 1960. Partap Singh Kairon, Gian Singh Rarewala and Kartar Singh jointly sponsored the 'Sadh Sangat Board' to fight the election against the Akali Dal. On May 1959, Master Tara Singh announced at Ludhiana that he would fight SGPC election on the Punjabi Suba issue only. The strength to the Akali demand of Punjabi Suba was again provided by the decision of the Congress High Command to bifurcate Bombay into two states—Maharashtra and Gujarat on 28 December, 1959, as Punjab remained the only state which was left bilingual. The emotional appeal and the environment which was created by the decision of bifurcation of Bombay turned the Sikh masses against the Congress supported 'Sadh Sangat'. The elections of the SGPC again proved the great support of Sikh Masses to the Akali Dal as it won 134 seats from total of 139. The Congress supported Sadh Sangat was badly marginalized winning to only 4 seats, while the pro-Communists Desh Bhagat Board failed to get even a single seat.[163]

The moment was captured by the taking oaths and making the strategy for the achievement of the Punjabi Suba by the Akali Dal immediately after winning the elections. The Working Committee of Congress decided to snap its ties with the Congress and directed all the Akali legislators to leave the Congress. But out of 24 Akali Legislators only Sarup Singh, Atam Singh, Harguand Singh, Udham Singh and Partap Singh resigned from the Congress. Master Tara Singh relinquished the office of the President of SGPC so as to devote his entire time to the movement for the creation of Punjabi Suba.[164] Dal decided to organise Shahidi Jatha (Martyr Groups) headed by Master Tara Singh. The Punjab Government reacted firmly to this new campaign. Master Tara Singh and other Akalis were arrested and charged with incitement to communal violence. While responding to the Demand of Punjabi Suba on the occasion of Independence Day on 15 August 1960, Nehru Said, "every Punjabi should himself consider learning both Hindi and Punjabi, but there could be no bifurcation of the Punjab."[165] Partap Singh Kairon started releasing Akali volunteers from jails to create the impression that they were reluctant. Agitating over the forced release by the government 4 Akalis were killed in firing by the police at Bathinda Central Jail.[166]

In the absence of Master Tara, his lieutenant Sant Fateh Singh became incharge of Morcha for Punjabi Suba. He introduced new convincing note into Akali agitation for Punjabi Suba by presenting this demand purely on linguistic consideration. He stated that "We do not seek a Sikh majority area; that we are not concerned with the percentage; that we want the Punjabi language is spoken; that it is immaterial whether the Sikhs are in majority or minority in such areas".[167]

Emphasizing over their determination not to settle for anything less than Punjabi Suba the Akali leaders warned mediators against any form of intervention and declared that they would enter into no discussion unless the government accepted the formation of Punjabi-Suba beforehand.[168] Proving their strong commitment to the demand of Punjabi Suba more than 57,000 of Sikh volunteers got arrested.[169] After failing to convince the government by constitutional and agitation means, Sant Fateh Singh pledged to achieve his mission through sacrifice so as to rise the concise of the authorities while highlighting his aim, he said, "You have closed all the doors for justice and fair play.... I am left with no way out but to go fast unto death so as to pick your conscience."[170]

As a result, Sant Fateh Singh started his fast on 18 December 1960 in the presence of a huge crowd, which had gathered at Gurdwara Manji Sahib. In his speech he directed the Sikhs to remain peaceful and adhere to four slogans namely: Punjabi Suba Zindabad, Hindu-Sikh Ekta Zindabad, Azad Bharat Zindabad and Jhulte Nishan Rehan Panth Maharaj De.[171] Although Fateh Singh included the agenda of national integration in his demand of Punjabi Suba, but the government did not responded to his call. Taking the account of the prolonged fast of Sant Fateh Singh and rising unrest in Punjab, prominent personalities like Principal Niranjan Singh and Gopal Singh approached Jai Parkash Narain to get Master Tara Singh. Jai Parkash Narain called on Nehru and Master Tara Singh was released on 4 January 1961. Tara Singh immediately arranged a meeting with Prime Minister also to discuss the creation of Punjabi Suba and unrest in Punjab but he failed to convince Prime Minister for the creation of Punjabi Suba. Scared of the growing popularity of Sant Fateh Singh which could challenge to his undisputed leadership of party, Master Tara Singh somehow convinced Sant to break his fast for the negotiation with the Prime Minister.[172]

On 23 January Sant Fateh Singh got a personal letter from Prime Minister inviting him to meet him at Delhi on 8 February 1961. The Working Committee of the Akali Dal discussed the draft for the bifurcation of the State on linguistic basis. A series of meetings between Nehru and Fateh Singh were took place but all the efforts of Fateh Singh and mediators failed to convince Nehru for the creation of Punjabi Suba. On 25 August 1961, Gurnam Singh accompanied Sant Fateh Singh where he announced that the talks failed. The government cleared its position both in Lok Sabha and Rajya Sabha on 28 and 30 August 1961 respectively, rejecting the demand for Punjabi Suba.[173] Hukam Singh opposed the Punjabi Suba with these words: "Punjabi Suba ... I had been on the floor of the House advocating this cause. Many a time, I stood and pleaded for it, but there are other reasons that outweight it at this moment. I consider Hindu-Sikh harmony is more important than getting this demand conceded at this moment."[174]

The Prime Minister while speaking in the Rajya Sabha the next day was more unequivocal when he said, "we come to firm conclusion that we cannot agree even in the principle to the Punjabi Suba demand."[175] He warned the House that if effect was given to the proposal of Punjabi Suba, it would be resisted. In the meantime, Master Tara Singh felt that the growing popularity of Sant Fateh Singh was going to prove as a setback to his leadership. He, therefore, decided to go fast unto death himself from 15 August 1961 for the creation of Punjabi Suba and the charges of discrimination against the

Sikhs. While announcing his fast unto death Master Tara said: "I will get a Punjabi Suba or I will die" But Master Tara Singh climbed down on the assurance of government through the Maharaja Patiala and Malik Hardit Singh among the others to appoint a Commission to look into Sikh grievances. Thus Master Tara Singh declared:

> "They have ended my fast but not my pledge to sacrifice my life for Punjabi Suba. Now either I shall die or see my pledge to achieve Punjabi Honoured".[176] It was felt that Master Tara Singh saved his life but killed his political career in the process. His own party, the Akali Dal expelled him from party membership and the Sikh Panth declared him Tankhahia (treacher). The Head Priest of Akal Takhat Sahib imposed on him the punishment to clean the shoes of the devotees of Sikh Shrines for five days.[177]

Although the breaking of fast by Master Tara resulted in a set back of the Akali Dal and particularly to the leadership of Master Tara Singh, however, Dal again decided to contest the elections of 1962 on the slogan of Punjabi Suba. In addition, Dal issued a 22 points Election Manifesto wherein, it opposed cooperative farming and high taxation though it favoured nationalisation of banks and industries to suit the interests of agriculturalist.[178] Dal contested on all the 154 seats but fared badly winning to 19 seats only. Its share of valid votes just remained 11.87 and it was unable to win the majority seats even in the Punjabi-speaking regions.[179]

This defeat was followed by a division of Akali Dal. Two rival Akali Dals led by Sant Fateh Singh and Master Tara Singh came into being. The division of the Akali Dal had its impacts on the supreme religious body of Sikhs. A tussle between Sant and Tara group started and finally Master Tara Singh was removed from the Presidentship of SGPC and Sant Chanan Singh the right hand of Sant Fateh Singh became the President of SGPC.[180]

TOWARDS THE FORMATION OF PUNJABI SUBA

The results of 1962 have not only divided the Akali leadership but it also left its prints on the political history of Punjab. The Sikh leadership which was in the hands of urban Sikhs (non-Jats) now shifted rural Sikhs (Jat Sikhs). The peasantry felt that their interests were not being protected by the urban leadership of Master Tara Singh. The emergence of this new rural leadership broad based the campaign for the achievement of the Punjabi Suba by secularising the objective of the demand.[181] Sant Fateh Singh condemned the separatist attitude of Master Tara Singh; he emphasized the age-old common bonds of the Sikh with Hindus, his primary concern with the unity and integrity of India.[182]

In the changed environment, the Hindu organization could not counter the demand of Punjabi Suba as the Hindus of Haryana and Himachal regions were not against the Punjabi language actually they were apprehending the Sikh domination and separatism. Secondly, the secular attitude of Akali Dal also got support from the people of Haryana region as they had also given their representation to the SRC for the formation of a separate state for the people of Haryana region.[183] They also alleged that they were being discriminated against the Punjabi people in all the fields of education, administration politics and commerce. Speaking in Lok Sabha on 23 December 1955, Pandit Thakur Das Bhargava presented the figures from various departments, ministries, and parliament and state legislatures to prove that the Haryana region Haryana region had on 5.5 representations in the government sector.[184] The Punjabi Hindus however, continued to oppose the demand and interpreted the new approach.[185] Sant Fateh Singh temporarily suspended the Punjabi-Suba Movement in the wake of Indo-Chinese war in 1962 and offered unconditional support to the government in war. Sant Fateh Singh constituted a separate Defence Council to mobilise the Sikh Community for defence efforts. He met Nehru and presented 50,000 rupees on the behalf of SGPC as contribution to National Defence Fund. This was an important factor to soften the official attitude. Meanwhile, Partap Singh leadership came under the clouds as a number of legislators' submitted a charge sheet against him to the President of Congress Party. A deputation of some opposition leaders had already met the President of India with over thirty charges of corruption, nepotism and favouritism against Kairon.[186]

The passing away of Nehru in 1964 and the ouster of Partap Singh Kairon from the Chief Minister office in Punjab after the death of Nehru further strengthened the Punjabi Suba Movement. Kairon was assassinated soon after his ouster from Chief Minister Office and Congress was also splintered into a number of factions in Punjab and its political will got greatly reduced. In the lack of leadership, some Congressmen from Haryana region also started pressing for separate Haryana. The Congress leaders from the Hill districts looking for the political opportunities also started demanding merger of their areas into Himachal Pradesh. More importantly, the assumption of power by Lal Bahadur Shastri as Prime Minister also modified the tough line that had been adopted by Nehru, ostensibly on the advice of Kairon. The change of regime at Centre brought a favourable climate as the new leaders were more receptive to the regional demands. Lal Bahadur Shastri had a round of talks with Sant Fateh Singh but reiterated the old position that the government was prepared to do everything for the advancement of Punjabi language and redressal of Sikh grievances but was not convinced for the creation of separate Punjabi Suba.[187]

At this juncture Sant Fateh Singh from the Akal Takht on 15 August 1965 argued, that he would go on a 15 days fast from 10 September 1965 inside the Golden Temple for the creation of Punjabi Suba. Sant threatened the Centre that if hunger strike could not kill him within 15 days he was going to immolate himself on the pyre which was built in the Golden Temple Complex. Meanwhile, the situation on Pakistan-Kashmir border which was already tense became more crystal clear for war. Fateh Singh was referred to the possibility of war with Pakistan by the Centre. But Fateh Singh refused to give up his agitation and reportedly said that *country was dear but Punjab was dearer*. Somehow, he was persuaded and agreed to postpone his plans when the Pakistan media started referring to him a suggestive of Sikh insurgency against the Indian State. Apparently the then Prime Minister Lal Bahadur Shastri had come to an unofficial deal with Akali leadership that their demand would be granted if they create no further problem during the period of conflict. During the war, the role of Punjabis in general and Sikh population in particular was highly appreciated. In view of all these developments, within two days of cease-fire, the central government appointed a three member Cabinet Committee consisting of Y.B. Chavan, Indira Gandhi and Mahavir Tyagi to examine afresh the demand for Punjabi Suba. To assist the Cabinet Committee a 22 Member Committee of Parliament was also set-up under the chairmanship of Sardar Hukam Singh, speaker of Lok Sabha.[188]

The formation of a cabinet sub-committee and a parliament committee to review the Akali demand marked a definite change in the attitude of the central leadership towards the Akalis. This change received further imputes with Indira Gandhi becoming Prime Minister after Lal Bahadur Shastri's death in January 1966.[189]

When Indira Gandhi became Prime Minister, the Congress was a faction ridden party and the state level bosses exercised a good deal of influence on the party apparatus. Not sure of support from her own party, Indira Gandhi needed support from outside, both to consolidate her position and to win the forthcoming election. For that she started looking towards regional parties. In Punjab she thought of Akalis. Thus she did not wait for the report of Cabinet and Parliament Committees appointed by the Shastri government and asked the Congress President to summon the meeting of the Congress Working Committee to discuss the issue. In the meeting, a resolution was passed requesting the government to form a new state of Punjab on a linguistic basis. Thereafter, the government promptly announced its acceptance of reorganisation. In September 1966, Parliament enacted the Punjab State Reorganisation Bill and a Punjab Boundaries Commission was appointed under the chairmanship of Justice J.C. Shah with Subimal Dutt and M.M. Philip as members. Finally, Punjab was reorganized on November 2, 1966 with the creation of Haryana. Its hill districts were merged with Himachal Pradesh on November 1, 1966.

The now truncated Punjab comprised of the districts of Gurdaspur, Hoshiarpur, Amritsar, Kapurthala, Jalandhar, Ludhiana, Ferozpur and Bathinda besides a part of Sangrur district and Ropar and Kharar tehsil of Ambala district. In theory, the new state was a Punjabi-speaking state but then it was also a Sikh majority state. The Union Government, however, took over Chandigarh as union territory and control and management Bhakhra and Beas dam projects. It also made provision for a common Governor and a High Court for both states. Common Electricity Board and Financial Cooperation were also retained. All these developments opened a number of vital questions immediately after the reorganisation of the state that we would be referring to in the following chapters.

Notes and References

1. "Punjab—Wikipedia, the free encyclopedia," en.wikipedia.org/wiki/Punjab, 2-4-2005.
2. H.K. Puri and Paramjit Singh Judge (eds.), 2000, *Social and Political Movements : Readings on Punjab,* Rawat Publications, New Delhi, pp. 12-13.
3. Dr. Fauja Singh, 1972, *History of Punjab,* Vol. 1, Publication Bureau, Punjabi University, Patiala, p. 65.
4. Eleanor Nesbitt, 2005, Sikhism: *A Very Short Introduction,* Oxford University Press, London, pp. 40-43. See also: "Sikhism", *Encyclopedia Britannica*, 2007, p. 44.
5. Punjab—Wikipedia, *op. cit.,* No. 2.
6. Dr. Harjinder Singh Dalgeer, 1989, *Sikh Twarikh (Sikh History),* Vol. V, Singh Brothers, Amritsar, pp. 60- 67. See also: Nesbitt Eleanor, 2005, *op. cit.,* No. 4, p. 74.

7. J.S. Grewal, 1980, *Sikh History from Persian Sources: Translations of Major Texts*, Saujana Books, New Delhi, pp. 210-20.
8. J.S. Grewal, 1998, *The Sikhs of the Punjab*, Cambridge University Press, New Delhi, pp. 97-99.
9. Man Singh Deora, 1989, *Guru Gobind Singh: A Literary Survey*, Anmol Publications, New Delhi, pp. 26-45.
10. The Manjis system was originated during the period of third guru. Under which the whole Punjab was divided into the 22 areas and guru appointed 22 preachers to preach Sikhism and collect the offering of devotees for the Sikh Shrines across the Punjab. The Manjis system came under the clouds due to the widespread corruption perpetuated by the preacher class and finally collapsed in the early period of ninth guru.
11. The Masand system was developed during the fourth guru under which some disciples were appointed by the guru to monitor the preaching of Sikhism, collection of offering and monitoring the construction work of Sikh shrines etc. The Masand system was ended by the tenth guru as he received complaints against some Masands for violating the principles of Sikhism and ordering the heavy offering to Sikh devotees in the name of guru.
12. Gopal Singh, 1979, *History of Sikh People,* World Sikh Publication, New Delhi, pp. 289-90.
13. *Ibid.*, pp. 305-10. See also: Sohan Singh Sheetal, 1968, *Prophet of Man, Guru Gobind Singh*, Lyall Book Depot, Chandigarh, p. 366.
14. Gurdev Singh, 1972, *Banda Bahadur*, New Academic Pub. Company, Patiala, p. 14.
15. Ganda Singh, 1990, *Life of Banda Singh Bahadur : Based on Contemporary and Original Records*, Punjabi University Press, Patiala, pp. 120-25.
16. Gurdev Singh, 1972, *op. cit.*, No. 14, pp. 223-30.
17. *Ibid.*, pp. 252-58.
18. Ram Narayan Kumar, 1991, *The Sikh Struggle: Origin, Evolution and Present Phase*, Chanakya Publications, New Delhi, p. 73.
19. Gurdev Singh, 1972, *op. cit.*, No. 14, pp. 271-76.
20. Fauja Singh, 1964, *Military System of Sikhs: During the Period 1799-1847*, Motilal Banarsidas, Patiala, pp. 169-75.
21. *Ibid.*, pp. 285-91.
22. *Punjabi Folklore*, Cited in, Khushwant Singh, 1991, *History of the Sikhs*, Vol. 1, Oxford University Press, New Delhi, p. 54.
23. Harbans Singh, 1994, *The Heritage of the Sikhs*, Manohar Publications, New Delhi, pp. 115-23.
24. *Ibid.*, pp. 148-55.
25. *Ibid.*, pp. 172-83.
26. Kartar Singh Duggal, 1989, *Ranjit Singh: A Secular Sikh Sovereign*, Abhinav Publications, New Delhi, pp. 15-19.
27. Kartar Singh Duggal, 2001, *Maharaja Ranjit Singh: The Last to Lay Arms*, Abhinav Publications, New Delhi, pp. 70-73.
28. *Ibid.*, p. 125.
29. Kartar Singh Duggal, 1989, *op.Cit.*, No. 26, p. 62.
30. J.S. Grewal, 1981, *The Reign of Maharaja Ranjit Singh: Structure, power, economy and society*, Panjab University, Chandigarh, p. 23.

31. *Ibid.*, p. 30.
32. Khushwant Singh, 1962, *Ranjit Singh Maharajah of the Punjab*, Allen & Unwin, London, p. 63.
33. *Ibid.*, p. *67.*
34. Jean-Marie Lafont, 2002, *Maharaja Ranjit Singh, Lord of the Five Rivers*, Oxford University Press, London, pp. 208-09.
35. *Ibid.*, p. *213.*
36. Khushwant Singh, 1962, *op. cit.*, No. 32, p. 67.
37. Jean-Mari Lafonte, 2002, *op. cit.*, No. 34, p. 212.
38. Jean-Marie Lafont, 2001, *Maharaja Ranjit Singh: the French Connection*, Guru Nanak Dev University, Amritsar, pp. 59-64.
39. Kartar Singh Duggal, 1989, *op.cit.*, No. 26, pp. 206-12.
40. Jean-Marie Lafont, 2002, *Fauj-I-khas Maharaja Ranjit Singh and his French Officer*, Guru Nanak Dev University, Amritsar, pp. 60-61.
41. *Ibid.*, p. 91.
42. Hari Ram Gupta, 1973, *History of the Sikhs: Sikh Commonwealth, Rise & Fall of Sikh Misls*, Munshiram Manoharlal Publications, Amritsar, pp. 66-69.
43. *Ibid.*, pp. 93-97.
44. *Ibid.*, pp. 302-08.
45. Khushwant Singh, 1991, *History of the Sikhs*, Vol. 2, Oxford University Press, New Delhi, pp. 90-94.
46. *Ibid.*, pp. 94-101.
47. *Ibid.*, pp. 109-14.
48. Bhupinder Singh Dhillon, 1969, *Pilgrim's Progress: The Translation and Punjabi of Padries*, Punjabi University, Patiala, p. 260.
49. *Ibid.*, p. 283.
50. J.S. Grewal, 1992, "Making of Sikh Self-Image before Independence", P.C. Chatterji (ed.), *Self-Images, Identity and Nationality*, Allied Publishers, New Delhi, p. 60.
51. Satish Kumar Sharma, 1985, *Social Movements and Social Change: A Study of Arya Samaj and Untouchables in Punjab*, B.R. Publishing House, New Delhi, pp. 54-58.
52. Rajwant Kaur, 1987, *Arya Samaj and Singh Sabha Movement*, M.Phil. Dissertation (Unpublished), Punjabi University, Patiala, p. 32.
53. N. Gerald Barrier, 2000, "The Singh Sabha Movement; 1875-1925", Harish K. Puri and Paramjit Judge (eds.), *op. cit.*, No. 2, p. 64.
54. Harjot Oberoi, 1994, *The Construction of Religious Boundries: Culture-Identity and Diversity in the Sikh Tradition*, Oxford University Press, New York, pp. 50-52
55. Harbansh Singh, 1973, "Origin of Singh Sabha", *Punjab Past and Present*, Vol. VII, No. I, April, p. 29.
56. Kahn Singh, 1981, *Hum Hindu Nahi*, Dharam Parchar Committee (SGPC), Amritsar, pp. 40-65.
57. N. Gerald Barrier, 2000, *op. cit.*, No. 53, pp. 67-69.
58. Bhai Nahar Singh and Kirpal Singh (eds.), 1995, *Rebels Against the British Rule*, Atlantic Publishers, New Delhi, p. 15.
59. Mohinder Singh, 2002, "The Gurdwara Reform Movement", H.K Puri *et. al.*, *op. cit.*, No. 2, pp. 175-76.

60. Mohinder Singh, 1978, *Akali Movement*, Macmillan, New Delhi, pp. 34-49.
61. Harbansh Singh, 1999, *op. cit.*, No. 23, p. 281.
62. K.L. Tuteja, 1989, *The Sikh Politics, 1920-40*, Vishal Publications, Kurukshetra, p. 139.
63. M.S. Sahni, 1996, *Sikh Politics: 1927-47*, Ph.D. Theses (Unpublished), Punjabi University, Patiala, p. 90.
64. *Ibid.*, p. 91.
65. Rajiv Kapoor, 1986, *Sikh Separatism: Politics of Faith*, George Allen and Unwin, London, p. 203.
66. M.S. Sahni, 1996, *op. cit.*, No. 63, p. 108.
67. Krishan Gopal Lamba, 1999, *Dynamics of Punjabi Suba Movement*, Deep & Deep Publications, New Delhi, pp. 6-8.
68. K.C. Gulati, 1974, *The Akali Past and Present*, Ashajanak Publishers, New Delhi, pp. 62-63.
69. P.C. Joshi, 1976, *A Punjabi Suba: A Symposium*, National Book Publication, New Delhi, p. 146.
70. *Ibid.*, p. 147.
71. Sunder Singh Majitha, *Papers, NMML*, New Delhi, Cited in, Krishan Gopal Lamba, 1999, *op. cit.*, No. 67, p. 9.
72. *Ibid.*
73. Davinderpal Singh Sandhu, 1992, *Sikhs in Indian Politics*, Patriot Publications, New Delhi, p. 118.
74. Khushwant Singh, 1991, *op. cit.* No. 45, p. 232.
75. Krishan Gopal Lamba, 1999, *op. cit.*, No. 67, pp. 11-12.
76. K.C. Gulati, 1994, *Akali Past and Present*, Ashajanak Publication, New Delhi, p. 77.
77. J.S. Grewal, 1998, "Sikh Identity, the Akalis and Khalistan", J.S. Grewal and Indu Banga (eds.), *Punjab in Prosperity and Violence: Administrative, Politics and Social Change*, K.K. Publishers, New Delhi, p. 61.
78. Balraj Madhok, 1985, *Punjab Problem: The Muslim Connection*, Vision Books Pvt. Ltd., New Delhi, p. 222.
79. *Ibid.*, 223.
80. J.S Grewal, 1998, *op. cit.*, No. 77, p. 66.
81. Jaswant Singh (ed.), 1972, *Master Tara Singh: Jiwan Sangarsh Te Udesh* (in Punjabi), Hardesh Printing Press, Amritsar, p. 193.
82. A.S. Narang, 1983, *Storms over Sutlej: The Akali Politics*, Gitanjali Publishing House, New Delhi, p. 70.
83. Young India, March 19, 1931, Cited in Ram Narayan Kumar, 1991, *The Sikh Struggle: Origin, Evolution and Present Phase*, Chanakya Publications, Delhi, p. 121
84. Shiv Lal, 1994, *Dateline Punjab: Lifeline Sikhs, Election Archives*, New Delhi, p. 110.
85. Krishan Gopal Lamba, 1999, *op. cit.*, No. 67, p. 26.
86. *Ibid.*, p. 28.
87. *Ibid.*, pp. 29-30.
88. Inderjit Singh Jaijee, 2002, *Politics of Genocide: Punjab 1984-98*, Ajanta Publications, New Delhi, pp. 4-5.

89. *Ibid.*, pp. 5-6.
90. Krishan Gopal Lamba, 1999, *op. cit.*, No. 67, p. 61.
91. Satya M. Rai, 1965, *Partition of Punjab*, Asia Publications, Bombay, pp. 251-52.
92. Guru Rattan Pal Singh, 1972, *The Illustrated History of Sikhs*, Punjab University Press, Chandigarh, p. 145.
93. Khushwant Singh, 1962, *op. cit.*, No. 32, Delhi, p. 299.
94. Ajit Singh Sarhadi, 1976, *Punjabi Suba: A History of Struggle*, U.C. Kapoor & Sons Publications, New Delhi, p. 165.
95. K.C. Gulati, 1974, *op. cit.*, No. 68, p. 147.
96. Manorma Kohli, 1985, "Protest Movements in Punjab: A Case Study of Punjabi Suba Agitation", *Punjab Past and Present*, Vol. XVII, No. II, August, p. 391.
97. *Ibid., 392.*
98. Dharam Singh Sahota and Sohan Singh Sahota, 1993, *Sikh Struggle for Autonomy (1940-92),* Guru Nanak Study Centre, Gardhiwala, p. 43.
99. Khushwant Singh, 1987, *History of Sikhs*, Vol. III, 1839-1947, Oxford University Press, New Delhi, pp. 302-05.
100. K.C. Gulati, 1974, *op. cit.*, No. 68, p. 151.
101. Krishan Gopal Lamba, 1999, *op. cit.*, No. 67, p. 63- 65.
102. Harish Puri & Paramjit Singh Judge, (eds.), 2000, *op. cit.*, No. 2, p. 296.
103. *Ibid.*, 301.
104. J.S. Grewal, 1991, *The New Cambridge History of India: The Sikhs of Punjab*, Orient Longman, Cambridge University Press, Cambridge, p. 193.
105. Harish Puri & Paramjit Singh Judge, 2000, *op. cit.*, No. 2, p. 297.
106. *Ibid.*
107. *Ibid.*, p. 298.
108. *Ibid.*
109. A.S. Narang, 1983, *op. cit.*, No. 82, p. 110.
110. Baldev Raj Nayar, 1978, *Minority Politics in the Punjab*, Princeton University Press, Princeton, p. 50.
111. Krishan Gopal Lamba, 1999, *op. cit.*, No. 67, p. 67.
112. *Ibid.*, p. 68.
113. A.S. Narang, 1983, *op. cit.*, No. 82, pp. 110-11.
114. Paul R. Brass, 1975, "Ethnic cleavage in Punjab Party System, 1952-77" Myron Weiner and Osgood Field (eds.), *Studies in Electoral Politics in the Indian States*, Vol. IV, Manohar Book Service, New Delhi, p. 17.
115. H.K. Puri and Paramjit Judge, 2000, *op. cit.*, No. 2, p. 301. See also: A.S. Narang, 1983, *op. cit.*, No. 57, p. 112.
116. Manorma Kohli, 1982, *op. cit.*, No. 97, pp. 392-93.
117. A.S. Narang, 1983, *op. cit.*, No. 82, p. 116.
118. *Ibid.*, p. 117.
119. *Ibid.*, p. 118.
120. Harish Puri and Paramjit Singh Judge, 2000, *op. cit.*, No. 2, p. 300
121. Krishan Gopal Lamba, 1999, *op. cit.*, No. 67, p. 72.
122. *Ibid.*, p. 71.

123. Gursharn Singh, 1992, "An Account of the Political Overturns on the Issue of Merger of PEPSU with Punjab in 1956", *The Punjab Journal of Politics*, Vol. IV, No. 1, p. 342.
124. Krishan Gopal Lamba, 1999, *op. cit.*, No. 67, p. 71.
125. Baldev Raj Nayar, 1978, *op. cit.*, No. 111, pp. 33-34
126. *Ibid.*
127. Krishan Gopal Lamba, 1999, *op. cit.*, No. 67, pp. 73-72.
128. G. Adhikari, 1995, *Sikh Homeland Through Hindu-Muslim-Sikh Unity*, People's Publishing House, Bombay, p. 120.
129. Krishan Gopal Lamba, 1999, *op. cit.*, No. 67, p. 96.
130. A.S. Narang, 1986, *Punjab Politics in National Perspective*, Gitanjali Publishing House, New Delhi, p. 33.
131. *Ibid.*
132. Gursharan Singh, 1992, *op. cit.*, No. 124, pp. 55-60.
133. Krishan Gopal Lamba, 1999, *op. cit.*, No. 67, p. 74.
134. Gursharn Singh, 1991, *The History of PEPSU: 1948-56*, Konark Publishers Pvt. Ltd., Delhi, p. 226.
135. *Ibid.*, p. 96.
136. *Ibid.*, p. 235.
137. K.C. Gulati, 1974, *op. cit.*, No. 68, p. 162.
138. Gurrattan Pal Singh, 1972, *The Illustrated History of the Sikhs*, Punjab University, Chandigarh, p. 167.
139. Karam Singh Jakhmi, 1978, *Rozana Akali Morache the Ithas* (in Punjabi), Panthic Tract Society, Amritsar, p. 26.
140. Satya M. Rai, 1988, "The Structure of Regional Politics in Punjab", Paul Wallace and Surinder Chopra (eds.), *Political Dynamics and Crisis in Punjab*, Guru Nanak Dev University, Amritsar, pp. 107-08.
141. *Ibid.*, 108.
142. *Ibid.*, 109.
143. *Ibid.*
144. Ajit Singh Sarhadi, 1976, *op. cit.*, No. 95, p. 55.
145. *Ibid.*, p. 77.
146. Krishan Gopal Lamba, 1999, *op. cit.*, No. 67, pp. 79-80.
147. J.S. Grewal, 1992, *op. cit.*, No. 50, pp. 190-91.
148. *Ibid.*
149. Ajit Singh Sarhadi, 1976, *op. cit.*, No. 95, p. 261.
150. J.S. Grewal, 1992, *op. cit.*, No. 105, p. 91.
151. *Ibid.*
152. Krishan Gopal Lamba, 1999, *op. cit.*, No. 67, p. 179.
153. *Papers Relating to the Hindi Agitation in Punjab*, 1957, Public Relations Department, Punjab, Chandigarh, pp. 9-10.
154. *Ibid.*
155. A.S. Narang, 1983, *op. cit.*, No. 82, p. 130.
156. *Ibid.*, p, 30.
157. J.S. Grewal, 1991, *op. cit.*, No. 105, p. 193.
158. Surinderpal Parmar, 1987, *History of Bhartiya Jana Sangh in Punjab*, Ph.D Theses (Unpublished), Punjab University, Chandigarh, p. 181.
159. *Ibid.*

160. P. Kashitish, 1984, *Storms in Punjab*, The World Publication, New Delhi, p. 120.
161. Krishan Gopal Lamba, 1999, *op. cit.*, No. 67, p. 99.
162. *Ibid.*
163. J.S. Grewal, 1991, *op. cit.*, No. 105, p. 197.
164. Manorama Kohli, 1983, *op. cit.*, No. 97, p. 127.
165. Ajit Singh Sarhadi, 1976, *op. cit.*, No. 95, p. 331.
166. *Ibid.*, p. 348.
167. K.C. Gulati, 1994, *op. cit.*, No. 68, p. 170.
168. *Ibid.*
169. Baldev Raj Nayar, 1978, *op. cit.*, No. 111, p. 250.
170. *Ibid.*, p. 259.
171. Ajit Singh Sarhadi, 1976, *op. cit.*, No. 95, p. 336.
172. *Ibid.*, pp. 356-57.
173. *Ibid.*
174. Krishan Gopal Lamba, 1999, *op. cit.*, No. 67, p. 164.
175. *Ibid.*
176. *Ibid.*, p. 190.
177. Rajinder Kaur, 1988, *Politics of Sikh Homeland, A case study of National Integration*, Ph.D. Thesis, Himachal Pradesh University, Shimla, p. 157. See also: Dhana Singh Gulshan, 1978, *Aj da Punjab Ate Singh Rajniti* (in Punjabi), Dhariwal Publishing House, Bathinda, p. 126.
178. *Ibid.*
179. J.C. Anand, 1976, "Punjab Politics of Retreating Communalism", Iqbal Narain, (ed.), *Politics in India*, Meenakshi Parkashan, Meerut, p. 264.
180. Manorma Kohli, 1985, *op. cit.*, No. 97, p. 400.
181. Ranjinder Kaur, 1988, *op, cit.*, No, 147, p. 157.
182. Harish Puri,1985, "Akali Politics: Emerging Compulsions", Paul Wallace and Surinder Chopra (eds.), *Political Dynamics and Crisis in Punjab*, Guru Nanak Dev University, Amritsar, p. 237.
183. Ventakeshwar Rao Adiraju, 1991, *Sikhs and India: Identity Crisis*, Hyderabad Sahitya Publication, New Delhi, p. 124.
184. Gulshan Rai, 1987, *Formation of Haryana*, B.R Publishing Cooperation, Delhi, p. 69.
185. A.S. Narang, 2000, "The Punjabi Suba Movement", H.K. Puri and Paramjit Judge (eds.), *op. cit.*, No. 2, p. 305.
186. Gurmit Singh, 1989, *History of Sikh Struggle*, Atlantic Publishers, New Delhi, p. 201.
187. Staya M. Rai, 1986, *Partition of Punjab*, Durga Publications, New Delhi, p. 310.
188. Mohan Lal, 1984, *Disintegration of Punjab*, Sameer Parkashan, Chandigarh, p. 319.
189. Ajit Singh, 1992, *Shiromani Akali Dal in Punjab*, Punjabi University, Patiala, pp. 107-13.

3

In Search of a Land of their 'Own': An Analysis of Ethno-regional Movement in Punjab

Contrary to the popular perception of Punjab witnessed more than a decade of turbulent period barely after the creation of Punjabi Suba. During the period, thousands of civilians got killed as armed insurgency engulfed the state. The armed militants driven by religious passion waged a war against the Indian state for the creation of an independent Sikh theocratic state called Khalistan (The land of purity/pure).

It would be pertinent to mention here that the running theme in the literature available on Punjab relating to the period of the militancy has been to connect the armed insurgency waged by the militants to the emergence of the leadership of Jarnail Singh Bhindranwale in the Sikh politics which led to the marginalization of the mainstream Akali Dal leadership for a considerable period of time in the panthic politics of the state. It has also been widely argued that the rise of Bhindranwale in Punjab politics can be attributed to the early encouragement of the Congress. The Congress aimed to use him to curtail the influence of the Akali Dal over the panthic politics and also to break its monopoly over the cash rich SGPC, the highest temporal seat of the Sikh community. It was proven a tactical move having most tragic consequences both for the state as well as the nation. There were not only selective killings by the militants and the atrocities perpetrated by the state agents but that also led to the massacre of thousands of the innocent Sikhs in Delhi and in other cities of India after the killing of the then Prime Minister of India Indira Gandhi by her own Sikh bodyguards. Punjab notably remained free from the communal violence though thousands of civilians belonging to both the Hindu as well as the Sikh communities got killed during the 1980' and 1990 at the hands of the militants and also due to the direct and physical violence unleashed by the state coercive agencies. The end of the dark shadow of violence and terror in the land of Punjab was noted with the killing of the Chief Minister of Punjab Sardar Beant Singh in its capital city. The personalizing and centralizing leadership of the Congress leadership at the centre, encouraged at the state level by the then chief minister Giani Zail Singh, did not realize that in its obsession with the aim to weaken Akali Dal, which prompted them to promote an obscure preacher heading Damdami Taksal named Bhindranwale in the early eighties, would have such disastrous consequences. The happening and the facts of the Punjab politics also showed that Bhindranwale had not much say in the Sikh politics to begin with. He gained prominence due to the active encouragement of some of the local congress leaders involved in internecine factional battles within the party as well as the policy of adhocism adopted by the centre while dealing with the demands of the Akalis. Thus it was mainly due to the lopsided policies of the centre and incompetent leadership that Bhindranwale was able to secure a place in Punjab during the turbulent period.

Even then the Sikh mainstream politics and the SGPC remained under the control of Akali Dal till the killing of Bhindranwale in Operation Blue Star. Bhindranwale could not secure the democratic space in the mainstream Sikh politics. This was illustrated during the 1978 SGPC elections as most of his candidates lost to the moderate Akalis candidates. Even his close associate Bhai Amrik Singh, the chief of All India Sikh Students Federation, was defeated in the area of Beas in the Majha region of Punjab.

The rise of Bhindranwale led Khalistan Movement could be attributed to his distinct emphasis on "Sikhism in danger". Bhindranwale made an initial impact over the masses by preaching the fundamentals of Sikhism and arguing that the vices like drinking and rampant consumerism that signified post-Green Revolution,

Punjab was posing grave danger to the tenets of Sikhism. He also evoked the issue of distinct Sikh identity and the alleged discrimination of the Hindu government of India.

The unexpected and swift fall of the movement within a span of three years in nineties and the subsequent period of peace and communal harmony in the state has reverted the Sikh fundamentalist agenda on the margin. However, the continuation of the violent movement for a long-time spanning one and half decade also raised serious questions against the then government's claims that this long period of turmoil was merely the result of divisive agenda of the communal forces which received its impetus from Pakistan. It was also not merely a law and order problem that could be solved militarily as we would see the peace returned to the state only after certain political initiatives, howsoever, inadequate they might be undertaken.

At the same time, the swift return to normalcy and the return of Hindu-Sikh unity and decline of panthic politics as illustrated in the long-term formation of Akalis and BJP alliance has also left many questions of the identity and political issues unresolved in this borderland state. The issues raised by the Sikh fundamentalist forces and also by the mainstream moderate Akali Dal leadership in Punjab before the collapse of the militancy are still to be resolved. These unresolved questions need a serious analysis of social, economic, political and religious circumstances along with the instant happening under which the Khalistan Movement emerged and collapsed. Most of the analysts trace the genesis of the militant movement in Punjab to two major incidents of the 13 April, 1978 which took place in the holy city of Sikhs (Amritsar) and the capital city of Punjab, Chandigarh.

The significance of 13 April in the Sikh history lies in the fact that it was on this day, as mentioned in the preceding chapter, that the tenth Guru had laid the foundation of the Khalsa Panth and given a distinct identity to the Sikhs on the great day in 1699 at Anandpur Sahib. On this auspicious occasion, the Chief of Nirankari (a religious sect) sect Baba Gurbachan Singh was holding a special Diwan at Amritsar with permission of the state government and a prominent leader of Congress Lala Jagat Narain was sitting in the Diwan. A Sikh Jatha (a group of Sikh devotees) of Bhindranwale followers protested against the Diwan of Baba Gurbachan Singh on the auspicious occasion in their holy city. Gurbachan Singh had allegedly used derogatory remarks against the Sikh faith earlier.

Nirankaris used fire arms against these Sikhs protestors, which resulted into the killing of 18 people, including 13 Sikh devotees, 3 members of Nirankaris sect and 2 bystanders. This incident caused a deep resentment within the Sikh community. It thus provided an instant opportunity to Bhindranwale to seize on wounded Sikh psyche and confront the moderate Akali leadership.[1] The bickering within the Akali leadership as it remained factionalised also helped the rise of radical mode of politics that used violence as a means for the political goal.

On the same fateful day, in another development, formation of the Dal Khalsa took place at Aroma Hotel in Capital city of Punjab. The formation of the Dal Khalsa was actually handiwork of the Congress to challenge the Akalis by encouraging the fundamentalists among the Sikhs. Giani Zail Singh in an interview to a Hindi weekly *Dinman* conceded that the Congress leaders like him were involved in encouraging the formation of Dal Khalsa with an objective to participate in the Gurdwara politics because the Gurdwaras were not the monopoly of the Akalis.[2] Pertinently Gurdwaras have been major source of income for the Akali Dal right from the beginning. In 1983, Dal Khalsa opened its branches in UK and Germany. The term Dal Khalsa reminded of the national army of the Sikhs which had succeeded in establishing sovereign Sikh state, as discussed in the preceding chapter. In 1979, it contested elections for the SGPC but without any success. In 1982 the responsibility for throwing the head of a cow in a Hindu temple was reported to be claimed by the Dal Khalsa activists.[3]

The idea of Khalistan was first mooted in the form of a call for its formation in an advertisement in the *New York Times* in October 1971 by Jagjit Singh Chauhan. He had enjoyed a short spell of power as a minister in the Cabinet of Lachman Singh Gill in 1967-68. At the time of publication of the call for separate Sikh theocratic state Chauhan living in England had no followers in the Punjab. His idea of Khalistan was treated mostly as a joke and was hardly taken with seriousness.[4]

In June 1980, Balbir Singh Sandhu announced the formation of Khalistan, claimed himself to be the secretary of the National Council of Khalistan with Jagjit Singh Chauhan as its President. This organisation existed only on paper. In March 1981, a US citizen Ganga Singh Dhillon, who was known to Chauhan, addressed the annual session of the Sikh Education Conference organised by the Chief Khalsa Diwan, who put forth the view that the Sikhs formed a separate 'nation' with the claim of their own political territory. The implication was that an independent state could be demanded on the basis. Soon afterwards, however, the Chief Khalsa Diwan disassociated itself from Dhillon's statement.[5]

Arguably, the two incidents mentioned above and also the hue and cry raised by the rootless Sikh leaders could not have been the bases for the rise of the movement alone. Socio-economic, religious and political circumstances also contributed. The ethno-regional movement having secessionist design could not emerge in a vacuum. There must be some socio-economic, political and historic reasons which need to be connected with the present socio-economic and political circumstances to gather the support of any section of the society.

As mentioned in the preceding chapter, the term Khalistan was first used by a medical doctor, V.S. Bhatti of Ludhiana in response to a pamphlet in 1940, published soon after the Lahore Resolution of All India Muslim League, properly known as the Pakistan resolution. It was primarily meant to counter the idea of Pakistan, supposed to be embodied in Lahore Resolution, covering much of the areas between the Chenab and Yamuna. Khalistan as conceived by Bhatti was meant to serve as a buffer state between India and Pakistan with Maharaja Patiala as its head. Khalistan to be a theocratic state consisting of several units, a corridor was to link it with Arabian Sea. Master Tara Singh (born in 1885 at Haryal village of Rawalpindi in an influential Hindu Khatri family converted himself as a Sikh and become Tara Singh from Nanak Chand), the then president of Akali Dal denounced the pamphlet for confounding confusion that has been already created by the Muslim League. Conferences were organized by Baba Gurdit Singh Kamagata Maru, a known supporter of the Congress party to popularize the idea of Khalistan. Maulana Abdul Kalam Azad expressed his disapproval immediately by stating that some Akalis were using the Congress as platform to propagate the ideas of Sikh state for scuttling the unity agenda of the Congress.[6]

As discussed in the preceding chapter, the idea of Khalistan was never appropriated by the Akalis but in their opposition to the idea of Pakistan in 1940's they did come out with counter proposal of a separate nation-state the Sikh community. With the freedom coming closer, their concern for the Sikhs' future increased with the worries of dominance by the other majorities. In March April 1942, Stafford Cripps conceded in principles that it was not obligatory for princely states to be part of an independent Indian State. The Akali leaders did not like to be subordinated permanently to the Muslim majority. The Sikh All Parties Committee submitted the proposal of a province with different boundaries and different proportions of the three major communities of the Punjab to the Cripps Mission.[7] The name given to the province of their occupation was Azad Punjab. Akalis gave an impression that it was meant not to be an independent state. They tried to sell this idea to the Hindus and Sikhs of Punjab. They explained then that this province was meant to be part of the Indian federation. The Term *Azad* was meant to suggest that each community of province would be free from domination by another community. Unlike Khalistan, the Azad Punjab was imagined to be part of India. It was also to have democratic constitution; the Sikhs could, hope to gain possibly an effective collaborative role in the affairs of Azad Punjab. The Azad Punjab remained on the political agenda of Akali Dal at least for two years.[8] The Sikh leaders in general and Akalis in particular tried to promote their idea of Sikh state in 1945. At the time of Shimla conference in June and July, Master Tara Singh met Lord Wavell and emphasized that the Sikhs were strongly opposed to the creation of Pakistan. Master Tara Singh expressed the Sikh view to the Lord that if the Pakistan was to be created then Jinnah should have agreed for the creation of separate state for the Sikhs. The efforts to stop the partition of Punjab and the creation of Pakistan by the Sikh's and Akali were continued by countering it by asking for the creation of Sikh sovereign state. Such efforts continued, as discussed in the preceding chapter, until the creation of Pakistan or the partition of Punjab.[9] Their demand and action for the creation of separate Sikh sovereign state, however, showed that they were never for the creation of a separate Sikh state. They were against the creation of Pakistan and division of India on religious basis as this could result into the oppression of the majority in the future India. Acceptance of a divided India as their homeland and their peaceful struggle for the creation of Punjab Suba for long time also supported the above argument about them not being really keen on a separate state for the Sikhs.

The problem of Sikh secessionism came within the two decade of the creation of Punjabi Suba for whom they had to struggle for two decades peacefully in the independent India. For about three decades the Sikh youths followed the Akali lines, of DharmYudh Morchas (the peaceful protests for the political and religious demand of the community). These Dharam Yudh Morchas remained the major tool of the Akalis to make a considerable pressure on the government. For protesting against the government policies until the Operation Blue Star, Dharm Yudh Morchas was the tool of Akali Dal protest. It remained a major tool of the Akali Dal even afterwards as militancy took roots and the mainstream Akali leadership came under the influence of the militant leaders. The Dharm Yudh Morchas also played a vital role in the formation of the modern Sikh identity and its religious institutions and customs either it was in the form of the Sikh Gurdwara Reform Movement for the formation of *Punjabi Suba*.

Although Bhindranwale was showing his influence in the Sikh politics since early 1980's, as mentioned above, the moderate Akalis still had the great following among the rural as well as in urban Sikhs. Even on the very day of Operation Blue Star, the Akalis had a great gathering in the golden temple to launch a Dharm Yudh Morchas for the boycott of movement of the grains to other parts of India and blocking the railway and roads lines for the purpose. Supporters of Akali Dal were arrested by the Indian Army along with Longowal and Jathedar Gurcharn Singh Tohra. Some of them reportedly also got killed in the cross firing during the Operation Blue Star.

Significantly at the community level, the Sikhs have not had any historical confrontation with the Hindus. Even the two communities have shared the religious festival, the *Guru Granth* (Holy book of Sikhs) and Gurdwaras had vital space both among the Sikh and Hindus in Punjab. Their demand for the recognition of their mother tongue Punjabi was also fulfilled with creation of Punjabi Suba on November 2, 1966. Then, how come some of Sikh youths fell prey to the hatred filled ideology and fundamentalism of Bhindranwale and others needs to be discussed as a vital question. It requires a serious analysis of immediate and constant happening of 1970's and 1980's along with the analysis of the political history of the Sikhs in the colonial and post colonial Punjab.

IMMEDIATE BACKGROUND TO THE RISE OF AUTONOMIST MOVEMENT

The Anandpur Sahib Resolution and a series of uninterrupted Akali agitations aimed at capturing political power in the state on the strength of the mobilisation of the majority Sikh community prepared the ground for the rise of armed politics based on secessionism/self-determination. What also contributed to the passing of resolutions were the politically motivated decisions and the response of the Congress Government at the Centre at that time.

It was between 1981 and 1984 that the Akali Dal led a series of peaceful mass demonstration to present a set of grievance to the central government. The core of the Akali Dal demands was based on a resolution adopted by the working committee of the Akali Dal at Anandpur Sahib in October 1973, outlying the policy and programme of the party. The issues raised by Akali Dal in the Anandpur Sahib resolution were religious, political, economic and social. The primary political objective stated in the Anandpur Sahib resolution was the pre-eminence of Khalsa through the creation of a congenial environment and a political setup.[10] The political goal stated in the resolution, the Akali pointed out, was not in itself new but a reiteration of the Akali Dal earlier objective, before India's independence, to preserve and maintain the distinct and independent entity of the *"Panth"*. In order to achieve this political goal, the resolution outlined seven key objectives. These were as follows:

- The transfer of the federally administrative city of Chandigarh to Punjab. It was argued that although the Punjabi Suba had been conceded in 1966, Punjab still shared its capital Chandigarh with the neighbouring state of Haryana.
- The readjustment of the state boundaries of Punjab to incorporate certain Sikh populated Punjabi-speaking areas, presently outside and contiguous to Punjab.
- The re-examination of the centre-state relations under the existing Constitution of India so as to grant provincial autonomy to all Indian states. The powers of the central government should be confined to external affairs, defence and communications.
- The call for land reforms. Loans to be provided to the farmers at the rates given to industrialists and non-remunerative prices to be fixed for agriculture produce. The rights of weaker section of the population are to be safeguarded. Further all the key industries should be brought under the public sector. The central government should invest in setting up heavy industry in Punjab, in order to alleviate the industrial stagnation of the state.
- The enactment of an All India Gurudwara Act that would bring all the historic gurudwaras in India under the control of SGPC.
- The Sikh minorities living outside Punjab to be provided protection.

- By reducing the recruitment quota of the Sikhs in the armed forces from 20 to 2%, The Indian government was keeping the Sikhs out of their traditional profession in its new recruitment policy.[11]

The text of the Anandpur Sahib Resolution became a subject of considerable controversy. As the rival factions of the Akali Dal adopted different versions and different interpretations of the Anandpur Sahib resolution are being made by the different religious sect of the Sikhs. On the question of Sikh political autonomy, the Akali Dal denied that the Anandpur Sahib resolution envisaged an autonomous Sikh state of Khalistan.

As the then President of the Akali Dal declared, 'let us make it clear once and for all that the Sikh have no designs to get away from India in any manner. What they simply want is that they should be allowed to live within India as Sikhs, free from direct and indirect interference and tampering with their religious way of life. Undoubtedly the Sikhs have the same nationality as the other Indians".[12] The meeting of the Akali Dal in 1978 endorsed the principles and objectives of Anandpur Sahib Resolution. In February 1981, the working committee of the Akali Dal reiterated that the party would strive for the implementation of the Anandpur Sahib resolution. Between August 1980 and September 1981, the Akali Dal organised a succession of seven peaceful agitations in which 25,000 volunteer's courted arrest in order to bring attention to their demands.[13] A set of forty five demands was submitted to the central government in September 1981. These demands reflected the core objectives of the Anandpur Sahib resolutions and two new demands were added. These were:

- The halting of reallocation of available river waters of the riparian Punjab to the other non-riparian states (under the arrangement regulated by the central government, 75 per cent of the river water of Punjab were being allocated to the other states; and further reduction in the government control over hydroelectric installations.
- The recognition of Sikh personal law.[14]

As negotiations between the Akali leaders and the central government began in October 1981, the list of 45 demands was reduced to 15. The core of these demands was concerned with the socioeconomic grievances over the centralization policies of the

Indian government, which were adversely affecting the rural sector of the society. The manner in which the centralization of the Indian government, concerning over the productive and development processes, propelled agrarian unrest in the Punjab in the late 1970s.There seemed nothing unconstitutional about the Akali demand to seek greater autonomy for all Indian states. However, these negotiations continued sporadically for a period of 2.5 years with the Akalis often accusing the party in power at the centre of intransigence, bad faith and deliberate delaying tactics.

Once again, the Akali Dal organised a mass agitation in order to pressurise the government. In April 1982, the Akali Dal organised the Nahar Roko Morcha (stop the canal construction protest) campaign to obstruct the construction of the canal that would divert river water to the neighbour state of Haryana and would deprive the Punjab's peasantry of the vital water resources. Agrarian interests seemed to be at the heart of the issue. Farmers were also urged to refrain from repaying the loans to the government as a protest. Each *jatha (*group of volunteers*)* would proceed daily to the site of construction and would be subsequently arrested. The Akali campaign continued unabated and by the September some 20,000 agitators were arrested. This campaign was suspended briefly for negotiation with the government, which were unsuccessful. In response, the Akali Dal announced a one new day Rasta Roko, (block the road), campaign in April 1983 to disrupt vehicular traffic on Punjab national highways. Similarly, the Akali leaders announced a 1day rail roko, or block the rails campaign. In August, Kam Roko, (halt the work), campaign to hamper functioning of the state administration was organised. These political demonstrations were inundated with volunteers from all over province made them remarkably successful. The Congress government in centre had grave apprehension of widespread Sikh unrest. In October 1983, the Punjab legislative assembly was dissolved bringing the state under the complete control of central government.[15]

The suspension of the legislative assembly and the call for Dharm Yudh against the centre was not a new thing. It was a general feature of the Punjab politics after the Independence. The launch of the Dharm Yudh Morchas and resurgence of identity politics in Punjab was accompanied by the rise of a charismatic Sikh preacher, Jarnail Singh Bhindranwale. Other important development was that for the first time the Akali Dal formed a coalition government with the Janata party in 1977, after the end of emergency at the state level.

This was after the Akali Dal had launched powerful campaign to protest against the imposition of a state of emergency by Indira Gandhi. The Akali Dal opposed the promulgation of the draconian Maintenance of Internal Security Act (MISA), which gave the police the power to arrest and detain people without trial. The Congress party therefore was desperate to break up formidable Akali Dal. It was looking for someone who could put challenge and put an end of Akali hegemony over the SGPC. Bhindranwale's position as the head of the historic Damdami Taksal and his popularity as a religious preacher made him a potential formidable political ally of the Congress in the eyes of a segment of the Congress leadership at the state level.

In the SGPC elections of 1979, Bhindranwale was promoted and supported by the Congress leaders and encouraged to put up candidates against Akalis. Bhindranwale's sect couldn't get a single seat in the SGPC elections in spite of the open support of the Congress Sikhs in Punjab. Nonetheless, Bhindranwale was to become an outspoken critic of the Congress party. In 1980, the Congress party was returned to power in the Punjab State Assembly elections.[16]

HISTORIC REASONS

As stated in the preceding chapter, the demand for the creation of Punjabi Suba was raised mainly by Shiromani Akali Dal on the basis of language as asking it on the basis of religion would have been unacceptable to the centre given the secular nature of the polity. However, Akali leadership could not exactly define its aims and objectives in plausible manners. The conflicting arguments advanced by the different leaders and groups at different times created misunderstanding and confusion. Master Tara Singh, the Akali leader demanded Punjabi speaking State and sometimes advocated "Self-determined political status for Sikhs" within the Indian union too. In an interview Master Tara Singh made it clear that the demand for Punjabi Suba "was a bid to protect the 'Khalsa Panth' from the Hindu religious and intellectual inroads."[17] Sant Fateh Singh's views were different about the concept and nature of Punjabi Suba. Fateh Singh declared, "We do not want a Sikh majority area, we are not concerned about the percentage."[18] He made it clear that he wanted the creation of Punjabi State purely on linguistic basis. The demand for unilingual (Punjabi speaking) state was on the pattern of other similar states reorganised on the same linguistic basis in the country.

Certain other Akali leaders made the demand in the name of Punjabi linguistic identity and distinct culture, but the real aim was to have a State which should be under the political control of the Sikhs.

The centre also played a dubious role by dithering over the issue thus creating a wedge amongst the different religious groups in Punjab. From the study of various sources it can be suggested that the government of India's inaction for the creation of the Punjabi speaking State underlined certain misgivings and apprehensions. The proximity of the Punjab's boundary to the neighbouring hostile Pakistan and a sense of mistrust towards Akali leadership real intent did not permit the government to accept the demand. This growing sense of mistrust, it may be said, distanced the Sikhs as outcastes and doubtful appendage within the Indian Union.

As far as Akali Dal is concerned, the demand for Punjabi Suba has important historical and social roots. The historical roots of the movement can be traced back to the birth of Sikhism and its formation as a separate religious community in the colonial period. In real sense the pronounced tendencies among the Sikhs for their identity had its beginning in 1909. This as a matter of fact was the reaction with the originated to counter the Muslim demand for a separate state in pre-independence Punjab. Throughout the period Sikh leadership made desperate attempts to save their community from the domination of Muslims. The Government of India Act of 1909 granted separate electorate to Muslims ignored the Sikhs despite their repeated pleas. However, the Act of 1919 incorporated separate electorates to the Sikhs which to some extent satisfied their initiating desire of maintaining the separate entity of the Sikh Panth. It marked the beginning of their efforts for procuring more concessions and safeguards for the community. The Sikhs emphasised their demands in the Lucknow Conference, before the Simon Commission and made a plea for their cause during the Round Table Conference. Dissatisfied with the attitude of the Congress, Muslim League and the British, the Sikhs came out with the scheme of 'Azad Punjab' as a counter move to Mohammad Iqbal's proposal of partition which later got the approval of Muslim League in the shape of Pakistan Resolution at its Lahore Session in 1940. The scheme of 'Azad Punjab' envisaged creation of new Punjab State by redrawing the boundaries of the exiting State in a way as to assure the Sikhs Majority. The scheme, however, did not find favour with the Cripps Mission, Cabinet Mission and Mountbatten Plan but the Sikhs were recognized as an important minority after the Muslims. The greatest handicap for the non-acceptance of the Sikh demand was the absence of compact territory where the Sikhs could claim themselves to be a majority.

The consequent partitioning of the country converted the Sikhs into a majority in the certain parts of the eastern Punjab. They became a pre-dominant majority in six districts and sizeable majority in five other districts. The population distribution was such that it would be feasible to have a Sikh majority State on the basis of Punjabi language. As such they raised the demand for the creation of Punjabi Suba. If we look into the past account of the long association of the Congress with the Akalis in their joint strive against the British and the promises of the Nehru and Gandhi to the minorities and particularly to the Sikhs for their role and status in the independent India, as briefly mentioned in the preceding chapter also, it can be recalled that the Congress had pronounced on the occasion for the unilingual state of Punjab in Independent India. The Sikh leadership had hoped that after independence it would be possible for the Congress to help them for the protection of their identity through constitutional safeguards. The partition of country on the basis of religion, however, changed the earlier view of Congress drastically in the Independent India. Partition anxiety about further balkanisation of the country loomed large in the minds of the Constitution makers of the country.

The demand of Punjabi Suba hanged for a long time due to the strong opposition of the RSS and the Hindu organizations of the Punjab. These organisations also gave communal colour to the demand of Punjabi Suba. The opposition to the creation of Punjabi Suba by the Hindu organisation went to an extent that they even denied the separate identity of the Sikhs and claimed that the Sikh Panth is part of the greater Hindu religion. It was argued by the Hindu communal forces that Sikhism as a *"Panth"* was created by the Gurus just to defend the Hindus against the Muslim aggression and in the present circumstances there was no need of distinct Sikh Panth.

PUNJAB POLITICS AFTER THE REORGANISATION

Finally, under the pressure of the Sikhs and people from the Haryana and Himachal region of the Punjab, Central government accepted the demand of the linguistic basis reorganisation of the state of Punjab on November 2, 1966. However, it did not meet the Akali leadership expectations. It seemed as half-hearted acceptance as the central government accepted it at the very crucial time of Indo-Pak war, when the government of India needed the Sikh support unconditionally. The Centre passed the Punjab Reorganisation Act just to invite new political problems and unrests as it ironically turned out rather than closing the issue.

It was for the first time in the history of independent India that a state was deprived of its rights over its capital city and the natural resources of water by putting them under the central government. Some of the Punjabi speaking areas were given to the newly created states of Haryana and Himachal. More importantly, the motive behind the linguistic reorganisation was also defeated as it could not end the communal mobilisation, which was earlier done along the religious and linguistic lines. Unfortunately it further surged into the new era of confrontation over the division of river water, Punjabi speaking areas and the capital city of Chandigarh between the newly created state of Punjab and Haryana. The manmade territorial reorganisation has remained a bone of contention for the people on the both sides i.e. Haryana and Punjab.

The reorganisation of the Punjab could not solve the problem of linguistic trifurcation of the Province of Punjab into separate state of Punjab, Haryana and Himachal. Instead it created the new problem of the redrawing of the boundaries of the Punjab. Some Punjabi speaking areas were merged into the newly created state of Haryana. A wedge between the people of Punjab and Haryana was also created due to struggle over the natural resources of river water and capital city, which was unfortunately linked with the religion due to the demographic set up of both regions.

Unfortunately the proclamation of Punjab Suba was immediately followed by the sporadic incidents of communal tension. Hindu-Sikh clashes took place in many towns. Government vehicles were attacked and burnt. A curfew was imposed in Amritsar, the epicentre of Akali struggle. In Panipat, three veteran Congressmen were burnt alive. These Congressmen, Kranti Kumar, D.C. Thakkar and Ram Lamba, had been close associates of Bhagat Singh, a revolutionary of Punjab in the days of anti-imperialist struggle.[19] The redrawing of the boundaries of Punjab had also resulted into the loss of the votes of Punjabi Hindus for the Congress, Bharatiya Jan Sangh as a large segment of Punjabi Hindus considered that the Congress Party was no longer defender of their interests. The agitation of the Punjabi Hindus against the reorganization of Punjab ceased quickly because it could not get support from the Hindu lobby of Haryana and Himachal Pradesh.[20]

The reorganization of Punjab was taken s another challenge by Sikh leadership (Akali Dal) as they were not agreed to the centre awarding some Punjabi speaking areas to the newly created states of Haryana and Himachal Pradesh and also were not ready to accept the union government control over the Punjabi capital and hydro water resources.

Within the first month of the redrawing of the boundaries of Punjab, Akali Dal demanded the merger of the Punjabi speaking areas into Punjab and handing over the Capital City of Chandigarh and the hydro water resources to Punjab as they were kept under the central control. Sant Fateh Singh announced his decision to commence a fast from December 17 and to immolate himself on December 27 if the above demands were not fulfilled. Mrs. Indira Gandhi immediately intervened and promised to consider the demands.[21]

The creation of Punjabi Suba and the larger support of the Sikhs to the Akali during the Punjabi Suba agitation could not establish it as the ruling party. Although it tasted the power and also became the ruling party but it was possible only with an uneasy alliance with the Jan Sangh and Communist parties. The support base of the Congress comprising of the Sikhs forced the Akali Dal to keep alive the issues of identity and injustice. Another addition to the already vitiated politics of the Punjab was the anxiety of the Hindutva leadership as they apprehended now that they would be dominated by the Sikhs, who constituted 60 per cent in the reorganised Punjab. Although the Dal was not able to get a clear majority despite having about 60 per cent population of the Sikhs in the newly created Punjab, but it got a good response to its call for various agitation campaigns.[22]

Thus in the first elections in reorganised Punjab, the Congress party succeeded in electing more Sikhs legislators than the Akali Dal. Akali Dal was, however, restricted to 26 seats in the total house of 104 members of the Punjab Legislative Assembly. Its voting percentage had significantly gone up in comparison to what it had got in the third general election in 1962. It was 24.1 percent in 1967 in comparison to 11.9% in 1967. The Congress Party, on the other hand, had still managed to win 43 seats. Even the combined strength of all non-Congress parties in the legislature was not enough to form the government. Yet a coalition government came about due to opportunistic politics. Some members of the Congress party and a block of Independent legislators joined the gratuitous alliance. It was their chance to become ministers in a government which could not be formed without defectors.[23]

The government was pulled down eight months later by the Congress party with the help of the Akali defectors. The government popped up with the help of the defectors once again was a government of short span. It could hardly govern. All it achieved was to set new distorted precedents in parliamentary practices like filibuster. The non-ethical alliance of the opposite ideologies based parties and defectors to occupy power with the help of corruption could not be sustained. Both the Akali Dal and the Congress were ready to cross all ethics and the precedents of the Parliamentary politics. Some of the examples of this could be found from the first session of the new Assembly in 1967, convened to elect the Speaker of the House. Three Congress MLAs voted for the candidates sponsored by the ruling coalition. The Congress established the new precedents of the parliamentary politics in the same session when the official motion of thanks to the Governor for his address to the Assembly was defeated in favour of an amended version which the Congress leaders introduced in the Assembly. The Deputy Speaker of the House Baldev Singh himself voted against the official motion. To forestall a no confidence motion against the government, the Chief Minister Gurnam Singh persuaded the Speaker to adjourn the assembly. When the assembly was reassembled on 6 April, 1967, the opposition demanded that the Chief Minister should step down and threatened to move no confidence motion. The speaker suspended the House sine die without putting the official motion for adjournment to vote.[24]

The house assembled again only when six Congress legislators Balwant Singh, Satnam Singh Bajwa, Jagtar Singh and Shiv Chand were made ministers. This happened on 4 May, 1967, a day before the House had to be convened for the Budget Session. On the first day of the Budget Session, the Deputy Speaker of the House, Balwant Singh, who had voted against the official motion of thanks to the Governor, was physically manhandled by Lachman Singh Gill, the then Minister for Education.

Lachman Singh Gill soon changed his loyalty from Akal Dal to Congress when he was offered a chance to become the Chief Minister of Punjab with the support of Congress Party. On 22 November 1967, Gill made the announcement that he together with sixteen legislators was breaking from the United Front Government. The Akali Chief Minister, Gurnam Singh had to resign.

Lachman Singh Gill had old association with the Congress Party. Until 1937, he was a member of the Party. Gill was sworn in as Chief Minister on 25 November 1967. One member of his ministry was Jagjit Singh Chauhan who later proclaimed the 'formation' of Khalistan. The government of Lachman Singh just lasted for eight months.[25] A mid-term poll to elect a new Assembly was held in February 1969 after the six months of the President rule over Punjab. Akali Dal, baffling as it may seem, substantially improved its strength in the Assembly. For the first time in the history of Punjab, Akali Dal emerged as the single largest party. It secured 43 seats. Clearly, the party emerged as the instrument of the ethno-economic aspiration of the Sikh landed peasantry which had started gaining economic muscles due to Green Revolution. A strengthened Akali Dal, however, could not yet form a government on its own as it still did not have a majority in the house. Once again it roped in the non-Congress legislators into a coalition arrangement and formed a government with Gurnam Singh as the Chief Minister.[26]

As a consequence of the cross-communal following of the Congress Party, the Akali Dal was forced to have alliance with the other parties. Although the percentage of votes to the Dal was increased but it could not manage more than 30 percent of the total votes in the five elections to the Punjab legislative assembly held between 1967 and 1980.[27] Akali Dal has had to compete with the Congress Party for electoral support from the Sikhs. The Akali Dal was ousted from power in the Punjab assembly held in 1972. In the election to the lower house of Parliament in 1980, the Congress won twelve out of thirteen seats in Punjab. This demonstrates the wider appeal of the Congress Party to voters in Punjab.

Coalition governments in one form or another had become an unavoidable aspect of Punjab politics. Political power had to be shared by the representative parties of the two dominant communities in proportion to their numerical strength. This applied also to the Congress government which ruled the State from 1972 to 1977 and from 1980 to 1985. From the creation of the Punjabi Suba in 1966 to 1980, the Akali Dal managed to come to power only by forming a coalition government as it had the core support base only among the Sikhs and there also the congress also had support base among the lower caste Sikhs. In the first election held in reorganised Punjab, Akali Dal succeeded in forming a coalition government in alliance with the Jan Sangh and the Communist Party of India (CPI). The Akali alliance with the Jan Sangh, the political arm of the Arya Samaj in the state, founded in 1951 and a party with essentially

Hindu communal appeal were particularly baffling because its president had gone on record to stating that "The Jana Sangh regards the Sikhs as part and parcel of Hindus." [28] Thus the creation of a Sikh dominated territorial unit did not ensure political power for the Akalis much to their disappointment.

The above nature of experiments in government formation, ludicrous as they may seem, proved to have serious implications for future of the state. It began to draw upon rank and file of the Akali Dal that governments formed by them in the state under the prevailing circumstances were only going to remain not only open to blackmail by the unreliable partners of an inevitable coalition, but would also remain susceptible to manipulation by the Congress party backed by Centre. Any government formed under the existing setup was doomed to expend itself in the exertions to survive against the subversive manipulations of the opposition parties. The experiences of being in the government had produced only one important outcome for the Akal Dal: Its leaders had been corrupted to betray the objectives which they championed for decades. The political power which they wielded while in the government, though far from absolute, had corrupted them absolutely.

What disappointed the workers and sympathisers of the party most was their leaders' failure to intervene effectively when Darshan Singh Pheruman went on fast unto the death for the transfer of Chandigarh to Punjab. Beginning his fast on 15 August 1969, he died seventy four days later. Darshan Singh Pheruman was a respected Sikh leader who had come under the influence of the Gadar party, launched by the Indian expatriates in the USA and Canada, when he was in Malaya in the early twenties. He returned to India to organise revolutionary groups to over throw the British government. He was arrested on a number of occasions and spent more than thirteen years in jails before India attained independence. He represented the Sikh cause before the Cabinet Mission in 1946, which had come to India to discuss the modalities of the transfer of power. He was a member of All Parties Council of Action which had been formed to oppose the dismemberment of Punjab. Later he was elected to the Upper House of Parliament for three terms from 1952 to 1962, as a founding member of Swantantra Party. Though not in Akali Dal, he chose to die for a cause, which the party had vociferously advocated as a plank for its election to government in February 1969. When the Union government refused to hand over Chandigarh even after death of Darshan Singh Pheruman, the Akali Dal government could at least resign in protest which they did not do. Evidently, the principles and party objectives had ceased to count for much to the Akali leaders who had now tasted power.[29]

GREEN REVOLUTION AND AFTER

Communal mobilisation along the lines of electoral politics was followed by the strain in its social and economic order due to the phenomenal agricultural growth in the state due to Green Revolution. The success of Green Revolution made Punjab the model state of agriculture across the globe. The prosperity of the Green Revolution and changing requirement of the agriculture under the new capital model of agriculture had both positive and negative impacts on the Punjabi society as community and individual. The agricultural development in Punjab created the contradiction between the different classes of the Punjab.[30]

In the post-reorganisation period, Punjab's economy like that of neighbouring newly created Haryana prospered within the broad framework of controlled capitalist development in India. Within this framework, Punjab had its own specific model of agrarian capitalist transformation. It was based on the capital development of agriculture accompanied by small scale industries in the production structure of commodities. It was facilitated by a relatively more developed tertiary in the service sectors. Punjab also gained from already existing canal system developed by the British. Punjab model of growth generated contradictions at two levels, first within itself between the rich farmers and the landless farm workers and second between regional dominant classes of Punjab and the dominant classes at all India level. Contradictions within the Punjabi society are generated by its nature of mode of production. Punjab has remained predominantly an agrarian economy. In 1980-81, agricultural live stock contributed 49.04% of the state domestic product at 1970-71 prices.[31] Agricultural sector employed 59.1% of total work force in 1981. Punjab agriculture experienced capitalist development at relatively a faster pace since 1965-66. A section of landed peasantry having greater command over land and capital resources has got transformed into capitalist farmers. In 1980-81 top 7.19% farmers owned. They cultivated 29.17% of cultivable area, 10 acres and more. Farmers with 4 hectare and more constituted 33.39% of total farmers and operated 71.98% of the area.[32] These farmers owned capital assets such as tractors, threshers, pump sets, more than proportion of the land held by them. Finding their family labour insufficient to carry on farm operations, these farmers depended mainly on hired labour often in the form of migrant ones.

A study of post-Green Revolution labour use pattern shows that all farmers with different level of technology hire labour power. The farmers owning tractors, pump-set, thresher and trolley hire labour to the extent 76.27% of their requirements.[33] Along with capitalist farmers there came into existence a class of agricultural workers who own neither land nor capital resources. They mostly belonged to the marginal social groups. They have had to depend on selling their labour power to farmers either as casual or attached labourers. This class constitute 38.6% of the total labour force, engaged in the agriculture as compared to 61.4% that of cultivators.[34]

The emergent irreconcilable contradiction between farmers and agricultural workers on the issue of wages has led to breakdown of the social order. Every year, there have been a number of cases of struggle of agriculture workers on the issue of wages in Punjab. There is sufficient documented evidence of this. The class of agriculture workers emerged from four sources: First, some workers existed in agriculture sector of the state on the eve of independence. Second, with the introduction of land reforms, the tenants were ejected from the land by the landlords fearing confiscation of the excess land by the state. As a result they joined the ranks of agriculture as lawless workers.[35] With the introduction of new technology, pure tenants became owners of land and tenants at will were ejected by the owners of the land. Third, with the modernization of rural society in the state, the traditional artisans have become redundant and majority of them joined the ranks of agriculture worker or they migrated to urban Punjab.[36] Lastly, with an increase in productivity and cropping intensity in Punjab, there increased a considerable flow of migratory labour from eastern Uttar Pradesh and Bihar and Madhya Pradesh. The local labour generally belonged to the scheduled castes. It had conflict with migrant labour which had been generally of peasant background and belonged to the middle or lower caste groups. Being migratory in character, the newly inducted migrant labourers who had no local roots was prepared to work for longer hours and for low wages. This factor was used by rich capitalist farmers many a times to disrupt the struggle of local agriculture workers.[37]

Capitalist transformation of Punjab agriculture had different effects on the different section of peasantry. Capitalist farmers became the largest beneficiaries and were now producing much more than what they required for family consumption. They produced surplus which are invested in agriculture and other income generating activities. The small and marginal farmers experienced some gains in their income initial period but unable to sustain it. Many small and marginal holdings became non-viable due to heavy costs involved. According to a survey in 1974 small farmers were running annually loss of Rs.125 per capita where as farmers with land between 5 and 10 acres were producing profit of Rs. 1200 per capita. Another survey covering 1976-77 to 1977-78 indicates that marginal and small households were annually running into average deficit of Rs. 1513.17 and Rs. 1648.19 respectively.[38] Consequently 24 per cent of small farmers and 31 per cent of marginal farmers were living below the poverty line by 197980 despite the Green Revolution.[39] With the rise of development crisis in agriculture, the small and marginal farmers found it difficult to survive. Between 197071 and 198081, a large number of operational holding in Punjab was 13, 75, 382 in numbers which declined to 10, 27,127 registering a decline of 25 per cent. Thus decline was contributed by marginal and small land holdings which were not suitable for capitalist farming. The marginal holding declined in the state by 61.9% whereas small holding declined 23.3%. The small farmers were compelled to sell out and to move to the cities.[40] As yet there was no evidence to suggest that the farmers giving up cultivation joined the ranks of agriculture labour. There was a strong tendency visible among the Jat Sikh cultivators of not joining the ranks of agriculture workers who often belonged to low caste Mazhabi Sikhs. The cultivators being relieved from agriculture were largely absorbed in the Industrial sector of the state as the rate of industrial growth in the state on an average was higher than that of Indian economy. [41] But here again the small industrial units absorbed largely migratory labour as they could be hired on low wages and can be easily hired and fired. In fact, wages were very low and the working conditions so unattractive that in small scale ancillary units local labour with peasant background was not prepared. Job opportunities in the other state of India and abroad have always been scarce for the unskilled local labour ousted from the agrarian sector and this applied to Punjab also.

Thus the cultivators being released by the capitalist development in agriculture in agriculture were not being absorbed outside it in the urban space and were experiencing redundancy. This force was accompanied by a large body of educated unemployed youth from rural areas. The youth had inflated aspiration and wanted to become rich over night like their kins abroad. Educated youth from poor peasantry found land holding of their parents economically unviable. They therefore, were in dire need of employment outside agriculture. There was less inclination to indulge in back breaking labour that their forefathers did willingly. The same was the position of retired army personal of lower ranks who were in their mid-thirties or early forties. Since jobs were scarce, a large number of youth and army personal were unemployed and their numbers were increasing by every year. This was the man power available for various uses and manipulations including violence unleashed by political processes.

The well off sections in rural areas that had cornered major part of the prosperity generated by the capitalist development had different sets of problems. They had initially gained from rise in agrarian production but also from the government's subsidies/ facilities in the name of rural development. They started taking over the land of poor peasantry on lease and mortgage or on sale. Big cultivators having land above 10 hectare constituted 5.01% of the total and operated 26.86% of the land in 1970-71 their proportion increased to 7.19% and they operated 29.17% of land in 1980-81. These farmers had surpluses with them which they invested in land. Very soon, however, returns from investments were falling making investment less profitable. The rate of return of wheat cultivator per quintal declined from 24.50% in 1970- 71 to 1.32% in 1977-78.[42] As a consequence, net income per hectare from wheat cultivation at 1970-71, price declined from 328 in the 197-71 to Rs. 54 in 1981-82.[43] Since agriculture was less rewarding for capitalist farmers, they were upset over it. Some of them invested their surplus outside agriculture particularly in transport, cinema and cold storage, etc. But these activities were also becoming less rewarding. It was very difficult to for them to enter business and industry. First, they didn't have the necessary expertise and experiences in the trading/business activities. Second, there was stiff competition by the established urban based businessmen and industrialists. Only traditional business communities and artisans particularly carpenter and blacksmiths (Ramgarhias) were able to enter the emerging industrial sector of the state. Thus there was lack of integration of agriculturalist in the urban based business and capitalists. The former felt alienated and deprived and had a feeling that despite feeding the nation had been left high and dry by the system. Anger was directed against centre as Akalis articulated it that way.

Capitalist development brought greater integration of agriculture to market net work. There was a great degree of specialization in production. Farmers grew mainly Rabi and Paddy, cotton and sugarcane in Kharif crops. This made farmers of different layers as commodity producers. They started selling a major part of output in the market. There was a considerable increase in the inputs like high yielding variety seeds, chemicals fertilizers, insecticides, weedicides, and pump sets, electronic thrashers, tractors, etc. Farmers sold a major part of their output to buy all major inputs and considerable goods from market. Market operations had an important effect on the income and life of the farmers. Therefore, price issue and smooth market were of direct relevance for the peasantry. In the market, farmers came in direct contact with the traders. Traders/commission agents were held responsible for unloading and bagging the produce, preparing it for sale, providing display space. Finding buyers and making sale, stitching the bags, weighing them, collecting payments from buyers and making them available to the farmers after making deduction for various intermediately charges and taxes. They also provided considerable amount of credit to the farmers both in the cash and in the form of inputs on differed payments. In the process there was predominance of the commission agents who exploit the farmer through various malpractices and usurious interest rate.[44] Farmers bought various inputs and consumer goods from the traders in the market places of urban areas where they were over charged. This established a contradiction between the farming community and trading community. Farmers became suspicious of traders and considered them as cunning exploiter. Traders looked at farmers as rustic, rash uneducated, and easy to cheat. In fact peasantry nourished a grudge against urban centres where traders, government officials reside. Class contradiction was also re-enforced by communal division in the society. A study based on 1971 census data shows that 69.37% of the Sikhs in Punjab were concentrated in the rural areas and are mainly cultivators, and 66.37% on the Hindus lived in urban areas and specialise in non-agriculture occupation such as trade, industry, service etc. In the urban based occupation Hindus were and are over represented and the Sikhs underrepresented thus bringing in the community issue.[45] Entry of the Sikhs in these occupations on a significant scale created communal polarisation. This explained contradictions between Hindus and Sikh traders and growing communalism among educated people during the period after Green Revolution.

There was a second set of contradictions between the Punjab and the Centre. With capitalist development in the agriculture, the class of capitalist farmers came to dominate the rural life, wielded decisive influence on political process and power in the state. The institution of Panchayati Raj network of cooperative institutions and state Legislative Assembly were increasingly controlled by people from this class. This class was using government machinery at state level to promote its interests. While using government machinery at state level it came into conflict with class in control of government machinery at central level. Against the growing assertion of this class it found administrative powers of the Central Government getting eroded. The growing economic and social role of administration was being monopolised by Central Government. Whether economic planning and diversification of financial institutions or Radio television communication system it was the monopoly of central administration. In this situation promotional role of class interest through administration at state level became extremely limited.

Major part of the surplus agriculture production was marked by capitalist farmers. The prices of agricultural major crops from the state such as wheat, paddy, sugarcane and cotton were fixed by the central government on the recommendation of agriculture prices and costs commission. There has been another agency named Bureau of Industrial Costs and Prices which advises Central government to intervene in the prices of industrial goods. The Central Government intervention in the pricing of various commodities under regulated price system has a capacity to change relative price system. Price system moved against the agriculture from 100 in 1970-72 to 81.8 in 1980-81. The fall had been sharp and consistent from 1974-75. Major part of the surplus wheat, paddy and cotton were procured by the Central agencies such as Food Corporation of India (FCI) and Competition Commission of India (CCI). Inputs as fertilizers, pesticides, insecticide, weedicides, tractors, pumping sets and electric motors were and still are supplied by Indian (Private and Government Sectors) and foreign monopolies. Any shift of terms of trade against agriculture results in transfer of economic surplus from capital farmers to industrial monopoly bourgeoisie. It is over the price issue and other market operations that a big agitation under Bhartiya Kisan Union (BKU) an organisation of capitalist farmers was fought in Punjab during the 18384.[46] Due to greater needs of centralisation of monopoly capital, greater encroachment of central government become possible in areas earlier demarcated for states under the constitution. This invariably lead to the blurring of the distinction between the central and state subjects. The centre's involvement in a state and concurrent list is both direct as well as indirect. The massive involvement of the centre is made possible by enormous amount of the financial resources at its disposal. Of the total budgetary resources of the Central and State governments made fifty-fifty by both centre and states. Thus states depend on Centre for their resources to the extent of one third.[47] This makes the position of state administration very precarious particularly when they are ruled by opposition parties.

It was under these circumstances that the issue of agriculture prices, marketing and development got connected with the other political issues in the troubled State. The Akali Dal which was already demanding more power to the states under the federal structure was abled to collect the huge support of the farmers and to present the problems of the agriculture as the problems of predominantly Sikh peasants mounted. The Anandpur Sahib Resolution under which the Akali Dal demanded more subsides on agriculture machinery and fertilizers, chemicals is the clear assertion of the farmers against central government's monopoly over the agriculture prices.

ANANDPUR SAHIB RESOLUTION: IDENTITY, ECONOMY AND CENTRE, SATE RELATIONS

It was under this back drop that the socio-economic and political programme of the Akali Dal were framed by the Working Committee of the Akali Dal on 17th October 1973, which was adopted at by the Akali Dal at Anandpur Sahib (the birth place of Khalsa Panth). The Anandpur Sahib resolution was a direct attempt of the capitalist farmers of the Punjab to link their economic demands with the Sikh identity by giving the religious name to the drafted resolution of their demands. In the Anandpur Sahib Resolution the Akali Dal emphasised the capitalist development of the Agriculture by demanding more subsidies on heavy machinery fertilizers and chemicals. Akali Dal claimed that the agriculture sector was systematically discriminated by the Centre although the mainstay of the Indian economy is agriculture. Despite the hard work of the larger number of farmers and their contribution to the development of the country the lever of power remained in the hands of industrialists, big traders, capitalist and monopolists due to the central control of political and economic resources. The party held that no political power who claimed to raise social structure on the basis of justice could afford to ignore this fact, yet this was a hard fact that the levers of economic power, continued to be in the hands of big traders, capitalists and monopolists.[48] Some marginal benefits might have accrued to other classes, but the real benefits of economic growth have been reaped by these categories during the last 26 years after the independence. The political power was also been misappropriated by these classes which were viewed as wielding the same for their own benefits. As such, any peaceful attempt to usher in a new era of social justice would have to break the economic and political strongholds of these categories' of the people. Akali position can be understood in the context of the party core support base coming from the landed Jat Sikh peasantry.[49]

The Shiromani Akali Dal consistently underlined the growing gulf between the urban and rural areas. In rural areas, the Akali Dal avowed to help the weaker classes, like the scheduled castes, backward classes, landless tenants, ordinary labourers, and the poor and middle class farmers. For such a purpose, it stands for meaningful land reforms which envisage a ceiling of 30 standards acres and distribution of excess land among the poor farmers as mentioned in the Anandpur Sahib Resolution.

AGRICULTURE CRISIS AND ANANDPUR SAHIB RESOLUTION : SOME OBSERVATIONS

Noting that agriculture sector had witnessed land reforms and Green Revolution, Akali Dal undertook to enrich the Green Revolution gains by an increase in yield per acre. It also promised to ensure perceptible improvement in the standard of living of all rural classes, more particularly of the poor and the middle class farmers, as also landless labourers. For such a purpose it planned to work on the following lines as envisaged in the Anandpur Sahib Resolutions:

a) Introduction of land reforms and measures to increase agriculture production with a view to remove growing gap between the rich and poor. For such a purpose the existing legislation on land ceiling would have to be revised and firm ceiling 30 standard acres per family would have to be enforced with proprietary rights to the actual tiller.
b) The Shiromani Akali Dal shall work for the modernisation of farming and would also try to enable the

middle class families to seek loans and inputs available by the different agencies.

c) The Shiromani Akali Dal shall fix the prices of the agriculture produce on the basis of return of middle class farmers. Such prices would be notified well before the sowing season and only the State government would be empowered to fix such prices.

d) The Shiromani Akali Dal stands for complete nationalisation of the trade in food grains and as such, shall endeavour to nationalise the wholesale trade in food grains through the establishment of State agencies.

e) The Shiromani Akali Dal strongly opposes the demarcation of food zones and attendant restriction on the movements of food grains. The whole country should be single food zone.

f) The party shall make special efforts to bring the Thein Dam and Bathinda Thermal plant to a speedy completion so that increased and cheaper power and irrigation facilities are availed. Efforts will be made for the establishment of an Atomic power station in the State.

g) Cooperative societies would be set up in the rural areas. In all those areas where canal water is no available small irrigation projects would be taken in hand.[50]

INDUSTRIAL SECTOR AND ANANDPUR SAHIB RESOLUTION

To facilitate the growth of agriculture, Akali Dal advocated for the state ownership of the key industries and the agro-based industrial development in Punjab and a balanced industrial growth sector in all the states. The party demanded the immediate nationalization of basic consumer industries to stabilise the process of the goods and to save the poor consumer from exploitation at the hands of industrialists and the middlemen.

A planned effort to establish agro-industries in the rural areas was to be made to relieve the growing population pressure in the urban areas. The industrial management was sought to be democratised by enabling workers to have said in the management and by fair distribution of profit between the Industrialists and the workers. The credit agencies especially the nationalised banks were to be directed to invest a fixed ratio of their deposits in the rural areas. Every industrial unit beyond worth one crore assets was to be brought under the public sector. The Akali Dal at that time stood for progressive nationalization of transport.

ECONOMIC DEMANDS

Shiromani Akali Dal demanded that the whole tax structure was to be revised in such a way that the evasion of taxes and flow of black money was completely eradicated. It stood for a simple and straight forward system of taxation. The present infrastructure of taxations weighed heavily against the poor and enabled the rich to bypass it. The party stood for a more realistic policy in this respect so that the black money running a parallel economy could be usefully employed.[51]

WORKERS, MIDDLE CLASS EMPLOYEES AND AGRICULTURAL LABOUR

The welfare of the agriculture and industrial labour was also proposed by the Akali Dal under the economic programme:

a) To fix need based wages for industrial workers.
b) To bring progressive improvement in the standard of living of government employees.
c) To reassess the minimum wages of agriculture labour and to standard of living for them.
d) To take necessary steps to provide roofed accommodation for the rural and urban poor.
e) The unemployed youth should be provided immediate employment or reasonable unemployment allowance.[52]

The Anandpur Sahib Resolution was clearly an attempt of the Akali Dal to garner the support of rural poor along with the capitalist and middle class farmer. The second most important objective of the Akali Dal was to capture the Congress traditional support base among the Scheduled Castes (SCs) and Other Backward Classes (OBCs) in the rural areas. Although the Anandpur Sahib Resolution attempted to broaden the base of Akali Dal among the rural poor, however, the demography of the Punjab again connected it to the Sikh religion as the absolute majority of the rural population either of the farmer or the farmer labour is belongs to the Sikhism. Simultaneously the issues of Agriculture crisis and the river water dispute and the issue of the resettle of the boundaries of Punjabi speaking areas between the Punjab and Haryana were coloured as the Sikh issues by the Dal.[53] After creation of Punjabi Suba, Akali Dal got an opportunity to get a huge support of Sikh masses by colouring the issues of Punjab as the alone Sikh issues due to the demographic change first time in the history of Independent India, although it was attempting to garner the support of Sikh masses along the communal from the very day of Independence, but the strong base of the Congress in particular in the farmer folk always created problems for the Akali Dal. Special campaigns for the "Unity of Panth" and propagation through "amrit parchar' was started by the SGPC on the request of Akali Dal to sharpen the political consciousness of the Sikhs masses along the religious lines, that could turn into electoral gains for the Akali Dal.

Realising the adverse impact of religious appeal of the Akalis, the Congress party also made extensive use of religious revivalism as a tool to keep its hold on the Sikh masses. Giani Zail Singh, as Chief Minister of Punjab during 1972-77 tried to mobilise the different sections of the Sikhs in favour of Congress by employing religious symbols and idioms. He even surpassed the Akalis in his effort to use religious plank for consolidating his personal as well as the Congress support base. He turned the State machinery into "glorified institution of Dharm Parchar." [54] A long road was built to connect the historic Gurudwaras and on its completion he himself headed a mammoth procession of devotees; descendants of the tenth Guru's horses led the congregation; the historic Sikh weapons were brought back from British with a great religious fervour.[55] He named various streets, highways, towns and institutions after names of Gurus. Thus, Giani Zail Singh used the upsurge of Sikh religious revivalism as a tool to consolidate the support base of the Congress party among the Sikh masses.

The Akali Dal at that time found itself beaten by the Congress with its own stick, i.e. the use of religious symbols and idioms. Therefore, it was constrained to look for some opportunity to launch an agitation which might rescue them from this precarious position that would have spelled doom for the party's future. The imposition of the national emergency by the Indira Gandhi June 26, 1975, provided a golden opportunity to the Akalis at the crucial time, when they have losing their ground on the religious issues to protest against the government.

The Akali leadership took upon itself the task of launching an agitation and a "Save Democracy Morcha" was launched by the Akali Committee at Amritsar on June 9, 1975 as per the resolution adopted by the party working committee at Amritsar on June 28-30, 1975. The resolution criticised emergency as "an onslaught on the civil liberties, freedom of press and freedom of speech, a rape of democracy and a great step towards dictatorship."[56] The top leaders of the party courted arrest from the Golden Temple after 9th July Morcha. While courting arrest the Sikh masses were reminded to their glorious historical traditions of sacrifice. The Dal also inspired the SGPC to take up the task of Amrit Parchar seriously. In addition to demonstrating throughout the state on regular basis, special cultural occasions such as Diwali and Baisakhi, as well as the first anniversary of the 'Morcha' on July 9, 1976 were marked with extra and special protest.[57] Although the fight against emergency excesses and for restoration of civil liberties was secular, yet the mobilization tactics applied by the Akali leadership remained imbued with religious symbols and idioms systematically.

When emergency was lifted and elections were announced in January 1977, the Akali Dal re-emerged as a party better equipped to particular to particular get re-established. The Janata Party and CPM also sought an alliance with the Akali party in order to carve out some place for themselves in the changed political situation in Punjab. The Assembly elections in June 1977 resulted in the emergence of the Akali Dal as a dominant partner of the alliance. During the two year period of the Akali-Janata coalition (1997), the Akali Dal and other Sikh organizations continued to make demands which would further consolidate Sikh identity. Though the Akali leaders avoided the excessive use of communal and religious symbols and idioms because of their alliance with Janata Party, yet they remained under pressure from the more extremist section and were never allowed to forget that in ultimate analysis, they were the representative of the Panth.

The Congress party led by Giani Zail Singh in order to undermine the religious base of the Akali Dal now tried to use the weapon of fundamentalism. In order to capture the imagination of Sikh peasantry, the Congress elite began to project a young dynamic fundamentalist Sikh preacher as the saviour.[58] The forces of fundamentalism struck for the first time in a decisive way, when on April 13, 1978, a band of Jarnail Singh Bhindarwale's followers clashed with the Nirankaris resulting in the killing of sixteen of his followers. Almost all those killed were Gurbani singers. The killing of the sixteen Sikh holy men by the Nirankaris was a great loss to the creditability to the Akali Dal among the Sikhs as the Akali government was in power. A Hukamnama (Religious order from the highest temple) was issued by the Akal Takhat Jathedar (head priest) asking the Sikh to boycott the Nirankaris. The Sikh *versus*

Nirankaris clash speeded up the resurgence of Sikh fundamentalism and paved the way for the rise of Jarnail Singh Bhindranwale, who symbolised the extreme type of fundamentalism.[59]

A militant organisation of the Sikh youth came to be established to further strengthen the fundamentalist forces engaged in a crusade against unorthodoxy among the Sikh masses and the "Hate Nirankari Campaign". This came in the form of Dal Khalsa.[60] Its inaugural session was held on 1978 at Chandigarh, and a scheme for the establishment of Khalistan was discussed in its meeting.[61] It was called as the "Mukti Sangathan" (Liberation Organisation) and "Supreme Panchayat". While the head office was kept at Chandigarh, a camp office was opened at Room no. 37, Guru Nanak Niwas in the Golden Temple complex, Amritsar with Gajinder Singh as its incharge. Dal Khalsa became the first militant organisation with the avowed object of demanding an independent Sikh sovereign state and to fight the Nirankaris. The main sources of inspiration of the Dal inspiration, for the demand of Khalistan on the basis of a separate Sikh identity, is said to be late Sardar Kapur Singh who had written extensively defining the concept of Khalsa and Khalistan or Sikh homeland.[62]

The Congress (I) in order to capture political power and erode the base of Akali Dal tacitly sided with the fundamentalist forces. As the SGPC played a great role in the Sikh politics and provided vast financial resources as well as an important platform for the mass mobilisation. Congress (I) tried to dislodge the Akali Dal by supporting the candidates of Bhindranwale and Dal Khalsa in 1979 in the election of SGPC. Akali Dal was able to retain its control over the SGPC when out of 140 seats, it won 136. Amrik Singh, a close associate of Bhindranwale and the President of All India Sikh Students Federation (AISSF) was defeated by Jiwan Singh Umranagal.[63] The defeat of the hardliners in the SGPC, however, did not result in the weakening of these fundamentalist forces. They succeeded in spreading their influence over the Sikh masses gradually but steadily.

The factional politics of Akali Dal, after Indira Gandhi came back to power at the centre in January 1980, led to their defeat in the State Assembly elections. Akali Dal could win only 37 seats against 63 seats of Congress (I) in a house of 117 members. The narrow political interest of party politics further strengthened the fundamentalist elements. The hate Nirankaris campaign of Jaranil Singh Bhindranwale had deeply impacted on the Punjab politics. Murder of Gurbachan Singh, the Nirankari Chief on April 24, 1980, gave a fillip to the cult of violence. The rift between Zail Singh and Darbara Singh factions within the Congress (I) played a role in encouraging communal and fundamental elements. It has widely been noted and commented upon in many Journals and books.[64]

While the fundamentalism was becoming entrenched into the Punjab politics, some other Sikh leaders settled abroad, found an appropriate time to strike with their secessionist slogans and the Sikhs as a nation theory. Jagjit Singh Chauhan, who had earlier raised the demand of Khalistan in 1971, but was not taken seriously by the mainstream of Sikh community, renewed his campaign in the late seventies and early eighties. In the changed socio-political atmosphere in the Punjab (in the wake of the resurgence of fundamentalism), Jagjit Singh Chauhan found a few supporters when he visited India in 1980. He along with his supporters hoisted a "national flag of Khalisatn" at Anandpur Sahib in March 1980. On June 16, 1980, at Amritsar, Balbir Singh Sandhu, a Sikh leader of Tarn Taran announced the formation of Khalistan, with Chauhan as its President. Sandhu declared himself as Secretary General of the National Council of Khalistan, which became another Sikh militant organisation. Since then Chauhan started issuing passports, currency and postage stamps from UK.[65] Chauhan announced the establishment of his government in exile.[66] As mention at the beginning of this chapter, in March 1981, another American born rich national Ganga Singh Dhillon, during his address to the 54th Educational Conference of the chief Khalsa Diwan at Chandigarh declared that "the Sikhs are a nation and they should seek the membership of United Nations on the lines of Palestine Liberation Organisation".[67] Soon afterwards, however, the Chief Khalsa Diwan disassociated itself from Dhillon Statement.[68]

The factionalism among the Akalis and the Congress support to the dissenters aiming to weaken the hold of the Akali Dal further complicated the situation as three versions of the Anandpur Sahib came out. Both the Akali Dal led respectively by Talwandi and Giani Ajmer Singh also came out with their own Anandpur Sahib Resolution with a stress over the Sikh Identity and self-determination. Although the moderate version of Anandpur Sahib Resolution of 1973 had also incorporated the theory of Sikhs as a nation, but it did not stress upon the separatism and total autonomy. The concept of "Sikhs are a nation", however, became handy to sharpen the separate identity of the Sikhs at the beginning of 1980's and the various sections of the Sikh leadership used it to keep their hold on the Sikh masses during the 1980's. The Sikh extremist section of the Akali Dal, led by Jagdev Singh Talwandi, openly supported-the Sikh nation theory. Dal Khalsa, the militant Sikh organization, came out in open on March 20, 1981 when over 60 Dal activists took up a procession led by Sikhs wielding swords and a banner with map of proposed areas of Khalistan at Anandpur Sahib on Hola Mohalla occasion.

After the procession, a saffron flag was hoisted and five shots were fired from a gun, in salutation. The Dal Khalsa activists were vocal and conspicuous during the tobacco–ban agitation, in the holy city of Amritsar from March 29 to 31, 1981, led by Bhindranwale. Again on 15 August, 1981, the day of India's Independence, over a dozen Dal volunteers hoisted the flag which had the map of the proposed Khalistan inscribed in the Centre. They even dared to raise the slogans of pro-Khalistan from the gallery of the Punjab Assembly, on August 17, 1981.[69]

In reaction to violence perpetrated by Dal Khalsa, certain Hindu revivalist organizations came into existence, particularly Jagdish Tangaris Shiv Sena at Ludhiana and Pawan Kumar Sharma led Hindu Suraksha Samiti at Patiala. The tails and heads of the Cows were put on a temple gates allegedly by Dal Khalsa activists and the packets of cigarettes thrown in Gurudwaras allegedly by Hindu communalists further deepened the divide in the perceptions of two communities and generated tension. In short, all this consolidated the distinct and separate identity of the Sikhs which came to be projected as the basis of secessionist demands.[70]

From 1981 onwards, the cult of militancy spread resulting in killing of Nirankaris or many others opposing the killings. Lala Jagat Narain, the manager proprietor of *Hind Samachar Group of Newspapers* at Jalandhar, repeatedly raised his voice against in his highly inflammatory articles and condemned Bhindranwale for his cult of violence. His editorials attacked not only Bhindranwale but also Akali Dal and contained warnings regarding "Khalistan". The *Hate Nirankaris* campaign of Bhindranwale was equally matched by "Hate Sikh" campaign of Lala Jagat Narain. Lala was allegedly murdered by Sikh militants on September 9, 1981 and in the FIR registered with police, Bhindranwale's name figured prominently. The warrant of his arrest was issued by the state government, but he refused to be arrested. Ultimately he agreed to court arrest but on his own terms and conditions. The "Sikh Sangat" was called to witness the arrest of Bhindranwale at Mehta Chowk on September 20, 1981. Soon after his arrest, violence broke out and about a dozen Sikhs were killed in police firing. Bhindranwale was released by the government within a Month on October 15, 1981, which created a god size image of Bhindranwale among the Sikhs and he was taken as the "saviour of Sikhs by a section of the community.[71]

The Akali Dal was constantly under the extreme pressure and got scared of the increasing support of Bhindranwale in the Sikh community. In order to win back the Sikh masses, Dal started an agitation in support of a set of demands. A long charter of demands numbering 45 was forwarded by the Dal to the Government in September 1981. The main demands submitted by the Dal fell into three categories: (a) demands concerning the Sikh community as a religious group, (b) demands concerning water and territorial issues, and (c), general demands. [72] Later on October 1981, the Akali Dal submitted the list of 15 demands. However, when the negotiations between the Akali Dal and Government of India failed (after meetings in October 1981, November 1981, and April 1982), the Akali Dal intensified its agitation from August 4, 1982 and called it *Dharm Yudh Morcha.* [73] Meanwhile militant killings continued unabated. Amrik Singh, President of AISSF and Tara Singh, manager of Mehta Chowk Damdami Taksal were arrested in July 1982 in connection with a case of attempt to murder. Bhindranwale and his supporters started a morcha for their release. At this time Akali leadership even when not agreeing to his political ideas and method of protest needed the support of Bhindranwale to strengthen their agitation against the government. Factional fights within Akali Dal also played a role. Hence, the President of SGPC, Gurcharn Singh Tohra and Harcharan Singh Longowal persuaded Bhindranwale to join the Akali Dharma Yudh Morcha. Bhindranwale not only agreed to join the Morcha but also promised to abide by the orders of Longowal, appointed as the Morcha dictator. The Akali Dal on its part included the demands of Bhindranwale in their charter.[74] Thus Akali Dal in a way allowed itself to be aligned itself with the fundamentalist and militant elements. It was a tactical blunder which led to the growing irrelevance of Akali Dal in Punjab politics as a credible opposition party and branded the party as panthic. It arguably led to the rise of extra-systematic politics in the state.

Before discussing the dynamics of the "*Dharm Yudh Morcha*" (1982-85), it would be pertinent to mention the background of Bhindranwale and his ideology as he was an iconic figure for the secessionist movement and played the central role in the rise of armed resistance to the Indian state.

Jarnail Singh Bhindranwale belonged to the Jaat community and his gotra was Brar. His family belonged to the twin villages called Rode Lande in the then Faridkot. He was born in 1947 and was second son of Joginder Singh. Joginder Singh was associated with Gurbachan Singh, the then head of the Dam Dami Taksal. Gurbachan Singh chose Jarnail Singh as his pupil.[75] Dam Dami Taksal is a religious sect from days of Guru Gobind Singh. The word 'Damdami' seems to be derived from the Punjabi word *dam* which means breathing and it is historically connected with the few days of rest that the tenth guru of Sikhs, Guru Gobind Singh, took after leaving Anandpur Sahib at Talwandi Sabo where the Gurdwara Damdama Sahib is presently located. The literal meaning of Taksal is mint and metaphorically, it would imply that the place from where the 'real Sikh' emerges. In other words, a Taksal is seminary where a man is trained right from the childhood into proper recitation of Gurbani and Kirtan (singing hymns). The story as to how the idea of having a seminary related to Guru Gobind Singh is found in the oral history of Damdami Taksal.[76] The story is woven around an incident that occurred when a Sikh, while reciting Gurbani pronounced some words wrongly, which led the tenth guru to intervene and explain to him that how the meaning could undergo a change if the words were pronounced wrongly. Since the Guru had advised the Sikh in the presence of others, one of the Panj Piara. Bhai Daya Singh approached the Guru to guide the congregation in this respect. However, Guru could not find time for it though he promised to do. When the Guru left Anandpur Sahib and reached and stayed at Talwandi Sabo, Singh reminded him for his promise. He told them to go to Dheer Mal at Kartarpur Sahib to get the Granth that had been prepared by the fifth guru so that the Gurbani of ninth guru could be included in it. Baba Deep Singh met Dhir Mall who challenged that if the tenth guru represented the charisma of the first guru, as was the case of fifth guru, then he could himself prepare the Granth.

Under such circumstances Guru Gobind Singh dictated the entire Gurbani to Bhai Mani Singh and he also undertook himself the task of interpreting it. Two of his devout Sikh followers, namely Bhai Mani Singh and Baba Deep Singh, were involved in the writing of the Granth. The dictation and simultaneously interpretation of the Gurbani took nine months and nine days. According to the story as narrated in the official history of Damdami Taksal, the tenth guru nominated the Guru Granth Sahib as his successor when he was at Nanded. When he was at Nanded, Baba Deep Singh returned to

Punjab, and started Taksal at Damdama Sahib. Bhai Mani Singh went to Amritsar. After Baba Deep Singh there was a line of successors who continued the tradition of Jarnail Singh Bhindranwale was fourteen. It may be noted that till the tenth head of the Taksal no head used the suffix of 'Bhindranwale'. The suffix 'Bhindranwale' began with Baba Sunder Singh who belongs to the village Bhinder Kalan in Ferozpur district.[77]

Sunder Singh died in 1930 and it is obvious that he was witness to the changes in not only the Sikhism but also the relations among the various religious communities. The influence of Tat Khalsa on its emphasis on five 'Ks' to carve out distinct Sikh traditions could not be ignored. Also, the establishment of new nomenclature, that is Bhindranwale, seems to suggest that before Sunder Singh there could be some contentions and contestations among the followers or between the followers and relatives of the deceased heads of Taksal. However, there could be another dimension. It has been found that most of the heads of Taksal were very active and mobile in spreading the "true interpretation of the Gurbani". They were able to establish many Gurdwaras at different places. Sunder Singh Bhindranwale, in comparison to other heads of such centres of learning, proved to be more charismatic as a result of which others got marginalized and their influence remained confined and localized. Gurbachan Singh Bhindranwale, the twelfth in the succession of heads of the Taksal, died in 1969 at Mehta in Amritsar district. Kartar Singh succeeded him who was more aggressive in his sermons and turned his religion to political space thus competing with various other such god men for influence. The example of Kartar Singh Bhindranwale substantiates the general view that political orientation of a religious leader helps in creating an ideology emphasising more and more Puritanism in the religious practice, even such an emphasis is political functional.[78]

Kartar Singh Bhindranwale shifted his headquarters from village Bhinder Kalan to Mehta where his predecessor had died. The reasons for shifting had something to do with the internal conflicts of the Taksal after death of Baba Gurbachan Singh. In spite of his credentials, the Akali leaders Chanan Singh, Fateh Singh, Justice Gurnam Singh and Gurcharn Singh Tohra conspired to make his rival Mohan Singh the Taksal head.[79] Unlike the earlier heads of the Taksal, he maintained the suffix 'Bhindranwala'. Immediately, after becoming the self-styled chief of the Taksal, Kartar Singh carried on his activities quite aggressively and in the process came into conflict with the Nirankaris. According to Kartar Singh, Nirankari sect was bogus, as it believed in living guru. He also became critical to the gurus of the Nirankari sect for imitating the Sikh gurus.

In fact, Damdami Taksal had been fighting a war of sorts with the Nirankaris since the time of Gurbachan Singh. Contrary to the general belief that it was the Taksal heads who launched the offensive, provocation had actually come from Niranjan Singh, a top ranking Nirankari. Niranjan Singh had tried to set-up Nirankaris Bhawan at various places in Punjab which at times put the Taksal in direct confrontation with the Nirankaris. For instance, he deliberately invited the Nirankari head Baba Gurbachan Singh to set up Nirankari Bhawan at the historic city of Hargobindpur, where the Kar Sewa was being carried out by then Taksal head Gurbachan Singh. This led to minor clashes.

At this juncture, political scenario began to change rapidly. Indira Gandhi had imposed emergency and was ruling over the country as an authoritarian leader. During this period the Akali Dal was among the opposition parties, which continued to protest against Indira Gandhi by sending jathas (Group of Volunteers) to court arrest. Opposition parties were in disarray as most of the leaders had either gone underground or were arrested.[80] The CPI was supporting the emergency as it had alliance with the Congress earlier elections. The dynamism of Kartar Singh could be noticed during the period of emergency. With him thus began the entry of seminary chiefs into political space. When most of the Akali leaders were in prison, Kartar Singh organised 37 processions. Kartar Singh Bhindranwale was a man of learning and during his whirlwind tour of Punjab he used to baptise a large number of Sikhs. It was during such journey that he met with an accident in August 1977 and died. With him ended an era of the Damdami Taksal during which Sikh orthodoxy was aggressively interpreted, preached and spread through the Khalsa principles. His successor Jarnail Singh exploited that space effectively and with the tactical ability of a politician created an unforeseen political instability in Punjab.

Most of the scholars, who have written on the life of Bhindrawale, have missed an important dimension of the social life of Punjab of which he was a typical instance. In the Sikh religious traditions, the respect of and veneration for the saints is a highly prescribed behaviour. There is a large number of maths or deras orthodoxy with a few exceptions. These saints are now collectively known as Sant Samaj. Damdami Taksal falls in this category of religious practice within the Sikhism. The deras also have an important function for the society as they provide employment to a large number of persons. For example, the Damdami Taksal trains young people in recitation of the Gurbani and after completing their training they become pathis and granthis. This tradition has been going on since its inception. Many families such as Joginder Singh gave one of their sons to dera largely due to hard conditions of their life. Obviously, Jarnail Singh was one such case. It seems now clear that the devotion and intensity of Jarnail Singh might have made him a special follower and loved one of Kartar Singh. The arrival of Jarnail Singh on the scene as the fourteenth head of the Taksal changed the direction of events, as he intensified his criticism of the Nirankaris that subsequently led to clash between the two.[81] It can be observed from the recent Samaj and Dera conflicts that the Bhindranwale taking on the Nirankaris was not a new thing in the religious domains of Sikhs and also it could not be held as the only reason for rise of Bhindranwale and Sikh fundamentalism. After all, as discussed in the preceding chapter, Akali leadership had won over the Mahants during the Gurdwaras reforms movement peacefully despite the use of violence by the Mahants. There were other reasons which were used to exploit the religious sentiments of the Sikhs in the designed politics of Punjab in a charged atmosphere under which Lala Jagat Narain got killed becoming among the first victims of the carnage that followed involving both Sikhs as well as Hindus. Subsequent burning of the office of the indicted Punjabi newspaper and the Sikh shops in Jalandhar by the mob has been more linked to the old ideological contradiction of the Arya Samaj and the Singh Sabha and its had greater implications over the Hindu-Sikh relations in the state at that moment rather than the Nirankaris and Sikh clash. The political parties and the electoral politics also had its share to contribute to the rise of Hindu and Sikh fundamentalism.

The immediate action of the government to arrest Bhindranwale on the alleged charges of being involved in the murder of Lala Jagat Narain and the escape of Bhindranwale from the Chando Kalan Gurdwaras in Haryana had a lot to do with the Akali and Congress politics. As the contingent of Punjab police that was dispatched for the arrest surprisingly took seven days to cover the distance of 300 kilometres.[82] By the time they arrived at the gurudwara, Bhindranwale had already left. The frustrated police men resorted to unprovoked violence. The villagers testified that the police set the vans on fire and burnt Bhindranwale sermons.

Bhindranwale was outraged, not because of his alleged complicity in the murder of Lala Jagat Narain, but because of the burning of his sermons by the government officials. He alleged that these actions amounted insult to the Sikh Guru.[83] Later on, he offered himself for arrest but as it is mentioned above his arrest added to his popularity and sympathy among the Sikhs. It was at this point that due to their own political calculation, the Akalis urged the Bhindranwale to join their Dharm Yudh Morchas as he had disassociated himself from the Congress.

It was for the first time when Akalis and Bhindranwale led-extremist forces joined hands to defeat the Congress and centre. The agitation proceeded unabated and in the period of 2.5 months 30,000 Sikhs had been arrested.[84] Many women and ex-Army men also joined the agitation. As the number of arrested ones surged, it became very difficult for the authorities to accommodate the protesting volunteers in the existing jails. In a conciliatory gesture the central government released all Akali volunteers and resumed negotiations with the Akali Dal. A settlement was believed to have been virtually reached. But the Chief Minister of Haryana played a critical role in sabotaging the talks and persuaded the central leadership to desist from implementing the promises made to the Akalis. Indira Gandhi failed to find a settlement and this was to have grave consequences.[85] It weakened the position of the moderate Akali leadership within the party. Akalis wanted to use Bhindranwale while negotiating with the centre and for collecting the huge gathering for their Morcha to negotiate with centre on the issue of language, water and identity. Entry of Bhindranwale and extremists like Jagdev Singh Talwandi, Gurcharn Singh Tohra, proved volatile for themselves. The differences between Bhindranwale and Akali leadership headed by Longowal began to surface soon. Bhindranwale was sceptical of the Akali leadership's capacity to negotiate with central government. He also mistrusted the intention of the Congress government to resolve the grievances of the Sikhs. These differences accentuated the division between the Akali Dal, headed by Longowal and the hardliners, who were supported by the young Sikhs through the All India Sikh Students' Federation (AISSF), which was under the patronage of Bhindranwale. While the Akali Dal was vulnerable to the carrot and stick policies of Indira Gandhi, Bhindranwale was adamant that nothing short of the Anandpur Sahib Resolution would be acceptable.[86] The militant groups under the direct orders of Bhindranwale were going ahead with unabated and indiscriminate killing in all parts of Punjab. His '*Hate Nirankaris*' campaign was replaced by '*Hate Hindu*' campaign. Many militants became active in annihilating Nirankaris, Hindus, dissenting Sikhs and even policemen. In April 1983, the extremist violence took a new dimension when D.I.G. Atwal was gunned down at the gate of the Golden temple where he had gone to pay his respect.

Akali expectation to surge ahead in terms of support base under which they had joined hands with him resulted only in the marginalization of Akalis. It was with connivance of Akalis that Bhindranwale shifted from his headquarter of Damdami Taksal of Mehta to Guru Nanak Nivas and later on to Akal Takht, buildings within the precincts of the Darbar Sahib. Longowal apparently wanted to use Bhindranwale as he thought that Bhindranwale will work as fear factor to centre and they will be able to get more gain also baffled.

RISE OF BHINDRANWALE

The entry of the Bhindranwale into the Guru Nanak Niwas and later on to Akal Takht had its own implications for the Sikh identity and the Sikh politics. The entry of Bhindranwale to the Guru Nanak Nivas as it provided him with the opportunity to have a discourse on the Sikh religion and contemporary politics at the central religious places of the Sikhs. Simultaneously the sacred complex of Golden Temple provided a strong cover to the violent acts of the Bhindranwale-led militants. The moderate Akalis became more vulnerable as Bhindranwale underlined the course of arms as a part of Sikh tradition. The Akalis found difficult to challenge Bhindranwale, when he eulogized and advocated the use of violence for the Sikh cause. More so, he was viewed by the Sikhs as a daring religious leader who was not guided by any lust for power and money and who was ready to take on 'Delhi Durbar'. The old strategies of the Dal to defeat the Congress by calling for the unity of Sikhs by the making the slogan of *Panth khatre vich hai* (The Panth is in danger), *Sikha nal Dhaka ho riha hai* (there is discrimination against the Sikhs) became totally irrelevant against the more sharpened and fundamentalist approach of Bhindranwale.[87] While utilizing the space which provided by the Akalis for the short span during *Dharm Yudh Morchas*, Bhindranwale let no stone unturned in his fight against the Centre and Hindus. He not only redefined the Hindu-Sikh relations in the contemporary context, but also reinterpreted the Sikh identity and Hindu and Sikh relations in the historical trajectories from the

Golden Temple Complex thereby trying his best to create cleavage between the two communities.

In his speeches to the Sikh gatherings in Guru Nanak Nivas and later on inside the Golden Temple complex, Bhindranwale emphasised over the masculine and martial culture of the Sikhs. While interpreting the Sikh relations with the Hindus and creating the other he presented the scattered incidents of treachery of Hindus with the Guru (the story of Gangu Brahmin, etc.). The 'other' (Hindus) was presented as a 'coward and ungrateful', who 'does not deserve any respect' as he 'doesn't believe in hard work and survive on the fruit of the labour of the *other.*[88]

MILITANT DISCOURSE ON THE CONSTRUCTION OF SIKH IDENTITY

Who are Sikhs and what does make Sikhs different from Hindus and Muslims? This was one of the favourite themes in the lectures of Bhindranwale. Bhindranwale in his first speech that he delivered to the Sikhs at Golden Temple, his main focus was over the Sikh identity in the form of *Sabat Soorat, that is, unshorn hair.* In his own words: "I wish to appeal to my young brothers. Whatever I am going to say shall have effects only if you accept what I am requesting. I wish to have promise from you and those who promise may raise their hands. Those brothers who have cut their hair and beard and have moved away from Sikhism, should swear that they would not do this in future and shall keep *sabat soorat* (unshorn hair and beard) ... If you are not prepared to keep unshorn hair and beard how you will get Khalsa Raj....Preaching is in the interest of religion and to save the suppressed generations from hell. I have preached to make Sikhs free from the Hindu imperialism. When we shall pray, we read following lines: *"Raj Karega Khalsa* (Khalsa shall rule)".[89]

The most striking feature of his speeches was his recognition of singular tradition in the Sikh tradition. Singh Sabha movement constructed this tradition in colonial Punjab. Singh Sabha movement had constructed this tradition as discussed in the preceding chapter. The word 'Khalsa' has been given a distinct meaning so as to signify every baptized (amritdhari) Sikh. In the popular perception, 'Khalsa' is also understood as a derivation of '*Khalis*' meaning pure. However, is difficult to ascertain whether the two are connected and to have some origin. In Sikhism, God has been signified as the true emperor (Sacha Patshah). In the light of this, it may be argued that Khalsa meant the people of God. Khalsa as the people of God makes more sense than all other meaning. The meaning, formation and the importance as the passing of the word 'Khalsa' through the many trajectories of history is already mentioned. Bhindranwala, however, simply emphasised the already established notion of the Khalsa.[90]

Bhindranwale's view that a Sikh was expected to be of particular appearance fell in line with the prevailing view within the community undergoing social and cultural churning as a result of the entry of what has been called 'chicken whiskey culture' due to the new found wealth that came with the green revolution. Bhindranwale insistence on following the true Sikh traditions and Maryada found ready acceptance among a large segment of the Sikhs.

Besides emphasising over the distinct identity of a Sikh, Bhindranwale in his speeches widely circulated in the form of tapes as well as newspapers (mainly in Punjabi) reports, also aimed at making a case for what he would like to present as evidences as the wrongs done against the Sikh community. In his hate speeches, majority Hindu community was projected as the ruling community. Ill-treatment meted out to the Sikhs by the Hindus rulers from the historical past would be narrated by him to create a wedge between the two communities. It would be worthwhile to quote from his first of the fiery speeches, which he delivered in February 1983.[91] "How are we slaves? I want to make the educated students aware of this fact. In the population of 66 crores when eighty year old Lala Jagat Narain is killed, its inquiry is completed within three days. But if one and half dozens of young Sikhs like you are killed, then its inquiry is not even completed in a year." [92]

Bhindranwale would argue that whenever the Sikhs demanded something, they had to struggle and had to make sacrifices. In comparison to the Sikhs, the Hindus had never had to sacrifice for any demand they raised, the argument would go. The sense of being historically wronged related to the question of Punjabi Suba for which the Akali Dal launched an agitation.

Linguistic reorganisation of states in India took place with the sole exception of Punjab. In Punjab, as pointed earlier, the politics of language entailed communal overtones. The objective of the Akali Dal was to create a Sikh majority state than the Punjabi-speaking state. The overlapping of the Punjabi language with the Sikh on the one hand and Hindi with the Hindus on the other was one of the consequences of electoral politics. The struggle for getting Punjabi Suba turned into a long drawn fight for the demand that ultimately succeeded after the Indo-Pak war in which, as is alleged by many, the Sikhs showed patriotism for which they were rewarded.

Interestingly, the 'other community' (read Hindu community) and its history had no relevance for Bhindranwale. He used derogatory remarks (What is the sign of Hindu? The Hindu in fact is an Arabic word, which means *thief*).[93]

With the above kind of hate speeches delivered by Bhindranwale and his disciples, the militants succeeded in getting a section of the community influenced by the argument that there was a conscious attempt to marginalise the Sikhs in the country and that it was a government of the majority community. Operation Blue Star and Operation Wood Rose strengthened such a perception, even when Bhindranwale was dead.

THE GOVERNMENT ATTITUDE TOWARDS PUNJAB PROBLEM

More than the hate speeches of Bhindranwale, the growing Sikh community's alienation arose from the perception of being wronged by the centre. The central government's inability in responding to the Akali Dal-led democratic protests did worsen the situation. It also weakened the Akali Dal position also as it was facing serious challenge from Bhindranwala in Punjab. The Akali's threat to disrupt the Asian Games in 1982, if their demands were not fulfilled was dealt severely causing great sense of hurt to the community's pride. The routes of Delhi were not only blocked for the Akalis, all the Sikhs who were going to Delhi from Punjab were taken as the Akalis. The chief Minister of Haryana Bhajan Lal issued blanket orders prohibiting the travelling of Sikh to Delhi through Haryana. No distinctions were made between the Sikhs and Akalis as if all the Sikhs were Akalis and also were going to their own country's capital for creating trouble. Haryana police maltreated every Sikh without inhibition, including the senior Congress leaders like Swarn Singh and Amarjit Kaur of Congress (I) who were harassed by the police despite their disclosing identities. The Haryana police was also accused of insulting a number of Sikhs including the military officers, some of them retired Major Generals. Avenging insult of the Sikhs by the Haryana police became emotional issue for some ex-army officers and they became the followers of Bhindranwale. A retired Major General was one of them.[94]

Ban on the militant organisation like Dal Khalsa also could not help the deteriorating law and order situation in 1982. The killing of the Deputy Inspector General (DIG) Atwal and resultant action of the state forces further alienated the Sikhs. The police raided the houses of suspects, allegedly beat up the inmates and even killed few of them in the "fake" encounters. Some of the Akali workers were also allegedly killed in the fake encounters. Both the Longowal and Talwandi groups of the Akali Dal brought out the lists of *Amritdhari* (baptised) Sikhs who were killed in the police lockup and fake encounters. The powers of the police forces were further enhanced by the Punjab Disturbed Areas Ordinance and Chandigarh Disturbed Areas ordinance by Congress government of Punjab headed by Darbara Singh.[95]

Simultaneously, the Akalis felt under pressure to retain their support base as the emotive appeals of Bhindranwale to the Sikh youth weaned away the traditional Akali supporters. Akalis came under physical threat also as the dead bodies stuffed in gunny bags started appearing in gutters outside the temple regularly.[96] Longowal at this point wanted to use the members of the Akhand Kirtan Jatha (Babbar Khalsa) to remove Bhindranwale from the Guru Nanak Nivas.[97] On the other hand the internal politics of the Akali Dal was moving in such a way that it led to the inevitable disastrous consequences. The entry of the Bhindranwale with the weapons in the Golden Temple could not be possible if they had resisted unanimously. But factional interest of the Tohra Group who was a weak third leader after Longowal and Bhindranwale in Sikh politics helped Bhindranwale as he wanted to become strong by getting the support of one from the two strong leaders of Sikh community.[98] After the killing of DIG Atwal, Longowal was cooperating with Punjab police which wanted to arrest Bhindranwala. At that time Bhindranwale was staying in Guru Nanak Nivas. Tohra began to nudge Bhindranwale to shift to the Akal Takht. Finally, Bhindranwale moved into Akal Takht on 15 December, 1983 after a clash with the members of Babbar Khalsa in Guru Nanak Nivas.[99]

The law and order condition had already deteriorated as all efforts of the Darbara Singh, led Congress government to handle the situation with the help of police forces and extraordinary laws failed. The negotiations became derailed as mainstream politics was getting marginalised. The media reports focused on a series of sensational murders and terrorists attacks, attributed to the Sikh separatism. On the night of 10 March, an abortive attempt was made to murder Ved Pal, Deputy Speaker of Haryana's Legislative Assembly near Ambala in Haryana. Darbara Singh escaped another bid on his life on 10 March when a Sikh gunman opened fire. On 28 March, Harbansh Lal Manchanda, the Chief of Delhi Gurdwara Management Committee was shot dead in Delhi. Some other prominent leaders also became victims to the violence of militants.[100] Punjab was under the sway of violence. On the other hand, the lack of any concrete concession to the Akali demands articulated in the form of Anandpur Sahib Resolutions ruled out any political solution. Worse it emphasised over the use of forces against the political protests of Akali Dal more than the fundamentalists like Bhindranwale and Dal Khalsa. The fact of central government's highhandedness was also proven by the dismissal of the Darbara Singh government by the central government after the killing of some Hindus by the terrorists in Moga in November 1983. The imposition of the President rule in Punjab had the larger implication over the regional and national politics as the dismissed Congress government in the state belonged to the ruling party.

OPERATION BLUE STAR AND NATIONAL SECURITY : SOME UNSOLVED QUESTIONS

Indira Gandhi was keen to consolidate power during her second stint in power after 1980 elections. She gradually allowed the decline in terms of support for her party from the traditional minorities support while she went for the consolidation of the majority Hindu vote using the ethnic violence in Punjab and Kashmir as the pretext. As the party continued to suffer from ideological and institutional decline, it also lost its organisation presence in the rural belt of Punjab. The results of the by-elections in the 12 states of the southern and northern India, held in the third week of May 1984, went against the Congress as the decline set in. It lost on many of the prestigious seats also. The election results had shown that northern India being swept by a wave of Hindu anger over the government inability to suppress the Sikh extremist movement in Punjab. The southern peninsular, on the other hand was under the sway of strong regional parties inimical to the Congress.

The by-election results convinced Indira Gandhi that unless she took a drastic action against the Sikh agitation, largely perceived by the Hindu population as being covertly secessionist and as a sign of Congress regime, she would not be able to win the forthcoming Lok Sabha elections. What followed was planning of a swift military operation, as the top brass of the Army apparently had promised to finish Bhindranwale and his band of followers entrenched in the Golden Temple complex, it was supposed to re-establish her credential as a strong leader, but also would restore her popularity through communal polarization.[101] The centre's action against Bhindranwale, however, was kept secret as the Congress government seemed to be the hand in gloves with Bhindranwale. While speaking on the Punjab issue in Chandigarh on 5 May, 1984, Rajiv Gandhi called Bhindranwale a Saint, who is without any political ambition.[102] On the other hand, the democratic protests of the Akalis were suppressed by central government by declaring Punjab a disturbed area on 24 May. In all thirty rounds of negotiations between the Akalis and the centre failed.[103]

It has been argued that the plan to attack on the Golden Temple was made much earlier. Inder Malhotra quotes General K. Sunderji, who commanded the operation Blue Star, as saying, 'I was told by Defence Minister to prepare for the operation on 15 January, 1984, on the occasion of Army Day.'[104]

OPERATION BLUE STAR

Subramanian Swami, then the leader of Janata Party and a Member of Parliament spent three days from 24 to 26 April, 1984 at Golden Temple complex a few weeks before the Army attack, speaking on the issue of centre Sikh relation with the Sikh leaders including Bhindranwale. He published an article on 13 May 1984 in the *Illustrated Weekly* of India. In his article he advised the government that any attack on the Golden Temple by the Indian forces would be a great folly. He wrote if firing was heavy and the temple or Akal Takht got damaged, India as an idea will be destroyed. In the same article Swami asked why the officers of various paramilitary and intelligence organizations surrounding the temple complex were not arresting the known criminals/terrorists walking in and out from the complex with total impunity. Ironically, the then Deputy Commissioner of Amritsar, Gurudev Singh said that he had categorically informed the highest officials of the Punjab Government that if they wanted to arrest Bhindranwale there would be no major difficulty in organizing it.[105]

On 2 June, 1984 Longowal announced that the Akalis would launch campaign of Civil Disobedience from 3 June, taxes would not be paid; food grains and trains would not be allowed to move out of Punjab. At the same time General Singh was appointed Security Advisor to Punjab Governor. On 2 June, 1984 the Governor summoned the Chief Secretary K.D. Vasudeva, Home Secretary, A.S. Punni, Inspector General P.S. Bhinder and Inspector Genral

Intelligence H.S. Randhawa at Governor House and had a meeting. They were unanimously agreed that Army should not be used to attack the Golden Temple.[106]

The Governor also agreed in the presence of all the officers. He also got through P.C. Alexander in charge of Prime Minister's Office on the hot line and informed him that he apprehended that the army might be sent into Golden Temple. They were against such steps being taken and that he himself endorsed their view. P.C. Alexander rejected the advice of the Governor of Punjab and instructed him to get a letter from Home Secretary of the state requesting army intervention in the State.[107]

On June 3, 1984, District Magistrate of Amritsar had not signed any formal request for army assistance but the army was already in Amritsar. Out of 13 districts of Punjab, not a single Deputy Commissioner had indicated that the law and order situation was not threatened, nor had they asked for army support. On 2nd June curfew was declared throughout the Punjab and telecommunication lined were cut. Army issued a "shoot at sight" order for curfew violation but after Chief Secretary Vasudeva and Punjab Police I.G. (Intelligence) H.S. Randhawa protested against the illegality of the orders, the orders were withdrawn.[108]

Without knowing the internal situation and bothering about the involvement of the civilian, Indian Army chose to surround the Golden Temple complex on 3 June. Then a large number of Sikhs pilgrims were gathered inside the Golden Temple to celebrate the martyrdom day of Guru Arjan Dev. Simultaneously, Akalis who had always used the religious occasions for pushing their political agenda also called the Akali volunteers on the very day to launch a morcha against the government.[109] Giving a detailed account of the happening in the Golden temple complex, Mark Tully wrote that the army started shelling the Golden without warning from the early hours of 4 June. The onslaught reached its peak two days after on the night of 5 June around 7 p.m. According to Giani Puran Singh, a priest at Golden temple who witnessed the whole operation, it was around 10 p.m. on 5 June, when tanks started entering the complex. The pilgrims trapped inside the complex could not understand that the tanks were coming. The heavy lights of tanks were reportedly taken by them as the lights of the vehicle of Fire brigade, which might be coming to take water from the holy pond to extinguish the fire in city. But they were shocked when these vehicles came down the *Parikarma* and started firing. From both sides of the complex the tanks started closing in from clock tower to *Brahm Butta* the tanks set fire to all rooms with desperate people collecting water from the *sarovar* to extinguish the fire. A vigorous battle ensued and Darshani Deori, Clock Tower and Atta Mandi, along with serai were under Army control by 10 am on 6 June. The militants who had been holding the forces fought till either they were killed or their ammunition was exhausted. Tully quotes another priest Giani Mohan Singh's statement that there were 13 tanks in the Parikarma.[110]

Another account of the events came from the teenaged daughter an SGPC employee, who luckily escaped during the turmoil. She is quoted by the team commissioned by Justice V.M. Tarkunde. "Then the tanks entered, we thought that ambulances had come to attend the dead and injured but it was turned opposite. The tanks went pass us. From the tanks came the announcement 'please come out, God's blessing are with you.' We will take you home absolutely safe and sound. There were some who were frantic for some water and they came out in open. In morning, I saw the dead bodies of them lying on the parikarma".

Brahm Chelly, the only foreign newspaper correspondent who managed to remain in Amritsar after the government had ordered all foreign correspondents out, reported the statements of the doctors and Police officials that many of the Sikhs killed in attack had been shot at the point-blank range with their hands tied behind the back.[111]

The death toll of the civilian and the army was not released by the government even after the establishment of the peace and democratic government till the date twenty-six years has been passed. The figures which have been quoted by the academics and journalists are varying in the same manner the army encounter with the civilians in general in the whole Punjab and inside the Golden temple during the "Operation Blue Star" is also varying. How many people lost their lives in the operation? That depends on whose figures one accepts. The government's 'White Papers' issued in July 1984, put the soldiers causalities 83 and civilian 492, whereas the injured included 86 civilians and 249 army men. 1,283 men and 309 women were arrested. In September of the same year, addressing the National Student Union of India session in Nagpur, Prime Minister Rajiv Gandhi mentioned that 700 soldiers had lost their lives in Operation Blue Star. Khuswant Singh and Kuldip Nayar quoted in their book *The Tragedy of Beloved Punjab* that the army got the more gallantry awards for Operation Blue Star than for combined awards for India's four wars of 1948, 1962, 1965 and 1971.[112]

Without confusing with the figures of how many were actually killed and detained, we should also look that how the persons were identified to be detained. More important is that how the Sikhs in general reacted to the Army operation of their religious places as the raids were conducted in other 40 historic Gurdwaras across the Punjab, an armed resistance to the Indian Army by the Sikhs was also reported.[113] As Inderjit Singh Jaijee wrote in his book *Politics of Genocide* that persons taken in the custody by the army were categorized into four groups: Elderly people, women, young and the dangerous groups. People wearing blue and saffron turbans, ceremonial daggers, flowing beard or generally unhappy looks identified as dangerous group. No woman constables were assigned to look after the women prisoners. Soldiers were their captors. There were rumours of large scale molestation and rapes. The looting of shops and shooting of the innocents in open streets near to the Golden Temple complex by the *Jawans* of Bihar Regiment and BSF are reported by the eyewitnesses. Some Journalists who dared to report of the abuse of power by the Army were also detained under the NSA after the brutal torture.[114]

For many days after the army action, the pilgrims taken into custody inside the Golden Temple continued to be held in the army camps and detention centre as prisoners of war. It was much later that on the advice of Punjab officials that the army stopped referring them as the 'prisoners of war' and began to call them terrorists and terrorists' sympathizers. Even the moderate leader like Longowal and Tohra were also arrested and sent to the jails under NSA.[115]

PUNJAB: AFTERMATH OF OPERATION "BLUE STAR"

The Sikh reaction against army operation on sanctorum of Golden Temple was very sharp and immediate across the globe. The army operation against the Bhindranwale was taken as an attack on the Akal Takht unfortunately. The patriot Sikhs of Punjab were for the first time not only became uncooperative to the army of their own country, but they also suspected their mission and became hostile to the army. It was observed during our field study of 10 villages in the most adversely affected districts of Tarn Taran, Amritsar and Gurdaspur that Bhindranwale became the cult figure as he was perceived as one who was fighting against the Indian army to defend the sanctity of the Golden Temple in the rural Punjab.

Special prayers for the victory of the Sikh fighter were organised in Gurdwaras of some villages. The leading Sikh men also took an oath to fight against the Indian Army to free the Golden temple. A large number of local Sikhs were also reported to march against the army with swords, dagger, axe, etc. but were forced to surrender or returned back from the outskirts of Amritsar when they saw the heavy deployments of the Army. The attack on the Golden temple was taken in the historic sense by the masses reminding them of the old attack of Ahemd Shah Abdali and the Dyer action at Jallianwal Bagh in Amritsar. The *Times of India* reported that 550 people were detained by the army for violating the curfew order and seven persons were arrested under National Security Act on 3 June, 1984 only in Ludhiana.[116] The detailed reports on the arrests and reaction of the Sikhs could not come out due to the sanction on the press in Punjab. In an emotional setback, around 1,438 Sikh Soldiers of Ramgarh Sikh Regiment revolted against the alleged Army action on the Golden temple complex. These soldiers with full of arms of their battalion started marching towards Punjab from Ramgarh in Bihar; however, they were apprehended after the minor resistance under which 23 soldiers were got killed and 46 were reported to be missing in their way to Punjab.[117] The deserter of the Sikh Regiments in Ramgarh Cantt. earned the title of *Dharmi Faujis* and some of them who either lost their service or got killed during their resistance to Indian Army were also rewarded with the services and social security to the families by the SGPC. Brigadiar Sukhjit Singh (retd.) is on the record saying that in the countryside the late Bhindranwale emerged as a martyr to the Sikh cause.[118] Delhi Akali Dal (Longowal) unit organised a march from Delhi to the Golden Temple in Amritsar. The Sikhs, led by Jathedar Natha Singh, were wearing black turbans and marigold garlands and raised pro-Khalistan slogans. The march was started from Gurdwara Bangla Sahib. Police took into the custody a group of 13 activists when they set out on a march. They were later awarded 15 days simple imprisonment.[119] There were other reports of the arrest in the other towns of Punjab and the other states of India.

Ostensibly to keep the Sikhs in good faith, Sikh officers were not only involved in the Operation but they were also given major charges. Lt. Gen. R.S. Dayal, Chief of the Army Staff of Western Command was appointed the Security Advisor to the Punjab Governor and also given the overall charge of the Operation Blue Star. Major General Kuldip Singh Brar was appointed as the Divisional Commander-in-Charge of the Army operations against the alleged hideouts of the terrorists in the sanctuaries of different

Gurdwaras across Punjab[120] and Lt. Gen. Bhupinder Singh was given the task to check the rebellion of the Ramgarh Sikh Regiment. Lt General J.S. Arora also explained the necessity of the Operation Blue Star to the anguished Sikhs to flush out the terrorists on 14 June, 1984, while speaking at a press conference convened by the All India Sikh Council. He said there was no other way to flush out terrorists in view of the conditions which prevailed in the Golden Temple complex recently. General also condemned the government for not taking timely action. He disclosed that terrorists had begun preparing for armed conflict since February last. He had condemned Bhindranwale action and misuse of Gurdwara for political purpose. Arora also questioned the Congress for making Bhindranwale powerful due for political interests. He also informed that Longowal and Gurcharn Singh Tohra were taken into custody after the commando action in Guru Ram Das Sarai and SGPC complex. Similar action could have been tried to force others to surrender, he said. Arora also tried to convince the fellow Sikhs by telling them that the army action though commendable was against Indian nationals and not against the enemy. Therefore, efforts were needed to be made to give healing touch to the Sikh community which felt hurt. Repeated press statements by army officers and political leaders did not cut much ice with the Sikhs as their sentiments were badly hurt by Operation Blue Star and a vacuum was created in the Sikh politics as the prominent leaders of Akali Dal and also anybody who dared to protest against the attack was thrown into jails.[121]

The Sikh community's historic sense of sacrifice received a boost as prominent Sikh personalities including the Sikh politicians, bureaucratic elite came out in open condemning the Operation Blue Star. Amrinder Singh and Devinder Singh Garcha quit the Lok Sabha membership and Congress (I). The former Defence Minister Sardar Swarn Singh expressed his unhappiness over the Army action. General Brar described the Deputy Commissioner of Amritsar as an ardent supporter of Bhindranwale. On June 2, after learning of the plan to use Army, Gurdev Singh telephoned the Governor and told him that conscience did not allow him to be part of it. The Governor immediately relieved Gurdev Singh of his post for three months and told him to go on long leave. Some other Sikh officers also reported to leave the prestigious positions as reported by the media. [122]

Sikh leaders from the seven countries, USA, Germany, Canada, Malaysia, Hong Kong, Britain and Mexico met at New Mexico to plan strategies in response to Indian army's raid on the Golden

Temple complex at Amritsar. The chief leader of Sikhs in the Western hemisphere, Yogi Bhajan Singh, called for unity in order to win more religious and political autonomy for Sikhs in Punjab.[123]

A large number of Sikhs in different parts of the country, particularly in Chandigarh, Punjab, Jammu and Kashmir, including Delhi, Bombay, Ahmedabad, observed the *Ardas Divas* (prayer day) for those killed in Army action in Punjab, particularly in Amritsar, in response to call given by Akali Dal leaders. Parkash Singh Badal was arrested under NSA a few hours after the announcement. In retaliation, at some places in Punjab and Haryana and in the Union territory of Chandigarh, people observed the "mourning day" in response to a call given by the Arya Pratinidhi Sabha to pay homage to the jawans killed in army action.[124]

Ved Marwah, then a senior police officer on the Prime Minister's select committee for monitoring Punjab affairs avers in his book, *Uncivil wars* that the majority of the Sikhs after the Operation Blue Star supported separatism. He, and other members of the select committed, saw the Punjab problem as essentially a Sikh problem. In his words: "The entire Sikh community considered the assault on the Sikh religion. A major section among the Sikhs sought to break all links with the Indian Union. What Bhindranwale had so far not demanded openly now becomes the main demand of the Sikhs".[125]

After the occupation of the Golden Temple complex and the other historic Gurdwaras, a massive combing operation condemned Operation Wood Rose was launched to search for the remaining militants under the command of Lt. R.S. General Dayal. It is argued by the researchers, academicians and journalists that the Operation Wood Rose contributed to Sikh alienation as they felt as an outsiders in their own country. The detainees of the Operation Blue Star and Operation Woodrose got the worst of their life from the Army of their own country. The innocent detainees of the Operation Blue Star included some children and women along with the youths who were detained by the Army due to their suspicious look, because they were baptised Sikhs or were keeping long beard.[126] Even the ex-army officers who criticised the Army action were not spared. The charges of sedition were filed by the Army against its own officers for criticizing army action and the accused declared absconders even when they were present in the city. Maj. Gen. Narinder Singh (retd.), Brig. Joginder Singh Dhillon (retd.) and Navrang Singh were charged with sedition. In the FIR registered against all of them they were said to have made provocative public speeches. The family members of the banned AISSF members along with the members suffered at the hands of the police.[127] Army was not ready to listen to even the University faculty and students who criticised the army highhandedness. Dean Students Welfare along with the two other faculty members were reported to be harassed by the Army without any fault of them in the Punjabi University, Patiala. The other case which was highly publicized in Punjab was the interrogation of a Young Sikh, who was disabled since childhood. He was picked up by the army during the search operation. His story is that his interrogator, an army ófficer, repeatedly abused Jarnail Singh Bhindranwale and Guru Gobind Singh. The young man told the officer that while he could abuse Bhindranwale as a fellow Indian why did he abuse the Guru? The major according to the villagers retorted "who told you that you are also an Indian? The young man's reply was that he had always thought that he was an Indian but now he was beginning to wonder if this is his country".[128]

The terrorists gunned down Haridial Singh, acting president of the Jalandhar District Congress (I) Committee Rural and hacked to death Mahant Chanchal Das of Dera Thukrala on the outskirts of village Athula. Meanwhile security forces arrested about 100 persons while attempting to cross Goindwal Sahib on Beas River on way to Amritsar. About 34 persons at different places in Punjab were also apprehended. Dr. Bhagel Singh, former Vice-Chancellor of Punjabi University, Patiala was also arrested. Meanwhile Takht Damdama Sahib in Talwandi Sabo in Bathinda district was opened to the public. However, tight security arrangement was made in view of the Akali call to observe June 17, as *Ardas Diva*" in memory of those killed in Army action in Amritsar[129]. The security forces apprehended 71 more terrorists including suspects and also recovered more arms and ammunition from the Golden temple complex, Amrik Singh Babbar, general secretary of Guru Singh Sabha Chandigarh was detained under National Security Agency (NSA).[130]

The Bombay police arrested 30 local Sikhs on charges of sedition. It is alleged that all of them had behaved frantically while taking part in a boisterous attempt made to take out procession from Darbar Singh Sabha to Raj Bhawan on June 13 last to record protest against the Operation Blue Star. In Amritsar the five Sikh priests gave a call to the Sikhs all over the world to observe July 15 as *Saheedi divas* (Martyrdom day) in the memory of those killed in the army action in Amritsar. [131] Maj. Gen. R.P. Gaur, spokesman of the Western Command disclosed that 4,220 persons were rounded up by the security forces, out of these 1,858 screened and 85, all employee of the SGPC, had been released. He gave the figures of army causalities as 92 killed and 287 injured including four Officers and four JCOs killed and 15 Officers and 18 JCOs injured. Mr. P.S. Bhinder, Inspector General of police also gave details of screening operation of those rounded up. Meanwhile night curfew was lifted in all towns of Ropar district and Ludhiana District and was also relaxed in Patiala city.[132] Terrorists' set fire to a place of worship in Mahalkalan village in Sangrur district even as security forces apprehended 156 extremists and seize a large quantity of arms and ammunition in Chandigarh and Punjab.[133]

In Uttar Pradesh a joint court of inquiry was set-up to screen out civilian who were apprehended along with the army deserters. The joint operations of the army and state police to apprehend army jawans who had run away from Sikh Regiment Centre at Ramgarh (Bihar) and had crossed over to Uttar Pradesh on their way to Punjab was discontinued. However, the police continued with the search in six districts of the state.[134]

The security forces in Punjab, during the cordon and search operations, apprehend 30 persons and militants killed a shopkeeper in Jalandhar district and robbed a person of Rs. 50,000 near Ferozepur cantonment[135] In Jalandhar one suspected militant, Malkiat Singh, was detained under NSA and the Haryana Police detained Jagjit Singh Fauji, an activist of the Akali Dal, at Shahbad Markanda in Kurkshetra for allegedly preaching communalism.[136] Security forces shot dead extremists in encounter near Tarn Taran in Amritsar district. Two persons were apprehended for setting on fire a shrine at Malhon village of Sangrur district. In Ludhiana a large number of persons were arrested on charge of indulging in anti-national activities. They had hoisted Khalistan flags at their house tops. A priest, Shri Ram was murdered with sharp edge weapon at Gardhiwal village in Hoshiarpur district.[137] Krishan Gupta, General Secretary of the Ludhiana District Bharatiya Janata Party, was arrested as a precautionary measure. He was the first BJP leader arrested since the Army action.[138]

Baba Nihal Singh Harianwelawale, a prominent Nihang Sect. Chief was arrested along with unspecified number of his associates and a large quantity of arms and ammunition is recovered by the security forces in Punjab. The securities forces arrested the Nihang Chief after a tip-off from a suspected terrorist and cordoned off his headquarter.[139]

Punjab appeared to be 'normal' and the authorities lifted ban on the movement of vehicular traffic which was imposed on 3 June when the army was called in to flush out terrorists. The ban continued in Amritsar and Gurdaspur district. The ban on motorcycle and pillion riding by males was not lifted.[140] The Gurdwaras except the Golden Temple and gurdwaras at Muktsar were opened to the devotees. Meanwhile, six workers of *Bharatiya Kisan Union,* including its block president, Gurcharn Singh Rafaela were rounded up in Samana on the charges of apprehension of breach of peace.[141]

During our field survey some old students activists of the Students Federation of India (SFI) revealed that the police arrested all the members of the Students Union either they were of the AISSF or SFI.[142] No distinction was made between the political commitments of the members of the Students Union whether they believed in militancy or not. Some of the activists of the SFI were also implicated into wrong cases and were sent to jails, after their illegal detentions for a month or so. An activist of AISSF Sukhwinder Singh Sangha, who later on became the Chief of Bhindranwale Tiger Force (BTF) told one of the inmates in jail (who was interviewed by me in village Tharu, Punjab) that he, was in jail without any fault, but if he was to come to jail again then there would be strong reason for it. It is believed that he joined the militant's outfits after his release from jail. The government of India's White Paper claimed that operation Blue Star and Wood Rose resulted in the apprehension of 4,712 suspects.[143] The blatant injustice of persecuting family members (even minors, women and old people) of missing persons including illegal detention, torture, humiliation alienated the people. It should be noted that according to the interviews and interaction with the villagers, especially in the border villages of Amritsar and Gurdaspur districts many young men absconded because of the occurrences of encounter killings in the districts of Amritsar and Gurdaspur. There was fear all around and trust in the state institutions broke down.

PUNJAB CRISIS AND THE NATIONAL POLITICS

The communal polarization on the issue and the political calculations to get the benefits from the Operation Blue Star both by the Akalis Dal, Congress and other political parties started with very dawn of the Army control over the Golden temple complex. The issuing of the statements by the leaders of the various political parties, Chief Ministers of the various states for and against the Blue

Star dominated the press and politics at the moment. Some of the Sikh political leaders while supporting the decision of Indira Gandhi blamed the Akalis for encouraging fundamentalism and allowing Bhindranwale to enter in the Golden temple complex. While addressing the media on the issue of Operation Blue Star, L.K. Advani, MP and General Secretary of the BJP admitted that the military action was "unavoidable and imperative". He, however, did not justify the government policy which had allowed the situation to slide to the position where such action was necessitated. He accused the centre of pursuing a policy of "deliberate drift" both in respect of action against terrorists as well as finding political solution to the river water and territorial problem of Punjab. The action, he said brought the nation on the brink of a disaster. He did not agree with the Government claim that arms accumulation was due to intelligence failure. It was a case of collusion between a section of police and administrators, [144] Shankar Dayal Sharma and Darbara Singh, both senior Congress (I) leaders, refuted BJP general sectary L.K Advani's statement that Indira Gandhi's remarks in the recent interview with BBC had established the Congress (I) party's link with Bhindranwale. They accused Advani trying to twist the Prime Minister's statement by quoting it out of context. She had, in fact categorically denied any type of support to or links between the Congress and Bhindranwale.[145]

Indira Gandhi, while addressing a delegation of the Citizens' Welfare Organisation, said that it would have been catastrophic if the government had not taken action to flush out terrorists from places of worship in Amritsar and elsewhere in Punjab. She observed that the government was left with no alternative. While appealing for communal harmony and maintaining unity and integrity of the country, Mrs. Gandhi disclosed that the government was aware that some arms had been smuggled from Pakistan through the border.[146] Mrs. Gandhi told that security forces could be withdrawn from the Golden Temple complex only after ensuring that all accumulated weapons from the complex were removed.[147]

The Central Committee of the Communist Party of India (Marxist) (CPM) while reviewing the Punjab situation noted that the situation "continued to be extremely grave" and called on "all democratic and patriotic forces to stand for the unity of the country." Criticising the government the party held that the developments in Punjab were avoidable and lamented that the government did not heed to the opposition parties' proposals which at one time was accepted by the Akalis. It called upon the government to withdraw the armed forces from the Golden Temple complex immediately. It also urged to accept the democratic demands of the Punjabis immediately. While issuing the party resolution Harkrishan Singh Surjeet criticised the government for humiliating the Sikhs.[148]

Chief Minister Farooq Abdullah, while addressing function at Srinagar, refuted the charge that arms were sent to Punjab extremists through Jammu and Kashmir. He described the charge as far from the truth. In fact he had been pleading for an amicable and negotiated solution to the Punjab tangle, he told. He knew that the aggravation of the Punjab problem would adversely affect the state's economy, he said.[149]

Pranab Mukherjee, Union Finance Minister talking to reporters at Calcutta on Punjab Situation said that it was difficult to say how long the troops would stay in the Golden Temple complex for mopping up operation of the extremists in Punjab. Stay in the Golden Temple complex was required for recovery of arms and ammunition. While ruling out the possibility of an early resumption of talks the Finance Minister said there was no scope or meaning for holding discussion with the Akalis until complete normalcy was restored. He also criticised the Akali Leadership projecting itself moderate but supporting always each move and action of extremists led by Bhindranwale. Mukherjee disclosed that had not the commandos rescued the Akalis and SGPC leaders from inside the Golden Temple complex they would have met the same fate as that of the first batch which had come out to surrender and subsequently shot dead by the extremists.[150]

Rajiv Gandhi, Congress (I) Secretary, blamed G.S. Tohra and Sant Longowal, presidents of the SGPC and Akali Dal respectively, for allowing the extremists to defame the sanctity of the Golden Temple and converting it into a fort. Referring to the opposition parties' criticism that the Army action in Punjab was uncalled for Rajiv Gandhi said that these parties were changing their stand now keeping in view the elections, but the Congress (I) did not believe in election prospects. It believed in national interest.[151]

The chairman of the Minorities Commission, Justice M.H. Beg, supported the army action in the Golden Temple complex. The action had saved the country from anarchy, disorder, destabilisation and design of international forces to create communal tension in the country. Bhiwandi riots, the issue of graves in Varanasi and the extremists' activities in Punjab pointed to this conspiracy, Justice Beg said. He disclosed that the Minorities Commission had sent its representatives to Punjab to meet various leaders who, however, refused to discuss the issue with them and said they would rather have talks with the government.[152]

While the politics over the building of the demolished structure of the Akal Takht was going on between the Congress Sikhs and the Akalis, the national politics also seemed to be connected too much on the issue as the political parties wanted to use the issue of Sikh fundamentalism and the Operation Blue Star for the gain of votes.[153] Although the prominent leaders of the SGPC and Akali Dal were detained, but the Dal was giving the tough challenge to the Congress and still seemed to holding a big power in Sikh affairs. Declaration of the World Sikh Convention by the Acting Chief of the SGPC to discuss the issue of reconstruction by Baba Kharak Singh, and resulted arrest of workers of Akali Dal and SGPC can be seen in the light.[154]

In the charged atmosphere Indira Gandhi was shot down by her own Sikh guards on 31 October 1984. Her assassination sparked off a widespread orgy of killing, plunder, rapes and arson directed against the Sikhs in Delhi and several other Indian cities. The killings were indiscriminate, unnecessarily cruel and carried out with meticulous planning and forethought, with the Sikh police was disarmed and taken off duty. Thousands lost their lives, honour, property and means of livelihood. Some migration of Sikhs to Punjab also took place. It was commonly believed then and later substantiated in many enquiry reports that the Congress Party and some of its senior leaders in Delhi were actively involved in incitement, instigation and planning carnage. Predictably the government action was tardy, listless, half-hearted and negligent. Few, if any, investigations were pursued with vigour and competence. The discriminatory handling of the anti-Sikh riots was another instance of the inept handling of the Sikh problem and a major step in the ongoing process of alienation of the Sikhs. [155]

Soon after the assassination of Indira Gandhi, Parliament elections were held in December, though the voting in Assam and Punjab was delayed until 1985 due to ongoing conflict. The Congress Party under Rajiv Gandhi leadership won the parliament election, with an unprecedented popular mandate to fight the "Sikh terrorism and secessionism", gaining 401 of 508 seats, the biggest parliament victory ever by any political party since India become Independent. After coming into power, Rajiv Gandhi released important Akali leaders from detention to negotiate with them a peace accord was signed with them, which he signed with Harchand Singh Longowal, the President of Akali Dal then, on 25 July 1985.[156] The Accord delineated eleven points of common consent, making the following main concessions. It promised: (a) to transfer Chandigarh to Punjab by 26 January, 1986; (b) to set-up tribunal presided over by Supreme Court Judge to adjudicate the river water and territorial dispute within the next months: and (c) to refer the Akali resolution for provincial autonomy to a Commission appointed to recommend Changes in the "centre State relationship to bring about the true federal characteristic of our unitary constitution." The Accord also promised a thorough inquiry into Delhi killing of November 1984: to withdraw the Armed Forces Special Powers Act; and to restore the rule of law and human rights in Punjab.

RAJIV-LONGOWAL ACCORD A CHANCE FOR PEACE: MYTH AND REALITY

The Rajiv-Longowal Accord was like a sudden burst of light at the end of dark tunnel. It was viewed as the return of sanity in an era of confrontation. The Anandpur Sahib resolution was no more regarded as secessionist. The focus was on identifying the negotiable demands not on symbolism. The massive turnout in the assembly elections soon after and unprecedented popular support for Akali Dal reflected people's verdict against the role of Congress leadership. "Congress had lost the elections" said Prime Minister Rajiv Gandhi but "country had won battle for unity.[157] In the retrospect, however, it was not more than a political posture for managing a serious conflict. Petty calculations again came into political picture as the central government backed down on the implementation of the terms of Accord.

The three developments immediately after the singing of Accord led to set a back to the peace process. One was the assassination of Longowal, second the release of extremists especially the nephew of Bhindranwale with his band of outfits. That encouraged, in parallel process, the more militant elements belonging to Dam Dami Taksal and AISSF to rally under the leadership of Bhindranwale old father Joginder Singh. After coming to limelight on 3 May, 1985 he announced that all the Akali factions had decided to dissolve themselves and to come together as a single group under his leadership. Longowal told the media that he had authorised Joginder Singh to take necessary steps to bring about a unity among all the Akali groups. Unfortunately the peace process was also followed by violence at large, series of bomb explosions, which started in Delhi and Haryana, on 10 May, 1985, left scores of innocent people dead.

In the wake of bomb blasts, Longowal announced his decision to quit the Presidency of the Akali Dal with the announcement that "he had been seeking a peaceful solution to the Punjab crisis but others had conspired to foment violence and undermine negotiation." Before resigning his position, Longowal said that he had been challenged last week by Joginder Singh, the father of Bhindranwale. The government quickly arrested 1,500 Sikhs. Soon the Longowal was shot dead by the extremists.[158]

Longowal was succeeded by Surjit Singh Barnala, a former Union Agriculture Minister. Barnala's success in transforming the 'Political Solution' into an enduring settlement depended on two factors: his ability to politically marginalise the militant Sikhs and their allies within the Sikh political system, the institutions and structure around which Sikh politics are organised.[159] To deliver effectively on the Rajiv-Longowal Accord, initially Barnala had a promising start. In September 1985 elections to the Punjab Legislative Assembly, Akali Dal (Longowal) won 73 and the Congress could not cross the number of 32 in the house of 117 member assembly while the militants boycotted the election.[160] The Barnala government was much threatened by sabotage from within his party as by the central government. Intra-elite conflict within the factionalised party took a heavy on the Barnala government to secure peace. More serious, however, was the challenge from the scattered militants after "Operation Woodrose" now hiding, either in Pakistan or in remote areas within India. The message given by the assassination of Longowal in a public religious gathering within a month of the Accord pointed towards challenges for the peace-makers in the beleaguered state.

DISMISSAL OF BARNALA GOVERNMENT

The *Sarbat Khalsa* congregation called by the Dam Dami Taksal on January 26, 1986, the event was in fact the regrouping of the militants inside the Golden Temple complex again. The *Sarbat Khalsa* call got a great response from the Sikhs as they were angry with the government over the demolition of Akal Takht and the recent anti-Sikh riots. The immediate pretext was the demolition of the government built Akal Takht and preparing the Sikhs to take the revenge. The moderate leadership of SGPC was silenced as the militants took over the banner of Damdami Taksal and AISSF, and the United Akal Dal displaced the Militants appointing a *Panthic Committee.* It is to note that after entering Akal Takht, competition for capturing the leadership of the militant took place between AISSF, *Dam Dami Taksal* and the President of United Akali Dal Baba Joginder Singh.

The announcement made by Makham Singh of Dam Dami Taksal regarding the appointment of the *Panthic Committee* and the replacement of the SGPC appointed *Jathedar* by the new appointees came as surprise to some of the prominent leaders. The members of the Apex Committee Gurbachan Singh Manochahal, Wassan Singh Zaffarwal, Aroor Singh, Dhanna Singh and Gurdev Singh were bunch of little known people, singularly lacking political sense or religious convictions, and they were chosen to serve as " pawns" of one group. Their daring vengefulness and predilection for violence were perhaps only qualifications. Jasbir Singh Rode was nominated as the Head Priest of the Akal Takht and his brother-in-law Gurjit Singh replaced the chief of AISSF. The brash manipulation by the kins of Bhindranwale to appropriate dominant position was resented by many militants.[161]

THE DECLARATION OF KHALISTAN AND THE OPERATION BLACK THUNDER

On 13 April 1986, Dam Dami Taksal, the United Akali Dal and the *Panthic* Committee convened a second Sarbat Khalsa at the site of Akal Takht inside the Golden Temple complex. The resolution was also called *Gurmata or* the verdict of the Guru, called on the Sikhs of Punjab "to break the shackles of the slavery and to strive for the *"Khalsa rule."* The Congregation demanded full implementation of the Anandpur Sahib Resolution; release of all detained Sikhs; punishment to the participants and the planners of anti-Sikh riots; rehabilitation of the Sikh army deserters; legal action against the officers responsible for "fake encounters" and an end to the building of the SYNL canal.[162] The newspaper reported that more than 6000 young Sikh gathered and many of them branding the guns, spears and swords passed a series of resolutions. There are reports that the Declaration of *Panthic* Committee claimed that the call for the foundation of Khalistan was given by Bhindranwale himself on June 3, 1984. The Sikh religion was to be regarded as the official religion of the 'State'. Sikhs living outside Punjab were called upon to migrate and settle in Punjab. It was alleged that those who did not agree with the programme the so-called "mercenaries and sold out to Kesh Dhari Hindus were causing obstruction. Mahabir Singh Chehru, a former Nihang Singh, a latter follower of Bhindranwale was appointed commander-in-chief of Khalistan Commando Force (KCF). Reproducing the text of the declaration, the Sipahi reported the violent incidents and commands issued to the Hindus to leave the Punjab." If they started leaving, there would follow riots against Sikhs outside the Punjab, make it difficult for them to live there. Perhaps this is precisely what the supporters of Khalisatn wanted.[163]

On the 30 of April, 1986, Barnala Government sent police force into temple to expel militants holed up there. It was discovered that all those who had operated from within the Temple for about four months had left soon after making the declaration of Khalisatn. Some of them such as Wassan Singh and Gurjit Singh reported to have crossed over Pakistan.[164] This operation was entirely carried out in the full view of media and it was also documented. But the decision of Barnala was proven to be a blunder for his political career as the dissident Akali leaders led by Prakash Singh Badal criticised as they claimed that neither a single terrorists nor any weapon found in the Golden Temple Complex. In protest against the entry of the police and NSG into the Golden Temple, 27 Akali Dal members of the Legislative Assembly formed a breakaway Akali Dal faction with Badal as the president and Amrinder Singh as the leader in the State Legislative Party. Gurcharn Singh Tohra, former SGPC president, also later joined hands with Badal. Chief Minister Barnala was left with little opinion but to rely openly on the Congress support in the Assembly. Barnala was projected as traitor to the Sikh cause by his critics as well as by the Sikh radicals.[165]

Barnala government had no respite as the Head Priest of Golden temple also refused to give moral support. Simultaneously the national media led by the Jalandhar press, gave wide publicity to the notice issued by the KCF under the former Punjab Police Sub Inspector Manbir Singh Chahedu, asking all Hindus of Punjab to leave the state or face the retribution. Unknown groups of armed persons hijacked the buses at gun points to mow down the Hindu passengers, including women and children. On the other hand the centre was not ready to implement the promise of the Rajiv-Longowal Accord. While his former colleague Badal and others, who broke from his government compared Barnala action against the Golden temple "a sacrilege comparable to Mrs Gandhi's army raid". It was stated that that the extremists could not be won over by violence but by love and affection".[166] Badal attended the last rites of all Sikhs killed in fake encounter and made strong speeches against the government. At this point the United Akali Dal headed by father of Bhindranwale merged with Akali Dal Badal group in February 1987. Three months latter, and with ever diminishing authority, the centre decided to terminate the Barnala ministry and impose President's Rule. Officially this action was approved on the grounds of the prevailing 'chaos and anarchy' in Punjab. Among the opposition, however, it was widely believed that the step had been taken to improve the Congress's fortune in the ensuring Haryana elections.[167]

Surprisingly Rajiv Gandhi's move to dismiss the state government was warmly welcomed by the United Akali Dal, the Taksal and the *Panthik* Committee, which described the dismissed government as an "unworthy ministry".[168]

The dismissal of the state government saw the government giving free hand to state police chief Ribeiro to catch and kill the terrorists in Punjab. He, however, failed to reduce the levels of violence. Within a month of the dismissal, the official who had clamoured for Barnala's removal began to link the ongoing violence and the communal tension. On the day Ribeiro assumed the office of DGP, Punjab, one shoot out in Ludhiana had left 13 civilian killed and 17 injured. Soon after Manbir Singh group, in a daring operation killed six escorting police constables in the civil court at Jalandhar and secured the release of 4 dreaded militants. The "Hate Hindu Campaign" was again strengthened. 48 Hindus were killed in the two shootouts in Buses in the month of November.[169] Within a short span of time after taking the charges of the Punjab police by the Ribeiro, the former Chief of Army Gen. A.S. Vaidya was killed by the militants. An aborted attempt on the life of the Prime Minister Rajiv Gandhi was made at Raj Ghat, New Delhi on 2nd October and the escape of DGP Ribeiro and his wife from a well planned attack inside the Armed forces complex the next day were the daring acts of the terrorists soon after the taking of command of the Punjab by the Centre.

The first ever remarks on the militant violence by Ribeiro was in support of the Bullet for Bullet policy. Extraordinary power to detain under the draconian law called Terrorists and Disruptive Activities (Prevention) Act (TADA), (1984) and impunity to the armed forces for eliminating the alleged militants, however, could not achieve much success in eliminating violence.

It is to be mentioned that the daring acts of the Sikh guerrillas were well received by the community through the old religious network of the *Ragi Dhadi Pratha*, in the Gurudwara. Some special songs like *Jago Singh Surme* (Be aware, Singh warriors) and a large number of songs in the Gurudwara and in the recorded castes were dedicated to the armed insurgents. Erecting of the *Nishan Sahib on the graveyard* of the militant and the large gathering over the cremation and in the Bhog ceremonies made the parents to feel proud over the killing of their sons as the slain ones were praised as martyrs which give them a prestige in the community. The tradition of *Shaheedi* (martyrdom) *in Sikhism* was one of the important factor which encouraged the recruitment of the fighters to the movement along with the other factors like police atrocities, unemployment, etc. Pettigrew also noted that all the guerrillas mention that it was the behaviour of the security forces towards them and their families that finally drew them to join the struggle.[170]

TABLE I

Recruitment of Militants

Year of Recruitment	*Amritsar*	*Majitha*	*Tara Taran*	*Batala*	*Total*
1979	—	—	—	1	1
1980	—	3	—	2	5
1981	1	—	1	1	3
1982	—	—	—	—	—
1983	—	—	1	2	3
1984	4	—	7	4	15
1985	2	1	5	2	10
1986	7	8	15	8	38
1987	11	8	14	4	37
1988	14	15	22	17	68
1989	7	12	30	13	62
1990	12	19	12	6	49
1991	7	8	5	4	24
1992	3	2	—	—	5
Year Not Known	2	1	—	—	3
Total	70	77	112	64	323

The data pertaining to the recruitment of the militants also shows that recruitment to the militant ranks increased to large a extent after 1986.[171] By the end of 1986, the number of people killed in the violence during the year rose to 520. Most of those killed were Hindus. Nearly double the numbers were killed in the following year. Then the Governor of Punjab Siddhartha Shankar Ray conceded in a talk with V.N. Narayan that the state government was paralysed. It were the terrorists who ruled by fiat and killing.[172] *Bullet for Bullet*, Ribeiro's controversial remarks, symbolised the desperation of the police. H.K. Puri, Paramjit Singh Judge and Jagroop Singh Sekhon in their co-authored book *Terrorism in Punjab Understanding the Grassroots Reality*, wrote "As the militants constituted a *Panthic Committee*, entered the Golden Temple and replaced all religious appointees of the SGPC and also proclaimed the formation of Khalistan, the government agencies appeared to have been shaken out of the existing weak balance. All political leadership in the community stood discredited at that time. It appeared to be beyond the capacity of the police forces to deal with the difficult situation. The grip of the militants over the Punjab and the situation was reportedly summed up by the then Governor of Punjab Siddhartha Shankar Ray as under: "There is a government in Punjab, but it is not in Chandigarh. It is in Amṛitsar. Room No. 45, 47, 48 of Guru Nanak Niwas. Like the jizhia of the Moghul day, the militants are sending show cause notices to people demanding money. These people, both Sikhs and Hindus, do not go to the police or to the D.C. They straight away go to the militants, pay the money and go off. The situation is simply this. If the terrorists want something to be done; it is done; if they don't want something to happen, it is blocked".[173]

THE FALL OF THE MOVEMENT AND THE RETURN OF PEACE : AN APPRAISAL

The highly intensified violent movement of the Sikh guerrillas to establish a sovereign theocratic Sikh State was at its peak in the year 1990, but suddenly it witnessed a great decline in 1991 and totally collapsed in the year of 1992. It is significant that following the end of militant violence what struck the people most was not only the collapse of the Khalistan movement but also the virtual disappearance of "the logic of the struggle", which the spokesmen of the movement had advanced. The sudden return of the peace and cessation of disenchantment of the Sikhs without gaining any thing from the centre after struggling for two and half decades through the peaceful as well as violent means, has left many questions unresolved. If the peace could be established by security forces and coercion, why it had not established earlier? Why the situation was allowed to deteriorate so much over the two decades? Was there any weight in the Akalis as well as the extremists' demands? Did the Akalis and later the extremists have any popular support for the issues they raised during and before the turmoil in Punjab?

Is the establishment of the peace by the security forces without any political solution makes everyone to think that the sudden return of the peace in Punjab is the return of 'real peace' or it is the 'forced peace'? Did the peace achieved have the support of people or they were silenced by the terror of state? How the government dealt with it? Was the problem of Punjab was just a law and order problem or had any political lineage? These questions need not only a serious analysis of the situation under which the Sikh militant movement emerged and collapsed, but also the strategy of the government which it adopted to counter the militant violence and their support in the Punjab.

The political view of the central government towards the Sikh secessionism is one of the important elements which need a comprehensive analysis along with the strategy of the security forces to win over the militant movement in Punjab. The alienation of the Sikhs due to impunity to the armed forces under the central government is also recognised by the former Governor of Punjab. Just before Punjab's Governor Nirmal Mukherji resigned on May 31, 1990, he told the *Times of India* correspondence that he felt the situation in Punjab was still retrievable and refused to withdraw parallel between Punjab and Kashmir. He felt the Punjab problem was primarily a Sikh problem which had been aggravated by the police. "The burnt of the police raj (police rule) was being felt by the Sikh masses that had no place to go for redressal of their grievances," he said. Writing in *Seminar* magazine of October 1992, Mukherji described Sikh alienation as the basic problem in Punjab.[174]

The remarks of the head of the state are pertinent analysis of the rise and fall of the movement. It is important to note that the distinctive identity of the Sikhs from the Hindus in colonial as well as in the post-colonial period has been a matter of considerable debate. A clear-cut demarcation between the Hindus and Sikhs is still not possible as the Hindu families have bearded and turbaned sons and the Sikh families too have clean shave sons, particular the practice to cut the hair and beard is common in the Jat-Sikh Community, the community involved most in the insurgency. Sikh Gurudwaras and *Guru Granth Sahib* have a vital space among the both communities. Simultaneously the Hindu Temples and festivals have a very vital place in the Sikh families. Still the inter-religion marriages between the Hindus and Sikhs belonging to the same castes are still in practice. It is also to be noted that the Punjab is only an exception for the Indian Union where it successfully toppled the secessionist movement. Peace has been well received by the community that was in such a rebellious mood and alienated from the Centre not long ago. The sudden elimination of the Sikh alienation and joining once again the Indian mainstream in the early 1990's also raised the serious question as to why the Sikh community feel alienated. Was this rebellion for a separate Sikh sovereign state or was it for some political concessions to which the community wanted from the centre or more importantly was it fallout of the centre's callous policy towards Punjab.

The above remarks of the former Governor of the Punjab have an important bearing on the fall of *Khalistan Movement,* which needs an analysis along with the social economic and political situation under which the movement emerged in early 1980's and failed in the early 1990's. In independent India, the struggle for the separate identity by the Sikhs was started during the constitution making when the Sikh leaders asked for the special safeguards for the Sikhs in the Constitution of free India. After failing to get the special constitutional protection, a struggle for the recognition of Punjabi language as a medium of teaching in the schools and instruction in the government offices was launched. The best efforts of the Akali Dal and Nehru to evolve a solution to the language problem by bi-furcating the provinces into Punjabi and Hindi-speaking zones also failed due to the strong opposition of the *Jan Sangh.* Later on the demand of the *Punjabi Suba* met with the same fate. The demands like the reorganisation of the demand of *Punjabi Suba,* the trifurcation of the Province into Punjab, Haryana and Himachal Pradesh and taking the control of the natural water resources for the production of hydro-power and the capital city in its hands along with the leaving out of some Punjabi speaking areas out of Punjab, remained unfulfilled. The vested interests of the political parties i.e., Akali Dal and the Congress under the designed politics, however, connected the issues of the struggling peasantry with the identity and autonomy issue in Punjab for their electoral gains.

As it is noted ending is always traced to the beginning, the success and failure of any movement dependent on the beginning, the cause and the support of the people to the movement. The beginning of the militant movement in Punjab is traced back to emergence of Bhindranwale in the Sikh politics. However, it is also noted that despite his good connection with ruling party leaders at centre intially and the Congress Sikhs in Punjab, Bhindranwale failed to get a democratic space in the Sikh community. His candidates lost the election of SGPC to Akali Dal in 1979. After that whatever reputation he got in the community was created from the two factors: first one was the Congress efforts to decrease the influence or eliminate the hold of Akali Dal on the Sikh politics by creating a counter-Sikh leadership. The second was the use of the brute force against the democratic protests by Akali Dal. The Sikhs got the impression that the democratic means and Akalis could not solve their problems.[175] Violence became the weapon of politics due to democracy deficit. Reneging on the concessions by the government for discrediting the Akali Dal also aggravated to the Problem.

The Sikh alienation had been aggravated after the Operation Blue Star, Operation Woodrose and anti-Sikh riots. The positive attempts of the Akali Dal Longowal to bail out Punjab from chronic crisis came to an end by the killing of Longowal. The extremists' attempts to derail the peace were rebuffed by the people of Punjab through their participation in the State Legislative Assembly Elections of September 1985. The Congress, however, could not digest the thumping victory of the Akali Dal. The release of the extremists along with the moderate Akalis appeared to be the dual policy of war and peace adopted by Rajiv Gandhi Government. It is to be noted that the extremists under the leadership of the Joginder Singh, the then president of Akali Dal openly appealed to the Sikh not to take part in the elections. It is important to mention here that the call of the extremist to Sikhs for boycotting the election was an attempt to keep away Longowal Akali Dal from winning the elections.[176]

Extremism received support among the youth due to the centre policy of the repression. Violation of human rights discredited the Akali government among the Sikhs and the centre by acting tough on Punjab tried to mobilise the Hindu community for the electoral benefits in the neighbouring states. The conciliatory measure of the Barnala government were set aside by the new appointment of the Siddhartha Shankar Ray as Governor of Punjab, former Chief

Minister of West Bengal with an infamous record of crushing the left wing extremists movement that flourished in his state in early 1970's. A week earlier, the government had appointed Julius F. Riberio, notorious for his "bullet for bullet" policy, as the Director General of Punjab police.[177] To make matter worse, several towns in Punjab witnessed the orchestration of anti-Sikh riots by Shiv Sena, a previously unknown organisation in the State, led by Ramkant Jalota and Jagdish Tandgri. To make a conspicuous show of support to Hindu minority in Punjab, the government announced the deployment of paramilitary forces.[178] The efforts of the Barnala government to handle the militancy were further degraded by Arun Nehru, Minister of the newly created Ministry of Internal Security who chose to work on a different strategy to justify its failures in implementing the Rajiv-Longowal accord.[179] The leadership taking recourse to the politics of symbolism heard the representatives telling them either 'to declare military rule or give us guns' and expressed deep concern about the failure of the State government.[180] However, the concrete actions to initiate peace process were missing. It was obvious that law and order approach was preferred over the democratic approach.

As discussed above, Barnala government was forced to take action or support the centre action called Operation Black Thunder against the militants who fled from the complex after making the Declaration of Khalisatn. The action of NSG and other government forces was fully covered by the media including the electronic media and nothing disrespectful against the Sikh traditions was done by the security forces. Dissident Akalis accused Barnala of being guilty of breaking the religious norms being the head of state government. Barnala government became the minority government as 27 MLAs under the leadership of Captain Amrinder Singh and Parkash Singh Badal broke away from the government. Under the situation Barnala government survived on the Congress support. The Operation Black Thunder clearly was designed by the Centre as it indirectly validated the Operation Blue Star though centre had learnt its lessons and received appreciation for its deft handling.

Maloy Krishan Dhar in his book *Open Secrets, India's Intelligence Unveiled* revealed that how the efforts of Barnala government to control the militancy were not fully backed by Rajiv Gandhi-led Congress government at the centre when the hardcore militants were approached by the Centre for secret negotiation. Based on his interviews with the senior officers of Intelligence Bureau, Ram Narayan Kumar narrates as to how the dreaded militants were roped into negotiation with the help of Tarlochon Singh Riyasti (veteran freedom fighter) and Sushil Muni, (a Jain Monk) and how the Militants of the different groups including Atinderpal Singh, a journalist turned separatist, Gurjit Singh, Chief of Dam Dami Taksal of AISSF, Avtar Singh Brahma, (chief of Tat Khalsa and Khalisatn Liberation Force and Gurdip Singh Bathinda, a follower of Jasbir Singh Rode, the incarcerated militant appointed *jathedar* of the Akal Takhat). This band of militants had been logged in Muni Ashram at Delhi for meeting with Prime Minister. Dhar, the government representative, who himself accompanied the militants to Delhi ruled out a meeting of this group of militants with the Prime Minister on the ground that the modalities of the intended talks had not been worked out.

Finally, Satish Sharma, an aide to the Prime Minister along with the Director of Intelligence Bureau, met with the group. Sushil Muni also joined the discussion in which Atinderpal Singh spelt out certain conditions, which were not different from Rajiv-Longowal Accord. Their demands included the declaration of general amnesty, release of all detainees and rehabilitation of the surrender terrorists.[181] Soon, Punjab was rife with speculations and rumours that whereas the police establishment in Punjab, led by Ribeiro charged the Akali government of being soft on the militants, the central government agencies were directly dealing with them. Barnala said that he had no objection to talks between the extremists and the centre if they could help bring peace and stability to Punjab. Badal and Tohra too had urged the government of India to initiate the dialogue with the extremist organisation including Dam Dami Taksal. Manjit Singh and Harminder Singh Sandhu, militant leaders, detained at Jodhpur jail, confirmed that they together with Harinder Singh Kahlon had been talking with the representatives of the Government of India to find durable solution of the Punjab problem. However, afterwards there was no further initiative of this kind from the centre.[182]

No further development was reported between the militants and central government. Just in the middle of all this, Ribeiro, the police chief of Punjab began to blame the Punjab government for impending the efforts of the police to arrest about 40 hardcore terrorists, who in the Punjab police force view, were responsible for organising violence in Punjab and could be involved in attempt to recruit 3000 to 4000 thousands for terrorist activities. Soon after the Ribeiro criticism of the Barnala government the president rule was imposed in Punjab.

Again a slender hope for peace arrived when the fourth *Sarbat Khalsa,* which was convened at the Golden Temple with support from the Akali Dal (Badal), the SGPC and Dam Dami Taksal, appointed Darshan Singh Ragi, a well-known religious leader famous for his singing hymns from Guru Granth, as the acting *Jathedar* of Akal Takht. Darshan Singh was also committed to the concept of just peace.[183]

Soon after becoming the acting head of the Akal Takht, Darshan Singh took steps to unify various factions of the Akali Dal. A note that he circulated among all the leaders and senior members of the party factions said; 'I feel that unity of the Sikhs, not just Akali unity will be the solution to all the present problems facing the Sikh community.... The demand for Khalistan was nothing but the echo of revolt by Sikh youth, which convinced that they had been reduced to the status of second-class citizen in the country.'[184] Along with this note, Darshan Singh also advised the leader of all the factions to submit their resignations, which they promptly did. Darshan Singh announced the formation of a new United Akali Dal, with Simranjit Singh Mann, a former IPS officer under incarceration as the Party President and a five-member presidium including Joginder Singh, Prakash Singh Badal, Jagdev Singh Talwandi, Surjan Singh Thakedar and Geja Singh of Dam Dami Taksal to run the affairs of the party until Mann's release.[185] The now united Akali Dal declared its goal to be "carving out a geopolitical environment which would reflect the aspiration and sentiments of the Sikhs and protect the independent identity of the panth. Its immediate specific goals included: (1) the declaration of Amritsar as "holy city"; (2) the release of Sikhs detained at Jodhpur and other jails; (3) the rehabilitation and reinstatement of Sikh army deserters; (4) a judicial enquiry into "fake encounter" used by the Punjab police; and (5) the withdrawal of false cases against Sikh youth.

Rajiv Gandhi appointed Acharya Sushil Muni and Sunil Dutt, a film star turned politician to hold talks with Darshan Singh Ragi and through him establish a framework of negotiation with militants connected with UAD, AISSF, Dam Dami Taksal and the *Panthic* Committee. Union Home Minister Buta Singh was to coordinate the initiative. Sushil Muni later explained the then failure of the mission in an interview he gave to Indian Express. Sushil Muni claimed that he had succeeded in persuading the militants to sign an accord of peace and to lay down their arms, following the official declaration of amnesty. Sushil Muni alleged that those within the establishment "who stand to gain by keeping on the brink of terrorism" scuttled the peace process. He also accused the "vested interest" of arranging the murder of Tarlochan Singh Riyasati, a former Minister who had been helping him out in establishing a rapport with the discontented hardliner groups. His own secretary too was murdered. Sushil Muni posed the question: "who could be responsible for acts of violence when the major extremists' organisations were all condemning them?" Sushil Muni added, "You must notice that during the earlier terrorists' killings there was no TV coverage. But look how quickly TV crew now reach the scene of a massacre and telecast them in detail all over India." Darshan Singh Ragi also made similar allegations.[186] Other insiders to the ongoing negotiation blamed Union Home Minster Buta Singh and the IB officials running a parallel course of negotiation with other militants and also of sabotaging the peace process.[187] Frustrated and feeling betrayed, Darshan Singh announced his decision to withdraw from the scene. Later, he also mentioned that the *Panthik* Committee was a creation of the central government's agencies to divide and destroy the Sikh struggle. He told the *Guardian* correspondence. "All the deaths are without exception the responsibility of the state or unnamed agencies created to crush the Sikh and to deprive them of their identity."[188] There was also a protest against the killing of the Bus Conductor by the CRF was going with a notable participation of the union members of the Punjab Roadways.[189] Ram Narayan Kumar in his book *Terror in Punjab: Narrative, Knowledge and Truth* argued that the Centre government reneged on the accord out of political calculations to placate the Hindu communal sentiments in Haryana. Also Rajiv Gandhi was personally under cloud following the revelation by the Swedish Radio that Bofors, the arms manufacturing firm had paid 5 million dollars of kickbacks to his officials to secure a weapon supply contract from the Indian Government Surrounded by scandals and fearing the fallout of a strong reaction against any appeasement with the Sikhs of Punjab back traced.[190] Spawning hypocritical postures in public sabotaged all possibilities of reconciliation with the moderate Akalis by spurning their exhortations to return to the terms and the spirit of the July 1985 record. Simultaneously, they also built bridge with the extremists.

Showing the flip flop approach of the government Malloy Krishna Dhar, who was part of the peace making efforts, has narrated his experience: " I received a feeler that an important Punjab terrorist incarcerated in Delhi's Tihar Jail wanted to meet me. Conducted to the maximum security cell by friendly jail officials, I was surprised to meet Jasbir Singh Rode, a Nephew of Jarnail Singh Bhindranwale and militant appointed *Jathedar* of the Akal Takht..... Jasbir Singh appeared to be a simple person whose faith in the separatist tenets of his uncle had started wearing thin. He was tired of the prison and longed to be home and to the gaddi of Akal Takht... I was accompanied, often by my controlling officer Kalyan Rudra. After three rounds of discussion, I submitted an Operation Project Report (OPR) that outlined a fresh round of peace negotiation with the *Panth*ik Committee headed by Gurbachan Singh Manochahal and Dam Dami Taksal, headed by Baba Thakur Singh. The project was approved and the Prime Minister designated Satish Sharma as the point man for liaison with the IB and the target individuals. It was very effectively guided by Kalyan Rudra and abundantly assisted by Taj Kaushik and Ajay Vali... We worked over a blueprint of the action and as the first step the Prime Minister Office (PMO) allowed the IB to transfer three terrorist high priests from Patiala jail to Tihar. They were flown in a special flight and were lodged in adjacent cells.[191] On 11 May 1987, as the dealing with the militants outfits seemed to be moving in the positive direction, the central government announced the dismissal of the Barnala government in Punjab, brining the state under the President rule.

As mentioned above, the dismissal was preceded by a significant public exchange in which the Akali ministers accused Ribeiro of upholding an extra-judicial approach in handling the separatist militancy; Ribeiro in turn accused them of offering shelter and support to the Sikh militants.[192] Some startling revelations came from Sampat Singh, Home Minister of Haryana. Speaking to press on 25 April 1989, the Home Minister claimed evidences to show that Union Home Minister and the Agriculture Minister patronized some groups of militants in Punjab. He promised to furnish complete evidence if Prime Minister cared to institute an inquiry. Rajinder Puri, a well known columnist, made similar allegations, suggesting that Indian intelligence organisation were themselves patronising rabid elements to discredit militants.

In his book, Ribeiro has mentioned several other undercover operations, planned by Amritsar SSP Izhar Alam and other senior officers of the Punjab Police. The book also narrates how KPS Gill, then Inspector General of the Central Reserve Police Forces (CRPF), reportedly thwarted Ribeiro's attempts to discipline the policemen who committed atrocities, by persuading the Union Home Ministry not to sanction their prosecution.[194]

The IB officials went on to meet with Baba Thakur Singh of Dam Dami Taksal for his approval of a peace pact with the government of India and Dhar personally met Gurbachan Singh Manochahal. The militants were divided and areas chieftains controlled their individual groups. There was no central command. Manochahal 'scribbled a cryptic note allowing Jasbir Singh to go ahead with the talks, subject to approval of the *Panthic* Committee, Dam Dami Taksal and a consortium of top terrorists' leaders." Dhar personally negotiated the terms of Jasbir Singh Rode's release. The terms included : (1) To arrange the installation of Jasbir Singh as the Jathedar of the Akal Takhat; (2) to provide adequate weapon to enable him to drive out those who oppose the deal; (3) to facilitate free movement and enable him to meet top militant leaders; (4) to arrange for the rehabilitation of the surrendered militants: and (5) to facilitate the holding of a *Sarbat Khalsa* at Bathinda on 13 April 1988 for announcing the final settlement with the government of India and formal scrapping of the declaration of the Khalistan.[195]

This formula was submitted to the Prime Minister in the early January 1988. The IB officials, assisted by Jasbir Singh Rode's relatives and associates, including Rajdev Singh Barnala who later became a member of parliament, met with the leaders of Dam Dami Taksal. "At least three leaders of *Panthic* Committee and militant leaders like Atinderpal Singh, Avtar Singh Brahma and Gurbachan Singh Manochahal too approved the formula. Baba Joginder Singh too endorsed the deal.[196]

Dhar further explained that after the release of Rode and his associates they were flown in a special DC3, escorted bẏ Kalyan Rudra and him. At the Amritsar Airport they were received by a huge gathering of militants and AISSF members and driven straight to Golden Temple. They were housed in a couple of rooms above the *parikarma*. Before their departure they were "supplied with a sizable quantity of licensed non-prohibitary weapons and ammunitions... Jasbir Singh Rode's crowning as the Jathedar of Takht was done on March 9, in a glittering ceremony attended by second rung members of the *Panthic* Committee, Dam Dami Taksal, AISSF, KCF, KLF and BTF and others. Two more consignments of the weapons and ammunition were also allegdly given to the Rode by IB officials in Amritsar and Anandpur Sahib. Maloy Krishna Dhar describes what happened after Rode's release:" As we prepared to leap on to the next assignment of facilitating establishment of firm contact between Jasbir Singh Rode and the members of the *Panthic* Committee, we faced insurmountable problem of eluding ever-vigilant operation by KPS Gill and shadow operations by my IB colleagues ... Both the Governor and Home Minister declined to declare a particular area near Goindwal safe zone. Satish Sharma suddenly became incommunicado. The Prime Minister was beyond my reach. A section in the Operations Cell of the IB adopted a hostile attitude. The Militant groups hold inside the temple meantime started erecting fortifications and bunkers at all conceivable defensive and offensive level.[197] Meanwhile the state forces successfully envisioned the guerrilla groups as some of the policemen reported to have joined the ranks of militants and some ex-militants became the informers of the police. The most important strategic arm of the KPS Gill who was elevated to Director General of Police in April 1988 to invasion the militant ranks.[198] Inderjit Singh Jaijee claimed that the Operation Black Thunder II was planned by the government before a month of the release of Rode. The Commandos of National Security Guards were carefully trained for the Operation and they were also advised to grow their hairs and beard so they could easily get the entry in the Temple Complex as the Sikhs. Just after the two weeks of Rode release the militants of the Punjab were reported to be armed with the Soviet made rocket launchers. The nature of police action, state plans and violence reached at the peak when 70 CRPF soldiers were reported to be killed in a single attack of rocket launcher allegedly propelled by the militants on the Vishwakarma Temple on the outskirts of Phagwara town. Human rights activists and foreign media refuted the state claims of the arming of militants and accused the state agents for using the high power weapons just to justify the extra-constitutional, extra-judicial methods to pressurise the Sikhs masses to support their action.[199]

During these months, the security forces were infiltrating men into Golden Temple Complex. In outward appearance they were Sikhs. By mid-April Security force personal began occupying rooftop pickets near Golden Temple. On May, CRPF DIG Sarbdeep Singh Virk went up to the rooftop of the building around the Temple *parikarma*. He was fired upon. Hearing of the firing and injury to Virk, the acting Jathedar of the Akal Takhat Rode hurried back from Patiala to Amritsar. On May 11 and 12, 1,000 commandos of Special Action Group of NSG were airlifted to Amritsar under the overall command of Brigadier Sushil Nanda. Rode requests for ceasefire to talks with the militants were accepted by the local administration and a 2 hour cease fire was announced on 11 May. Along with his associates Rode went inside to talk with militants, meanwhile the CRF were replaced by NSG special rangers.[200] The two hours ceasefire was in actual a strategy of the state forces to strengthen its strategic position by apportioning the NSG commandos in place of CRPF jawans.[201] When rode came to know the reality he protested against the firing on the complex when the militants were ready to talk. Rode and his companions were immediately arrested for violating curfew. Some of infiltrators were also reported to surrender before the police acting as the militants.[202]

At the very beginning, when the concept of Khalistan and movement for the freedom emerged in the psyche of the Sikhs of Punjab, it lost the leadership. A significant number of political leaders had been eliminated in the "Operation Blue Star" and Operation Woodrose, and many survivors went underground for fear of harassment and torture by the paramilitary forces. Attempts to resurrect the guerrilla movement were initiated by those who had some trade union experience or the members of the splintered AISSF or those associated with the religious seminary Ḍam Dami Taksal. After that was at every moment the lack of central command, uniform opinion on the strategies of struggle and political negotiation with the government were noted.

Between 1989 and 1991, civilian casualties rose from 54 per cent to 73 per cent of the total number of killings and ordinary Sikh villagers were targeted in an unprecedented orgy of violence.[203] The wealthier families migrated to cities, often abandoning their land holdings in fear of abduction or extortion. A situation of general lawlessness prevailed and the scale and nature of violence suggested the wider breakdown in social relationships in the province. The lumpen elements of society, such as smugglers and criminals indulged in the intimidation of the people already caught between the security forces and the militants. Armed bands plundered the land of farming families and the rural masses were subjected to brutal attack on their lives and property.

By 1988, a serious rift occurred between the main guerrilla organisations over the issues of policy and tactics. The core of the ideological differences was whether to raise the social reform, notably an anti-dowry and an anti-alcohol campaign, during the armed struggle. Divisions in the resistance increased between 1990 and 1991.[204] Once the paramilitary forces had succeeded in eliminating the ideologically committed cadre, the weakness in the organisational structure of guerrilla group became evident. The average life span of a militant was not more than 3 years, and this induced the guerrilla organisations to draw in fresh recruits continually.[205] The method of recruitment was based on traditional associations of kin and friendship. Moreover, in an attempt to broaden their mass base, the militants had inducted recruits without proper scrutiny and much recruitment had not undergone on ideological training or training in surveillance tactics. All these factors encouraged many guerrillas to secure local power base and in the process many of them accrued considerable financial assets. Another factor that propelled the militants to seek self-limited goals through violence was the failure of the prevailing institutional structure, both modern as well as customary, to give them a measure of power. Another noteworthy feature of the movement is that the rural population of the province sought the intervention of militants to settle disputes and render justice. The schools, colleges, hospitals and other public services particular in the rural areas became dysfunctional creating people's dissatisfaction.[206]

THE ELECTIONS IN 1989

A little hope of peace for the people of Punjab lighted once again when the parliament elections were declared in 1989. The Congress central government was confident to get the ground in the Punjab again. The Akali Dal for a long time had been faction ridden and ruthless. With the moderate leaders languishing in jails and their organisations being doldrums, they could not pose serious challenge to the Congress establishment. Simranjit Singh Mann was popular but had no organisational base to convert his popularity into electoral gains. The militant and their activities too were very confusing. Simranjit Mann had been in jail for nearly five years, suffering physical and mental torture. His all candidates were raw to the field of politics and many of them belonged to the families that had suffered terrible human rights abuses, including custodial torture, summary execution and enforced disappearance. Yet, the campaigns remained democratic. Mann's candidates talked about the imperatives of Hindu-Sikh unity and a common search for an end to the atrocities and injustice. Mann himself, despite all he had gone through and long before the elections were over, not only clearly spoke against violence but also profess faith in the possibility of resolving the Punjab tangle within the framework of the Indian Constitution. In an interview to *India Today* published in April 989, Mann categorically declared that he was "against all the killing.[207]

The parliamentary elections in Punjab, contrary to all expectations, were brisk and peaceful. The Chief Electoral Officer declared that he had not received a single complaint of irregularity and intimidation from any constituency. The results of elections, announced in the last week of November 1989, were astonishingly clear. They also radically falsified the predictions of *political pundits* that the division in the Sikh vote would benefit the Congress party. The group under the leadership of Simranjit Singh Mann swept the polls by bagging six seats out of total thirteen. Four additional constituencies elected independent candidates who had Mann's backing. Mann himself created a record in his constituency of Tarn Taran by taking the largest number of votes secured by any candidate ever in India: 527,707 votes out of the total of 591, 883.[208]

At the national level, the Congress party lost its majority in Parliament retaining only 194 out of 397 seats it held in 1984 elections. The Janata Dal, which gained 142 seats, formed a National Front government, with the parliamentary support from the Bharatiya Janata Party (BJP) with its 88 seats under V.P. Singh as the new Prime Minister The Communist Party of India (Marxist) CPI (M) with 33 seats and Communist Party of India (CPI) with its strength of 11, also decided to support the government.[209]

Immediately after losing parliamentary elections but before quitting office, Rajiv Gandhi's government in Delhi seemed to have changed its perception radically claiming that a "fairly peaceful atmosphere" had returned to Punjab and that the "fair and peaceful elections" held in the state showed that "every section of the people of Punjab was striving for peace and amity." Governor Siddharth Shankar Ray went to the extent of suggesting that the time had come for the restoration of popular government in the state.[210]

The government immediately withdrew the case the conspiracy which had been registered earlier. The Janata Dal government also decided to release all the arrested Akali leaders including Badal and Tohra. Governor Ray went on to praise Mann publicly by calling him "the leader of the vast majority of the Sikhs".[211] The first expression of the Mann was the solution of the Sikh grievances through the constitutional ways. He refuted the violence. While addressing a huge gathering in Amritsar, which assembled to greet him, Mann called for the support of Punjabis from all corners.[212]

Mann set out the following conditions for the government to fulfil before he could resume negotiations on more basic issues of the Sikh discontent. His conditions were: (1) Expression of repentance for army assault on the Golden Temple; (2) adoption of a motion in both houses of parliament to condole the Sikhs who had been killed during the November 1984 carnage; (3) pardon for the Sikh soldiers who had mutinied in the wake of Operation Blue Star; (4) Institution of criminal cases against the officials in Punjab who routinely practiced custodial torture and summary executions and (5) repeal of the laws for Punjab that violate fundamental rights of citizens.[213]

In the beginning, there were hopeful signals suggesting a new harmonious beginning to end the Punjab crisis. Prime Minister V.P. Singh went to Amritsar to offer prayer at Golden Temple. His reception at Amritsar by the Sikhs of Punjab was tumultuous.[214] Prime Minister said: "We have come on a pilgrimage to offer prayer and seek blessings to overcome all hurdles and gave a healing touch to the hurt psyche of the people.... It is a solemn occasion and a new era had begun. We shall win the hearts of the people with love and not with bayonets".[215]

The first sign of trouble that was lying ahead came when on 21 December 1989, the security personnel at parliament house refused permission to a newly elected Sikh member, Dhyan Singh Mann, to enter the House along with the 'sword'. The incident triggered a media controversy and Mann himself refused to enter Parliament unless the government allowed the newly elected members to carry their swords with them. The issue resulted in a split in the parliamentary group under Mann. Three members including Beant Singh's Widow Bimal Kaur and Atinderpal Singh, who had faced trail with Mann, took oath without swords. Another member of parliament, Jagdev Singh Khudian was found missing on 28 December 1989. The police found his dead body from a canal two days later. Mann said that official agencies had organised his elimination.[216] Maloy Dhar, former Joint Director of IB who coordinated some of the clandestine operations in Punjab, himself admits that Atinderpal Singh and Rajdev Singh Barnala of Sangrur, who had earned his ticket of parliament by defending victims of human rights abuses and other 'extremists' implicated in cases under draconian laws like *Terrorists and Disruptive Activities* (Prevention) Act (TADA) and "few other friendly Sikhs in Parliament had been working for the Indian intelligence establishment".[217]

The peace initiatives unfortunately again erupted into the controversies and centre found Mann a tough Mann for the peace deal. Mann asserted that the democratic rights of the Sikh citizens and the forced disappearance of 20,000 Sikh youths by the Indian forces.

He suddenly started comparing Rajiv Gandhi with Hitler and Mussolini and went on to propose that if India does not know how to establish peace, he would like to invite former American President Jimmy Carter to mediate a settlement in Punjab since he had been a successful peacemaker in several parts of Central America and Ethiopia's Eritrea province.[218] The hopes for the return of peace were again derailed by the centre which initiated silence over the forced disappearance to which Mann claimed before the foreign media[219]. Political analysts in Punjab and Delhi argued that the government of Prime Minister V P Singh liked to find a more cooperative candidate to head the state government before allowing the elections to take place in Punjab.[220]

The time was indeed running out for V.P. Singh-led Janta Dal government and apprehensions that Barbara Crosset expressed would soon come true. On 2 October, *Financial Times* of London published an article describing the situation in Punjab: "Police vehicles bristling with automatic weapons tour the streets of Amritsar now a shabby, run down city demoralised by continuing conflict-making themselves familiar a feature of the urban landscape the taxis belching black smoke or the auto rickshaw[221]. David Housego, who wrote article, talked to the people on a subject that would soon lead to their elimination: "At Sunsing, a large village close to the border of Pakistan, three terrorists silently observe the foreign journalists talking to a family in the courtyard of their house". When the "boys" come here I willingly serve them food, said Surinder Singh, the head of the family, as he looked towards the militants with a look that expressed both fear and support. The Article also referred to Prime Minister V.P. Singh regret. "Talking to reporters this week, Prime Minister V.P. Singh conceded that he had let slip the chance of fresh beginning to find a political solution in the Punjab that was provided by a new administration coming to power in Delhi in November". One thing I will regret all my life, he said "is of not holding elections for the state assembly in the Punjab within six months of my government taking office". The article explains why Singh was unable to go ahead and keep his pledge: "The holding of elections now is opposed by the Hindus in the province, who account for 40 percent of the population and most of the non-Sikh political parties." "The boys will come to power and it will practically be a government of Pakistan" was another fear that was articulated by Vijay Chopra, editor of the *Hind Samachar* newspaper group."[222]

Chandra Shekhar's Initiative again failed due to the unstable future of his government. As a weak government it could not take any decision on Punjab although Chandra Shekhar had held discussion with Mann and other radicals. The problem of holding the Parliament elections in Punjab was resolved through the network of the IB and militants. The AISF (Manjit Singh), *Panthic* Committee members, former MP Gurtej Singh, former Secretary SAD (M) decided to support civic elections.[223]

The unconventional strategies to defeat the political process in Punjab, referred to by Maloy Krishna Dhar, were successful. The groups under Manochahal and Zaffarwal and AISSF (Manjit Singh) decided to field their candidates. Their manifestos identified their objectives to 'spread the ideology of Bhindranwale' and to 'create home land for the Sikhs with complete ownership and freedom'.[224] Independently, Mann's Akali Dal also decided to participate "with the objective for securing freedom for the Sikhs." The old Akali Dal leaders like Badal, Tohra and Amrinder Singh, who had earlier accepted Mann's leadership but parted company with him, joined the fray by separately fielding their own candidates.[225] Their Manifesto was in favour of decentralising India into a "Union of sovereign States with independent representations in UNO." Even this group did not remain cohesive: Amrinder Singh, now the President of Punjab Congress and Congress Chief Minister of Punjab from 2004-2009, and the scion of Patiala royalty and a personal friend of late Rajiv Gandhi, floated his own Akali Dal. The faction of the Akali Dal, loyal to Surjit Singh Barnala was also contesting the elections separately. None of these factions were, however, cohesive. They broke up in quarrelsome splinters over dispute regarding the selection of candidates.[226]

It is difficult to predict about the outcome as elections were never held. On 22 May, 1991, Rajiv Gandhi was assassinated in the South by a woman belonged to Tamil separate group from Sri Lanka.[227] Indeed, it was by far the most violent election campaign in the history of India comparable to the elections in Assam in 1983, with the most killings of the Akali candidates in the Punjab.

The Congress was returned as the single largest party in Parliament, but fell short of majority in the Lok Sabha in 1991. Narsimha Rao became the Prime Minister. It is alleged that Election Commission Under the instruction of central government cancelled the polls in Punjab just 24 hours before they were scheduled to be held.[228] Outgoing Prime Minister Chandra Shekhar labelled the postponement as a "dangerous move which had far reaching consequences". Simranjit Mann said that it was a fascist move. Governor O.P. Malhotra himself resigned in protest.[229] The new Congress government in Delhi under Rao appointed Surendar Nath, a former police officer who had been orchestrating some of under-cover operations since 1983, as the new Governor of Punjab. Nath had become prominent actor in Punjab imbroglio following his appointment as the Governor's advisor in February 1984, three months before the Operation Blue Star[230]. K.P.S. Gill came as Director General of Punjab police.[231]

The last hope for the political settlement by consensus demised in December 1991, when all the Akali leaders refused the invitation from the Union government to attend an all party meeting to discuss a solution to the Punjab problem after it became clear that the centre had no intention to transfer Chandigarh to Punjab.[232] Badal explained their boycott. "We have been engaged in discussion for decades now and it has always proved to be frustrating and futile rehearsal. There is nothing to discuss any longer and the centre should take steps to find a just, definite and a permanent solution to the Punjab problem."[233]

In January 1992, even before the government announced the holding of elections in Punjab, the *Panthic* Committee and the militants forced the Akali leaders to unambiguously announce their decision to boycott the elections. All the Akali leaders met and announced their decision to stay away from polls. On 8 February 1992 the then Defence Minister announced that soldiers were doing rounds of 12,000 villages to ensure that the terrorists did not interfere against the people right to franchise. With the majority of Akalis behind the bars, the polling took place on 19 February. [234]

Tim Megirk, a correspondent from *The Independent* from London captured the picture of a rural polling station in Amritsar: "A shawl was draped around the Punjab police officer's turban and his breath was sour from the cane liquor he had been drinking since dawn. He pointed to a queue of sullen farmers outside a school room that had been turned into a polling booth for election. 'Don't panic them, please,' the drunken policeman told the two newsmen. It has taken me since four this morning to round them up for voting and I don't want them all to run away. It was 7.30 a.m. In Meharbanpur, a village outside Amritsar, and the police was forcing villagers to cast their votes. Sikh extremists had vowed to disrupt the polls but with the army patrolling in jeeps filled with machine gunners wearing goggles and bandannas, violence was kept down. More than 250,000 soldiers, police and an array of paramilitary descended on Punjab.... With the main Sikh parties boycotting election, the field is open to the Congress party, which will scope up votes from the Hindus who make up 42% of Punjab's 13 million voters." [235] The voting turn out in the rural area remained 5 to 20 percent and in the urban areas 25 to 45% voting turn out was reported. Some of the rural constituencies were reported to register much less turn out. The results lacked legitimacy due to low turnout. The elections saw the return of the Congress in power with two-third majority in the State Assembly. Congress won 87 out of 117 assembly seats contested and also won 12 out of the 13 parliamentary seats. Beant Singh became the new Chief Minister of Punjab.[236]

RESTORATION OF NORMALCY

The transformation of Punjab was swift and dramatic. A noted journalist Kanwar Sandhu, writing for *India Today*, described the situation, exactly one year after Beant Singh had taken over: "Punjab descent into terror and chaos was gradual. Its recovery has been defeated by the militant gun power. Not much was expected from Beant Singh government which somewhat lacked legitimacy. But the state as well as Beant Singh has managed to thwart the prophets of doom... The killing fields are back to being the granaries of the country. The migrants are returning, claiming their factories. Folk songs are back on the feisty Punjabi's lips. The state highways are roaring with vehicular traffic and petrol pumps and *dhabas* (roadside cafes) are open to business till late in the night. The vendor of terror has clearly packed up. The guns are there but they belong to the police. The militants press handouts and threatening calls to newspaper offices have ceased... Now, for the first time in a decade, Amritsar and Gurdaspur districts (near the border with Pakistan) have not reported any terrorist strikes in the past three months.[237] It was too early to predict the miracle of peace. The Governor of Punjab Surendra Nath along with 9 members of family died in a mysterious chopper crash in August 1994. The reports of his death revealed that the officials discovered more than unaccounted stacks of money in his official residence.[238]

In January 1995, Jaswant Singh Khalra exposed the ghastly practices of the Congress government in Punjab involving enforced disappearances of the suspects followed by secret cremations of the unclaimed bodies. The human rights organisation started raising their voices against the state repression during the dark days.

On 31 August, 1995 the Chief Minister of Punjab Sardar Beant Singh was killed in a bomb explosion just outside his own heavily guarded office. K.P.S. Gill characterised the blast indicating a serious lapse in the Chief Minister security. On 6 September, 1995, Khalra was abducted from his house. Ajit Singh Sandhu, the SSP of the Tarn Taran, committed suicide while facing the charges of fake encounter and killing of Jaswant Singh Khalra in police custody along with the other police officers of Tarn Taran district. Intelligence agencies are of late expressing their apprehensions on the revival of the militancy. Some of militants like KCF chief Paramjit Singh Panjwar and some other daring are still reported to be residing in foreign countries like Canada, Europe and Pakistan waiting for the right moment to become active. Even after twenty years having lapsed, the cases of human rights violation committed by the state agents are still pending in the courts and many parents are still waiting the news of the whereabouts of their missing children.

Notes and References

1. H.K. Puri, *et. al.*, 1999, *Terrorism in Punjab: Understanding the Grassroots Reality*, Haranand Publications, New Delhi, pp. 36-37. See also: Ram Narayan Kumar *et. al.*, 2003, *Reduced to Ashes: The Insurgency and Human Rights in Punjab, Final Report,* Vol. 1, Published by South Asia Forum for Human Rights, Kathmandu, p. 52.
2. J.S. Grewal, 2009, *The Sikhs: Ideology, Institutions and Identity*, Oxford University Press, New Delhi, p. 305.
3. Sangat Singh, 1996, *The Sikh History*, Greater Kailash, New Delhi, pp. 201-02.
4. *Ibid.*, p. 304
5. J.S. Grewal, 2009, *op. cit.*, No. 2, p. 290.
6. Ram Naryan Kumar, *et. al.*, 2003, *op. cit.*, No. 1, p. 52. See also: Sangat Singh, 1996, *op. cit.*, No. 2, p. 49.
7. Shiv Lal, 1994, *Dateline Punjab Lifelines Sikhs, Election Archives*, New Delhi, pp. 70-71.
8. J.S. Grewal,1998, "Sikh Identity, the Akalis and Khalistan", J.S. Grewal and Indu Banga (eds.), *Punjab in Prosperity and Violence: Administrative, Politics and Social Change,* K.K Publishers, New Delhi, p. 64.
9. Krishan Gopal Lamba, 1999, *Dynamics of Punjabi Suba Movement*, Deep & Deep, Publications, New Delhi, pp. 89-91.
10. Khuswant Singh, 1991, *History of the Sikhs,* Vol. 2, Oxford University Press, New Delhi, p. 346.
11. "Anandpur Sahib Resolution," en.wikipedia.org/wiki/Anandpur Resolution, 29-9-2009.
12. Mark Tully and Satish Jacob, 1987, *Amritsar Mrs. Gandhi's Last Battle,* Jonathcape, London, p. 50.
13. Khuswant Singh, 1991, *op. cit.*, No. 10, p. 350.

14. *Ibid.*, p. 353.
15. Harnik Deol, 2000, *Religion and Nationalism in India: A Case Study of Punjab*, Routledge, London, p. 103.
16. Khuswant Singh, 1991, *op. cit.*, No. 10, p. 352.
17. Satya M. Rai, 1986, *Punjab Since Partition*, Durga Publications, New Delhi, p. 310.
18. K.C. Gulati, 1974, *The Akali: Past and Present*, Ashajank Publications, New Delhi, p. 166.
19. Ram Naryan Kumar, and George Sieber, 1991, *The Sikh Struggle: Origin, Evolution and Present Phase*, Chankaya Publications, New Delhi, p. 185.
20. *Ibid.*
21. *Ibid.*, p. 186.
22. *Ibid.*, p. 187.
23. A.S. Narang, 1983, *Storm Over the Sutlej: The Akali Politics*, Gitanjali Publishing House, New Delhi, pp. 181-82.
24. Ram Naryan Kumar and George Sieber, 1991, *op. cit.*, No. 19, p. 188.
25. *Ibid.*, pp. 188-89.
26. *Ibid.*, pp. 190-91.
27. R.A. Kapur, 1986, *Sikh Separatism: The Politics of Faith*, Allen and Unwin, London, p. 217.
28. Paul R. Brass, 1974, *Language, Religion and Politics in North India*, Cambridge University Press, Cambridge, p. 333.
29. Ram Naryan Kumar and George Sieber,, 1991, *op. cit.*, No. 19, p. 191-92.
30. Sucha Singh Gill and K.C. Singhal, 1984, "Punjab Problem: Its Historical Roots", *Economic and Political Weekly*, Vol. XIX, No. 14, April 7, pp. 603-06.
31. Vinod Kumar, 1981, *Impact of Technology Change on Farm Employment: A Case Study of Punjab*, M.Phil. Dissertation (Unpublished), Department of Economics, Punjabi University, Patiala, pp. 444-50.
32. *Ibid.*, p. 451.
33. *Ibid.*, p. 455.
34. Vinod Kumar, 1981, *op. cit.*, No. 31, p. 455.
35. Nirmal S. Azad, 1976, "Punjab Agricultural Wages", *Economic and Political Weekly*, Vol. XXII, No. 25, June 19, pp. 2161-71. See also: Master Hari Singh, 1980, *Agriculture Workers, Struggle in Punjab*, People Publishing House, New Delhi, Aminder Singh, 1979, "Farmer Workers *vs.* Rich Farmers: Class and Caste in the Punjab Villages", *Economic and Political Weekly*, Vol. XIV, No. 43, October 27, pp. 2112-17.
36. Sucha Singh Gill, 1980, "Land Reforms and Peasant Movement in Punjab", *Mainstream*, June 14, pp. 27-30.
37. Sucha Singh Gill, 1982, "Impact of Economic Development on Rural Artisans in Punjab", *Economic Analyst*, Vol. XXVI. No. 7, December 7, pp. 42-50 .
38. Nirmal Singh Azad, 1980, *Small Peasantry in Punjab: An Analysis of Production Conditions*, Ph.D. Thesis (Unpublished), Punjabi University, Patiala, p. 306.
39. G.S. Bhalla, and K.G. Chadha, 1982, "Green Revolution and Small Peasantry: A Study of Income Distribution", *Economic and Political Weekly*, Vol. XVII, No. 2, May 22, pp. 870-78.

40. *Ibid.*
41. *Ibid.*
42. Rajbans Kaur, 1982, *Agriculture Price Policy in Developing Countries with Special Reference to India*, Ph.D. Thesis (Unpublished), Punjabi University, Patiala, p. 275.
43. Dalip, S. Swamy and Ashok Gulati, 1986, "From Prosperity to Retrogression Indian Cultivators During the 1970's", *Economic and Political Weekly*, Vol. XXI, No.25, June 21-28, pp. 556-59.
44. H.S. Aulakh, 1983, *Changing Foodgrains Market Structure in India*, B.R. Publishing Corporation, New Delhi, pp. 50-60.
45. Victor Disouza, 1982, "Economy, caste, religion, and population distribution and analysis Communal tension in Punjab", *Economic and Political Weekly,* Vol. XVII, No. 19, May 8, pp. 113-17.
46. Sucha Singh Gill and K.C. Singhal, 1984, "Farmers' Agitation—Response to Development Crisis of Agriculture", *Economic and Political Weekly*, October 6, pp. 603-06.
47. K.K. George and I.S Gulati, 1985, "Centre-State Resources Transfers 1951-84: An Appraisal", *Economic and Political Weekly*, Vol. XX, No. 7, February 16, p. 3472.
48. M.C. Bhardwaj, 1983, *State Autonomy and Anandpur Sahib Resolution*, Jaspal Printing Press, Amritsar, pp. 93-97.
49. *Ibid.*, p. 99.
50. Anandpur Sahib Resolution Authenticated by Sant Harchand Singh ... www.satp.org/satporgtp/countries/.../anantpur_sahib_resolution.htm, 29-9-2009. See also: Varinder Grover, "Anandpur Sahib Resolution", Varinder Grover (ed.), 1995, *The Story of Punjab Yesterday and Today : Documents, Treaties and Exhaustive Bibliography*, Deep & Deep Publications, New Delhi, pp. 307-321.
51. *Ibid.*
52. Rajinder Kaur, 1992, *Sikh Identity and National Integration*, Intellectual Publishing House, New Delhi, pp. 84-87.
53. Paul R. Brass, 1974, *op. cit.*, No. 28, pp. 292-93.
54. T.V. Sathyamurthy, 1984, "Crisis within Crisis", *Seminar*, Vol. 294, February, pp. 11-17.
55. K. Gujral, "The Sequences", Patwant Singh and Harjit Malik (eds.), 1985, *Punjab: The Fatal Miscalculations*, Crescent Printing Works, New Delhi, p. 233.
56. Spokesman News, 1978, "Akali Lauched Save Democrarcy", *Spokesman Weekly*, Vol. 27, No 19, January 2, p. 67.
57. Paul Wallace, 1981, "Religion and Secular Politics in Punjab", *Punjab Journal of Politics*, Vol. III, No. 1, January-June, p. 20.
58. Rajinder Kaur, 1992, *op. cit.*, No. 52, pp. 70-72.
59. H.K. Puri, *et. al.*, 1999, *op. cit.*, No. 1, pp. 56-57.
60. The term Dal Khalsa served as a reminder of the national army of Sikhs which had succeeded in establishing sovereign Sikh during the late eighteen-century. Zail Singh is said to have blessed the Dal Khalsa, J.S. Grewal, 2009, *op. cit.*, No. 2, pp. 305-07, Harshimran Singh of Chandigarh was made the "Mukh Panch" the top functionary of the

organisation. The other members were Harbhagat Singh Nanagwal, Gajinder Singh, Satnam Singh and Jaswant Singh, and Chanchal M. Singh, Indian Express News Service (IENS), 1981, "Khalisatan-Origin and Growth", *The Indian Express*, (Sunday Magazine), October 4.

61. *Ibid.*, p. 305.
62. *Ibid.*
63. Attar Singh, 1985, "Management of Gurudwaras", Amrik Singh (ed.), *Punjab in Indian Politics: Issues and Trends*, Ajanata Publications, Delhi, , pp. 196-97, See also: H.K. Puri, *et. al.*, 1999, *op. cit.*, No. 2, p. 37.
64. T.V. Sathyamurthy, 1984, *op. cit.*, No. 54. See also: J.S. Grewal, 2009, *op. cit.*, No. 2, pp. 288-90. See also: H.K. Puri, *et. al.*, 1999, *op. cit.*, No. 1, pp. 10-15.
65. Ramjilal, 1998, "Khalistan: A Dilemma of Akali Politics", *Research Journal of Arts and Humanities*, Vol. XXII, No. 4. pp. 213-18.
66. Rajinder Kaur, 1992, *op. cit.*, No. 52, pp. 72-73.
67. J.S. Grewal, 2009, *op. cit.*, No. 2, p. 304.
68. *Ibid.*, p. 305
69. "Dal Khalsa: Militant Slogans", 1981, *India Today*, October 31, p. 34. See also: Satpal Dang, *et. al.*, 2000, *Terrorism in Punjab*, Gyan Publishing House, New Delhi, pp. 13, 17, 71, 82.
70. Rajinder Kaur, 1992, *op. cit.*, No. 52, p. 75.
71. *Ibid.*, p. 80. See also: Gubinder Singh,1990, *Religion and Politics in Punjab*, Deep & Deep Publications, New Delhi, pp. 342-50.
72. "White papers on Punjab", 1984, Presented by the Government of India in Parliament, 10 July, pp. 3-7.
73. B.K. Chum, 1983, "The Punjab: A War of Nervous", *The Indian Express* (Sunday Magazine), May 8.
74. Gopal Singh, 1994, *Politics of Sikh Homeland (1940-90)*, Ajanta Publications, New Delhi, pp. 10-15.
75. Harkanwal Korpal, 2001, *Genesis of Damdami Taksal*, Bhai Gurdas Foundation, Amritsar, p. 176.
76. www.damdamitaksal.org/index.pho=com, 23-4 -2009.
77. "Damdami taksal The official website," www.Damdamitaksaal.org, 23-4-2009.
78. Harkanwal, Korpal, 2001, *op. cit.*, No. 75, pp. 223-27.
79. Harminder Kaur, 1990, *Blue Star Over Amritsar*, Ajanta Publications, New Delhi, p. 52.
80. Paul R. Brass, 1991, *Ethnicity and Nationalism*, Sage Publication, London, p. 90.
81. It is pertinent to mention that the clash between the Nirnarkaris and Sikhs was not new thing in the religious domain of the Punjab. The rivalry between 'Sant Samaj' and 'Deras headed by Babas/Gurus' has been a continuous feature of the political economy of religion in Punjab. The recent Dera Sacha Sauda and Sikh conflict and the verdicts of the Sikh Samaj against the other Deras like Gyan Jyoti Peeth, and the assassination of Baba Ramanand in Vienna, (Austria), the deputy chief of Dera Baba Sarwandas Sach Khand Ballan and attack on the chief of Dera Sacha Sauda can be seen as the continuation of the Samaj Dera conflict in

the post-militancy Punjab. Surinder Singh Jodhka and Parkash Louis, 2003 "Caste Tension in Punjab: Talhan and Beyond," *Economic and Political Weekly*, Vol. XXXVIII, No. 28, 18 July, pp. 2923-26. See also:Surinder Singh Jodhka, 2002, "Caste and Untouchabilty in Rural Punjab", *Economic and Political Weekly*, Vol. XXXVII, No. 19, May 11, pp. 1814-16, Surinder Singh Jodhka, 2009, "The Ravidasis of Punjab: Global Counters of Caste and Religious Strifes", *Economic and Political Weekly*, Vol. XLIV, 24, 18 July, p. 79-85, Surinder Singh Jodhka, 2004, "Sikhism and Caste Question: Dalit and their Politics in Contemporary Punjab", *Contribution to Indian Sociology*, Sage, New Delhi, Vol. 38, Nos. 1&2, January-August, p. 182, Surinder Singh, 2006, "Caste and Democracy Assertion and Identity among the Dalits of Rural Punjab," *Sociology Bulletin*, Sage, New Delhi, Vol. 55, No. 1, January-April, p. 11. Ronki Ram, 2004, "Untouchability and Dalit Consciousness and Ad Dharm Movement on In Punjab", *Contribution to Indian Sociology*, Sage, New Delhi, Vol. 38, No. 3, pp. 323-28. See also: Ronki Ram, 2007, "Social Exclusion, Resistance and Deras: Exploring the Myth of Casteless Sikh Society in Punjab", *Economic and Political* Weekly, Vol. XLII, No. 40 October 13, pp. 4065-67, Ronki Ram, 2007, "Ravidass Dera and Social Protest: Making Sense of Dalit Consciousness in Punjab", *The Journal of Asian Studies*, November, Vol. 67, No. 4, p. 896, Surinder Singh, 2009, "Deras Caste Conflict and Recent Violence in Punjab", *Mainstream*, Vol. XLVII, No. 26, p. 34.

82. Khuswant Singh, 1991, *op. cit.*, No. 10, p. 75.
83. Mark Tully and Satish Jacob, 1987, *op. cit.*, No.12 , p. 68.
84. *Ibid.*
85. Harnik Deol, 2000, *op. cit.*, No. 15, p. 105.
86. *Ibid.*
87. Paramjit Singh Judge, 2005, *Religion Identity and Nationhood*, Rawat Publications, New Delhi, pp. 55-56.
88. 37th Speech of Bhindranwale, cited in Paramjit Singh Judge, 2005, *Ibid.*, pp. 132-41.
89. Narain Singh, 2003, *Singh Garj: Speeches and Interviews of Sant Jarnail Singh*, Gurmat Pustak Bhandar, Amritsar.
90. Paramjit Singh Judge, 2005, *op. cit.*, No. 87, pp. 88-89.
91. *Ibid.*, p. 130
92. Paramjit Singh Judge, 2005, *op. cit.*, No. 87, p. 130.
93. *Ibid.*, p. 141.
94. Harish Puri, *et. al.*, 1999, *op. cit.*, No.1, pp. 30-40. See also: Inderjit Singh Jaijee, 2002, *Politics of Genocide: Punjab 1984-1998*, Ajanta Publications, New Delhi, p. 22.
95. *Ibid.*, pp. 32-33: See also: Sachidanand Sinha, 1984, *Army Action in Punjab Prelude and Aftermath*, Pub. Samta Era, Delhi, pp. 42-50, 79-84.
96. Harish Puri, et. al., 1999, *op. cit.*, No. 1, p. 45. See also: Inderjit Singh Jaijee, 2002, *op. cit*, No. 94, p. 35.
97. "The Knights of Falsehood," www.satp.org., 21-12- 2010.
98. H.K. Puri, *et. al.*, 1999, *op. cit.*, No. 1, pp. 39-40.
99. Inderjit Singh Jaijee, 2002, *op. cit.*, No. 94, pp. 30-31.

100. PTI, 1984 "Terrorist attacked Deputy Speaker", *The Tribune*, 11 March. See also: TNS, 1984, "Terrorists tried to kill CM" *The Tribune*, 20 March, TNS, 1984, "Major accident averted: Rail Track blown up", 29 March, Delhi, 1984, "DSGPC Chief shot at", 3 April.
101. Ram Naryan Kumar, 2003, *op. cit.*, No. 2, p. 28.
102. Inderjit Singh Jaijee, 2002, *op. cit.*, No. 94, pp. 20-21.
103. In theirs book, *Mrs Indira Gandhi Last Battle*, Mark Tully, and Satish Jacob, 1987, Amritsar Mrs Gandhi's Last Battle, Jonathcape, London, coded that the CPM leader Harkrishan Surjit told them: "Three times in six months agreement was reached between the Akalis and centre but Prime Minister backed out at the last moment all in the three times."
104. Inderjit Jaijje, 2002, *op. cit., No.* 94, p. 44.
105. *Ibid.*, p. 15-16. See also: Amarjit Kaur, *et. al.*, 1984, *The Punjab Story*, Roli Books International, New Delhi pp. 42-50.
106. *Ibid.* See also: Giani Kirpal Singh, 1999, *Eyewitness Account of Operation Blue Star: Mighty Murderer, Our Army Attack on the Golden Temple Complex*, Pub. Bhai Chatter Singh Jiwan Singh, Amritsar, pp. 23-26.
107. Inderjit Singh Jaijee, 2002, *op. cit.*, No. 94, p. 19.
108. *Ibid.*, pp. 38-40.
109. Harbir Singh Bhawra, 1985, *Diary de Panhey* (in Punjabi), Hamdard Printers, Jalandhar, pp. 5-10.
110. Harminder Kaur, 1990, *Blue Star over Amritsar*, Ajanta Publications, New Delhi, pp. 52-63.
111. Santokh Singh, *et. al.*, 1992, *Great Betrayal*, Guru Nanak Mission, Patiala, p. 51.
112. Kuldeep Nayar & Khushwant Singh, 1984, *The Tragedy of Punjab*, Vision Books, New Delhi, p. 31.
113. Inderjit Singh Jaijee, 2002, *op. cit.*, No. 94, pp. 60-62.
114. PUDR, 1985, "Black Laws in Punjab: Report of an Enquiry", *Economic and Political Weekly,* Vol. XX, No. 9, May 11, pp. 826-30.
115. Inderjit Singh Jaijee, 2002, *op. cit.*, No. 94, pp. 64-68.
116. PTI, 1984, "530 Persons are detained: Army" , *Times of India*, 16 June.
117. UNI, 1984, "Sikh Regiment surrendered to Army," *Hindustan Times*, 14 June.
118. PTI, 1984 "Army action damaged the Army Image in Countryside", *Hindustan Times*, 15 June.
119. H.T. News, 1984, "Jathedar Natha Singh and 13 protestors sent to prison", *Hindustan Times*, 16 June.
120. H.T. News, 1984, "Operation against the terrorists hideout is continue: Army", *Hindustan Times*, 16 June.
121. H.T. News, 1984 "Army action against Bhindranwale was necessary: Lt. General Arora," *Hindustan Times*, 28 June.
122. Inderjit Jaijee, 2002, *op. cit*, No. 94, pp. 75-78.
123. Man Singh Deora, 1992, *Aftermath of Operation Blue Star*, Anmol Publications, New Delhi, p. 47.
124. H.T. News, 1984, "Badal Arrested for announcing Ardas Divas", and "Arya Pratinidhi Sabha call for Mourning day" *Hindustan Times*, 18 June. See also: IENS, 1984, Communal Tension prevailed over Ardas Diva and Mourning day: Badal arrested", *Indian Express*, 18 June.

125. Ved Marwah, 1995, *Uncivil Wars: Pathology of Terrorism in India*, Deep & Deep Publications, and New Delhi, p.196.
126. Harji Malik, 1984. "A Punjab Report", *Economic and Political Weekly*, Vol. XIX, No. 37, September 15, pp. 1522-25.
127. PUDR, May 11, 1985, *op. cit.*, No. 114, pp. 826-30.
128. Harji Malik, 1984, *op. cit.*, No. 126, p. 608.
129. PTI, 1984, "Terrorist killed Congress Leader, Security Forces nabbed 100 suspects" and "Vice Chancellor of Punjabi University Arrested" , *Indian Express*, 17 June.
130. PTI, 1984, "71 more terrorists are arrested : More ammunition and arms recovered from Golden Temple by Army", *Hindustan Times*, 18 June.
131. PTI, 1984, "30 Sikh protestors were arrested on Sedition charges", *Tribune*, 21 June. See also: Tribune News Service (TNS), 1984, "Sikh priests gave call for Shaheedi Divas", *The Tribune*, 21 June.
132. TNS, 1984, "Army explained the Punjab Situation and Operation Blue Star," *The Tribune,* 21 June.
133. UNI, 1984, "Terrorist targeted the religious place: More arms and ammunition seized", *The Times of India,* 21 June.
134. PTI, 1984, "Court of Inquiry is set to identity of the Civilians arrested with the Army deserted: Search for army deserted continue in U.P.", *Hindustan Times*, 20 June.
135. H.T. News, 1984, "Terrorists Killed a Shopkeeper; Army arrested 30 more", *Hindustan Times*, 22 June.
136. PTI, 1984, "Security forces shot dead extremists in encounter", *Times of India,* 22 June.
137. IENS, 1984,"Temple Priest Murdered" *Indian Express*, 25 June.
138. PTI, 1984, "BJP leader arrested in Ludhiana" *The Tribune,*28 June.
139. TNS, 1984, "Baba Harianwelawale arrested with a large quantity of weapons" *The Tribune*, 28, June.
140. TNS, 1984, "Punjab: The situation becoming normal", *The Tribune*, 22 June.
141. PTI, 1984 "Member of Bhartiya Kisan Union held for breaching peace", *Times of India*, 22 June.
142. Interview of Bhagwant Singh, former Member of *Student Federation of India* of Kala Afgana Government College in the District of Gurdaspur, Conducted on 15-5-2008. Interview of the former President of All India Sikh Student Federation, Hardial Singh of the same College, both were arrested at the time of Operation Blue Star under preventive detention interview conducted on 16-5-2008.
143. White papers on the Punjab Agitation, 10 July, 1984, *op. cit.*, No. 72, p. 11.
144. IENS, 1984, "Why the situation was allowed to deteriorate: L.K. Advani", *Indian Express*, 16 June.
145. TNS, 1984, "Congress leaders rebutted Advani for criticising government over Operation Blue Star", *The Tribune*, 22 June.
146. IENS, 1984, "Prime Minister appealed for Communal Harmony" *The Indian Express*, 21 June.
147. H.T. News, 1984, "Security forces will remain in the temple complex still: PM", *Hindustan Times*, 21 June.

148. IENS, 1984, "Senior CPM leader criticised Congress over Operation Blue Star", *Indian Express*, 20 June.
149. IENS, 1984, "The Punjab Problem can be solved through the dialogue : Farooq Abdullah", *The Indian Express*, 27 June.
150. PTI, 1984, "Finance Minister ruled out the possibility of any negotiation with Akalis before the restoration of normalcy", *The Tribune*, 25 June.
151. H.T. News, 1984, "Rajiv Gandhi blame Akalis for supporting Terrorists" *Hindustan Times*, 3 July.
152. UNI, 1984, "Beg Supported the government on Blue-Star", *Times of India*, 26 June.
153. H.T. News, 1948, "Janata Party Chief Chandra Sekhar sought an interview with Sant Longowal in Jail", *Hindustan Times*, 19 August. See also: TNS, 1984, "B.J.P. President and General Secretary visited Golden Temple", *The Tribune*, 19 August.
154. Amritsar, 1984, "World Convention to discussed the validity of Kar Sewa in Golden Temple", *The Tribune*, 20 August. See also: Amritsar, 1984 "District Magistrate turned down the permission to hold the World Sikh Convention", *The Tribune*, 28 August, UNI, 1984, "Security Forces made Preventive Arrests of the Akali and SGPC Workers", *Times of India*, 29 August.
155. Amiya Rao, 1984, "When Delhi Burnt", *Economic and Political Weekly*, Vol. XIX, No. 49, December 8, pp. 2066-69.
156. en.wikipedia.org/wiki/Indian general election 1984, 12.10.2009.
157. H.K. Puri, *et. al.*, 1999, *op. cit.*, No. 1, pp. 47-48.
158. *Ibid.*, p. 182.
159. S.S. Thandi, 1996, "Counter-insurgency and Political Violence in Punjab", G. Singh and Talbot (eds), *Punjabi Identity; Continuity and Change*, Manohar Publication, New Delhi, p. 165.
160. *Ibid.*
161. H.K. Puri, *et. al.*, 1999, *op. cit.*, No. 1, pp. 49-50.
162. D.P. Sharma, 1996, *The Punjab Story: Decade of Turmoil*, APH Publishing Corporation, New Delhi, pp. 93-94.
163. The day when Indian Army attacked on the Bhindranwale with his band of terrorists inside the Golden Temple was declared the day of the Sikh struggle for the establishment the sovereign Sikh state called Khalisatn, "Declaration of Khalistan", *Sant Sipahi*, 1986, June, pp. 25-27.
164. H.K. Puri, *et. al.*, 1999, *op. cit.*, No. 1, p. 50.
165. TNS, 1986, "Barnala Faces Crisis", *The Tribune*, May 2. See also: TNS, 1986, "Cong. (I)-BJP offer Support: CM claims 55 MLAs support", *The Tribune*, May 7.
166. Ram Naryan Kumar, 2008, *Terror in Punjab: Narrative Knowledge and Truth*, Shipra Publications, New Delhi, pp. 215-16.
167. Gurpal Singh, 2000, *Ethnic conflicts in India: A Case Study of Punjab*, Macmillan Press, London, p. 142.
168. Ram Naryan Kumar, 2008, *op. cit.*, No. 167, p. 224.
169. H.K. Puri, *et. al.*, 1999, *op. cit.*, No. 1, p. 50.
170. Joyce Pettigrew, 1995, *The Sikh of the Punjab: Unheard Voices of State and Guerrilla Violence*, Zed Book, London, p. 139. Other Prominent Studies

on the Movement Like: *Religion and National In India: The Case of the Punjab*, Harnik Deol, *The Sikh Unrest and The Indian State*, Ram Naryan Kumar, *Terrorism In Punjab: Narrative Knowledge and Truth*, Ram Naryan Kumar, *Reduced to Ashes: The Insurgency*, Ram Kumar Naryan *et. al., Politics of Genocide, Inderjit* Jaijee etc, presented the same view.

171. Harish Puri, *et. al.*, 1999, *op. cit.*, No. 1, p. 55.
172. K.S. Dhillon, 1998, "A decade of Violence, 1983-92", J.S. Grewal and Indu Banga (eds), *Punjab in Prosperity and Violence,* Institute of Punjab Studies, Chandigarh, p. 105.
173. V.N. Naryan, 1996, *Tryst with Terror: Punjab's Turbulent Decade*, Ajanta Publications, New Delhi, p. 27.
174. Inderjit Jaijee, 1999, *op. cit.*, No. 94, p. 31.
175. The bitter examples of the repression of the democratic repression the Akalis protest were the mishandling of the Sikhs during the ASIAN games in 1982. When the Haryana police did not spare the high Sikh dignitaries even the MP of Congress and Sikh army men of the Maj. Gen. Rank (personal interview with Major General Narinder Singh at his residence in Chandigarh, on 23 December, 2004), who became sympathies to Bhindranwale.
176. Ram Kumar, 2008, *op. cit.*, No. 167, p. 191.
177. *Ibid.*, p. 211.
178. Suman Dubey, 1986, "Shiv Sena: Fighting Back", *India Today*, 15 April, p. 34.
179. It is to note that the Rajiv Longowal Accord was political impractical as the third party the State of Haryana which was to be effected by the terms of the accord was even not consulted at the time of the signing of the accord. Latter on the Chief Minister of Haryana openly demanded the completion of SYNL and also questioned the transfer of the Capital city of Chandigarh to Punjab. Moreover the Barnala government was also dismissed to show the strong action of the centre against the violence in neighbouring state for the electoral gains in the Legislative Assembly Election of Haryana in 1987.
180. Ram Kumar, 2008, *op. cit.*, No. 167, p. 211.
181. Maloy Krishan Dhar, 2005, *Open Secrets: India's Intelligence Unveiled*, Manas Publications, New Delhi, p. 325.
182. Gobind Thukral, 1986, "Akali Dal Badal's Bid", *India Today*, 15 June. See also: Gobind Thukral, 1986, "Punjab Militant Poses and Terrorism Turning the Tide", *India Today,* 31 July, pp. 34-38.
183. Tavleen Singh & Gobind Thukral, 1987,"Punjab Held to Ransom", *India Today*, 15 February, pp. 10-14. See also: Tavleen Singh & Gobind Thukral, 1987, "Darshan Singh Ragi Double Edge", *India Today*, 28 February, pp. 36-39.
184. Gobind Thukral, 1987 ,"Punjab: Militant Win", *The Tribune*, 14 January.
185. TNS, 1987, "Akal Takht Jathedar announced the formation on United Akali Dal", *The Tribune*, 4 February.
186. IENS, 1988, "Killing part of conspiracy: Ragi", *India Express* , 28 January.
187. Maloy Krishan Dhar, 2005, *op. cit.*, No. 182, p. 343.
188. Ram Kumar, 2008, *op. cit.*, No. 167, pp. 209-10.

189. Vipul Mudgal, 1987, "Punjab in Bind", *India Today*, 15 October, pp. 16-19. See also: Vipul Mudgal, 1987, "Punjab Locked Horns", *India Today*, 31 October, 23-27.
190. Ram Kumar, 2008, *op. cit.*, No. 167, p. 222.
191. Maloy Krishan Dhar, 2005, *op. cit.*, No. 182, pp. 329-30.
192. TNS, 1986, "Barnala on the right track" , *The Tribune*, 21 July. See also: TNS, 1986, "The hardcore identified", *The Tribune*, 30 July, TNS, 1986, "PM for free hand to police", *The Tribune*, 18 August, TNS, 1986,"Police given six months to finish terrorists: Police wants more powers", *The Tribune*, 12 February, PTI, 1986, "BSF pins hops on operation bird", *The Tribune*, 5 October, UNI, 1987, "Akali Dal (B) leaders praise assailants of PM, Ribeiro", *The Tribune*, 15 May.
193. Ram Kumar, 2008, *op. cit.*, No. 167, p. 226.
194. Julio Ribeiro, 1998, *Bullet for Bullet: My Life as a Police Officer*, Penguin Book, New Delhi, pp. 350-52.
195. Maloy Krishna Dhar, 2005, *op. cit.*, No. 182, pp. 331-32.
196. *Ibid.*, pp. 332-30
197. *Ibid.* p. 336.
198. Inderjit Jaijee, 1999, *op. cit.*, No. 94, pp. 78-79.
199. Ram Kumar, 2005, *op. cit.*, No. 167, pp. 230-40. See also: Inderjit Jaijee, 1999, *op. cit.*, No. 94, pp. 78- 79.
200. Ved Marwah, 1995, *op. cit.*, No. 125, p. 191.
201. *Ibid.*
202. *Ibid.*, p. 189.
203. Joyce Pettigrew, 1995, *op. cit.*, No. 171, p. 77.
204. *Ibid.*, pp. 136-38.
205. H.K. Puri, *et. al.*, 1999, *op. cit.*, No, pp. 1. See also: pp. 89-91. Joyce Pettigrew, 1995, *op. cit.*, No. 171, pp. 70-100.
206. *Ibid.*, 57-61.
207. Kamaljeet Rattan, 1989, "Interview with Simranjit Singh Mann: I am against all killings", *India Today*, April 30, pp. 2-7. See also: Harnik Deol, 2000, *op. cit.*, No. 15, p. 113.
208. Kavita Shetty & Kanwar Sandhu, 1989, "Regional Parties: Growing Clout", *India Today*, 15 November, pp. 9-12. See also: Kanwar Sandhu, 1989, "Punjab: Rebels Win", *India Today*, 15 December, pp. 7-9.
209. Meenu Roy, 1999, *Elections: A Continuity in Coalition*, New Delhi, National Publishing House, New Delhi, p. 25.
210. Kanwar Sandhu, 1989, "interview with S.S Ray: "Acrimonious Departure", *India Today*, 31 December, pp. 6-9.
211. *Ibid.*
212. Ram Naryan Kumar, 1997, *The Sikh Unrest and the Indian State*, Ajanata Publications, New Delhi, pp. 275-76. See also: Kanwar Sandhu, 1989, "Interview with Mann, 'I pray to all to help the government'", *India Today*, 31 December pp. 12-14.
213. Kanwar Sandhu, 1989, "Punjab: Flickers of Hope", *India Today*, 31 December, p. 1-4.
214. Maloy Krishan Dhar, 2005, *op. cit.*, No. 182, p. 384.
215. *Ibid.*, p. 385.

216. TNS, 1991, "Khudian Case remains a mystery", *The Tribune*, January 31.
217. Maloy Krishan Dhar, 2005, *op. cit.*, No. 182, pp. 332-33.
218. Ram Naryan Kumar, 2008, *op. cit.*, No. 167, p. 276.
219. *Ibid.*, p. 277.
220. *Ibid.*, p. 278.
221. *Ibid.*, pp. 279-80.
222. *Ibid.*, pp. 281-82.
223. Maloy Krishan Dahr, 2005, *op. cit.*, No. 182, pp. 410-14.
224. TNS, 1991, "Militant realigning"', The *Tribune*, 19 April. See also: TNS, 1991, "AISSF (M) to contest the elections", *The Tribune*, 20 April. TNS, 1991, "AISSF promises homeland", *The Tribune*, 3 May.
225. Kanwar Sandhu, 1991, "Interview with Manochahal: We will not budge an Inch", *India Today*, 15 September, pp. 5-8.
226. TNS, "AISSF (M) Dal talks suffer setback", *The Tribune*, 24 April, 1991. See also: TNS, 1991, "Badal revolts against Mann", *The Tribune*, 24 April, TNS, 1991, "Dal (B) draft for union of states", *The Tribune*, 17 May, Staff Correspondence, 1991, "Amrinder floats Dal (Panthik)" , *The Tribune*, 29 April, TNS, 1991, "Dal Longowal also breaks away", *The Tribune*, 25 April, TNS, , 1991, "AISSF (M) unit revolts", *The Tribune*, 30 April 1991, "Kahlon group quit AISSF(M)",*The Tribune*, 6 May.
227. TNS, 1991 "Army curfew in several areas: How Rajiv began his fateful day", *The Tribune*, 23 May. See also : UNI, 1991, "Plastic belt bomb killed Rajiv Gandhi", *The Tribune*, 23 May.
228. Kanwar Sandhu, 1991, "Punjab: Perilous Poll", *India Today,* 31 June, 1-5.
229. Kanwar Sandhu, 1991, "Punjab: Floundering Move", *India Today*, 14 July, pp. 6-9.
230. TNS, 1991, "AISSF (M) Dal talks suffer setback", *The Tribune*, 24 April. See also: TNS, 1991, "Badal revolts against Mann", *The Tribune*, 24 April, TNS, 1991," Dal (B) draft for union of states', *The Tribune*, 17 May, PTI, 1991, "Amrinder floats Dal (Panthik)" , *The Tribune*, 29 April, TNS, 1991, "Dal Longowal also breaks away", *The Tribune*, 25 April. TNS, , 1991, "AISSF (M) unit revolts", *The Tribune*, 30 April, 1991, TNS "Kahlon group quit AISSF (M)", *The Tribune*, 6 May, UNI, 1991, "Army curfew in several areas: How Rajiv began his fateful day", *The Tribune*, 23 May, UNI, 1991, "Plastic belt bomb killed Rajiv Gandhi", *The Tribune*, 23 May. Kanwar Sandhu, 1991, *op. cit.*, Nos. 219-220. Ram Kumar Naryan, 2008, *op. cit.*, No. 167, p. 297. TNS, 1992, "Top Akalis held under TADA", *The Tribune*, 11 February. See also: PTI, 1992, "Election boycott march foiled", *The Tribune*, 12 February.
231. *Ibid.*
232. Ram Kumar Naryan, 2008, *op. cit.*, No. 167, p. 297.
233. *Ibid.*
234. PTI, 1992, "Top Akalis held under TADA", *The Tribune*, 11 February. See also: PTI, 1992, "Another case against Tohra, Badal, Mann", *The Tribune*, 17 February.
235. "The Independent, Tim Megirk, Scared Punjabis are shepherd to the polls", 20 February, 1992, coded in Ram Kumar Naryan, 2008, *op. cit.*, No. 167, p. 298.

236. TNS, 1992, "Peaceful poll, low turnout", *The Tribune*, 20 February, See also: TNS, 1992, "Lowest turnout, uneven spread", *The Tribune*, 24 February, TNS, 1992, "Two third majority for Congress', *The Tribune*, 21 February, TNS, 1992, "Record majority for Congress", *The Tribune*, 22 February.
237. Kanwar Sandhu, 1993, "Punjab: Normal Life at Last", *India Today*, 28 February, pp. 11-15.
238. Ram Kumar Naryan, 2008, *op. cit.*, No. 167, p. 299.

4

State, Militancy and Human Rights in Punjab : An Appraisal

The violent protests against the state are always deemed to be threat to the national integrity, security and the political stability by the governments. If incidents of the violence are related to the demands of a particular community, which is also residing in a particular region under a state, then these violent incidents are taken as the part of secessionist conspiracy. The states have always resorted to violence against any form of political opposition. Democratic states have also not been an exception in using violence whenever their existence has been in danger or when their authority has been challenged. However, the establishment of the rule of law, protecting human rights, as well as minorities' rights in a democracy pose a serious challenge to the age old strategies based on coercion by the state agents. Use of direct/visible or structural/invisible violence by the democratic states has come under critical scrutiny in the present era of democratization with emphasis on regime of human rights. The now widely accepted concept of human governance, human security and the equal rights of all along with the due process of law and equality before the law has been dominating the democratic political set-ups in these days. But the state is still confused with its constitutional commitment and its strategic planning while dealing with the violent movement based on collective claim making either for autonomy or for substantive equality and justice.

In the modern era it has been one of the continuing dilemmas of democratic states as to whether or not terrorist violence can be combated with the help of equally intense counter violence. Can it be done without altering the fabric of normal democratic legal structure and procedures? The democratic states have been circumspect in the use of counter violence as democratic mode of governance is supposed to be based on dialogue among and accommodation of the interests of the different collectives.

Stansfield Turner, former Director of US Intelligence Agency, emphasised during the discussion about the mode of the working of the US Task Force on combating terrorism that "in the name of defeating terrorism we don't become terrorist".[1] A whole corpus of what may be described as "counter-insurgency" or counter-terrorism" literature is now available which refers to the moral of dilemma any modern democratic state faces while meeting the challenge of the militant violence against the state or the helpless people.[2] Terrorists' crime is now increasingly being viewed as a special crime which required an apparatus and procedure different from the normal to deal with it irrespective of the fact that the political regime is democratic or not.

The central weapon of terrorism is fear and as a Scottish scholar Wilkinson has emphasised, its wider target is the public. So the victims of ensuing violence may largely be non-combatants who are soft targets and the terrorist action may have the most dramatic intimidating effect. Terrorism thrives on propaganda that creates a climate of fear. Their actions may be unpredictable. Terrorism also denies evidence to the state's prosecuting agency; evidence that would stand up to judicial scrutiny in a court of law. State tends to operate by intimidation of the police and magistracy, as also by penetration in their ranks which is the greatest scourge of the state. State is therefore inclined to view terrorism/militancy as anti-national "warfare" rather than crime in the legal sense of the term. Long drawn terrorism often thrives under the cover of public support. That may be the result of fear and intimidation or due to the sympathy with the cause and appreciation of heroism of those taking on the state. Social constructions of the struggle, the cause for which the terrorists claim to be fighting, play a crucial role in winning the public support and sympathy. The prevalence of anti-state militancy in a community is the life blood of terrorism aiming at the dismemberment of the state. Equally significant is the clandestine support from a hostile enemy state. Another significant element is the media writing, unwitting or coerced publicity of terrorist proclamations and deeds. Propaganda is the very oxygen of the sway and success of terrorism. In the process, the state responses to civil and political rights creates the popular alienation among the ethnic communities on one hand and a popular demand to suppress the agitation for the civil and political rights of the community which is in conflict with the state from the national perspective. The human rights discourse generally dominated by the state concerns of national unity and integrity.

The counter-insurgency measures by the state are aimed at the above mentioned sources of support and cover for terrorists. The present chapter focuses on a concrete case study of Punjab. Study of the secessionist violence perpetrated by the militants and the state's response and the issue of human rights in militancy prone Punjab is taken up for discussion.

It is to be noted that the Punjab is the only state where the government of India is claiming to curb the secessionist movement successfully. After witnessing violence for more than a decade that saw more than 20,000 deaths Punjab has become peaceful. The armed movement started with the "Operation Blue Star" and reached to its zenith with the killing of India's Prime Minister and ended with the killing of the Chief Minister of Punjab, besides the sacrifices of the thousands of men of the security forces, innocent civilians, the armed insurgents. Punjab since then has remained peaceful and the Sikh community no longer seems to be alienated politically. Hindu-Sikh community level relationship which came under strain due to the targeted killings of the Hindus by the militants has now been cordial as always.

The return to the 'normal', however, does not mask the critical issue of human rights violation. State response to the secessionism has remained under scrutiny. The collapse of Khalistan movement remained wrapped in unresolved mysteries. As discussed in the preceding chapters, the question of justice to the victims of the human rights abuses and the involvement of the ruling political party in the anti-Sikh riots in the 1984 remains a simmering emotive issue in Punjab politics.[3] At the same time, the means of struggle adopted by the armed militants in the Sikh ethno-nationalist movement also needs a comprehensive analysis while relating it to the human rights concerns.

The present chapter is structured around the life and times of militancy in Punjab. The focus of the chapter is as to how the demand for autonomy by a political community asking for an autonomous territorial homeland within Indian Union was denied. Subsequently, the autonomist movement turned into the fight for the realisation of the right to self-determination. It witnessed anti-systemic mode of politics based on terrorist violence. The movement for the autonomy for the state was viewed as a challenge by the Indian state to its unity and integrity leading to the use of state violence. As the state showed the unwillingness to concede the collective demands, the movement degenerated into violent one inviting much more strident response from the state. The net outcome was the gross violation of human rights of the people of Punjab. This was the period when faced with the militant violence, Indian state made attempt to settle the 'Punjab problem'. However, due to the lack of political will as well as the hardliners among the movement leaders, the turmoil continued unabated for more than a decade before the political leadership of Beant Singh saw the end of militancy. End of militancy, however, came not due to dialogue or negotiation but with the help of the unprecedented state violence against the suspected militants without following the democratic regime of rights. The state's response to the militant violence need to be analysed along with the ideological and human rights perspective.

STATE RESPONSES TO MILITANCY IN PUNJAB AND HUMAN RIGHTS

The democratic Indian state's response to the problem of the secessionism and human rights in Punjab may be analysed at three levels: one at the political level, second at the legislative level and third at the level of coercion.

POLITICAL RESPONSES

The analysis of the political responses and initiative of the Centre to solve the Punjab problem and the Akali demand has been attempted in the preceding chapter. The tough attitude of the centre against the democratic struggle of Akali Dal for the demand of autonomy over the natural resources of state and merger of some Punjabi-speaking areas in the neighbouring states are enough to vitiate the atmosphere in Punjab, as discussed in the preceding chapter. The mishandling of the fundamentalist and secessionist forces in Punjab meant that the terrorists came into picture. The opportunity to achieve political solution to the problem evaporated the moment the Indian Army launched the "Operation Blue Star" to get the Bhindranwale and his followers from the highest temporal stage of Sikhs. The damage to Akal Takht wounded the Sikh psyche. Although the Army action was necessary to flush out the Bhindranwale and his followers from the sanatorium of Golden Temple, But the operation had some miscalculation and the political leaning which resulted not only killing of the thousands of innocents who were gathered in the Shrines (rest-houses) and in the complex on the occasion of Martyr day celebration of fifth Sikh Guru. Akali protestors who came there to launch a civil-disobedience were also victims of the state violence. Moreover, the Operation Wood Rose and Anti-Sikh riots with the alleged support of the ruling party further eradicated the space for dialogue and negotiation. Although the moderate Akali leadership led by Sant Longowal and S.S. Barnala tried their best for the political solution but dissent of the Sikhs against the centre and extra-constitutional working of the armed forces was so high that either the moderate leaders like Longowal or Balwant Singh were killed by Sikh terrorists at the early stage of the conflict or the leaders like Barnala were marginalised due to the flip-flop policy of the centre towards Punjab. There was a certain degree of ad-hocism and later on the efforts of the Barnala government to find out the political solution of the problem also failed due to the alleged high-handedness and free hands of the armed forces provided by the extraordinary laws and the central government in the name of protecting the unity and integrity of a nation-state.[4]

The issue of Jodhpur Detainees, harassment of the Sikh masses by the Army and extra-judicial killing and the non-implementation of the Rajiv Longowal Accord, became the major reasons for the militants to win over the Sikh masses in the countryside. It was the Operation Blue Star and the Operation Wood Rose that arguably started the era of militancy in Punjab. It was after this that Bhindranwale cult received adulation.

LEGISLATIVE MEASURES AND THE HUMAN RIGHTS

As discussed in the preceding chapter, in October 1983, Punjab was put under President's rule. This was followed by a spate of extra-ordinary laws limiting the fundamental rights of the citizenry in the name of restoring peace and democracy in Punjab. These laws were namely *Punjab Disturbed Area Act, 1983, The Chandigarh Disturbed Area Act, 1983, The National Security Act, 1984, The Armed Forces Special Powers Act, 1983, the Code of Criminal Procedure (Punjab*

Amendment) Act, 1983 and finally *Terrorists–Affected Areas (Special Court) Act, 1984* and *Terrorist and Disruptive Activities (Preventive Act)* enacted in 1985 with lifetime limited to a period of two years. These laws gave extraordinary powers to the army, police and the judiciary and had the effect to by pass all safeguards incorporated in the ordinary criminal laws to ensure fair trial and legal justice.

To understand the depth and reach of the draconian mandate accorded to the security forces in Punjab by the Indian state, it would be pertinent to examine the provisions of arrest, detention, trial, prosecution and conviction in context of the due process of law fair trial and human rights.

The National Security Act, 1980, claimed as necessary legislation to tackle militancy was amended by the Act 24 of 1984, especially with the reference to "the extremist and terrorist elements in the disturbed areas of Punjab and Chandigarh". Government with the help of the Act aimed to deal with "anti-social and anti-national elements". The draconian Act provided detention without charge or trial for one year in all parts of the country and two years in Punjab. It was quite contrary to the letter and spirit of the Articles 19 and 21 of the Constitution of India.

The Armed Forces (Punjab and Haryana) Special Powers Act 1983 and The Punjab Disturbed Area Act, 1983 empowered the security forces to enter and search any premises, and to arrest any person without a warrant. It also allowed security forces to destroy any place on the suspicion of being a "terrorist hide out" and "shoot and kill" a suspected terrorist with immunity from prosecution. *The Terrorist Affected Areas (Special Court) Act, 1984* and *Disruptive Activities (Prevention Act)*, the Union government promulgated the *Terrorist and Disruptive Activities (Prevention) Ordinance issued by the President* under Article 22 of the Constitution in May 1987 on the ground that the police required special powers of the Act because, "on the basis of the experience, it was felt that in order to combat and cope with terrorist and disruptive activities effectively, it is not only necessary to continue the said law but also to strengthen it further." The May 1987 ordinance was replaced with the Terrorist and Disruptive Activities (Prevention) 1987, TADA in September 1987. The life time of the Act was prescribed as two years, but on the due dates of expiry in 1989, 1991 and 1993, TADA was extended for further period of two years.

The Act defined a terrorist as (1) whoever intent to strike terror in people. Or adversely affect the harmony amongst different section of people does any act...by using bombs, dynamite or other explosive substances or inflammable substance of firearms or other lethal weapon or poisons or noxious gases or other chemicals or by any other substances. In such a manner as to cause death or injuries to, any person destruction of property and supply of services...or detain any person and threaten to kill or injure such person in order to compel the government or any other person to do abstain from doing an act, commits a Terrorist Act; (2) whoever conspires ...or advocate, abets, advises or incites or facilitate the commission of terrorist act or any preparatory to a terrorist act; (3) Whoever harbours or conceals, or attempts to harbour or conceal, any terrorist.[5] Under the Act, *abetment of a terrorist act meant*: (1) Communication or association with any person. Who is engaged in assisting...terrorist or disruption; (2) the passing on or publication of any information likely to assist the terrorist or disruptionists ... and publication of or distribution of any document matter obtained from them.[6]

Disruptive activity was defined as any action taken, whether by act or by speech or through any other manner: (1) which questions, disrupts or is intended to disrupt, whether directly or indirectly, the sovereignty and territorial integrity of India; (2) which is intended to bring about or supports any claim, whether directly or indirectly, for secession of any part of India .. from the Union; (3) which advocates, advises, suggests or incites or predicts, prophesies or pronounce or otherwise expresses in such manner as to incite, advise suggest or prompt the killing or destruction of any person bound by oath under the Constitution to uphold the sovereignty and integrity of India.[7]

Punishment for the Act were: (1) Death or imprisonment for life, also liable to fine in an act was resulted in the death of any person; (2) In any other case, the act was punishable with imprisonment for a term not less than five years and extending to imprisonment of life, also liable to fine. [8]

Possession of unauthorised arms, ammunition or explosive and helping terrorists or disruptionists to possess them was punishable with imprisonment for a term not less than five years, extending to imprisonment for life, also liable to fine.[9]

Every offence punishable under the Act was to be tried only in the designated court constituted by the Central or State governments. The government also appointed the presiding judges and additional judges with the concurrence of the chief justice of High Court. These judges continued in their offices even after attaining the age of superannuation under the rules.[10]

JUDICIAL PROCEDURE AND POWERS OF DESIGNATED COURTS

The central government could with the concurrence of the Chief Justice of India transfer any case pending before a designated court in a state to any other designated court within that state or any other state if in its opinion such transfer was necessary for the requirement of a speedy trial, or safety of the witness the prosecutor and the judge, or in the interest of justice.[11]

A designated court on receiving a complaint or a police report could take cognizance of any offence, without the accused being committed to trial. It may also proceed with the trial in the absence of the accused or his pleader and record the evidence of any witness.[12]

All proceedings before the court could at the discretion of the court be conducted in camera. The designated court could take necessary measures to keep the identity and address of the witnesses' secret. It could also decide the place where to hold proceeding of the trial and suppress the name and address of the witness from its orders, judgments or in any record of the case. Further, the court could issue directions that the identity and address of the witnesses would not be disclosed and the proceeding of the court would not be published in any manner. An appeal against any judgments, sentence or order of a designated court could only be addressed to the Supreme Court within a period of 30 days from the date of order.[13]

When a person was convicted of an offence under the Act, the designated court could order that all his properties be attached during the period of his trial. If the trial ended in the conviction, the attached property would were to be forfeited to the government free from all encumbrances. If the court was satisfied on receiving a report from a police officer or an officer of central government specially appointed to arrest, investigate and prosecute any person under the Act was absconding or was concealing himself from apprehension, it could publish a written proclamation requiring him to appear at a specific place and at specified time not more than 30 days from the publication of such proclamation. At the non-compliance of the order, the person was to be declared a proclaimed offender.[14]

ARREST, INVESTIGATION AND EVIDENCE

When a person had been declared a proclaimed offender, the evidence regarding his identification by witness from his photograph had the same values as the evidence of a test identification parade;[15]

No person accused under TADA could avail the remedy of anticipatory bail under section 438 of the Code of Criminal Procedure, (CrPC), in 1973.[16] A person arrested under TADA could be produced before any judicial magistrate, executive magistrate or special executive magistrate, under Section 167 of the CrPC, who could then authorise, irrespective of his jurisdiction, the detention of the accused for the purpose of investigation under the police custody for a maximum period of sixty days.[17]

A person arrested of any offence under the Act could be detained without bail for the maximum period of one year to enable the prosecution to complete investigation against him.[18]

Even at the expiry of this period, the accused under trial could not claim bail unless the court on reasonable grounds was satisfied that he had neither committed any offence under the Act and was likely to commit any while on bail.[19]

Confession made by an accused, co-accused, abettor or conspirator before a police officer of the rank of superintend of police, either in writing or recorded in any mechanical device, was admissible as evidence at trial. If the prosecution established that arms or explosives were recovered from the possession of the accused, or that his finger prints were found at the site of the offence, by the evidence of the expert, or that accused had confessed his offence before any person, the designated court had to presume, unless the contrary was proved, that the accused had committed the offence.[20]

The recording of confession and statement, under section 164 of the Code of Criminal Procedure 1973, could also be made by metropolitan magistrate and special judicial magistrate, executive magistrate and special executive magistrate whether or not they had jurisdiction in the case, at the instance of an officer investigating a case under TADA.[21]

No government and its officers could be taken to any court in any form for any action which they had in good faith done or purported to have done in the pursuance of the Act.[22]

POINT AND COUNTERPOINT : SUPREME COURT UPHOLDS TADA

Even the above cursory examination of the provisions of TADA shows that they were not only excessively harsh with ample scope for misuse and abuse of the fundamental rights guaranteed by chapter III of the Constitution at the hands of the state agents; they also demolished the buffer of procedure (CrPC) and Indian Evidence

Act. Many writ petitions, criminals' appeals and special provisions in the Terrorist Affected Areas (Special Courts) Act (No. 51 of 1984) and the TADA remained under purview for long years adding to the sufferings of the detainees, which the court finally disposed of through the common judgement of *Kartar Singh* v. *The State of Punjab* pronounced on 11 March 1994.

The Judgement can be scrutinized in two parts: first in relation to the main arguments that challenged the legality of TADA for destroying the traditionally established safeguards of the criminal procedural regulation; then with reference to the arguments around the larger issue of legislative competence of Parliament to enact law. For the sake of brevity, we shall examine the judgment only in the first part of arguments by assembling those under three main principles of procedure destroyed by TADA: (1) The burden of proof; (II) Judicial independence; and (III) Fair trial. Below, we first present the argument given against TADA, and then the Court's response to these arguments in *Kartar Singh* v. *the State of Punjab*.

THE BURDEN OF PROOF

Arguments

Under traditionally established rules of criminal trial system in India, no offence is proven nor any charge formulated unless warranted by legal evidence. It is the prosecution's burden to furnish the evidence. According to section 111 of the Evidence Act, the accused are presumed to be innocent until the prosecution, on its onus, establishes the contrary. Section 21 of TADA, as far as it commanded the presumption of guilt against the accused, inverted this principle. This aberration from the established legal tradition received a permanent place in the evidence a permanent in the Evidence Act through the insertion of section 111 (a), which attended the passing of the Terrorist Affected Area (Special Court) Act.[23]

The definition of the word "abetment" in section 2(1)(a) of TADA eliminated the proof of criminal intention of the principle of "mensrea". It repudiated the explanation in sections 107 and 108 of the IPC that presupposed wrongful intention as an essential ingredient to the offence of "abetment". Thus, TADA destroyed the essential conditions of penal liability in the old maxima "actus non facit reum, nisi mens sit rea," meaning "the act alone does not amount to guilt, it must be accompanied by a guilty mind." Section 2(1) also overturned several decisions of the Supreme Court requiring the concurrence of the intent and act to constitute an offence of abetment.[24] Thus, TADA was unconstitutional and contrary to the principles of fairness and reasonableness.

Section 15 of TADA allowed a police officer of the superintendent's rank or above to record confessions of the accused person in custody and its sections 22 allowed for photographic identification. These provisions violated the "procedure established by law" as they removed the armour of the Evidence Act under sections 24, 25, 26 and 27, which have prohibited the admission of such evidence in trial since the Act came into operation in 1872. Section 164(a) of the CrPC also absolutely bans the recording of confession by police officers even when they are confirmed with magisterial powers. The TADA also violated the clear command of Article 20(3) of the Constitution that no person accused of any offence shall be compelled to be a witness against himself."

The police officers in India are known for their oppressive behaviour towards suspects in their custody and for compelling them under physical torture to make self-incriminating confessions. This has been a colonial legacy as at that time police was viewed as the coercive agency of a law and order administration whose main job was to suppress all the dissenting voices. The National Judicial Commission's fourth report notes with concern, "the inclination of even some of the supervisory ranks to countenance the practice in bid to achieve quick results ... Even well-meaning officers are sometimes drawn toward third degree methods..." Also, the Law Commission's working papers on the "Custodial Crimes" states that the abuse of power against detainees has become a concern for international community.[25] Thus the conclusive evidence of custodial crimes that exists against the Indian police and the expert finding on the psychology and consequences of custodial interrogation categorically prohibit the power that section 15 of TADA bestowed on senior police officers from the rank of superintendent.[26] This section of TADA also defined the unanimous judicial verdict, not only from America and Britain but also from India, that custodial disclosure are anathema as evidence in criminal trial.[27]

Section 20(7), 20(4)(b) of TADA were tarnished by the same inseparable presumption of guilt as impeachment preclusion of anticipatory bail by 20(7) destroyed the protection offered by section 438 of the CrPC to the innocent against the manifest abuse of police power. The protection under section 438 does not offer an unequivocal right; it only empowers the judiciary to exercise the discretion of bail, conditional to the satisfaction that the availing person is neither likely to abscond nor obstruct the investigation pending against him. Section 20(4) of TADA allowed 60 days of police custody of an accused under interrogation and one year of judicial remand without bail. The prosecution was given this period to complete its investigations and file charge -sheet against the accused for trial before the designated court. In contrast, section 167(2) of the CrPC permits an accused to be held in police custody for a maximum period of 15 days and for 90 days in judicial custody, to allow the prosecution to complete the investigation. The extended period of remand under TADA, which also plugged bail, vitiated the doctrine of "speedy trial", recited as the main objective justifying the legislation. At the end of the period even when the prosecution was unable to submit charge-sheet, the accused was still effectively barred from the benefit of bail under section 20(8) of TADA. This section required that "no person accused of an offence under TADA" would be released on bail unless the designated court was satisfied on "reasonable grounds" that he is not guilty of such offence and that he is not likely to commit any offence while on bail. In the absence of charge-sheet, neither could the accused produce the evidence of his innocence, nor could the designated court authenticate his guiltlessness ahead of the actual trial, let alone certify that he would not "commit any offence while on bail". Thus, section 20(8) ensured that no one accused under TADA, irrespective of the span of time he may already have spent in custody as an under-trial, could secure bail unless the prosecution was gratified to allow it.

THE JUDICIAL RESPONSE

Let us now refer to the Supreme Court of India' reasoning in response to these specific objections raised against TADA in *Kartar Singh* v. *State of Punjab* decision.

The Supreme Court held that the provisions of TADA, aiming to provide for speedy trial of terrorist and disruptive offences, were drastic in nature because the normal procedure of criminal trial was inadequate in fulfilling this objective. The stern stipulation of TADA was inseparable form and necessary for reaching this legislative objective. The transfer of the burden of proof to the accused, as well as other stringent provisions of TADA such as enhanced punishments, dispensation of the committal proceedings, summary trial, in-camera proceedings of the court, trial in the absence of accused his lawyer, admission of confessional evidence, were all seen as consistent with the main postulate of speedy trial, which derives from the Magna Carta and Sixth Amendment of the American Constitution. According to the Apex court the Parliament had the competence to enact laws whose procedure deviated from, even overrode, the rules of the Code of Criminal Procedures and the Evidence Act. Stringency and harshness of such provisions was seen as a matter of legislative wisdom, and court could not question it if it was based on a reasonable classification of offences and offenders for separate treatment. By fulfilling this criterion, TADA became unassailable on the ground of invidious discrimination.

The exclusion of "mens rea" from the definition of "abetment", according to the Additional Solicitor General appearing for the state, aimed to fulfil the objects of the Act in the period of escalated terrorism when it may not have been possible to prove the "intention" while establishing the physical facts. This position was seen as contrary to the established view that knowledge was an essential ingredient of the offence. However, the court can and did go beyond the ordinary grammatical meaning of the words to detect the actual intention of the legislature and to decide whether the presumption of knowledge should be imported into the definition of abetment, although it was verbally missing there. As the substantive provisions of the Act required the intention of offence, it was logical to assume that this ingredient of knowledge was silently implied also in the definition of abetment. To remove the anomaly which crept in from the lexical deficiency in the actual definition and this presumption of immanence, the court directed "that the actual knowledge or reason to believe on the part of a person to be roped in with the aid of that definition should be read into it instead of reading it down".

Regarding the admissibility of confession recorded by senior police officials, the Court was first inclined to expunge it for infringing the basic procedural safeguards in the criminal trial system. However, after examining the issue in the light of legislative competence to alter the procedure of trial, the meaningful objective of the legislation, and the gravity of terrorism, the court felt convinced that "the impugned section cannot be said to be suffering from any vice of unconstitutionality." The court cited the National Police Commission's fourth report from June 1980, which makes an ardent plea for the removal of the exiting ban on the entry of confessional statements recorded by police officials in to the area of judicial proceedings. Of course the Court had frequently dealt with cases of police atrocities. "We remorsefully like to state that on few occasions even custodial deaths caused during interrogation are brought to our notice. We are very much distressed and deeply concerned about the oppressive behaviour and most degrading and despicable practice adopted by some police officers..." But according to the court, the mere possibility of abuse was not a valid ground to challenging the validity of a statue. Section 15 of TADA, did not offend either Article 14 or Article 21 of the Constitution. The Court, however, expected the police officials to follow its guidelines on recording confessions that they were not tainted with vice.

The abolition of anticipatory bail by section 20(7) of TADA was seen as consistent with legislative mandate to rigorously quell the terrorist and disruptive menace. The provision of anticipatory bail under section 438 of CrPC was newly introduced in 1973 at the recommendation of the 41st report of the Law Commission and, therefore, was not give the difference of established tradition. Likewise, the extended period of pre-trial detention under section 20(4)(b) could not be attacked on the ground that it discredit the doctrine of speedy trial. Terrorists and saboteurs of national sovereignty belonged to secret societies and their activities covered large areas, both domestically and internationally. Investigation of their crimes justifiably required longer period and, as held by the American Supreme Court in *Beavers* v. *Haubert* case the right to speedy trial is necessary relative. It is consistent with delay and depends upon circumstances. It secures rights to a defendant. It does not preclude the right of public justice. Similarly, the contention the section 20 (7) of TADA made it impossible for even the innocent to get bail and therefore it violated Articles 21 and 14 of the Constitution guaranteeing the rights to life, liberty and equality before law, failed when compared to the terrorist threat to the society. All deprivation of liberty was validated by social defence. The court was fettered by the wisdom of a competent legislature and it had no option but to refuse bail unless it was *prima facie* established that the case did not fall within the scope of TADA. The Supreme Court had no doubt come across many cases where the prosecution unjustifiably invokes the provisions of TADA with an oblique motive of depriving the accused persons from getting bail. But the court hoped that the public prosecutors would learn to act like prosecutors on behalf of the public and not the police, and also the judges of the designated courts would discharge their functions as the repositories of human rights enshrined in the constitution. Unless this happened, the court warned, it cannot be said that the provisions of TADA are enforced effectively in consonance with the legislative intendment. Be that as it may, the conditions for the grant of bail imposed by section 20 (7) of TADA were constitutionally sound.[28]

JUDICIAL INDEPENDENCE

Arguments

The following provisions of TADA substantially undermined the principle of judicial independence: [a] the powers vested in the executive to appoint judges for the designated courts who could continue to serve even after attaining the age of super-annuation, under section 9(4) and (8) of TADA; [b] The power of transfer any case from one designated court to another, within or outside the state, under section 11; [c] the delegation of judicial functions to executive magistrates under sections 20(3); and (4); and finally [d] The eradication of high courts' jurisdiction over the designated courts under sections 19(1) and (2).

From the outset, judges are government appointees, with the chief justice of the concerned high court only formally concurring. Designated judges of the special courts continued to hold office even after attaining the age of superannuation during the pleasure of the executive. The executive could terminate their service when it liked. In reference to the Special Courts Bill, 1978, the Supreme Court had had held that appointment of a retired high court judge to a special court, even if made in consultation with the Chief Justice of India, was invalid because if fostered the pleasure doctrine, subversive to the independence of the judiciary. The "ratio decidendi" of this decision that the judicial service must be coterminous with the age of superannuation was clearly violated by section 9(7) of TADA.

Under section 11(2) of TADA, the transfer of a case from one designated court to any other designated court, within or outside the state, was not a matter of judicial but executive decision. The necessary concurrence of the Chief Justice of India in the government's motion to transfer a case was only a formal requirement, a statutory obligation to help an executive decision. Section 11(2) did not even give the Chief Justice of India the power to hear the person affected by the executive motion of transfer before giving or refusing this concurrence. Thus, section 11(2) of TADA not only vitiated the principle of judicial independence, it also destroyed the important rule of "Audi alteram partum" which means that a person who is going to be affected by an order must have prior notice and an opportunity to be heard before it is enforced.

Section 20(2), (3) and (4) of TADA surreptitiously imported executive officers, appointed under sections 20 and 21 of the CrPC, to render important judicial services to the prosecution at sensitive stages of the proceedings immediately after arrest: To authorize periodical custody under interrogation and to record confessions under sections 164 and 167 of the Code of Criminal Procedure. Section 20 of the CrPC allows the government to appoint even police officers as special executive magistrates to perform particular functions in particular areas for such terms as it may think fit.[29] Thus, it is obvious that these provisions of TADA altogether destroyed the scheme of Separation of the judiciary from the executive, as Article 50 of the Indian Constitution enunciates.

Finally, sections 19 (1) and (2), read conjointly with sections 9, 11 and 12, abrogated the high courts' powers over the designated courts. These powers, under Articles 225, 226, 227, and 228 of the Constitution and sections 439 and 482 of the CrPC, are to make rules, to regulate proceedings, to issue writs, to superintendent the working of and to expropriate cases involving substantial questions of law pending before the subordinate courts, to grant bail or to prevent abuse of judicial process in any court. Confirmed by the Supreme Court in the *Usmanbhai Dawoodbhai Memon* v. *State of Gujarat* case this eradication for the high courts' powers in relation to the Designated Courts had the effect of raising a quasi-judicial apparatus in the service of the executive, encroaching on and destroying the hierarchy of courts in their independent sphere as envisaged by the Constitution.[30] The high courts, although required to concur in the appointment of judges to the designated courts, ceased to have any administrative or judicial supervision over their subsequent conduct, whose judgments and orders could be challenged only before the Supreme Court. In reference to the Special courts Bill. 1978, the Supreme Court had held that the Constitution did not permit the establishment of a criminal court that was not subordinate to the high court. The Supreme Court had said: "It is not permissible for Parliament or a state legislature to ignore or bypass that scheme of the Constitution by providing for the establishment of a civil or criminal court, parallel to a high court in a state, or by way of an additional or extra or a second high court, or a court other than a court subordinate to the high court. Any such attempt would be unconstitutional and will strike at the independence of the judiciary which has so nobly been enshrined in the Constitution and so carefully nursed over the years."[31] Application of this decision should have certainly required the sections 9, 11, 12 and 19 of TADA be repudiated as unconstitutional.

Section 9(7) which allowed the judges of the designated courts to continue in their position after reaching the age of superannuation did not offend any constitutional provision as per the court response. According to the Supreme Court, the reference to the Special Courts Bill, 1978 was futile since the court had only overruled the proposal to nominate already retired judges to preside over special courts. TADA did not provide for such appointments, there was no illegality involved. However, the Court recommended that the judges appointed to designated courts should already have had sufficient tenure of service so that their seniority was not in doubt and their continuance after the age of superannuation was not remonstrated.[32]

The power of the government to transfer a case from one designated court to any other, within or without the state under section 11(2) of TADA, was shielded by the condition of obtaining the concurrence of the chief Justice of India. This absolved the government's orders from motivations of bias and mala-fide intention. Of course, the concurrence was not an order of transfer passed by the government. It was an important statutory condition, an imperative, even when it did not adjudicate any "lis" or determine any issue. Therefore, the principle of "audi alteram partem" did not apply. Also, the applications of this principle could paralyses or even frustrate the nature of the action contemplated by the government. Consequently, Parliament in its legislative competence had excluded the rule. However, in exceptional circumstances, the issue was open to examination by the Chief Justice of India, and the court could obtain the view of the accused.[33]

Sections 20(2), (3) and (4) of TADA permitted the construction of reference to "metropolitan magistrate or judicial magistrate" to include executive and special executive magistrates, who could carry out committal proceeding, also record confessions, whether or not they possessed jurisdiction in a case under investigation. According to the Court, the argument that the inclusion of executive magistrates and special executive magistrates in important judicial spheres destroyed the separation of the judiciary, failed when examined against concrete legal positions. Section 6 of the CrPC includes executive magistrates in one of the classes of criminal courts. No doubt, judicial functions they perform are very few, and part 4(b) of section 3 in the code seems to limit their work to matters of an administrative nature. However, the code itself includes them in the performance of quasi-judicial functions in investigating and preventing branches of peace etc., under sections 107 to 110, and others. These functions are revisable in the sense of "judicial proceedings". It is true that the code does not associate special executive magistrates, by their designation, with any of these functions. But it does say that under section 21 that they are appointed for a term that the government thinks fit "for particular areas or for the performance of particular functions." This means that they are by no means persona non grata within the machinery of criminal adjudication. Therefore, their inclusion by sections 20(2), (3) and (4) of TADA to perform committal proceedings and to record confessions along with other judicial magistrates did not violate the principles of criminal jurisprudence.

The second related question was whether the grant of judicial functions of these magistrates visited the principle of separation of the judiciary from the executive under Article 50 of the Constitution. The Supreme Court had repeatedly held that executive magistrates, while they perform judicial functions, are judicial officers. In *Ram Jawaya Kapur* v. *State of Punjab*, the Court held that while independence of judiciary was sacrosanct, "the Indian Constitution has not indeed recognized the doctrine of separation of powers in its absolute rigidity..." The executive was also involved in departmental or subordinate legislation, as well as in judicial functions in a limited way. Thus, the Court maintained that it followed that sections 20(2), (3) and (4) offended neither Article 50 nor Articles 14 equality before law, and 21—protection of life and personal liberty—of the Constitution. It would always be desirable that judicial magistrates record confessions. But when there were completing reasons, the court found that the executive or special executive magistrates could also do so.[34]

Section 19 provided that the right of appeal against any judgment or order of the designated court could only be exercised before the Supreme Court. Of course, the provision took away the right of appeal to the succession of appellate and revisional courts, which the CrPC provides, and also the right of appeal to the Supreme Court on the grant of leave under Article 136 of the Constitution, both at the remedial and procedural levels. The Court found that although the provision affected the jurisdiction of the high court; it was in conformity with the doctrine of speedy trial and did not suffer from constitutional invalidity. However, the provision created inconveniences for persons acquitted by the designated courts for offence under TADA, but convicted under other panel laws. Even in this situation the aggrieved were denied the regular procedure of appeal, and the Supreme Court was beyond their reach either because of financial constraints or because they lived in far-flung areas. Therefore, if a person was acquitted of the offences under TADA, he had to have the right of appeal before the next appellate court.[35]

The question of high courts' power under Articles 226, 227 and sections 439, 482 was more intricate. Some of the High Courts had taken the view that their jurisdiction even in regard to cases under TADA could not be whittled down. Apparently this view contradicted the manifest intention of Parliament to exclude high courts jurisdiction in TADA matters. The vastness of powers which the high courts enjoyed under Article 226 also imposed on them the responsibility to exercise them with circumspection. The TADA was a special Act that aimed to meet the challenges arising out of terrorism and disruption. It provided that an appeal against any order of the designated courts had to lie only before the Supreme Court. According to the court, the High Courts would defeat the clear intent of Parliament if they exercised their powers under Article 226 to obstruct this provision, or entertained bail applications under other provisions of the constitution and the CrPC. It was, therefore, necessary that in relation to TADA matters, the high courts exercised their powers under Article 226 most sparingly and only in extreme circumstances: "What those rare cases are and what would be the circumstances that would justify the entertaining of applications under Article 226 cannot be put in strait-jacket. However, we would like to emphasise and reemphasise that the judicial discipline and comity of courts require that the high, courts should refrain from exercising their jurisdiction in entertaining bail applications in respect of an accused indicated under the special Act."

FAIR TRIAL

Arguments

The TADA used the dogma of speedy trial as an all-encompassing cover to destroy the fundamental principles of fair trial. A part from the power of the government to transfer a case from one designated court to any other, within or without the state, without giving the accused the opportunity to present his viewpoint, the following provisions offended the fundamental principles of free and fair trial: (a) Section 14(5) allowed the designated courts to proceed with the trial even in the absence of the accused or his pleader; (b) Provisions of section 16 allowed the designated courts to hold the trial in camera, to suppress the identity of the witnesses against the accused, and to prohibit the dissemination of the proceedings in any manner; and (c) Section 8 permitted the attachment of the property belonging to an accused, and its forfeiture without encumbrances, at his conviction.

THE USE AND ABUSE OF TADA IN PUNJAB DURING MILITANCY : A NARRATIVE

The fact finding team of People Union for Democratic Rights when it visited Punjab during the militancy it found that the provision of TADA were grossly being abused. In order to avoid the long process of investigation and presenting the cases before the courts on regular basis, the Punjab police imposed TADA in the cases which were wholly disconnected from the terrorist activities and organised crimes. For instance, the team discovered a case pending under TADA in the court of Additional Special Court Judge G.L. Chopra which related to a murder case committed in a village. The incident occurred on the night of January 7/8 1985, at village Kathu Nagal PS, District Amritsar. FIR No. 9/85 recorded that Mahendar Kaur, her husband Dayal Singh and their elder son had gone to tube well to irrigate their fields. Their elder son was away. The husband and wife were sleeping in tube well room with door open when one Kewal Singh and another man alleged to have entered and hacked Dayal Singh with 'dater' (sickle). Another case, FIR No 97/84 also pending before the Additional Special Court at Amritsar, involves a dispute between two brothers of village Jethuwal. One of them Karnail Singh is alleged to have given Kirpan (sword) blow to his brother, niece and sister-in-law. This case came up at Jalandhar Special Court and later was transferred to the Additional Special Court of G.L. Chopra at Amritsar. Again case FIR No. 250/84 of August 29, 1984 relates to dispute over sharing of land within the family at village Sidhar, PS Beas; district Amritsar, leading to murder. The son daughter-in-law along with two grandsons of the deceased has been arrested. Their case came before the Jalandhar Special Court and from there it was transferred to the Additional Special Court at Hoshiarpur 200 KM from Amritsar.[36]

Each case first came up before the Special Court at Zonal level and then it was transferred to any of seven additional special courts. All the criminal cases involving offences in the schedule were to be tried by these Special Courts. The police could present the *challan* within a period of one year without possibility of bail or recording the confession. This opened avenues for the police to make money by accepting bribes in order to present challan. A person found himself in jail without conviction for a year in offences where if he found guilty he would be given a maximum of few months' imprisonment.[37]

In New Delhi, the Patel Nagar police picked up Karam Singh, Harnik Singh, Santok Singh, Major Singh, Baldev Singh, Ujjagar Singh, Kulwant Singh, Surinder Singh, Amarjit Singh and J.S. Dhillon in 1987. They were charged under Section 3 and 4 of TADA. Confessions of three of them, Baldev Singh, Ujjagar Singh and Karam Singh were apparently recorded by the DCP in September 1987. These confessional statements formed the basis of the prosecution case. More than 12 years later, the additional session judge R.C Yaduvanshi before whom the case was brought, ruled on January 9 that these confessional statements were 'untrustworthy' and 'unreliable'. He observed that " the DCP is not aware about the place where the statements were recorded, by whom they were recorded and in fact that there is nothing on record to show that sufficient time was given to the accused. In short, nothing to dispel doubts that the accused had made the statement voluntarily. The DCP concerned, Amod Kanth, became the Joint Police Commissioner (south range) Delhi, when hearing started in this case. He claimed that the statement was recorded by somebody else on his instance. But somehow he could name the scribe on seeing the confessional statements. He was unable to say who had produced the accused before him and by whom they were identified. To cap the courtroom farce a police officer, Inspector Datta Ram, himself came forward to say that he had recorded the confession at the direction of DCP, so after languishing in jail for 12 years the 10 alleged 'terrorists' were finally acquitted.[38]

This was the milieu of legislative and judicial approval, in which the security forces in Punjab, throughout the period under scrutiny, were able to carry out their anti-insurgency operations. By all available accounts, they were employing the extra-ordinary powers made available to them under the new legislations like TADA to the maximum possible extent. According to the National Human Rights

Commission (NHRC), the Punjab police registered 17, 529 cases under TADA since its promulgation in 1985 to the end of July 1994. In October 1993, according to the Union home ministry, the conviction rate of those tried by designated courts was 0.81 per cent. In Punjab, according to the same source, the conviction rate was 0.37 per cent. On 24 August 1994, former minister of state for home minister Rajesh Pilot disclosed that approximately 67,000 individuals had been detained since TADA came into force. Out of these, only 8,000 were tried and only 725 were convicted. Some 59,509 people had been detained with no case being brought against them. The TADA Review Committee found that TADA was wrongly applied in more the 50,000 cases. According to Sitaram Yechuri, the general secretary of the Communist Party of Indian (Marxist), "Of the 76,036 people arrested by mid-1994 nearly 99 per cent of 75,200 were at different stages of trial or had not been produced before any court at all. In Jammu and Kashmir, where 20,000 arrests were made since TADA's inception, not a single accused has been convicted to this day.[39] This failure of the security forces and the police forces in Punjab to bring militants to book despite TADA and other draconian legislation seemed clearly to be a result to their obsession with extra-judicial activities to the negation of arduous and lustreless tasks of regular police work.

COMMENTS OF THE UN HUMAN RIGHTS COMMITTEE ON THE USE OF EXTRA-ORDINARY LAWS AND INTERNATIONAL PROVISIONS FOR HUMAN RIGHTS

While referring to the Armed Forces (Punjab and Chandigarh) Special Powers Act and the state of human rights in strife torn Punjab, the Human Rights Committee while examining India's second report about the measures it had taken to implement the rights guaranteed in the International Covenant on Civil and Political Rights (ICCPR), expressed their concern to the representative of the Indian Government that the provisions of the NSA contained derogations from the rights guaranteed in the ICCPR of which the Committee ought to have been notified. They were particularly concerned about the fact that under the NSA, imposed in Punjab as elsewhere, there was no need to disclose the grounds of detention to a person detained under the Act and that it might take up to 7 weeks after the date of arrest before the Advisory Board reviewed the detention. One member added that these were periods "very considerably longer" than would be compatible with Article 9(4) of the ICCPR. The National Security Act's provisions for review by an Advisory Board within seven weeks are held as inconsistent with ICCPR Article 9(4) which stipulates that anyone who is detained is entitled to take proceedings before a court which should decide without delay on the lawfulness of detention. Similarly, Sections of the TADA specified in this report are inconsistent with ICCPR Article 14(2) which lays down the presumption of innocence and ICCPR Article 14(1) which provides that hearings should be fair and public, the Covenant not permitting an obligatory provision to hold all trials in cameras stipulated in the TADA. ICCPR Article 6 prohibits arbitrary deprivation of life and, contrary to the immunity from prosecution provided in the Armed Forces (Punjab and Chandigarh) Special Powers Act; ICCPR Article 2(3) (a) provides that all victims of human rights violations have the right to an effective remedy, notwithstanding that the violation has been committed by persons acting in an official capacity.[40]

THE FIELD ACTION OF THE ARMED FORCES AND HUMAN RIGHTS

The success of the state to win over the secessionist terrorism in Punjab is attributed to the police strategies to combat the terrorists and the terrorist violence.[41] The then Director General of Punjab Police K.P.S., Gill[42] under whom the whole operation against terrorism was launched under the leadership of chief minister Beant Singh became a national hero and super-cop for suppressing terrorism and secessionism successfully. But the strategies of this super cop to tackle with the terrorism and secessionism came under bitter criticism of human rights experts and human rights activists as they accused that Mr. Gill's policy of giving free hands to the armed forces in Punjab had resulted into corruption and criminalisation of the armed forces which resulted into the violation of human rights at large. It is also argued that Mr. Gill allowed his officers to adopt extra-constitutional methods while taking on the terrorism in Punjab.[43]

The prolonged policy of the police was to cut the civilian support to terrorist with the carrot and stick policy and countering the violence of terrorist with the state violence. Extra-judicial prosecutions and arrest of the suspected sympathisers and terrorists in private vehicles and private uniform were done to avoid the longer route of legal and constitutional procedure. Most of the arrests were unwarranted and unacknowledged, which resulted into the elimination of the suspected persons if they confessed their role in any terrorist activities. The non registration of FIR facilitated custodial torture as well as even death as police was not afraid of being held responsible. Rewards and promotions to the security forces personnel for apprehending the terrorists and extra-judicial killing was another method. Supporting and strengthening of the civilians who opposed the terrorists or who even provided information about the suspected militants to the police were provided the state security for protection. Government weapons were given to fight against the terrorist on the behalf of police. Infiltration in the terrorist organisation and setting up of the private vigilant groups were the strategies adopted by the security agencies.[44]

A celebrated senior police officer of the time, Izhar Alam at a press conference held in Patti on October 1, 1987 (reported in *The Tribune*) admitted that "terrorists who had committed five or more murders were killed by the police after they were caught." Elaborating on this he said that "the police had to resort killing terrorists because the possibility of their being punished by law was remote due to lack of evidence."[45] In his book *Tryst with Terror*, V.N. Narayanan, Chief Editor of the *Hindustan Times*, quotes the same police officer "The Judicial process was dead. We kill 70 per cent of terrorists we catch because presenting of them before the court means to bail them out. Bail is the rule, jail is the exception."[46]

REWARDS, PROMOTION FOR APPREHENSION OF TERRORISTS AND EXTRA-JUDICIAL KILLINGS

The police force in Punjab, as a retired senior officer observed, was known since the colonial days for its "Servility and Oppression".[47] Making it an effective instrument seemed to require appropriate incentive. That it indulged in staging "fake encounters" acknowledge by the governor of the Punjab when he publicly appealed to the Police officers "to stop fake encounters". An important innovation, however, was an official order of the Director General of Punjab Police issued on 30 August 1989 to all district superintendents of police. It promised to the police personnel handsome rewards in cash for apprehension/liquidation of 53 specially described terrorists/extremists.[48] In another circular issued on April 1, 1990 the word "liquidation" was repeated making the intent very clear as far as the police command' wish was concerned.[49]

Besides financial rewards, quick promotions in rank were promised to be given to the killers of terrorists. In certain cases, an officer of the rank of an inspector gained two out-of turn promotions in two years, soon becoming the head of that district police.[50] The rewards and promotion led to hasten the desire among the lower ranking officers to liquidate a wanted terrorist, because in case of arrest the reward was likely to be "grabbed" by some higher officer by killing that terrorist. The expected rewards not only encouraged the police/paramilitary forces to fight and kill the terrorists, but it converted the constitutional forces into bounty killers. The objective of the state to give the extraordinary power to the state armed forces was defeated due to the moral and professional corruption that set in among the armed forces. The extraordinary laws like TADA, declared awards and promotion opened the "Pandora Box", thousands of youths were arrested tortured and some of them were killed during the torture and some were killed as their parents could not pay the extortion money to the police. The gravity of the situation can be understood from the fact that the even the terrorists who were declared to be killed in the encounter twice by the two districts of police have now been traced as alive. Then whom the police killed in the place of these terrorists remains a mystery.[51]

SETTING UP OF THE VIGILANTE GROUPS AND INFILTRATION INTO TERRORIST ORGANISATION : LEGAL AND HUMAN RIGHTS CONCERNS

An under cover operation policy to suppress the militancy was started by the Punjab police during the time of the DGP Rebeiro in real earnest. But these under-cover operations came under the strong criticism of media and civil society groups as the officers in command forgot the legal and professional norms while making these groups. The persons who were chosen by the state forces to counter the terrorists were neither from the intelligence service and nor from armed forces, they were smuggler, criminals and ex-terrorists. The logic to give them money and rewards for the elimination of terrorists was that they knows the terrorists, their modes of functioning and network. The under-over agents of the state were provided with logistic support by the police for night under cover operation and even in the day they were allowed to use force to eliminate the terrorists at any place. Although the strategy of the under cover operations helped the state forces to get the militants but it resulted into extortion, killings of the innocents and the family members of the terrorists families. Once these criminals were provided with the sophisticated weapons they even went out of the hands of police force itself becoming dreaded ultras, a law unto themselves. The issue of infiltration and setting of extra-legal groups to counter the militants is still haunting the Punjab Police as the CATs, who were working under the cover operation of the armed forces were shown to be killed as dared terrorists are now traced by the media as living some where in Punjab and other parts of the country.[52]

WEAPONS TO INDIVIDUALS/FAMILIES AND RELIGIOUS INSTITUTIONS/GROUPS

It was considered to be fair to give the sophisticated government weapons if someone was considered helpful in the fight against terrorists by the police forces and civil administration in Punjab. Politically connected persons as well as any one who had enmity or had any dispute with a militant could also be considered for being given weapons by the government in the name of self-protection. It did not matter if the concerned person misused the weapon for his personal gains or for settling his personal score. Providing of government weapon to individuals/families reportedly resulted in lot of innocents killing at the hands of the persons to whom police provided the weapons. In some cases the police registered the cases against these families and individuals and booked them for judicial prosecution, however, there were some cases where the police remained not only spectator but also helped the alleged criminals who helped it during the terrorism. One among these cases was the case of the Baba Ajit Singh Poohla the chief of Taruna Dal (a *Nihang* sect).

Poohla was regarded as a politically well connected person. He was reported to have formed a hit squad of his followers to take on the militants. The base camp of Poohla was in Kartarpur near Butala in Majitha Police district. He and other leaders of Taruna Dal consistently opposed the terrorist movement in this area which was a stronghold of terrorist. Poohla was heavily armed with sophisticated weapons provided to him by the state government besides a bullet proof car and security guards. His activities took the shape of direct enmity with Joga Singh, a Lt. General of Khalistan Liberation Army. The reason of their enmity was their competing interest relating to control of Gurdwaras. This led to a chain of killing of each other's followers. In an ambush laid by Joga Singh men's three Nihang followers of Ajit Singh were killed and Poohla himself was injured. In a revenge attack Nihang attacked and killed the seven members of Joga family including women and children. Poohla was also responsible for the killing of families of other terrorists raping some women and killing of his fellow who wanted to leave him. The terror of Poohla was so high that no one dared to speak against Poohla even after the end of Terrorism. He was arrested after a long legal battle and a campaign by the Majha Ex-Servicemen's League, led by Col. G.S. Sandhu on the murder charges and inquiries in the other cases was taking place. But Poohla was burnt alive in the Amritsar Central Jail by two under- trial prisoners. All the crimes Poohla did with the alleged support of some officers in Punjab. [53]

An another case narrated by Harish Puri and others in their book *Terrorism in Punjab: Understanding the Grassroots Reality*, is of Giani Piara Singh of village Basarke-Bhaini, who used to sell illicit liquor and was known primarily as a police informer. In the local language of rural area he was a "police tout" In other words, he was a low level gangster who would inform the police about various illegal activities and served as a "prosecution witness" -in -reverse whenever the police required his services in a court of law. As a result he exercised a certain dubious influence in the village; He also controlled the holy place of Sufi Saint and land attached to it known as *theh* (mound). On every Thursday, a considerable number of devotees visited the place to earthen lamps and make some offerings. Piara Singh used to have some income from this source.

During their discussion with the villagers over the killing of 35 members of the village community, the team members found that Piara Singh had killed 19 members of the family of terrorist Jagir Singh due to the personal enmity over a *theh*. Earlier Jagir Singh and Paira Singh were friends and both had their land around the *Theh*. But Jagir Singh started encroaching in the *Theh* land which was under the possession of Paira Singh as the land was legally attached with the religious shrine. When Piara Singh stood against the encroachment both came into the confrontations. As the conflict sharpened and factions developed, Jagir Singh joined the KCF (Z) to avenge the accusation or to confront the possibility of an armed threat. Piara who had already secured the weapons from police for protection against any attack as he was serving as informer decided to eliminate the whole family of Jagir Singh with him. He was looking for a chance and the marriage of the younger brother of Jagir Singh provided him the opportunity to take the revenge. Before the marriage party to depart for bride's place, Piara Singh reached Jagir Singh' home with his gang. Without any warning they opened fire and killed 19 members of Jagir Singh family at spot. Jagir Singh was booked by the police and he was rewarded with capital punishment by the court.[54] In this case like many other cases killings had the origin in the personal vendetta.

ARBITRARY AND UNACKNOWLEDGED ARRESTS AND TORTURE

Amnesty International had received many complaints of arbitrary arrests by the police and paramilitary forces operating in Punjab during the militancy period. According to these reports, arrests were made without warrant. The security forces agents made the arrests. They, however, refused to identify themselves and the arrested person or the relatives were seldom informed the grounds of the arrest or the specific charges against the arrested person which is mandated by Article 22 of the constitution. In many cases, the arrests were not recorded in the daily registers of the police stations.[55]

CUSTODIAL TORTURE

The custodial torture was one of the key instruments which were used by the police during the unacknowledged and arbitrary arrest of the suspects for confession and giving the self-incrimination statements by the armed forces in Punjab. Special interrogation centres were established by the police to interrogate the suspected ones across Punjab. The human rights organisation reported the killings of the suspected ones in the interrogation centre.[56]

The evidence of illegal arrests and torture were not only reported by the media and human rights organisation, even the judiciary recognised the excess committed by the armed forces against the innocent civilian and the suspects. Justice S.S. Sodhi, who carried out an investigation during a routine inspection of Amritsar Central Jail in February 1989, found that many of the detainees then awaiting trial complained that police had detained them illegally for weeks before formally arresting them. In his unpublished report the High Court judge has reportedly criticized official behaviour in the registration of cases against detainees under the Arms Act for allegedly "harbouring terrorists" and "raising anti-national slogans". Justice Sodhi observed: "A stereotyped set pattern of their content emerges, almost as if there is a prescribed Performa where names etc. are filled in. What is more, one has to strain one's credibility to accept the version given in these reports". Many detainees told Justice

Sodhi that they were tortured during the initial period of unacknowledged detention, and that when they were finally granted bail the police immediately re-arrested them on fresh charges. Such claims continue to be made. For example Hardev Singh, son of Gurmail Singh of Nandpur village, Ludhiana, claimed in a sworn statement of 29 October 1990 that, just after he had been released on bail by the local court on 21 September 1987, "I was picked up by the police right outside the prison gate ..." He claimed that between September 1987 and March 1989, he was illegally detained by police no less than 38 times.[57]

Another reported case of torture of the villagers at the large level of five villages near Kathunangal—Talwandi Phuman, Chachowali, Farrar, Gujarpura and Pangli. It was on 30 August 1990, when the CRPF cordoned off these five villages and rounded about 200 residents of these villages. They were badly beaten by members of the CRPF and that some young men among them were later taken to Thiriawal CRPF station and tortured. The incident, apparently a reprisal action, took place the day after a landmine had exploded, damaging a patrol jeep. Journalists who saw the villagers reported that: "Many of them could not walk and showed injuries on the limbs electric shocks were given to some of them".[58]

FAKE ENCOUNTER AND EXTRA-JUDICIAL KILLINGS

Narrative

To illustrate the dismal state of human rights in strife torn Punjab, we may refer to the story of a young man called Surjit Singh who was picked up like countless youth in those years by the police from his farmhouse in Valtoha village of Tarn Taran police district on 15 October 1993. After 16 days, a sub-inspector of Punjab Police brought his "body" to the civil hospital at Patti. According to police, the body was of a militant who was killed by police in an encounter with police and body was brought there for post-mortem examination. When the policemen left and the doctor began the examination it was discovered that militant was not dead. Someone in the hospital recognised that it was Surjit Singh who had been grievously injured. The patient was put on life-saving devices. As the information reached the concerned ASI, he returned to the hospital with few constables and forcibly took away the injured Surjit Singh apparently for "better treatment" at Amritsar. After a few hours the body of Surjit Singh was brought back to the hospital. Now it was surely a dead body for which the post-mortem was necessary.[59]

Using civilian as shields is prohibited under International Law but it had been a routine tacit of security forces in Punjab. On June 14, 1992 a report carried in *The Telegraph* described how The Bhindranwale Tiger Force (Manochahal) Deputy Commander Surjit Singh Behla and his accomplice Madan Singh Madhi were hiding in house of Manjinder Singh, a former member of Punjab Legislative Assembly (This was widely known as Behla incident). Police kept house under fire for 28 hours. Some 1600 security personnel including one Army battalion assisted by a helicopter were involved in the operation and had even been video-tapped. After trading shots for more than a day the forces decided to go in. The militants sprayed bullets on the group as it approached. When it was all over, the police claimed that Surjit Singh Behla, deputy chief of BTKF, Madan Madhi, and Niranjan Singh advisor to the militant outfit, Sakatar Singh and area commander and five other unidentified militants had been gunned down in a 28 -hour encounter while no civilian had been killed or injured. The Tarn Taran SSP claimed that a bunker had been specially built under the house. Curiously, only three weapons were recovered but the police insisted that more would be found when the debris was cleared. Subsequently, details showed that one Ak-47, one Mouser pistol and one SLR were recovered. The SLR belonged to Parkash Chand, a Jawan of Dogra regiment who was killed in the encounter. When journalists got into Behla, they found the details their observation did not match the police version. To begin with, there was no bunker nor had any additional arms been found. The residents of village identified five of nine men killed in the encounter as ordinary villagers with no militant links. They identified them as Niranjan Singh Dodhi (65) (a dairy farmer) and his son Sikatar Singh (25), a cart owner Kartar Singh (35) and two farmers Ajit Singh (40) and Lakhwinder Singh (18) and a local mason. There was one whose identity was not established. Sukhchain Singh another son of Niranjan Singh was seriously injured and taken to hospital. Three other men were used as human shield but miraculously escaped: they were Gurdeep Singh (65) and his grandson Bhupinder Singh (17) and a local granthi father-in-law. The villager's story is that on the morning of June 8, 1992. Niranjan Singh, Sikatar Singh and a mason were constructing a room at their tube well just outside the village. Ajit Singh just had arrived with a carload of bricks. Police and CRPF men arrived and ordered the five men to come along with them to Manjinder Singh house. On the way Bhupinder Singh and granthi's (Priest) father-in-law was forced to join the police. At the house, the security forces put them in front of them to open the every room and ascertain that no militant was hiding inside. After searching almost all rooms they directed the men to stand by the stairs along with few police and CRPF men. Other security personnel went upstairs. All of sudden there was a burst of gunfire in which five or six personnel including one constable were killed. The police, CRPF and Army officers refused to comment on the villagers' version and no inquiry was ordered. SSP Ajit Singh's declaration that those killed were all militants belonging to BTFK was dispelled by the report of the Intelligence Bureau. When K.P.S. Gill was asked to comment he said that he had ordered an inquiry into the matter and that "justice would be done at any cost". But police had initially declared the seven victims as militants; their families were not legally entitled to any compensation. No further actions appeared to be taken.[60] Such incidents were fairly common in the then Punjab showing the highhandedness of police looking for fake encounters in order to gain recognition and rewards.

HUMAN RIGHTS ORGANISATIONS AND HUMAN RIGHTS ACTIVISTS: POSITION AND NARRATIVES

The repression against the human rights organisation, activists and the voices could be noted from the fact even the Amnesty International was not allowed to enter into Punjab by the government during the counter-insurgency operations.[61] Punjab government institutions equated human rights activists with sympathisers of the terrorists and consistently used the insurgency to justify their actions against them. Monitoring of the human rights situation was simply not on the agenda of the democratic government. In Punjab Involving unclaimed dead bodies and mass cremations case discussed below, the response of the Punjab police and government of Punjab has been to portray demands for a full accounting of abuses as negating the contributions of police in fighting insurgency. The Punjab police also associated human rights activists with Pakistan's Inter-Services Intelligence (ISI).[62]

THE FAITH OF HUMAN RIGHTS ACTIVISTS

Besides the prominent case of forced disappearance of human rights activist Jaswant Singh Khalra by the Punjab Police after the establishment of peace there were many similar cases of the torture, illegal detention and forces disappearance of the other human rights activists. Some reported among these are: Kulwant Singh Saini; aged 38, was a resident of Ropar and practiced law at the Ropar district courts. He often represented cases taken into custody on suspicion of involvement with militants and had been repeatedly warned by the police not to represent such cases. On January 25, 1993, the Ropar police picked up one Manjit Kaur and her son from Budha Bhora village 4 km from Ropar. Panchayat of her village came to Saini and requested his help in obtaining their release, vowing that the mother and son had committed no offence. On the afternoon of January 25, at about 4 p.m. Saini telephoned Ropar DSP Jaspal Singh and asked the DSP why they had been arrested and what could be done to get them released. The DSP asked Saini to come to his residence. Saini went there but the DSP had left. In the evening Saini consulted Bar Association President K.P.S. Rana and advocate Santokh Singh Gill as to how to get Manjit Kaur released. He said that he would speak to DSP at the police station if he was not available at his home. Santokh Singh advised him not to go to the police station alone. Around 9 a.m. that evening Saini contacted the Ropar Police Station House Officer and related his earlier conversation with the DSP. The SHO instructed him to come to the police station and take Manjit Kaur and her son. Acting on Gill's advice, Saini took his wife and infant son and drove to the police station in his white Maruti Car (DAQ 3804). Before leaving he informed his father that he was going to the police station to bring back two persons and was expected to return shortly. It was about 9:30 p.m. when they left home. They were never seen again. When they did not return home Saini's father, Jagtir Singh got worried. In the morning he met Santokh Singh Gill, and related the story. On January 27 Jagir Singh Gill and Rana met the Ropar SSP, Sanjeev Gupta. The SSP denied that the Ropar police had any information as to Saini's whereabouts but directed the DSP to inquire into the matter. The same day Jagir Singh also met M.M. Mittal, MLA and Punjab BJP President and told him what had happened. The Ropar Bar Association went on indefinite strike and subsequently the Bar Association of Punjab and Haryana High Court and Supreme Court went on Strike. In response to the lawyers demand of an inquiry into Saini's disappearance, the Ropar SSP issued a statement declaring: "Saini was harbouring Khalsa International activist a KLF militant Jaspal Singh, *alias* Tani, who frequently visited him; the wife of the slain KLF militant Jagrup Singh Khalak was staying in the advocate's house and he was involved in a plan to blow up Ropar Thermal Plant". SSP claimed that information came to light during interrogation of an arrested militant Harpreet Singh, *alias* Lucky. This man was the son of Manjit Kaur whose release Kulwant Singh had sought. The SSP said Lucky wanted to surrender but Saini threatened him with death if he did so and therefore Lucky and another man, Surjit Singh, Kidnapped the advocate and his family and threw them in the Bhakra Mainline Canal near Sirhind.[63] Immediately after signing a confession that he killed Saini and his wife and child, Surjit consumed cyanide and died. In March 1993, Saini's car was pulled out of Sirhind canal but no bodies were recovered. Another advocate Sukhwinder Singh Bhatti practiced law in the Sangrur district courts. On May 12, 1994, police took him off the bus in which he was returning home from court, forced him into vehicle without registration number, and he was never seen again.[64] Ram Singh Billing was both a journalist and a human rights activist (Secretary of the Sangrur District Punjab Human Rights Organisation), a correspondence of *Ajit*, a widely circulated Punjabi daily, was last seen on January 4, 1992, in the police lock-up at Lohat Baddi police post, district Sangrur, but no document have ever been produced to show that he was ever charged with any offence or ever arrested. The fabrication of the retired Justice Bains from Punjab and Haryana High Court under TADA and hand-cuffing him in public was one instance of silencing the voices of human rights groups in Punjab.[65] Justice Bains was released by the High Court after holding of a Judicial Inquiry, which found that Justice Bains name was corroborated in a FIR of sedition along with ten other persons, but originally when the FIR was registered against these ten persons Justice Bains name was not written in the FIR.

MILITANTS' IDEOLOGY, STRATEGIES AND HUMAN RIGHTS CONCERNS

No movements can go for a long time and can sustain credibility among the masses if the movement lacks a strong ideological base and also shuns humanitarian concerns during its struggle. The analysis of the success and failure of the every movement is always done along the ideological and strategic lines. So for an analytical study of the 'Khalistan Movement', one should have a fair knowledge of the Sikh history and culture that was sought to be used unsuccessfully by the militants. The immediate concerns of the movement and the strategy of the movement also need attention.

In the above light an ideological analysis of the movement becomes necessary along the line of Sikhism. The Sikh gurus spread the message of human co-existence, multiculturalism, human equality and doing justice to the weak. The so-called land of Khalistan (land of pure) did not cohere with the notion of pure as preached by the ten Gurus of the Sikhs.[66]

As for the strategic analysis of the movement, it can be done along while referring to the immediate demands and the methods adopted by different terrorist organisations. The analysis of the rise and fall of Khalistan Movement by the various analysts has proven that the violent movement of Sikh guerrillas could not secure the mass support from within the Sikh community. The militants, as mentioned before, could not win a single seat in the Mini Parliament of Sikhs (Shiromani Gurdwara Prabhandhak Committee) even during the period of Bhindranwale.[67] Second most important factor was the 37% non-Sikh population of the state was in any case against whom the proclaimed land of Khalsa as they feared themselves becoming the inferior 'others'. The Sikhs are themselves not a homogeneous community. Besides the caste divisions, there are different sects within the community.[68] How the militant movement was sustained for such long period is a matter of fact which needs to be analysed from the human rights perspective. The first attempt of the terrorists was to create a fear psychosis among the people and the target was 37% of Hindu population in state. They were prime targets of the terrorists for indiscriminate killing because without their displacement the aim of dreamed land of Khalistan could not be achieved. The militants also wanted to bring the 27% population of Sikhs living outside the state to Punjab.[69] The killings of the innocent Hindus were always carried to silence the society as a whole or as a measure of revenge against the government. Violence against the Sikhs in the other states of the Indian Union after the assassination of Indira Gandhi also became the basis for killings.

The second most notable factor was the forced social reforms and issuing of edicts on the power of gun. Whosoever ignored the edict had to face the verdict the majority of the time the minor resistance and delay resulted into violence.[70] The scenario of the country side infested areas in Punjab has been well depicted by H.K. Puri and others in their book. "They issued the edicts, firmons and orders which are scrupulously obeyed because of the fear of AK-47 rifles which were very much evident in the villages as the terrorists openly moved about in groups with these rifles slung on their shoulders". Some of the militant dictates were:

(a) Each farmer must cultivate half an acre of sugarcane per every five acre and this sugarcane cut unless the wheat crop grows up.
(b) All dogs should either be killed or to be kept chained.
(c) There should be no light in the street and in the houses at night.
(d) Teaching of Hindi in the schools was banned. Anybody violating the ban was to be killed.
(e) The singing of National Anthem stood banned in many schools.
(f) The students, both boys and girls were to wear a particular type of dress especially yellow turbans or dupatta.
(g) After killing of every militant by the police or as a result of mutual infighting, hand written orders were pasted and all shops in the area were ordered to be closed for 4 days or a week or even a fortnight. In some areas of Tarn Taran, Majitha and Batala police districts, shops hardly opened for a few days in the month.
(h) A ban on having more than eleven people in marriage party.[71]

The people who violated the militants dictate were killed or tortured. One mild punishment was to humiliate them publicly by making them to take dip in the village pond of dirty water. Another more important aspect was the local connections of the fighters and their involvement in the local disputes, which resulted into horrible consequences. The local people used their connection with the militant organisations while setting their personal scores. The wide-spread extortions and snatching of weapons by the militants in the name of purchasing the weapons for their struggle was also reported at large scale.[72]

Even the farmers were forced to give their tractors (agriculture machinery) to the militants for their movement and some of the farmers reported that their tractors were never returned. If in case the militant got killed by the police while they were on tractors then farmers never approached the police due to the fear of arrest and torture by the police as the farmer could not register their complaints to the police for the snatching of their tractors due to the fear of militants.[73]

NATIONAL HUMAN RIGHTS COMMISSION: FORCED DISAPPEARANCE AND STATE RESPONSES

While the much water has flown over the Sutlej; over the years since the peaces has been established, there was total political silence over the issue of illegal abduction and forced disappearances of the thousands of youths across the Punjab by the armed forces. The parents who were convinced that their sons were abducted and killed by the armed forces remained silent at home due the fear of police harassment. There was no one to give them a voice. Jaswant Singh Khalra, General Secretary of the Akali Dal Human Rights Wing and Jaspal Singh Dhillon done a commendable job to release copies of official documents that showed that the security agencies in Punjab had secretly cremated thousands of dead bodies after labelling them as "unidentified/unclaimed."[74]

It was alleged that dead bodies were of the youths who were abducted by the Punjab police and other security forces from their homes and anywhere in Punjab and they were allegedly killed by the police in fake encounters. All the allegations were based on survey of the number of missing persons in the district and an investigation of the record of the three crematoria in Amritsar district—one of the 13 other districts in the state. In their press release, it was claimed that an investigation would reveal a similar state of affairs at other crematoria in the state.[75]

In January 1995, Jaswant Singh Khalra and Jaspal Singh Dhillon filed a writ petition in the Punjab and Haryana High Court to investigate their discovery of mass illegal cremations in three crematoria in Amritsar district. The High Court dismissed the petition on grounds of vagueness. On 3 April, 1995: The Committee for Information and Initiative on Punjab (CIIP) moved the Supreme Court, in a writ petition under Article 32 of the Constitution to demand a comprehensive inquiry into the allegation of disappearance and subsequent, illegal cremation by the police in Punjab.

Before the Supreme Court could hear the matter Khalra was abducted by Punjab Police from outside his house. Paramjit Kaur, Khalra's wife, immediately filed a *habeas corpus* petition in the Supreme Court, hoping the Court could secure the release of Khalra before the police executed him. Unfortunately, like the victims Khalra himself had investigated, the police did not spare him. On 15 November 1995, Supreme Court instituted two inquiries to be conducted by the Central Bureau of Investigation (CBI).[76] First Inquiry aimed to determine what happened to Khalra. The second inquiry was to establish the substances of the allegation that Khalra had made. In July 1996, the report of the first inquiry held CBI categorised 2097 cremations into three lists of 585 identified, 274 partially identifies and 1,238 unidentified corpses.[77]

After receiving the C.B.I. report, the Supreme Court, in its order dated 12 December 1996, noted that it "disclosed flagrant violations of human rights on mass scale." Instructing the C.B.I. to investigate criminal culpability and to submit a quarterly progress report, the Court appointed the National Human Rights Commission (NHRC) to determine and adjudicate all other issues and to award compensation. The court clearly orders that since the matter is going to be examined by the NHRC at the request of this court, any compensation awarded shall be binding and payable."[78]

The NHRC in January 1997 asked all the parties appearing before it to make preliminary submission on "the scope and ambit" of the reference made to it by the Supreme Court and on the capacity in which the commission functions, i.e., whether the commission had limited powers vide the Protection of Human Rights Act, 1993, or whether it was, for the purpose of this reference, a *sui-generis* designated of the Supreme Court, with powers to adjudicate on the issue entrusted to it by the Court, without being fettered by the limitation contained in the act.

On 4 August, 1997, after hearing at length all the views placed before it, the NHRC, in a detailed order on the preliminary contention, held that it was a *sui-generis* designated of the Supreme Court, appointed to carry out the Court's mandate and vested with all of the powers of the said Court under Article 32 of the Indian Constitution. It also concluded that the Supreme Court had referred the whole matter to the commission, with no territorial or other limits on the nature and scope of inquiry. On the same date, by a separate order on "Proceeding", the NHRC stated that in view of the large number of alleged cremation it would be appropriate to invite claims by public notice. After ascertaining the extent of culpability of negligence on the part of the state and its authorities, the basis for quantification of compensation could be formulated, NHRC stated.[79]

STATE V. HUMAN RIGHT : POLITICISATION OF THE HUMAN RIGHTS ISSUE AND NATIONAL INTEGRATION : SOME QUERIES

It is to be mentioned that enquiry being conducted by National Human Rights Commission (NHRC), under the jurisdiction of the Supreme Court, in disappearance and illegal cremations in Punjab, showed the deep social division that influenced the prospective of justice and peace in the state. Every attempt to bring justice to the victims, reform the institution in order to achieve transparency, structural equality and democracy was sought to be frustrated by the powerful persons linked with the previous administration that perpetrated the horrible abuses in the mistaken belief of defending the integrity of the state. Their demand for amnesty had found support in the highest quarter of the Indian government.

Looking into the possibility of the action against the security forces for violating the human rights by the NHRC, central government immediately became active and on the 4th of September, 1997 stayed the NHRC proceeding by filing a 'clarification petition before the Supreme Court queering whether the 12 December, 1996 order of the Court empowered the NHRC to function as a *sui-generis* designate of the Supreme Court, untrammelled by the provision of the Protection of Human Rights Act, 1993. The application also challenged the NHRC's view that the Supreme Court's order of 12 December 1996 gave it unfettered jurisdiction to investigate human rights violation in Punjab. It was contended in the application that such an interpretation would result in "thousands of claims". Supreme Court dismissed the Union government clarification petition and upheld the NHRC's view of mandate conferred upon it. During the court proceedings the Supreme Court rule that the National Human Rights Commission was to be given a free hand and was not be circumscribed by the conditions.[80]

The most volatile was the response of the senior officers of the Punjab police and a campaign for their defence against the alleged charges of committing excess and violating the human has been started at very early stage by the police officer.[81] The counter and direct responses of the officers from the Punjab police against the filing of the human rights petition started from the very day of the disclosure of the report to the press by Khalra. On 18 January. 1995, DGP K.P.S. Gill addressed a press conference in Amritsar to rebut the allegation made by Khalra. He told the media persons that "thousands of Sikh youths who had left for foreign countries under the names and documents were claiming to be missing persons killed by the security forces in encounters". Gill said that police had compiled lists of "missing persons" and had discovered the most of cases, these persons were "missing with the consent of their parents and relatives and their whereabouts were known to their families. "He further said that "Some of these persons according to the DGP were shifting from one country to other by changing their names and address."[82] The claim of the DGP was challenged by Khalra on the very next day by holding a counter press conference in Amritsar and by putting forth the evidences.[83] To divert the media attention as the reports particularly in the Asian age were focusing on the issue of mass cremations.[84] K.P.S. Gill, DGP of Punjab police ordered the Inspector General of Punjab Dr. Bhatti to investigate the report but also stated at the time that most of the bodies mentioned in the lists prepared by the human rights activists might actually had belonged to the score of out-of-state terrorists victims like migrating Bihari labourers in brick kilns and on farms. He claimed that 95 per cent of those who were killed in encounters with the security forces were identified persons. N.V. Subramanian in his report on disappearance in Punjab quotes quoted ex-DGP Gill as saying: "We did a study. Many of them were Bangladeshis sneaking into Pakistan killed by their forces or ours. If still there were unidentified bodies, they would be of terrorists that we did not return to their families because of the ban we had imposed then on bhog ceremonies."[85]

OTHER MEANS OF STATE VIOLENCE

When other means seemed to be failing to get rid of the issue of human rights violation; then the police adopt the method to which it used during the period of counter-insurgency: First was giving threats to the human rights activist Mr. Jaswant Singh Khalra and when he did not submitted to the threats he also became an unidentified dead body but not be burnt. His dead body was not to be burnt but to be drowned into the Harike Canal Head Works, to eliminate all the records and to correct the mistakes to which police has committed earlier.[86] The transfer of the officers to same police districts and the police station to threaten the families which were filing the petition against the police is revealed by Ram Naryan Kumar and Inderjit Singh Jaijee in their works.[87]

SUICIDE BY THE FORMER SSP OF TARN TARAN AND THE STATE RESPONSE

On May 24, 1997 several national dailies reported that SSP Ajit Singh Sandhu committed suicide by throwing himself in front of a moving train. Sandhu had been imprisoned for few months on charges established by judicial inquiries that involved illegal abduction torture and custodial death of Kuljit Singh a close relative of Bhagat Singh. He was the prime accused in the cremation case and 42 other cases of extra-judicial and custodial killings.[88] The circumstances of his reported suicide were suspicious and reported by news papers and contented by human rights groups. He had consumed alcohol, had driven to the railway track in his own car, and a short note that he left behind said, "it is better to die than to live in shame."[89]

The suicide by Sandhu who fuelled the anti-human rights campaign by the Punjab Police. K.P.S. Gill was retired by the time. It gave an opportunity to him to launch his campaign against "an utterly compromised human rights lobby." He called a press conference on 25 May, 1997, a day after Sandhu was found dead, "not to express grief, but to discuss the larger political and policy issues that arose from Sandhu's suicide. The newspapers across the country carried the full text of his statement that lambasted the nation for showing ingratitude towards its "heroes" like Sandhu who have saved India from the brink of disintegration. It castigated the people for permitting the human rights activities "who will work with any cause serves their personal ends, whether criminal, political or secessionist to thrive on Indian Soil. The statement chided the state for not educating itself on how to tackle individuals and groups trying to destroy it, and went on to urge the Parliament to bring about the necessary legal amendments that would protect other courageous officers of Punjab police from the kind of humiliation that apparently drove Sandhu to suicide. The statement said that the bud of Khalistan had been nipped through the achievements of officers like Sandhu, which prevented the loss of Kashmir and eventually balkanisation of India.[90]

The campaign launched by Gill avalanched into a crusade. Responsible political leaders began to NHRC of being prejudice against the police. Jaswant Singh wrote, "Sandhu was just left to fend himself. The state has abandoned him and–to my mind, much worse—his incarceration and humiliation were used to deflect attention". Tavleen Singh, a senior journalist explained in her column: "Murderers of Sandhu are the human rights wallas." They have been unable to see that there was war in Tarn Taran. In fighting if Sandhu broke a few rules, there was no other way. In his subsequent letter to the Prime Minister Gill asked for a legislation that defines "appropriate criteria to judge the actions of those who fought this war on behalf of the Indian state." Until necessary criteria is sufficiently debated, defined and legislated, immediate steps should be taken to ensure that the pattern of humiliation through litigation and trials by the media is prevented forthwith. He repeated that insinuation that "for those who were comprehensive defeated in the battle of Khalistan, public interest litigation had become the most convenient strategy of vendetta.[91]

On 19 August, 2001, the Union Home Minister spoke at function, organised by *Hind Samachar* group of newspapers at Jalandhar to announce that the government was "contemplating steps to provide legal protection and relief to the personnel of the security forces facing prosecution for alleged excess during anti-insurgency operations" in Punjab, Kashmir and north-eastern provinces of India according to report published in *Asian Age*, the Union Home Minister indicated "some form of general amnesty" and suggested that forces deployed to combat terrorism anywhere in the country must be given special rights and powers.[92]

This rhetoric of morale and the national security is evidence of attempts to thwart the process of accountability. In his foreword to book titled *Human Rights and Indian Armed Forces,* Gill criticised the "systematic adoption of human rights litigation as a weapons against agencies of the state by criminals and by violent groups who themselves reject democracy and seek the overthrow of lawful and elected government." According to him, "An overwhelming proportion of public interest human rights litigation is today being initiated by front organisations of criminals' conglomerates and virulent underground terrorist movement in a systematic strategy to harass and paralyse security forces and the police.[93] The Punjab police have also associated human rights activists with Pakistan's Inter-Services Intelligence (ISI). [94]

COMPENSATION TO THE VICTIMS: CIVIL SOCIETY RESPONSES

The procedure to compensate the victims of the mass cremation was completed in the seven phases. The first phase of inquiry started on 13 January, 1999:

The Commission undertook an inquiry into the cremation of 2097 (on re-examination 2059) dead bodies in three crematoriums of Amritsar, Tarn Taran and Majitha during the decade 1984-94 from human rights perspective on the Remit from the Hon. Supreme Court of India with a view to award compensation to the next of kin of the deceased in deserving cases.

During the course of inquiry, CBI on the directions of the Commission submitted three Lists—List 'A' showing 582 out of those 2097 deceased as fully identified, 278 as partially identified and 1237 as unidentified dead bodies. Public notice inviting claims from the interested parties was issued in the news papers in January 1999. Pursuant to the said public notice, only 88 claims were received. With a view to ensure that justice is delivered in as many cases as possible, the Commission in 2004 decided to issue fresh public notice in the newspapers to invite claims in relation to those 2097 dead bodies. Pursuant to the subsequent notice, 1796 claims, besides those earlier 88 claims were received.

Noticing that only 582 dead bodies were fully identified, out of 2097 dead bodies cremated in three crematoriums under the dubious circumstances, the Commission decided to undertake an exercise for identifying as many dead bodies as possible and with the help of State authorities and the parties to the proceedings, the Commission was able to identify as many as 1245 dead bodies as against 582 initially identified.

On the basis of inquiry, the Commission came to the conclusion that 194 deceased out of those 2097 dead bodies were admittedly either in the custody or deemed to be in custody of the police authorities immediately before their death and cremation. Since the police had failed in their duty to safeguard those persons who were in the custody of police, the Commission extending the principle of strict liability of "Duty of Care" held the State vicariously liable for violation of human rights of those 194 persons and awarded compensation of Rs. 2.5 lakhs each to the next of kin (NOK) of those 194 deceased vide its order dated 11th November, 2004 and subsequent orders from time to time. Pursuant to the orders a sum of Rs. 4,85,00,000 has been deposited by the State Government for disbursement.

As regards the remaining 1051 deceased persons who have been fully identified, pursuant to the exercise undertaken by the

Commission, the Commission on inquiry found that those dead bodies were unceremoniously cremated by the state authorities in violation of the rules framed for cremation of unidentified dead bodies. The Commission took the view that the aforesaid acts of authorities amounted to violation of dignity of dead and also hurts the emotions and sentiments of the next of kin of the deceased persons who would have preferred to perform the last rites of their near and dear ones in accordance with their religious and customary beliefs. Thus, for violation of dignity of dead and the right of the next of kin of the deceased persons to give an honourable farewell to the departed soul, the Commission has awarded a sum of Rs. 1.75 lakhs (one lakh seventy five thousand only) each to the next of kin of those 1051 deceased persons. Total amount of Rs. 18,39,25,000 have been directed to be deposited by the State of Punjab within three months for disbursement to the NOK. 814 dead bodies out of 2097 dead bodies still remain to be identified. The Commission, with a view to dispense justice to NOK of those unidentified deceased persons also, has decided to make one more effort to identify as many dead bodies as possible. Accordingly, it has now decided to appoint a Commissioner of the rank of retired High Court Judge to hold an inquiry with the assistance of the claimants, State Authorities and the petitioners to fix the identity of as many dead bodies out of those 814 dead bodies as possible, so that monetary relief, if justified, can be awarded to the NOK of those deceased persons also as a solace. The Commissioner has been given eight months time to complete the inquiry which shall be held at Amritsar.[95]

VICTIMS' TESTIMONIES AND CIVIL SOCIETY RESPONSES: AN APPRAISAL

The defenders of impunity in Punjab have been vocal against the human rights litigation they seek accountability and restitution of hideous abuses of power. The procedure and working of NHRC on the issue of mass cremation in Punjab has been a matter of the writ petition and debate of civil society from the very inception of its work. The Committee for Information and Initiative on Punjab (CIIP) and *Ensaaf* working particularly on the human rights issue in Punjab during the militancy holds that the working and the verdict of the NHRC on Punjab mass cremations is influenced by the state. In its application against the NHRC inviting of application only from NOK of 2,097 in the three crematoriums of district Amritsar, and limited the inquiry only to the crematoriums, CIIP requested that the limiting of inquiry to the three crematoriums would deny justice to the large number of families. CIIP had argued that the illegal abduction and resulted cremation are not limited to the three crematoriums. But NHRC dismissed its application for the review of its earlier order. The review petition of CIIP was also dismissed by Supreme Court on the grounds that NHRC is appointed by the Supreme Court as a *sui-generis authority and Supreme Court is not prepared to interfere before the NHRC.*[96] The second most important issue which is raised by the civil society groups and human rights organisation is giving the compensation to victims without recognising the wrong doing of the security forces.

Although NHRC differentiated the victims into two categories—one in which their custody with the security forces was established before their death and another where the victims were just cremated by the security forces and their custody with the forces before their death were not established. The alleged role of the police to protect its officer by presenting the doctored FIR's and not providing the relevant information to the commission was underlined by the human rights organisation and activists.[97]

7 July ,1997, Ajyab Singh, a fifty -five year old farmer from Amritsar district, drank poison and killed himself inside the Golden Temple at Amritsar, six and half year after his son had been abducted and apparently killed by the Punjab police. The suicide note that he left said: "Self-annihilation is the only way out of tyranny that leaves no chance for justice... My son Kulwinder Singh was abducted and disappeared..... He had not committed any crime. He had not been absconding from..." I resent that no one ever confirmed my son's death. I never even received his ashes. Otherwise, I would have gone in vain to the High Court for justice.[98]

The decade of violence left behind a large number of victims who are still seeking justice even after the lapse of two decades. These victims have remained trapped in a web of fear, rumour and myth. They need to be released from psyche of the victimhood. But their journey from bewilderment of shattered lives under a complex political conspiracy to a position of powerful survival is not possible without acknowledgement of tragic happenings. The complex denial of truth not only serves the purpose of making atrocities invisible, it also makes the experiences of atrocities irrevocable among the victims.

The intensity of the direct and physical violence which was used by the state machinery to suppress the movement can be measured from the fact that there were many 'militants' who were killed by the state forces are now being traced as alive by the media after many years of the collapse of movement. In fact, some of militants, who were supposedly 'killed' twice by the state forces and their rewards were also received twice, are still alive and living with their families. The pertinent question is as to who were killed in place of these slain militants. It remains a mystery as state has not been keen to find out the truth. The issue has been given a decent burial. Democratic state in India has yet not come out with an credible explanation. The mystery over the unidentified dead-bodies and disappearances of youth is continuing even after the Investigation of the CBI (most premium investigation agency of the Indian State). Immense literature and facts about the fake encounters, unidentified dead-bodies, recorded statements before the courts and the government investigating has been completed.[99] The trails of most of the accused are almost complete. The extraordinary laws are no more applicable. The search of the disappeared youths in Punjab is also almost complete now. The issue of extra-judicial killing at large in Punjab during the period is almost recognised by government. Moreover, the charges of extra-judicial killings of the innocents by the police officers for rewards, promotion and personal enmities have also been widely reported and have received credence even if the Central Government has remained in denial mode. The people of Punjab, however, are still waiting for the state's adequate response on the violation of the human rights during militancy after a long period of the collapse of the Khalistan movement in Punjab.

Notes and References

1. H.K. Puri, *et. al.*, 1999, *Terrorism in Punjab: Understanding the Grassroots Reality,* Har Anand Publications, New Delhi, p. 112.
2. Some of the significant writings are N.C. Leites and Charles Wolf, 1970, *Rebellion and Authority: An Analytic Essay on Insurgent Conflict,* Makham Publishing Co., Chicago, Sir Robert Thompson, 1966, *Defeating Communist Insurgency,* Makham Publishing Co., Chicago. (Though the author deals with the ways of tackling communist insurgency, their ideas at the theoretical level are relevant).
3. Joginder Singh, 2006, *Myth and Reality of the Militancy in Punjab,* Shree Publications, New Delhi. See also: Anju Agnihotri & Sarabjit Singh, 2007, "The Big Picture: A Radical Change", *The Indian Express,* (Sunday Magazine), July 15.
4. Rajinder Kaur, 1992, Sikh Identity and National Integration, Intellectual Publishing House, New Delhi, pp. 72-75, 12-13.
5. TADA 3, [1], [3], [4].

6. TADA (2), [a], I, II & III. T.
7. TADA (4), (2), I-II (3), A-B. The restriction imposed on the communication and privacy are violative of the International provision provided under UDHR Article 18 freedom of opinion and expression, A.ticle 18 of ICP.
8. TADA (3) (2) I-II, (3) (4). The capital punishment is the violations of the ICCPR and the Optional Protocol to the ICCP, Art. 2, 3, and 4.
9. TADA (4).
10. TADA, 5 & 6.
11. TADA 11 (2) A-C.
12. TADA (14) 1, 5.
13. TADA (16) 1-3 (19) 1-3.
14. TADA (8) 1-3 (22) 17 of TADA Rules, 1987.
15. TADA 22.
16. TADA (20) 7.
17. TADA (20)4.
18. TADA (20) 4-b.
19. TADA (20) 8 a & b. These provisions are contradictory to the provision of effective remedies and right to equality before the Law under UDHR, Art 6, equality before the law and equal protection of law, Art. 7, right to an effective remedy, and to the ICPR, Art. 14, protection against retroactive criminal legislation, Art. 15, right to recognition as person before law.
20. TADA (15) 1-2 (21) 1a-b.
21. 21TADA (20) 3 violating the principles of fair trail provided under (Art. 9) of UDHR and (Art. 18) of ICPR which made provisions for the right to fair trial and public hearing by an independent and impartial tribunal.
22. TADA (26).
23. Supplement to the evidence act 1872, Sec 111(a); The terrorist affected areas (Special Court) Act 1984. Substance of the relevant sections 121—waging or attempting to wage war, or abetting the waging of war, against the government of India 121(a) conspiring to commit certain offences against the state, Concealing with intent to facilities a design to wage war.
24. Inder Sain *v.* State of Punjab (1973), 2 SCC 372; 1973 SCC (Cri) 813—(SCC, p. 378, para 20) State of Maharashtra *v.* M.H. George (1955) 1 SCR 123; AIR 1965 SC 722 (1965) 1 Cari LJ 641 (SCR p. 139) Nathulal *v.* Satate of AM.P. AIR 1966 SC 43: 1966 Cri LJ 71 (AIR p. 45); Srinivas Mall Bairoliya *v.* King -Emperior, AIR 1947 PC 135; 49 Bomb LR 688 (1947), 2 MLJ 328; Ravula Hariprasada Rao *v.* State, 1951 SCR 322; AIR 1951 SC 204; 52 Cri LJ 768; Sarjoo Prasad *v.* State of U.P. (1961), 3 SCR 324; AIR 1961 SC 631 (1961) 1 Cri LJ 747.
25. Quoted in Kartar Singh *v.* State of Punjab (1994), 3 SCC 569, Paras 252 & 382.
26. Kumar Amarasekera, Confessions: Recent Developments in England and Australia, *International and Comparative Law Quarterly*, Vol. 29, (1980), pp. 327-29.
27. Andrew R. Mallory *v.* USA 354 USA 449: 1 L Ed 2d 1479 (1957); Winston Massiah *v.* United States 377, US 201: 12 L Ed 2d 246 (1964);

Wlliam Mallloy *v.* Patrick J. Hogan 3788 US 1: 12 L Ed 2d 653 (1964); William Murphy *v.* Water front Commission of New York Harbor, 378 US L Ed 678 (1964); William Murphy *v.* Waterfront Commission of New York Harbor 378 UYS 52; 212 L Ed 2D 678 (1964) Emesto A .Miranda *v.* State of Arizona *v.* Robertson 486 US 675 (1988) Periyaswami Mooppan *v.* Emperior, ILR (1931) 54 Mad 75: AIR 1931 Mad 177: 32 Cri LJ 448; Pakala NarAYan Swami *v.* King Emprior 66 IA 66, 81; AIR 1939 PC 47: 40 Cri LJ 364; Nazir Ahmad *v.* King Emperior, AIR 1936PC 253: 37 Cri LJ 897; Bhuboni Sahu *v.* King, AIR 1949 PC 257; 76IA 147: 50 Cri LJ 872, Palvinder Kaur *v.* State of Punjab 1953 SCR 94, 104; AIR 1952 SC 354 SC 300: 1954 Cri LJ 865; Ram Chandra *v.* State of U.P., AIR 1957 SC381; 386; 12957 Cari LJ 559; Tahsildar Singh *v.* State of U.P., AIR 1959 SC 1012, 1059 Supp 2 SCR 875; 1959 Cri LJ 1231; Raja Narayanlal Bansilal *v.* Meneck Phiroz Mistry (1961) 1 SCR 417; AIR 1961 SC 29; (1960) 30 Comp Cas 644; State of Bombay *v.* Kathi Kalu Oghad (1962) 3 SCR 10; AIR 1961 SC 180; (1961) 2 Cri LJ 856; Hari Chand Kurmi and Jogia Hajam *v.* State of Bihar (1964) 6 SCR 623; AIR 1984 SC 1184 *(1984) 2 Cri LJ 344; Nandini Satpathyh *v.* P.L. Dani (1978) 2 SCC 494 1979 SCC (Cri) 155; AIR 1978 SC 1675; Sheela Barsa *v.* State of Maharashtra (1983) 2 SCC 96: 1983 SCC (Cri) 353; air 1983 SC 378; Special Court bill, 1978, Re (1979) 1 SCC 380; AIR 1979 SC 478, 518, (1979) 2 SCR 457, V.M. Ranga Rao *v.* State of A.P. (1985) AP LJ 361; State of Maharashtra *v.* Sukhdev Singh (1992) 3 SCC 700; 1992 SCC (Cri) 703; JT (1992) 4 SC 73.

28. Kartar Singh *v.* State of Punjab, *Ibid*, Paras 90, 19, 320, 326, 341, 347, 352. Citations: Beavers *v.* Haubert, 198 US 77, 87: 49 L Ed 950, 954 (1905); Gurbaksh Singh Sibbia *v.* State of Punjab, (1980) 2 SCC 565: 1980 SCC (Cri) 465: (1980) 3 SCR 383; Bimal Kaur Khalsa *v.* State of Punjab, AIR 1988 P&H 95: (1988) 93 Punj LR 189: 1988 Cri LJ 169; Usmanbhai Dawoodbhai Memon *v.* State of Gujarat (1988) 2 SCC 271: 1988 SCC (Cri) 318; State of Maharashtra *v.* Anand Chintaman Dighe, (1990), 1 SCC 397: 1990 SCC (Cri) 142.
29. V.M. Range Rao *v.* State of A.P., (1985), 3 APLJ 361.
30. Usmanbhai Dawood bhai Memon *v.* State of Gujarat, (1988), 2, SCC 271: 1988 SCC (Cri) 318.
31. Special Court Bill, 1978. (1979), 1 SCC 380: AIR 1979 SC 478, 518 (1979), 2 SCR 475—SCC pp. 455-56. Paras and 151.
32. Kartar Singh *v.* State of Punjab, *Ibid*, Paras. 165, 168.
33. Kartar Singh, *Ibid*, Paras 173-91, The Court referred to the precedence of the following judgments: Satya Vir Singh *v.* Union of India. (1985) 4 SCC 252: 1986 SCC (LYS); C.B. Gautam vs. Union of Indian, (1993) 1 SCC 78; R *v.* Cain, (1975) 2 All ER 850, (1975) 3 WLR 131.
34. Kartar Singh *v.* State of Punjab, *Ibid*, paras 302, 305, 306, 308, 310-317. The court relied on the following citations: Subramanian *v.* Commissioner of Police, AIR 1964 Mad 185: (1964), 1 Cri LJ 519; Directorate of Enforcement *v.* Deepak Mahajan, (1994) 3 SCC 440; JT (1994), 1 SC 290; Statesman (P) Ltd. *v.* H.R. Deb. (1968), 3 SCR 614: AIR 1968 SC 1495; Shree Hanuman Foundries *v.* H.R. Deb. Matter No. 120

of 1961, decided on July 28, 1965; Shri Kumar Padma Prasad *v.* Union of India, (1992), 2 SCC 428 SCC (LYS) 56 (1992), 20 ATC 230; Chandrz Mohan *v.* State of U.P. (1967) 1 SCR 77; AIR 1966 SC 1987; Ram Jawaya Kapur *v.* State of Punjab, AIR 1955 SC 549: (1955) 2 SCR 225.

35. Kartar Singh *v.* State of Punjab, *Ibid.*, paras 291-297: Citations: Syed Qasim Razvi *v.* State of Hyderabad, 1953, SCR 589: AIR 1953 SC 156: 1953 Cri LJ 862 V.C. Shukla *v.* State, 1980 Supp SCC 249: 1980 SCC (Cri) 849: AIR 1980 SC 1382.

36. The Special Courts violate Art. 14 (right to equality before the law) and 21 (personal liberty) (1) Ordinary criminals in other pare not tried by Special Courts. (2) Keeping accused in jail over such long periods amounts to violation of the first principle of criminal law-accused is presumed to be innocent until found guilty. (3) The Special Courts do not distinguish between classes of offenders, i.e., between the people accused of being terrorist and people accused of offences arising out of family dispute, rent, etc., (4) The ordinary class alleged offenders are being denied : (a) anticipatory bail, bail in bailable or non-bailable cases as under ordinary criminal law, (c) the witness can remain anonymous and thus cross-examination is defeated, (d) the trial in camera, so protection of open trial is denied, (e) the trial does not take the place in place where offence is supposed to have been committed (where cause of action arose) but at far away places making it difficult for lawyers, witnesses and the defence, and (f) right to appeal within 30 days instead of having the opportunity of moving the High Court and Supreme Court within 30 days . Besides the appeal time is 90 days normally.

37. PUDR, 1985, "Black Laws in Punjab: Report of an Enquiry", *Economic and Political Weekly*, May 11, pp. 826-30.

38. Ujjwal Kumar Singh, 2005, "TADA: Hard Law for Soft State", *Economic and Political Weekly*, March 25.

39. Ram Naryan Kumar, *et. al.*, 2003, *Reduced to Ashes; The Insurgency Operation and Human Rights In Punjab, South Asia Forum for Human Rights*, Kathmandu, Nepal, pp. 107-08.

40. The United Nations Human Rights Committee is a United Nations body of 18 experts that meets three times a year for four-week sessions (spring session at UN headquarters in New York, summer and fall sessions at the UN Office in Geneva) to consider the five-yearly reports submitted by 162 UN member states on their compliance with the International Covenant on Civil and Political Rights, ICCPR, and to examine individual petitions concerning 112 States parties to the Optional. Protocol,en.wikipedia.org/wiki/United Nations Human Rights Committee, 12-3-2009.

41. A former DGP of Punjab Police, K.S. Dhillon, 1995, stressed that the enactment was never really made use in the courts. Actually it only meant more powers to the police and an assault on the freedom of the common man." *The Indian Express*, March 2, p. 5.

42. While writing on the super cop for his role in suppressing the terrorist violence, H.K Puri *et. al.*, 1999, in their book, *Terrorism in Punjab: Understanding the Grassroots Reality*, pp. 121-22, wrote that K.P.S. Gill

had the distinction of having all the qualification to head the process of suppressing terrorism in Punjab. He is a Jat Sikh. He belongs to a well-to-do family. He had the experience of handling insurgency in Assam. Above all, he was a tall and handsome: the qualities that made him attractive for magazines and Television. Throughout the counter-insurgency period he was projected as the "super cop" who was planning and executing various strategies to suppress or "eliminate" terrorists. He was able to marginalize bureaucrats and politicians in public relation exercise. If the period of 1980 and 1984 belonged to Sant Bhindranwale as the most talked about the feared person in Punjab, then K.P.S. Gill, The Director General of Punjab Police was the hero of the period 1991-96. One may however be reminded of Clausewitz famous comment that war was too serious a matter to be handed over to the generals. It may be stated that counter-insurgency operation and strategy are also too serious and complex a business to be handed over totally to a police officer.

43. Ajay Bharadwaj (26 October 2008)." super–cop Gill floats new party" Daily News & Analysis. http://www.dnaindia.com/report.asp?newsid=1201142, 10-3-2011. Jyotsna Singh (8 May2002). "Profile: KPSGill". BBC News. http://news.bbc.co.uk/1/hi/world/south asia/1975997.htm,10-3-2011, http://www.tribuneindia.com/2005/20050217/punjab1.htm.. 31-5-2009, "Kanwar Pal Singh Gill:National, hero". Profiles.allindiansite.com. http://profiles.allindiansite.com/kpsgill.html., 28-9-2009.
44. H.K. Puri, 1999, *et. al. op. cit.*, No. 1, pp. 115-17, 168-80.
45. Inderjit Jiajjee, 2002, Politics of Genocide Punjab, 1984-98, Ajanta Publications, New Delhi, pp. 108-09.
46. V.N. Naryan, 1996, *Tryst with Terror Punjab's: Turbulent Decade,* Ajanta Publication, New Delhi, p. 36.
47. K.S. Dhillon, 1996, *"Servility and Oppression: Twin Legacies of Police in India"*; Paper presented at a Seminar organised by Institute of Punjab Studies, Chandigarh, 26-28 February.
48. H.K Puri, *et al,* 1999, *op. cit,* No. 1, p. 118. Endgame in Punjab: 1988-93," Gill describes how he developed "a radical policy of postings and promotions." K.P.S. Gill, "Endgame in Punjab: 1988-93," 2001, South Asia Terrorism Portal, http://www.satp.org/satporgtp/publication/faultlines/volume1/Fault1-kpstext.htm, 5-4-2007.
49. Akali Dal filed a writ petition against this in the Supreme Court. Their main objection was that Mr. Gill had actually exhorted his staff in that circular to "liquidate" the wanted terrorists. Citing the circular as an instance of state terrorism in Punjab the Akali Dal concluded that Mr. Gill's appropriation of the power was a violation of the right to life guaranteed by the constitution. The petition filed on February 6, came up for first time on February 21. The government counsel was present on the day and sought two weeks to file a counter affidavit. But when the second hearing took place on March 12, the government was still not prepared with an answer and obtained a reprieve of four more weeks. During this period the National Front government appears to have

devised a strategy to pre-empt any argument on the legality of the circular. Accordingly DGP of Punjab Police issued anew circular on April 1, superseding the earlier one. The word "liquidation" was duly dropped from the fresh circular, which instead calls only for arrest or apprehension. By the time 12 of the men in the first list were missing and presumed dead. Inderjit Singh Jaijee, 2002, *op. cit.*, No. 45, pp. 109-11.

50. Ajit Singh Sandhu the then SSP of Tarn Taran who committed suicide allegedly due to human rights violation charges was a Sub-inspector and he was promoted to the rank of SSP due to his strong actions against the terrorists., Inderjit Singh Jaijee, 2002, *op. cit.* No. 49, p. 98, Shekhar Gupta and Kanwar Sandhu, 1993, "K.P.S. Gill: True Grit: DGP Gill promoted the best officers", *India Today,* 1993, April 15.

51. Dharmendra Rataul, 2007, "Dead but Living"', *Indian Express* (Sunday Story), May 6. Manraj Grewal and Kamleshwar Singh, 2007, "Proxy Deaths", *Indian Express* (Sunday Story), May 6. *Tribune News Service* (TNS) 2007, "Using 'cats' to fight terror not unusual: Amrinder", The *Tribune*, and September 11. Dharminder Rataul, 2006, "Punjab police 'cats' on the prowl; Many terrorists -turned-informers enjoy milking their influence", *Indian Express*, February 23. Prabhjot Singh, 2005, "Wants only sitting SC judge to probe militancy : Badal replies to Amrinder", *The Tribune,* August 19. Staff Correspondence, 2005, "Punjab to review cases of those detained on terrorism charges: Cases of police personal allegedly in excesses also under study", *The Hindu*, April 20. Rubinder Gill, 2005, "6 convicted for killing rights activist Khalra", *The Tribune*, November 19. Kanwar Sandhu, 2005, "Shadow over the police"', *Hindustan Times,* November 26 TNS, 2006, "Dead terrorist runs away", *The Tribune*, January 17. Staff Correspondence, 2006, "Dead men walking continue to haunt the Punjab police; Fake Killings, Killed militants have returned to nail the lie", *The Indian Express*, February 17. Arun Sharma, 2006, "Sukhi 'victims' ask for police cover", *The Tribune*, February 19. Varinder Singh, 2006, "Sukhbir trying to rake up controversy, says Sukhi", *The Tribune*, February 20. "DGP fears threat to Sukhi's life", *The Tribune,* February 20, 2006, TNS, 2006, "Dead" terrorist embarrass Patil", *The Tribune,* February 22. PTI, 2006, "Khalsa Dal chief denies link with Sukhi's", *The Tribune*, February 22. PTI, 2006, "Dead terrorists issue echoes in LS", *The Tribune*, February 23. Staff Correspondence, 2006, "Dullo flays DGP on Sukhi issue", *The Tribune*, February 23. TNS, 2006, "PIL seeks names of persons declared dead", *The Tribune*, February 23. TNS, 2006, "Story behind Sukhi's death", *The Tribune*, February 23. Ajay Banerjee, 2006, "SAD attacks Cong on graft terrorism", *The Tribune*, February 24. Prabhjot Singh, 2006, "KPS Gill writes to CM, defends DGP Virk", *The Tribune*, February 24. Staff Correspondence, 2006, "Amrinder's no to CBI probe into Sukhi case", *The Tribune,* February 24, 2006, Varinder Walia, 2006, "100 ultra llisted as living under assumed names", *The Tribune*, February 27. Staff Correspondence, 2007, "SSP told to appear in person; Sukhi Case", *Hindustan Times,* February 28. Dharminder Rataul, 2006, "Punjab Police 'cats' on the prowl: Many terrorists-turned-informer enjoy milking their

influence", *Indian Express,* (Sunday Magazine) February 23. Amarjit Thind, 2006, "SGPC wants list of youths killed by police cats", *The Tribune,* March 2. TNS, 2006, "Cops accused of extra judicial killings to be protected: Singla", *The Tribune,* March 22. Ajay Banerjee, 2006, "No protection for cops who killed for personal gains", *The Tribune,* March 23. Dharminder Rataul, 2007, "Declared dead by police former ultra is still alive: former associate of Bhindranwale Gurnam Singh Bandala claims an innocent youth was killed in his place in 1994", *Indian Express,* April 24. Dharminder Rataul, 2007, "Killed' in 1993, encounter alive now", *Indian Express,* April 26. PTI, 2007, "It was not my duty to probe Bandala's alleged death: Former Batala SSP", *Indian Express,* April 25. *Indian Express News Service* (IENS), 2007, "Fake killings: Bhattal wants govt. to reply", *Indian Express,* April 26. IENS, 2007, "Probe the killing of 300 innocents", *Indian Express,* April 27. IENS, 2007, "Dead man walking, yet again: Bhatti says he was declared 'killed' by the Jagraon police", *Indian Express,* April 27. Navjeevan Gopal, 2007, "Dead" man is alive", *Indian Express,* April 27. Staff Correspondence, 2007, "Dead" militant moves HC to seek probe", *Indian Express,* May 8. TNS, 2007, "Punjab to probe fake killings", *The Tribune,* May 4. TNS, 2007, "Fake encounter probe to cover more cases", *The Tribune,* May 8. TNS, 2007, "Majha Human Rights Front to probe by HC judge", *The Tribune,* May 13. "Navjeevan Gopal, 2007, "Dead" man is alive in PO gallery", *Indian Express,* April 27. IENS, 2007, "Dead" militant moves HC to seek probe", *Indian Express,* May 8. TNS, 2007, "Punjab to probe fake killings", *The Tribune,* May 4. Staff Correspondence, 2007, "Fake encounter probe to cover more cases", *The Tribune,* May 8. TNS, 2007,"Majha Human Rights Front to probe by HC judge of extra-judicial killings by police", *The Tribune,* May 13. Staff Correspondence,, 2007, "Jhuthe puls mukablaya di janch laye raftar mathi: rasmi meeting ton bad koi karvai nahi", *Punjabi Tribune,* May 24. Staff Correspondence, 2007, "Farzi maqubalaya de sach ne puls prasashan nu hulaya", *Punjabi Tribune,* May 14. "Farzi Maqubalaya ton parbhayat parivara ne Rab da insaf keha: I.G. Mishra de maut da mambla", *Punjabi Tribune,* May 24, 2007, Anju Agnihotri, 2007, "Sukhi booked for fraud under passport Act", *Indian Express,* May 2. Upneet Lalli, 2007, "Encounter Killings: Truth commission needed", *The Tribune,* June 6. "Cops as criminals: Cleanse the police of such elements", *The Tribune,* June 26, 2007,, Sarbjit Dhaliwal, 2007, "Panel on fake encounter", *The Tribune,* May 14.

52. The vigilant groups included "Alam Sena" created by SSP Amritsar Mohammad Izhar, Cats (militants who surrender to the police) Ex-D.G.P. of Punjab Police Ribeiro concedes in his book Bullet for Bullet, which he authored after his retirement, Rebeiro writes "In Punjab there were some persons with criminal propensities, who were known to the police officers at various levels. They were approached and few of them agreed to form groups which would move in the guise of terrorists and confront the real militants in their dens...The police give them financial and logistic support, but their demands grew to an extent where it was impossible to satisfy them within our resources. Besides they were very

greedy people, with criminal tendency, who began to prey on law-abiding rich citizens on the assumption that the police were indebted to them and so would do nothing to stop them. One such man, recommended to Ribeiro by GurIqbal Singh Bhullar, a senior police officer, was a smuggler who had once been a police constable. He was reinstated and located in Patiala to search pot and neutralize dreaded militants, with the permission to use force. Once he drove into Ribeiro's official residence in Chandigarh to escape a police chase after he shot dead two bye-standers at a bus stand in the city. Ribeiro later found out that his operative, along with the policemen who constitute his squad, had been committing robberies, not only in Punjab but also in the neighbouring States. Ribeiro wanted to weed him out of the counter- insurgency set-up. But before he could do anything, the operative was reportedly killed after he shot down Pataila SSP. and his subordinate in their office. In his book, Ribeiro mentions several other undercover operations, planned by Amritsar SSP Izhar Alam and other senior officers of the Punjab Police. The Book also narrates how K.P.S. Gill, then inspector General of the C.R.P.F., thwarted Ribeiro attempts to discipline police who committed atrocities, by persuading the Union Home Ministry not to sanction their prosecution. Julio Ribeiro, 1998, *Bullet for Bullet: My Life as a Police Officer,* Penguin Books, New Delhi, pp. 310, 349, 350, 351.

53. Perneet Singh, 2004, "Poohla booked on abduction, murder charges", *The Tribune*, October 18. Varinder Walia, 2004, "Tension in Poohla village SGPC threat to 'liberate' gurdwara", *The Tribune*, March 10. Varinder Sareen, 2006, "Poohla, 8 aides acquitted: Cleared of charges of murder of Nihag in 2002", Hindustan Times, October 12. TNS, 2007, "Poohla, six others held", *The Tribune*, April 10. IENS, 2007, "Poohla, six others arrested, sent to judicial remand till April 23", *Indian Express*, April 10. IENS, 2007, "More trouble for Poohla: Ex-servicemen's body says it will expose Poohla links with top police officers, points fingers at former DGP Virk", *Indian Express*, April 12. Varinder Walia, 2008, "Poohla helped police to kill 7 in fake encounters, say kin", *The Tribune*, August 4. Staff Correspondence, 2008, "Poohla shifted to Ludhiana Jail", *The Tribune*, August 8. Staff Correspondence, 2008, "Controversial Nihang chief, Ajit Singh Poohla: facing trial for rape, murder and other heinous crime burnt alive", *The Tribune*, August 29. Anuja Jaswal, 2008, "Poohla dies", *The Tribune*, August 30. "Neo-Nihang Poohla Burnt to Death. Justice served", www.panthic.org/news,125,ARTICLe/.../2008-08-29.html- 23-6-2011.
54. H.K. Puri, *et. al.*, 1999, *op. cit.*, No. 1, pp. 104-05.
55. Amnesty International (AI). Break the Cycle of Torture And Impunity In Punjab, http://web.amnesty.org/library/Index/ENGASA200022003? Amnesty, January 23, 2010, International (AI). Persecuted For Challenging in Justice: Human Rights Defenders in India, http://web.amnesty.org/library/Index/ENGASA200082000?open&of=ENG-IND, January 23, 2010. UNI, 1989, 'Amnesty cannot visit Punjab', *The Tribune*, March 22.

56. Some of the infamous torture centres were Mal-Mandi (Cattle Market) Tarn Taran, Algo Kotho Bhikhiwind, Police Chowki Naushera Panua, Canal Rest House Ria, Thana Jhabal, all these places were for interrogation in the single police District of Taran Taran. In case of Amritsar, there were more places for interrogation in Amritsar then Tarn Taran, as the area under the Amritsar Police District is more than Tarn Taran Police District. Some of the infamous places were Mal-Mandi Amritsar, B.V.N., Model School, Verka, Gharinda Police Station, Khasa Police Station, Attari Police Station, Interrogation Centre in Khemkaran, Police Station at Jandiala Guru, etc. The same is true in the case of Gurdaspur.
57. *India Today*, 1989, "Prisoners were tortured by Police", *India Today*, September 30, p. 18.
58. IENS, 1990, "Villagers were Tortured", *The Indian Express*, and September 11. It is to mention that torture for the self-incrimination statement is not only prohibited by the Article 21 and 22 of the Indian Constitution by also by the Article 1(1) of the UN Convention on Torture and other Cruel, Inhuman Degrading Treatment or Punishment,1984 defines the torture as: "Any act by which severe pain or suffering, whether physical or mental, intentionally on a person for such purpose as obtaining from him or a third person information or a confession, punishing him for act he or third person has committed or is suspecting of having committed, or intimidating or coercing him or third person or, for any reason based on discrimination of any kind, when such pain or suffering is inflicted by or at the instigation of or with the consent or acquiescence of a public official or other person acting in an official capacity. It does not include pain or suffering arising only from, inherent in or incidental to lawful sanctions." Article 2 obligates the state parties to the Convention to take effective legislative, administrative, judicial or other measures to prevent acts of torture in any territory under their jurisdiction. The state may not invoke any exceptional circumstance whatsoever, whether a state of war or a threat of war, international political instability or any other public emergency, in order to justify torture.
59. H.K. Puri, *et. al.*, 1999, *op. cit.*, No. 1, p. 120.
60. Ram Naryan Kumar, *et. al.*, 2003, The Tribune (Chandigarh). "PHRO Dy Chief Threatened by SSP", 23 May, 2001, http://www.tribuneindia.com/2001/20010523/punjab1.htm#14., 25 May 2009.
61. During the counter insurgency in Punjab, the centre government not only rejected the reports of international human rights organizations on widespread abuses of human rights in Punjab but also stopped them from entering the Punjab. In a letter issued to Amnesty International that denied the permission to visit Punjab, the Indian Embassy stated: "The only turmoil in Punjab are the acts of violence by terrorists who have been indiscriminate in their butchery of innocents of all communities." The letter further stressed India's sovereignty and its antipathy to foreign interference in its domestic affairs.' UNI, 1989, "Amnesty cannot visit Punjab", *The Tribune*, March 22.

62. K.P.S. Gill, 1997, "By other means: The litigation weapon against the police and the state", *Frontline*, June 27, pp. 7-8.
63. Inderjit Singh Jaijee, 2002, *op. cit.*, No. 45, pp. 160-62.
64. *Ibid.*, p. 170.
65. Human Rights Watch/Asia and Physicians for Human Rights, Dead Silence; Human Rights Watch, India-Punjab in Crisis: Human Rights in India (New York: Human Rights Watch, 1991; Amnesty International, "Human Rights Violations in Punjab; Use and Abuse of the Law," May 1991, http;//amnestyusa.org/document.php?id=8d63FE02A44B98C 8802569A600600B91., 5-12-2009.
Amnesty International,. "Punjab Police: Beyond the Bounds of Law," April 1995, 1http://www.amnestyusa.org/document.php?id=3D24566 B3D60358B802569A50071504, 5-12-2009.
66. The origin of Khalistan is from the Persian world Khals which means a pure and it has nothing to do with the religion.
67. H.K. Puri *et. al.* 1999, *op. cit.*, No. 1, pp. 37-38.
68. Harjot Oberoi, 1994, *The Construction of Religious Boundaries: Cultural Boundaries and Diversity in the Sikh Traditions,* OUP, New Delhi.
69. On October 21, a massacre of Hindu rail passenger was occurred in Gobindgarh, September 22, 1984, 8 Hindu bus passengers were killed in Batala, February 10, 1986, 15 persons were killed and many were injured in indiscriminate firing at Nakodar, March 28, 1986, 13 Hindus were killed in indiscriminate firing at Ludhiana, March 29, 1986 in Mallian (Jalandhar), March 29, 1986, 20 innocent migrant labourers were killed, July 25, 1986, 15 Hindus were gunned down in Mukatsar, October 31, 1986, 8 migrant and local Hindu-industrial workers gunned down at a Dhaba in Ludhiana, March 3, 1988, 18 members of a Rajput family shot dead in village Theh Rajbah under Harike police station, large number of Hindu families were forced to sale their lands, close the business and leave their homes due to the fear of terrorists particularly in Amritsar and Gurdaspur districts, Data on forced migration and the reasons is given in, H.K. Puri, *et. al.*, 1999, *op. cit.*, No. 1, pp. 139 -163. In our field study, we found that the absolute majority of the Hindu families particularly in the rural areas were forced to flee from the Punjab due to the terrorism and the worship places of the Hindus and the Muslims were also damaged by the terrorists.
70. H.K. Puri *et. al.* 1999, *op. cit.*, No. 1, p. 112.
71. Satyapal Dang, *et. al.*, 2000, *Terrorism in Punjab,* Gyan Publishing House, New Delhi, pp. 161-62. see also: Joyce Pettigrew, 1995, *The Sikhs of Punjab: Unheard Voices of the State and Guerrilla Violence,* Zed Books, London, pp. 90-92, 153-54, K.S. Dhillon, 1998, "A Decade of Violence", J.S. Grewal and Indu Banga, (eds), *Punjab in Prosperity and Violence,* Institute of Punjab Studies, Chandigarh, p. 120, Kanwar Sandhu, 1996, "Buthcher or Saviour", *The Indian Express* (Magzine), January14. Paul Wallace, 1995, "Political Violence and Terrorism in India: The Crisis of Identity," Martha Crenshaw (ed.), *Terrorism in Context*, Pennsylvania University Press, Pennsylvania, pp. 354-55, Sataypal Dang, 1989, *Genesis*

of Terrorism: An Analytical Study of Punjab Terrorists, Patriot Publishers, New Delhi, pp. 39, 52, 402, 412, Gurpreet Singh, 1996, *Terrorism: An Analytical Study of Punjab*, Sehghal Books, New Delhi, p. 11.

72. *Ibid.*
73. Common observation from ten villages of Tarn Taran, Amritsar and Gurdaspur as the villagers reported that Bhai ji koi jina nahi, see, scooter moter cycle te dur di gal oh te tractor v nahi see chad de, pind chu sab loka ne dar de mare scooter motor cycle vech dite see. 'Brother Keeping of scooter and motor cycle was a distant dream during the militancy; even tractors were snatched by the militants for their movement.' All the scooter and motor-cycles were sold by the villagers as the cases of their snatching by the militants were very high.
74. Ram Naryan Kumar *et. al.*, 2003, *op. cit.*, No. 39, p. 8.
75. Documents India : "A Mockery of Justice: The case concerning the "disappearance" of human rights defender Jaswant Singh Khalra severely undermined," www.amnesty.org/en/library/asset/.../asa200071998en.html, 10-2-2010.
76. "Mass cremation of un-identified/un-claimed bodies by Punjab police in the police districts of Majitha, Tarn Taran and Amritsar," hrln.org/hrln/index.php?option=com...id...Punjab, 23-7-2010.
77. "The Murder of Human Rights Defender Jaswant Singh Khalra," www.ensaaf.org/programs/legal/khalra, 23-7-2010.
78. Punjab Mass Cremations Case, http://www.ensaaf.org/programs/legal/pmc, 16-12-2010.
79. "The National Human Rights Commission (NHRC) has justified limiting its investigation in the Punjab mass cremation case to ..." www.expressindia.com/ie/daily/19991018/ige18040.html, 1-12-2011.
80. *Ibid.*
81. As the campaign for human rights started in media a group of senior police officers including IG (Border) Dr. Bhatti and other three DIG's and 16 SSP, from all police districts met Punjab Chief Minister with request that the police should not be victimised for certain executive actions. They pointed out that they had done what they were sanction at the highest level and had succeeded in restoring normalcy to the state. IENS, 1995, "Police officer met CM", *The Indian Express*, April 28.
82. TNS, 1995, "Missing Persons were not killed: Gill", *The Tribune*, January 19. TNS, 1995, "Former DGP of Punjab Police said the centre condoned and positively encouraged the policy to commit excess", *The Indian Express*, March 1.
83. H.S. Bhanwar, 1995, "Khalra Challenges: K.P.S. for Open Debate", *Punjabi Tribune*, January 20.
84. PTI, 1995, "Thousands of Youth Killed in Police Custody", *The Asian Age'*, January 17. "Mass cremations: Inquiry Ordered by the DGP", *The Tribune*, February 8, 1995.
85. Subramanian, 1995, "Disappearance In Punjab", *Hindustan Times* (Sunday Magazine), published a report on May 25, quoting some senior police officers as saying; "About the policy of bullet for bullet, it was in the full knowledge of political high-ups that most of the terrorists were already

in police custody and they were killed in contrived encounters, 1995, "Bullet for Bullet", *Hindustan Times,* May 25, p. 5.

86. PTI, 1995, "Senior Tarn Taran Police officers rebut allegations", *Akali Patrika*, August 5. Satinder Bains, 1996, UNI, "I heard two shots I ran back: Khalra had stopped breathing", *The Indian Express,* May 5. Staff Correspondence, 1997, "Shame on Indian Police", *The Pioneer*, May 26. "Enforced Disappearance, Arbitrary Execution and Secret Cremation: Victim Testimony & India's Human Rights obligations—Interim Report by the Committee for Coordination on Disappearance in Punjab, released in July 1999. Amnesty International, A Mockery of Justice: The Case concerning the "disappearance of human rights defender Jaswant Singh Khalra severely undermined." AI index ASA 20/7/1998 http://www.webamnesty.org/ai.nsf/index/ASA200071998, 23-4-2011.
87. Inderjit Singh Jaijee, *op. cit.*, No. 45, pp. 99-100. Ram Naryan Kumar *et. al.*, 2003, *op. cit.*, No. 39, pp. 55-57, 64-65.
88. TNS, 1997, "Sandhu Committed Suicide", *The Tribune*, May 24, Hindustan Times News Service (HT News) 1997, "SSP Sandhu Committed Suicide", *Hindustan Times,* May 24. IENS, 1997, "Facing Human Rights Trials: Sandhu Committed Suicide", *The Indian Express,* May 24.
89. However, on May 4, 2007, *The Rozana Spokesman* of Chandigarh printed SSP Ajit Singh Sandhu's story, as disclosed by Col., Sandhu of the Indian army that he is alive and living in Halifax, Canada, under a fake identity. "SSP Ajit Singh Sandhu's Suicide a hoax?" The Sunday Indian the sundayindian.com/en/story/ssp-ajit-singh-sandhus...a.../6520, 24-4-2011.
90. PTI, 1997, "Sandhu was left to die: Gill", *The Poineer*, May 26. PTI, 1997, "Government should protect the police officers who fought for nation; Gill", *Indian Express,* May 26. Staff Correspondence, 1997, "Human rights cases against Sandhu dragged him to take the step: Gill", *The Times of India*, May 26. TNS, 1997, "Human rights cases was reason of Sandhu suicide: Gill", *The Tribune*, May 26.
91. Ram Naryan Kumar *et. al.*, 2003, *op. cit.*, No. 39, pp. 64-65.
92. The government assurance to police for protection regarding the human rights litigation against the police excess during the terrorism is continue phenomena in Punjab, TNS, 2006, "DGP fear threat to Sukhi's life", *The Tribune,* February 20. Prabhjot Singh, 2006, "K.P.S. Gill writes to CM defends DGP Virk", *The Tribune*, February 24. On the occasion of passing-out parade at Punjab Police Academy: Finance Minster Surinder Singla said that the Chief Minister of Punjab, Amrinder Singh would soon announce the procedure and method which will save the officers who had taken extra-judicial measures to combat terrorism. He said that the proposal has been mooted by DGP Virk in backdrop of Sukhi police CAT's case. TNS, 2006, "Cops accused of extra judicial killings to be protected: Singla", *The Tribune*, Mach 22. TNS, 2006, "No Protection for cops who killed for personal gains". *The Tribune,* Mach 22.
93. Ranvir Kumar & Capt. Sharma, 1998, *Human Rights and Indian Armed Forces,* Sterling Publication, New Delhi, On 8 June 2001, K.P.S. Gill published an article in *Hindustan Times* titled "Man in Uniform Demands

Justice". The article argued that "those who risked the lives in the defence of the State" are being subject to humiliation process of prosecution in a multiplicity of the cases that were intentionally and maliciously lodged.... As a strategy of vendetta by the front organisation of the defeated terrorists' movement". Gill asked: "How long will men continue to fight and die for India, if no one in the country speaks for the men in uniform? Can the power of the state survive the erosion of the confidence and authority of those who protect it?"

94. K.P.S. Gill, 1997, "By other means: The litigation weapon against the police and the state", *Frontline*, June 27, p. 115.
95. The details of cases with the affidavits of the Next of Kin (NOK) and the state responses and every case with the orders of dated, 11-11-2004, 4-10-2005, 8-3-2006-15-5-2006 and 09-10-2006, of compensation and pending cases are available on the website of NATIONAL HUMAN RIGHTS COMMISSION, "Punjab Mass Cremation orders" ... http://nhrc.nic.in/disparchive.asp?fno=855, 12 -3-2011, TNS, 2006, "570 more victims of mass cremations identified", *The Tribune,* April 4. TNS, 2006, "Mass cremation; relief orders for kin of 45", *The Tribune,* May 16. Dharminder Rataul, 2006, "Justice cremated, 185 families collect ashes of compensation", *Indian Express,* August 26. PTI, 2006, "Punjab to pay 1.75 lakh to1,051 families: NHRC names HC ex-judge Bhalla to identify remaining 814 families", *Hindustan Times,* October 11. "KMO leads protest march", *Hindustan Times,* November 27, 2006, Kuldip Mann, 2006, "Justice Bhalla urged to expand scope ; Rights activists want killing carried out to rehabilitate police cats' probed too", *Hindustan Times,* December 16. Kanwar Sandhu, 2007, "Wrong Punjab lessons", *Hindustan Times,* February 3. Kuldeep Mann, 2007, "Police out with 'doctored' FIRs: Withhold names of official involved in fake encounter", *Hindustan Times,* April 2. Ram Naryan Kumar, 2008, "Human rights: Justice Bhalla' Mandate is limited", The Tribune, December 31. P. K. Jaswant, 2007, "Mass cremation: Bhalla panel chastises police", *The Tribune,* March 4. S.S. Negi, 2007, "Move NHRC for equal relief, widow told, Illegal cremation by cops during militancy", *The Tribune,* April 10.
96. "Successive NHRC orders undermined the victim families' hopes of justice," http://hrln.org/hrln/index.php?option=com content&view+article&id+67:punjab-disappearance-mass, 27-1-2010, creamtioncase&catid=10:pils-a-cases<emid=147, 27-1-2010.
97. TNS, 2006, "570 more victims of mass cremations identified", *The Tribune,* April 4. "Mass cremation; relief orders for kin of 45", *The Tribune,* May 16. Dharminder Rataul, 2006, "Justice cremated, 185 families collect ashes of compensation", *Indian Express,* August 26. PTI, 2006, "Punjab to pay 1.75 lakh to 1,051 families: NHRC names HC ex-judge Bhalla to identify remaining 814 families". *Hindustan Times,* October 11. "KMO leads protest march", *Hindustan Times,* November 27, 2006, Kuldiip Mann, 2006, "Justice Bhalla urged to expand scope; Rights activists want killing carried out to rehabilitate police cats' probed too", *Hindustan Times,* December 16. Kanwar Sandhu, 2007, "Wrong Punjab lesson's", *Hindustan Times,* February 3. Kuldeep Mann, 2007,

"Police out with 'doctored' FIRs: Withhold names of official involved in fake encounter", *Hindustan Times,* April 2. Ram Naryan Kumar, 2008, "Human Rights: Justice Bhalla' Mandate is limited", *The Tribune*, December 31. P.K. Jaswant, 2007, "Mass Cremation: Bhalla Panel Chastises Police", *The Tribune*, March 4. "Move NHRC for equal relief, widow told, Illegal cremation by cops during militancy", *The Tribune,* April 10, 2007, *Amnesty International* (AI). "BREAK THE CYCLE OF TORTURE AND IMPUNITY IN PUNJAB, http://web.amnesty.org/library/Index/ENGASA200022003?Amnesty, January 23, 2010, International (AI), PERSECUTED FOR CHALLENGING INJUSTICE: HUMAN RIGHTS DEFENDERS IN INDIA "http://web.amnesty.org/library/Index/ENGASA200082000?open&of=ENG-IND, January 23, 2010.

Amnesty International (AI) "PERSECUTED FOR CHALLENGING INJUSTICE: HUMAN RIGHTS DEFENDERS IN INDIA (26 Apr. 2000), http://web.amnesty.org/library/Index/ENGASA200082000?open&of=ENG-IND, January 23, 2010.

Human Rights Watch (HRW). "India: Justice Eludes Families of the 'Disappeared' in Punjab: National Human Rights Commission Should Investigate", http://www.hrw.org/press/2003/06/india061003.html, January 23, 2010.

Human Rights Watch (HRW). "India: Justice Eludes Families of the 'Disappeared' in Punjab: National Human Rights Commission Should Investigate" (New York: 10 June 2003), http://www.hrw.org/press/2003/06/india061003.htm, January 24, 2010.

98. Ram Naryan Kumar, 2001, A complex Denial, SFHR Paper Series 10, Kathmandu-10, Kathmandu: South Asia Forum for Human Rights, pp. 20-25.

5

Visiting the Families of the Victims in Punjab : A Field Report from Tarn Taran

TARN TARAN

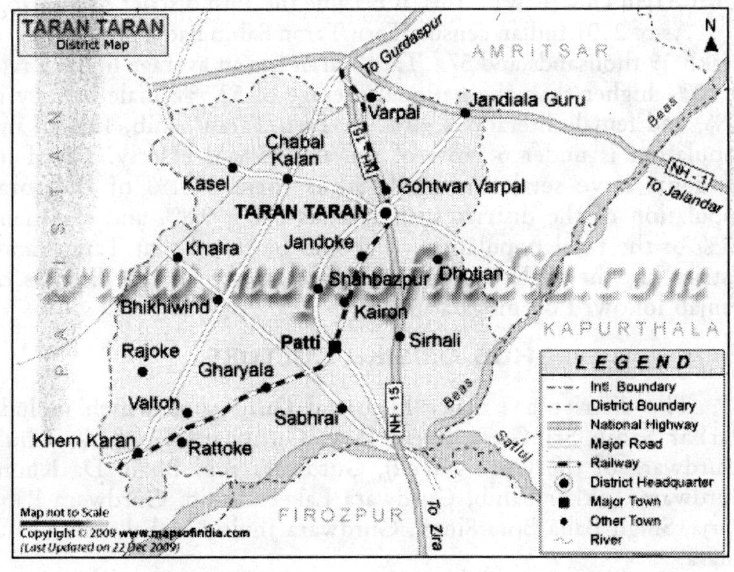

Tarn Taran was founded by the fifth Sikh Guru Shri Guru Arjan Dev Ji (1563-1606). He laid the foundation of Shri Tarn Taran Sahib Temple.[1]

Tarn Taran Sahib was Part of the Bhangi Sikh Dynasty Ruled by a Powerful Sikh Family of Dhillon Clan From 1716-1810.[2]

In 1947, the year of Partition of India, Tarn Taran was the only *tehsil* (district) in Punjab along with Sheikhupura, Ludhiana, Jalandhar, Hoshiapur, Kapurthala, Amritsar, Lyallpur, Patiala with a majority Sikh population. The city was a center of the Sikh insurgency during the 1980s and early 1990s. Tarn Taran Sahib was suggested as the capital of *Khalistan*, the proposed Sikh independent nation.[3] The main occupation in this area is agriculture and agroindustry with very few other industries.[4] The Industrial backwardness of this Sikh majority district also became the issue of the Parliament election in 2008. The Congress nominee Rana Gurmit Sodhi (An Industrial tycoon in Punjab) made the issue very alive for to the people of Tarn Tarn but somehow he lost the election and could not break the old hold of Akali Dal despite being the use of money and influential comapigns for the development of Tarn Taran.[5]

Tarn Taran district was formed in 2006. The declaration to this effect was made by Captain Amarinder Singh, Ex-Chief Minister of Punjab, during the celebrations marking the martyrdom day of Sri Guru Arjan Dev Ji. With this, it became the 19th district of Punjab.[6]

As of 2001 Indian census, Tarn Taran Sahib had a population of 9 lakh 39 thousands and 57.[7] Tarn Taran has an average literacy rate of 70%, higher than the national average of 59.5%: male literacy is 60%, and female literacy is 40%. In Tarn Taran Sahib, 12% of the population is under 6 years of age and 15% is elderly. 3% of its residents have settled abroad. Sikhs form 89.1% of the total population of the district with Hindus being 9.8% and christians 1.1% of the total population. It should be noted that Taran taran district has the highest sikh percentage among all the districts of Punjab followed by moga at 87%.[8]

HUB OF SIKH CULTURE

The district has many historical Gurdwaras which include Darbar Sahib Sri Guru Arjan Dev, Gurdwara Guru Ka Khuh (Gurdwara of the Guru's Well), Gurdwara Bibi Bhani Da Khuh, Gurdwara Takkar Sahib, Gurdwara Lakeer Sahib, Gurdwara Baba Garja, Singh Baba Bota Singh, Gurdwara Jhulna Mahal, and Thatti Khara.

Demography 2001

Total population	Religion	Population	Total Rural	Total Urban	Religion-wise Urban population		Reliogion-wise Rural population	
(1)	(2)	(3)	(4)	(5)	(6)	(7)	(8)	(9)
903957	Hindu	66823	829593	112464	Hindu	57732	Hindu	14410
	Sikh	837134			Sikh	52413	Sikh	774819
	Muslim	1876			Muslim	1537	Muslim	339
	Christian	16975			Christian	16975	Christian	15409

Statistical Abstract, 2001, Economic Advisor to Government Punjab, 2010, p. 72.

The main religious hub at Tarn Taran is Sri Darbar Sahib Tarn Taran, built by Sri Guru Arjan Dev Ji. The Gurdwara Sri Darbar Sahib Tarn Taran has the largest *sarovar* (holy tank) in the world.[9]

Other Gurdwaras in the district of Tarn Taran are at Goindwal Sahib, namely Gurdwara Baoli Sahib, at Khadoor Sahib, at Baba Buddha Sahib (Bir Sâhib) and those at Amritsar. Goindwal Sahib, situated along the River Beas, is 23 kilometres from Tarn Taran Sahib. It is an important center of Sikhism, as Guru Arjan Dev ji was born there. This district always remains the hub of socio-religious activities of the Sant Samaj, as the majority of the heads of Sants, like Kar Sewa Baba Tara Singh, Baba Jeewan Singh, Baba Jagtar Singh Sant Bhooriwale, Baba Shaheed, Sant Malkit Singh, Nanaksarware, Sant Khadoor Sahib wale, Baba Khark Singh ji Babe Budhe wale, Sant Chhapri Sahib wale, Baba Daya Singh etc from the Jat-Sikh clan of the different villages of the district Tarn Taran. Satyapal Dang found that the main reason of the Tarn Taran being the hot bed of terrorism was the Kar-Sewa run schools and colleges, where no Hindu Teachers were recruited and the teachings in the schools and collges was heavily influenced by the Sikh fundamentalism.[10]

Tharu

'Tharu' was the first and the most troubled village of my survey. It is located at the periphery of the District town of Tarn Taran, with the population of 3500 which includes both the Hindu and the Sikh families of different castes. It is one of the developed villages of Tarn Taran district. Initially, I was a little suspicious about the villagers since the village seemed to be divided into various factions. However, the Sarpanch of the village extended the desired help from the very day of my arrival. Looking into the situation, I decided to build a rapport with the villagers by visiting them regularly at the commonplace where the elders and youngsters of the village used to sit in the afternoon. A fair interaction with them broke my every myth regarding those people.

The wounds and sufferings of the violence during the militancy soon became clear, and the stories of suffering, heroism, atrocities, and wickedness were many. The names of the youths who joined the militants and members of village community, and who were either killed by the militants or by the state agents during the black days were on the tips. The hidden secrets of the violence and the damage done by militants and the state were also revealed during a series of dialogues with the respondents. A common narrative has been developed with the help of my friends and my cousin.

It was only after getting the factual information of the village set-up and the impact of the Khalistan Movement on the village, I came to know that Tharu has had long associations with the Khalistan Movement; and the youths of this village were also associated with Saint Bhindranwale (the founder of Khalistan Movement). It produced two Lieutenant-Generals of the Khalistan Commando Force (KCF). Tharu has a grim record of suffering and contribution to violence from the very beginning of the Khalistan Movement. Near about eight members of this village were killed in the Operation Blue Star. Besides the killings of these innocents (a fugitive from the village), Ajit Singh also got killed while fighting against the Indian Army during the Operation. The Lieutenant - General of KCF Ranjit Singh Rana (a mechanic with Punjab Roadways) and Ajit Singh were friends and both became baptized disciples of Bhindrawale in the early 1980's. Ajit Singh left his job from Army and started living with Saint Bhindranwale. Ajit got killed during the Operation Blue-Star but Ranjit Singh managed to escape as he was on his duty in Punjab Roadways.

The police search for Ranjit Singh Rana began after the operation Blue Star. According to the villagers, police found his photographs with Bhinranwale and wanted to arrest him. Although he was not involved in any activities of terrorism, he became a follower of Bhindranwale's ideology. The police haunt for Rana and his fear of torture and fake-encounter forced him to join the militants. He became the hero of Khalistan Commando Forces (KCF) and got the rank of Lieutenant General of KCF. He never returned and did nothing for his family which was suffering from poverty at that time. The police raided his home and the harassment of the family further deteriorated the family conditions. But Ranjit Singh did nothing to his family as the other boys of the village had done. There was nothing which was beyond the knowledge of the government and public. The culprits of the violence and looters had already become the agents of the police and the innocents were being killed by the police. The criminals made money by settling their personal feuds and finally became the agents of police as the villagers told me.

The cases of harassment and detention caused by the Fauj (Army)[11] immediately after the Operation Blue Star also came into limelights. Though the reasons of the arrest and detention were closely ascribed to the Akalis and Congress politics, their immediate connections were of the baptized and vocal character of the detainees to whom the military took as a threat and the ideologues of Khalistan and Bhindranwale.

This village is also the first village in the vicinity to erect a *Nishan Sahib* in the memory of those who lost their lives in Golden Temple during the Operation Blue Star from the Village. After the Operation Blue Star, Tharu became the hub of militant and criminal activities. Not only the degradation of the movement and the indulgences of the adherents of the Khalistan movement into local feuds and criminal activities like killing and the harassment of the villagers, the village also witnessed the cases of forced disappearances and of militants who surrendered to the police. The most tragic story of the village is of the three old mothers who are still waiting for the news of their Sons who went to nearby town of Tarn Taran with a promise to be back in home by evening but they never returned. The old parents are still searching the whereabouts of their sons and till date they have not received any news.

Interviews

The first respondents from this village were Tarlok Singh and his son Hardip Singh who were the victims of the police torture. It was only after getting assurance from his son Hardip Singh and checking of my authority letter issued by the University for the Field Survey, Tarlok Singh asked me to sit down and listen to their plight.

Singh explained that he did nothing wrong and had never been to the police station in his whole life before. He said, 'I believed in hard work and was a happy man blessed with two daughters and a son. I had never felt small in the eyes of community, though I had just one acre of land. I fulfilled all my responsibilities in respect to my family. I provided the necessary education to my children and settled them in their lives. But it was at the age of 55 in the year 1993 when I felt that I should die because in that black summer police cordoned our village off and took my family on the suspicion.'

He further added, 'One morning police announced at the Gurdwara Mike that they have doubts that some terrorists have entered in the village last night. Actually, the militants had fired on the police naka at village Nurdi and had escaped previous night. Nurdi is very near to Tharu. In a fit of fury, Police attacked on the village and a man from Nurdi was injured in the police firing. Police believed that it was the act of Bohar Singh (a militant from our village). All the males of the village were made to gather at one place and police inquired about the owners of 'Chubaras' (multi-stories houses) because they wanted the fortification of village before commencing the search of the village. Police had doubts that terrorist might be hiding in the Chubaras. Before entering these houses, police wanted to ensure the safety of all the cops. So they made the owners of the Chubaras escort the police[12], while going for a search in their houses. Villagers heaved a sigh of relief when the search of whole Chubaras completed peacefully.' To his ill luck, Tarlok was not aware of the tragedy that was knocking at their doors.

Suddenly police took the brother of Bohar Singh in their custody and was immediately taken to a room for interrogation. He was interrogated and he named Hardip because he had a verbal confrontation with him a day before. The brother of Bohar Singh confessed to the police that his brother had come to home last night and Hardip was accompanying him when he left the home. So Hardip knew his Brother's hideouts. Hence, police caught Hardip who was serving tea to the people at that time.

Hardip explained that after he was taken to police custody he was ordered to remove his clothes. Station House Officer (SHO) Gurbachan Singh seized the arms of Hardip and asked him tell the hideouts of Bohar Singh. He threatened Hardip without considering his pleadings. Hardip beseeched him that he did not know anything about Bohar Singh and his brothers and that his brother is taking revenge because he dared to speak against him.

Then SHO ordered his men to interrogate me (Tarlok) while Hardip was requesting him to enquire from the elders about his character and also to see the poor condition of their house. Hardip entreated the SHO that he and his father did lot of hard work to pay the debt which they had taken on the marriage of his sisters and if he had any association with the terrorists, they would definitely have got enough money for his sister's marriage. Afterwards my father was also taken for questioning by the SHO, Hardip added. Meanwhile a head constable showed some mercy and told him to cry loudly so that the policemen did not beat me more. He said, 'My father and I were standing naked before each other in the village school where we were taken for the interrogation.

Hardip and his father were nearly unconscious when the head-constable who had got pity on Hardip asked him to confess that Bohar came to their house. He told him that police was not going to let them go and their confession could escape them from more torture. Both the father and the son confessed. As the confession was not real rather forceful both told the different version of stories to police about the visit of Bohar Singh to their house. Hardip informed the police Bohar Singh had come last night and went back after taking milk. On the other hand his father confessed that Bohar Singh had come the previous night and went back after taking tea from their house. The police and military officers looked for some clues in their house and also beat the mother of Hardip for providing milk to terrorists, which she plainly refused.

Hardip said that God was perhaps with them as an Army colonel M.S. Kochar who also visited their home; saw the photographs of my Sisters' husbands in uniform. Fortunately, Colonel Sahib asked his mothers that whose photos these are? She told him that both were the Son-in-laws of the family and they were serving in 10 Sikh Battalion.

Then police tied their hands and foots and took them for further interrogation at City-Police Station in Tarn Taran. The village was the sole witness of this ruthless act. Hardip saw that SHO Gurbachan Singh was abusing and slapping his mother and forcing her to tell about the hide-outs of Bohar. With folded hands, she was convincing them that nobody did come to their place last night. Then Hardip cried and asked her mother to confess whatever the policemen were saying otherwise they would insult her all the more. Fortunately, the elders dared to request the Senior Superintendent of Police (SSP) Operation Khubi Ram for not to take his mother to the police station as all the males of the house had already been taken to the police custody.

Hardip said that they were lucky as both of his brother-in-laws were on leave and were at home. His mother visited them immediately after the police had taken Hardip and his father with them. His mother narrated the whole story to her son-in-laws and also told them about the colonel who was asking about their photographs. They immediately visited Jhabal where the battalion was camped during the militancy and approached their Colonel to see the case personally to have a fair inquiry.

Colonel M.S. Kochar immediately called the SSP Khubi Ram and told him that he wanted to see Hardip and his father because they were his relatives. Hardip said, 'Had his brothers-in-law not come for their rescue, he and his father would have been killed by the police in a fake encounter because they neither had any money to give nor they were near to any influencial personality who could save them.

It was on the same night that the police ordered them to come out from the cell with two other detainees, who were then killed by the police in mund area (riverside). However, the SHO ordered the policemen to send Hardip and his father back to the cell as they were known to Colonel Sahib. He told them that the Colonel had taken up their case personally with SSP and found that all the confessions made by them were contradictory. For instance, Hardip confessed that Bohar Singh and his associates left their home after taking milk; his father confessed that they came and left after taking tea; and his mother informed that they came to take water and went back. Colonel understood that all the confessions were made under duress and the arguments of the police carried no weight. He pursued the SSP to free them and called the brother-in-laws of Hardip to get them back.

Hardip's relatives immediately came and took them out from the police lockers, but they were hardly in the position to walk themselves because of immense swelling on foots and legs. They were admitted to a hospital directly and it took them two months to walk properly. His father is still not able to sit to pass stools, and they had to arrange a western toilet for him although they were not in the position to spend on this expensive item. He poignantly said, 'Although I managed to recover soon as I was young at that time, I have not been able to do any laborious task afterwards.

The torture inflicted upon them by the police not only broke them physically but also economically. Then we were forced to sell a plot to meet the medical expenses of Rs. 30,000 then. Secondly they were from lower peasantry and their only asset was physical labour but they had been made to feel unfit for the rest of their life, unable to earn their livelihood.

'We are fortunate that the battalion of my brothers-in- law remained in Punjab for some time and Colonel M.S. Kocher too was convinced of our innocence otherwise we would have been again caught and ultimately killed by the militants. The SHO of Jhabal Police Station, Dilbag Singh again marched into our house and put pressure on us to become police informer and give him the information about the activities of Bohar Singh who was our neighbourer. We requested him that although Bohar is of our neighbour but we don't know anything about his activities. He slapped me and said, 'I am sure that Bohar Singh visits your home.' He then left after giving me warning that he needed firm information of Bohar Singh from us and will be visiting us soon,' Hardip said.

'We again approached Colonel Sahib and he called SSP and asked him not to disturb us, as we were innocent. But Dilbag Singh did not bother and within a week he cordoned us and asked me about the task which he had given to us last time. I requested him that how could I know about him when the other villagers din't know. He again slapped me and told my father that if they wanted to save my life, they should supply the information of militants activities in the village otherwise he will kill me and he is sure that I am a close associate of Boahr Singh. We escaped from him earlier because of Colonel but now he will not spare us. Again he left while warning my father to get ready for my death or to become informer.' He further added, 'This time my father and I both went to Colonel Sahib and my father narrated the whole story to Colonel Sahib. He immediately called the SSP and reported him about the act of SHO. The Colonel Sahib told the SSP that we were known to him and he didn't want any harassment to them by the police again. My father was so afraid that he sent me to my sister's place and asked me to stay there. But circumstances did not allow me to stay at my sister's place as the police cordoned her village also for the search of militants and I was again caught by the police as outsider in the identity parade. Somehow luck favoured me as the father-in-law of my sister was standing with me and told the police that I am one of his relatives and came to meet my sister on yesterday. Again I was forced to come back to my village. The ultimate sigh of relief came only with the absolute end of militancy when the powers of the police were trimmed down by the government.'

The second respondent from this village was a 95 years old Ruar Singh, the father of Tejinder Singh who was a victim of forced disappearance. Being illiterate and old he could not recollect the dates of arrest and killing of his son but he showed daunting courage in narrating the real stories of militancy and unfair treatment of the people of Punjab during the militancy period.

This old man was sitting alone in his house when I visited to meet him. I greeted him and explained the purpose of my visit. He asked me to sit down and take water from the pitcher if I wanted. After getting the basic information of the victim, I moved to my questionnaire.

Bappu ji eh Bhana kado te keve Vapraya?
Grandfather, how and when did this incident happen?

Put eh rolaya vele di gal hai jad puls ne us nu Panjwar to us di daktri di dukan ton chukaya see. Mai us nu ek ver Ambarsar jail ton Jmanat ve Karva Laya see, par fer Sita Ram Thanedar fadd ke le gya te Ambarsar Jail chu band kar dita.

Son, it was during the time of militancy when the police arrested him from Panjwar village from his clinic. I got him out on bail, but Sita Ram, an SHO with Punjab Police, again arrested him and he was then sent to Amritsar prison.

Bapu ji je tanhu tareek da nahi pta ta mainu us saal ja mahenay bare das sakde oh?

Grandfather, if you don't remember the date of the killing of your son, can you tell me the month or year of this incident?

Nahi put hun Te lamba Sama ho gya, mai ek te buda banda nale unj anpad wa kethe yaad rehada ah mohal vele de gal va. Hun te uh di maa ve mar ge rondi-rondi nahi uh te das hi dendi.

No son, it has been so long now. It is very difficult for me to remember everything for I am both old and illiterate. But surely it was during the time of crisis in Punjab. His mother would have told you about this but she has also died because she cried much for him.

Bapu ji us de bhog de koi Nishani ja koi photo hai tuhade kol?

Grandfather, do you remember when you performed his Bhog ceremony or do you have any of his photograph?

Ha put Yaad aaya chhote ne us de vadi photo banvai see uh petti chu paye ae/Us de maa rondi see te mai udo luka diti see? Mai denda wa tainu kaad ke?

Yes Son, I remember that his younger brother got made a large sized photograph of him at his bhog ceremony. But I cloaked it in a big trunk because her mother used to cry when she saw it. I just show you.

He went to the room and called me to help him open the big trunk to get the photo out. I found that the photo was especially made for bhog ceremony of the victim as the name and the date of the death of Jatinder Singh was written on it.

After taking the photo of Jatinder, we sat in the veranda again. After a short pause, I asked:

Bapu ji Uhno police ne ek ver hi phadaya see ja ek to jayada ver.

Grandfather, how many times police caught him?

Nahi put oh nu eke ver Panwar ton us de haspital di dukan ton phad le gaye mur nahi chhadya. Udo uh nu Bhikiwind Thane le gaye see, mai pechhe gaya, us nu Jhubal le gaye, bade bade bande vich paye par pher us tu Tarn Taran Mal Mandi le gaye te pher us Ambarsar wali jail chu Band kar dita, Udo mai us de Jmanat karva layee ve kosis kiti par Thanedar Sita Ram ne nahi hon diti., Bahut Hosiar see mera put keve jarda kade phel nahi see hoya das jumta pad ke Daktri ve kiti see us change paisey kma ke ghar leyoda see,

For the first time he was caught at his Clinic in village Panjwar and then he was taken to Bhikhiwind Police Station. I approached some of the influential persons and went to Bhikhiwind police station to get my son released. But I was told that he was in the custody of Jhabal Police Station then. I went to Jahbal they told me to visit Tarn Taran as the police took him to Mal Mandi[13] From there he was sent to Amritsar. I tried to get him out on bail but Sita Ram did not let it happen because he was jealous of my son because as he had very intelligent. He had studied ten classes and had also done medical practices. He used to earn good amount of money also.

Te Bapu ji police ki kehandi see kyo nahi chadna us nu

Grandfather, what were the logics that the police gave for not releasing your son?

Oh kehanday see ke attwadian nu dwai denda, wada hamdard ban da uhna da assi bna de va vada daktar ehnu

They told us that he had been showing sympathy towards the militants by providing medicines to them. He will now get his rewards for showing sympathy to the milltants.

Tusi Daso Bhla jad koi goli le ke aa jau te tusi keve na kar do ge? Uh ta ose vele hi mar dende see nahi wadi gal tula ne a jade see marn. Nale uhe dukan ve ta karni see, kethe chla janda chhad ke, penda chu te Mundya da ghar see. Aap te dardi mari puls raat nu pind chu var de nahi see, Te mere put nu kehande see ke uh attwadian nu dwai kyo denda wa?

You tell me how you can disobey a person who comes with weapons. They used to kill on the spot to the person who would defy them. Moreover, he was to run his shop to earn his livelihood so he did not escape anywhere. The police was afraid of entering the village in the late evening. My son was accused of providing medicines to the militants.

Te bapu ji uhno Ambarsar wali jail Chu kina ku Cher rakhya?

Grandfather, for how long he had been caged in the Amritsar jail?

Wa wa Cher put ten char saal, etho oh us nu Nabhe ve la gaye see. Mai uthe ve janda reha mulkat karn. Koi ten char mehaney uthe reha fer us nu Ambarsar le aye. Ehto us nu Nabhe khar de see tareek bhagtaun, ek din khar de see te dusre din vapas le ke ayondey see. Uhna us nu Ayatver khadya see te Somver rah chu mar dita.

Well he was in jail for quite a long time, about three to four years. He was then transferred to Nabha jail. I used to visit Nabha jail to meet him. Then they again shifted him to Amritsar jail. From there they used to take him to Nabha for trials. Generally the hearing of his case would take two days as police used to take him out of jail one day in advance to reach Nabha. Finally police took him out on Sunday as his hearing was on Monday and killed him on the way to Amritsar.

Bapu ji Tahnu keve pta laga us di maut da, kene dasya?

Grandfather, how did you come to know about his death, who informed you?

Put Puls hi aaye see aglian tukala nu

Son, Police came to us on the next evening to inform us.

Oh ki kehandey see, ki uhna dasya see ke us di maut keve hoye.

What did they say about the death of your son?

Kejanday see tuhade munday di death ho ge, Ambarsar aa ke muh vekh Mulaja ho reha wa us da.

They told that your son is no more, if we want to see his face for the last time, we will need to go to Amritsar immediately as post-mortem of his deadbody is going on.

Par bapu ji tusi police ton Puchhya na ke us di maut keve koi?

But grandfather, didn't you ask the police about the reason of your son's sudden demise?

Put tu oh mahul nahi vekhe odno puls da raj see, koi nahi see push sakda puls kolo, uhna te sanu us di maut bare ve agle din sham nu dasya ke asi saskar ten a pahuch sakye, udo te las ve nahi dendey see.

Son you have not seen those times. Police were ruling the roost then. Nobody did have the right to ask any question to police. In fact, we were informed about the death of my son at the eleventh hour on the next evening so that we could attend his funeral. People were even not given the dead bodies at that time.

Te Bapu pher kaun gaya tuhade nal?

Grandfather, who did then go along with you to Amritsar?

Pind de do char Siane Bandey bhana Sun ke tur paye see.

Only three to four old men of the village went along with me.

Uhdi Maa, Bhra ja koi ristedar nahi gya uh di lash nu vekhan?

Didn't his mother, brother or any other relative go to see his dead body?

Bhra Te dardey Marian ne luka laye, uh ta jwan mundaya nu nahi see chhad de rsiteydara no ve betha lande see, Utho raat hon karke us di maa nu ve nahi khadya nale ki pta see ki beetni see ease kar us di maa nu ghare hi rahen ta.

His brother couldn't go because of the fear of the police, the police used to detain the young boys in those days. The relatives were also the target of the police. His mother was not taken because it was a night time so we were not sure that what would happen over there. So his mother was left at home only.

Te Ma nai gaye apne put nu vekhan?

What about his mother, didn't she cry to see the face of her son for the last time?

Uh te bahut vaste paundi see, main sochaya ke pta nahi police ne kithe le jana nale raat ser te see, jo hona see oh te ho gya uhnu kethe dhake paune see.

She was appealing to take her along, but I was not sure that we would be able to see his funerals. Moreover, the night was approaching and I was suspicious about the behaviour of the police. So I decided to leave her at home because whatever had to happen had already happened.

Te Bapu ji pher Ambarsar Kithe pahuchey?

Where did you go in Amritsar, Grandfather?

Put Pehla ta Ambarsar wale hospital pahuchay, uhna dasya ke police ta uhdi loth nu bara vaje de lay gaye, assi chheti nal maria wal daudey, par jad uthey pahuchey uh ta pura bal chukya see. Assi ta bus siva he vekkh sake, pher assi peche ek verandey Chu vade jith aasi panj chhe munde chhaney to pay vekhe, uh kaun see pata nahi laga? Pata ke lagna see uh ve sade put vang puls ne mar ke lehandey see. Kehande see oh Bijli wali bhati see, jithe uhna chheya to ekathe hi paya see, tena de muh ek pase te tena de muh ek pase san.

Son, first of all we went to Amritsar hospital. From there we came to know that police took the dead body of my son around 12 pm. Then we hurridly rushed to the crematorium but it was too late his body had already been burnt. Police took us to the heap of a wood which was also burnt we had only the glimpse of burning of the remaining wood. After some time, we entered to a veranda in the crematorium where we saw six more dead bodies of young boys lying on the electric heater.

Bapu oh lasha kehna dian san koi pta nahi laga?

Grandfather whose dead bodies were those?

Oh ve sade put vang kise durbhage de put hon ge. Thoda mulk marya Eahte Sade pind de suay te ve mar ke khad de rahe mundaya nu koi darda bolda nahi see.

They must be the sons of some ill-fated fathers like us. That was a bad time. The police killed innumerable youths. A Number of youths were also killed on the Canal side of our village. It was their rule so nobody could utter a single word against them.

Te bapu tusi police de Virudh kise kacheri ja adalt de vich nahi Gaye? Ja koi manukhi adikara wala ve nahi aya tuhade kol?

Grandfather, didn't you approach any court for justice or any human rights activists visit you?

Nahi koi nahi aaya put nale udo kehadi koi sunvai hundi see, Ha hun jarrorr Sarkar ne jaroor 2.5 lak rupaya dita jine de munde mare wa uhna nu. Sade pind Chu mainu ae ekale nu milaya wa. Aive kaha hor kise nu nahi milia vare loka de mund mare ne mere vangu, par paisey ekaley mainu hi miley ne.

No one ever visited us and justice was not done in those times. However, now I have got 2.5 lakh from the government, which has been given to those whose sons were killed during those days. I am the only one to receive this amount from my village, although there were many cases of killing in my village. But they got nothing from the government.

Bapu ji tahnu keve milay eh paisey kaun aya see tuhade kol. Koi sarkari Aadmi aaye si ja munkhi adhikara vale aaye see?

How did you get this money, who visited you? Did any government official visit you or any human rights activist?

Sarkar nu ki lod see, oh ta tuhadey warge log see, Jo push they push de mere ghar aa gaye uhna kol sara pata see. Uh ta kehandey nu ke 10 lakh da hirjana deve sarkar, oh 2.5 Te nahi san mane kehandey ne shayed uhna ne aagey ve case kar dita wa eh ta party di gal va vekho ki niberu.

Why would the government come to me? Actually, some persons like you came to me. They had got all the information. They did not agree to reimbursement of 2.5 lakh and were demanding 10 lakh each as compensation. I heard that they approached the above authorities, let's see what comes out.

Te Bapu oh bandey kehadi party de ne jina appa nu muawza dewaya?

Grandfather, do you know the persons who got you the reimbursement?

Nahi put nahi yaad

No son I don't remember.

At last he asked me to visit more houses which were ruined by the violence during the militancy.

Victims of the Militants

Sl. No.	Name of Victim	Father Name	Age	Sex	Date of Killing	Caste
(1)	(2)	(3)	(4)	(5)	(6)	(7)
1.	Bawa Singh	Ajit Singh	23	M	(Family left the village)	Nai-Sikh
2.	Gopal Singh	Ram Singh	50	M	(Wife left the village)	Mazhabi Sikh
3.	Gobind Singh	(Outsider and was living in village Gurdwara)	45	M	Consatbale in Punjab Home Guard	Mazhabi Sikh
4.	Nirmal Singh	Satwant Singh	35	M	5-7-1991	Jat-sikh
5.	Mehanga Singh	Piara Singh	39	M	16-3-1992	Jat-sikh
6.	Dalbir Singh	Beant Singh	50	M		Jat-sikh
7.	Jaspreet Kaur	Dalbir Singh	14	F	Sept. 1990	Jat-sikh
8.	Jagbir Kaur	Dalbir Singh	14	F	Sept. 1990	Jat-sikh
9.	Manjit Kaur	Dalbir Singh	40	F	Sept. 1990	Jat-sikh

Militants from the Village

Sl. No.	Name of Victim	Father Name	Age	Sex	Group	Live/ killed	Caste
(1)	(2)	(3)	(4)	(5)	(6)	(7)	(8)
1.	Ajit Singh	Bakshis Singh	35	M	BTF	Killed	Nai Sikh
2.	Baljit Singh	Shamsher Singh	22	M	KCF	Killed	Jat-Sikh
3.	Baljit Singh	Avtar Singh	25	M	KCF	Not known	Jat-Sikh
4.	Ranjit Singh	Gurdip Singh	23	M	KCF	Killed	Jat-Sikh
5.	Gurusewak Singh	Ajit Singh	17		Not Known	Not known	Nai-Sikh
6.	Bohar Singh	Tara Singh	25		(KCF)	Surrendered to Police	Jat-Sikh

Victims of Forced Disappearance

Victim Name	Father's Name	Age	Caste	Date
Ajit Singh	Roor Singh	35	Jat-Sikh	1988
Surjit Singh	Inder Singh	25	Jat-Sikh	July 1993.
Inderpal Singh	Gurdip Singh	17	Jat-Sikh	1988
Harpreet Singh (Tishu)	Gurdip Singh	16	Jat-Sikh	1988

Victim of Cross Firing

Victim Name	Father's Name	Age	Caste	Date
Harbhajan Singh	Lakha Singh	40	Jat-Sikh	19-6-1990

Photos of the Victims of Violence

VILLAGE PADHRI

Padhri was the second village of my Survey. It is situated 8 Km away from the International border of India and Pakistan with 4000 population in total. It is a village compromising eight castes and 711 of family units. The village has suffered a lot. There are many heard and unheard stories of suffering and victimization of the villagers. Padhari has lost its 35 members to the violence of black days. The members of this village not only became victims to the violence but they also joined the culprits. The village has the cases of every kind of violence and barbarity. A dialogue with a small gathering of villagers at the historic Gurdwara of Baba Vir Singh revealed not only the identities of the victims and the culprits but also gave insights to know the reasons of killings that were delibrately concealed by the families from me and also from the government during the interviews.

This village not only has the youths who joined the Singhs (Militants) but also lotus (the youths who managed to procure weapons and did some acts of extortion and burglary). The stories of killing of these youths by the police and militants after picking them were also revealed. The cycle of killings in this village started in 1987, when an influential Jat-Sikh Arjan Singh and his two sons were killed by Avtar Singh Brahma (A dared Militant and Lieutenant-General of KCF and who was known as the Robinhood), on the evening of 27.12.1987. The research of this case from the villagers revealed that the three members of this family were killed by the Brahma to avenge the murder of his friend's son from near village, Sursingh to whom the Arjun Singh and his two sons had killed and buried his body under the near drain when he had come to collect the money of the opium that his father had sold to Arjun Singh.

Then an unending chapter of killings started in the village. Another family in the village of the Gian Singh also became victim of the similar faith of local feud and lost all the children and women of the family. Only three male members of the family were able to survive as they had gone out of the house at the time of that incident. A shocking incident of the killing of three women in the dreadful night of 20.7.1990, who were alleged to have violated the moral code, came into limelight also. This agony continued until the end of militancy in Punjab and by that time the death toll crossed 35.

Tales of the families whose members and relatives fell prey to violence in Padhri

The first house of our survey in village Padhri is now traditionally known as Piar Kaur da ghar house which is now known with the name of an old woman, twenty years back this house was known with the name of her husband Arjan Singh and her sons. In the words of the village Chowkidar, '*Appa pehla Piar Kuar walh jande wa aaje ghar hi honi wa murke pta nahi kithe tib jave*'. Lets go to Piar Kaur's home first as she will be in her home and it would be very difficult to locate her afterwards. Cleared her position in the village after the loss of male members of the house, she was woman of an influential family, with three well built men and handsome landholding in the village once.

The Chowkidar appeared to be right because the door of her house had been bolted from outside, when we visited her house. Fortunately, the Chowkidar spotted her on the other side of a pound near to her house. The Chowkidar called her; I greeted her and explained the purpose of my visit. She was looking old and feeble and I decided to collect the information while sitting and talking her informally.

She started her story from the dreadful night of winters when all the males of her family were killed.

> *"Put ajje 7 ku da time see assi chule chowke Chu see, ki bahron awaz pai, Bhau ji. Vadha buha kholan Gaya see maut da, uhnu Te uthe hi goli mar diti, pher Sara tabbar gher laya, chhote nu phar he paudian Chu batha Liza, jad goli maran lage ta us ne akhan agay hath de laye see. Phir us nu andron kad ke mar dita, uh bhana vekh luk Gaya see. Ek tan kehanda see ki es de potare ve mar do par dusare reham kar Gaye. Assi Noh Sas uhane te pyaran te chuni rakh ke bacahya di jaan di bheekh mangdian rahia, te kahidian rahia ke bachian da ki kasoor hain. Vadha Jo udon 2 saal da sees, uh appane mare chache de pyara Chu diga Ronda see, chhuta ajje 7 ku mehanya da see. Pher uhana de dil mehar paye te sanu chhad ditta assi dardian ander luk gayian uhna chu ek kahen laga ehnu bahr kad ke ehade mare put vikhao. Par uhna chon ek kahen laga koi nahi us vekh hi lane wa, uh phir chale gaye." Phir pata nahi kujh chir bad mere man Chu dar aaya ki uh phir na aa jaan. Mai Nuh nu keha munde te kambal la ke gharo bahar kite luk jayee kite phir aa ke sanu ve na maar jaan. Phir assi es chhapar chu munde lupate ke luk gayian, dhian ta ghar dian bruhan chu see, uh ghar mare*

payee see te aasi Nuh, Sas... munde luko ke chhapar chu bathian sa. Hai adhi ku ki raat nu ek Banda mai ghar vad da vekhaya see, pata nahi uh kaun see, put udon jaan muthi chu aa gaye see, uh vehare chu pher ke nikal gaya pind de bahar nu. Pher saveray te vehra loka nal bhar gaya see.

Chowkidar police nu das aaya see, te uh lotha mulaze vaste le gaye Tarn Taran. Sab Bhain Bhra ve aa gaye te tikali Sanskar kar ghar aa gayian, vehalian ho ke Put!

Assal te uhana de tur jaan da pata Bhog wale din laga. Jad kurm, meri Noh nu kahen laga put munde chuk te mere nal chal pind nu. Par meri Nuh ne dil kad aapane pau nu keh dita, nahi Papa ji meri bibi ekali reh jau, ruldi mar jave gee, Loki mere munde chuk ke le jange. Asi Nuh Sas jo sade bhagan chu hai kat lava gian!

Put sadi halt kutian wali ho gayee see, koi darda kvauda nahi see, je kise de ghar chale jadian ta, Cha Pani puchhna te dur di gal koi baithan layee ve nahi see kehanda, darda mara". Hun Piar Kaur dian ankha chon hanzu nikal aaye san te mann kujh halka ho gaya lagda see. Mai us di halt nu sadharn hunde vekh kujh jarori sval puchhane shiru kar dite.

Te Maa koi ristedar ve nahi lage laga? Nahi put", kudi de peke ve nahi", "kehdi kudi!" Teri Nuh ma", "nahi put, jeheda kol aaye uh ve khan layee.

Te maa Sarkar ja police ne ve koi madad nahi keti?

Eh paise hi ditey ne hor kujh nahi, ja ek ver Thanedar Brar aaya see eh dekhan laye ke, assi keve rah-rahia va, bina kise sahre ton, Kehanda see maa dar nahi lagda keve ekalian reh rahian je es mohal vich?". Udon sham da time see mail Loon nalh roti kha rahi see, mai keha vekh lao loon nalh roti kha ke gujra kar rahian va, nale hun sade juan marn chon ki farq hai, mar den ge ta uhna kol chale java gian, nahi te ethe payian va".

Te Mata mur kade Aatvadi nahi aaye?

Nahi put ave kaha mur kise ne kujh nahi keha".

Ma ji police wale ve mur kade halh nahi puchhan aaye?

Nahi put aaj de dina tak koi nahi aya.

Te Maa aapa nu paisay kina ku time baad mile see es bhane ton baad?

Wa wa time lagh gay see 6, 7 Mehaye, uh ve meri bhateji kha gee methi ho ke. Paise Milan ton bad uh sanu Nariangarh, (Amritsar) aapane kol la gaye, sanu ve sahara see, us ne paisey udhar mang laye meri te mat kam nahi see kardi, Nuh ve ajje Niani see msa 20 -22 sala di, uh ve us dian gal vich aa gaye, us ne ajay tak nahi moray, vekh la". "Ah hun vade potare nu Food Supply Mehakme chu Naukri mili ae, nika vichara Bara pad ke bhaja pher da, uhde vi inquiree ho rahi pata nahi kado kam bane".

"Mata pata nahi laga ki kis ne mare san apane bande?"

"Nahi putt udon kaun puchh da sees".

"Kise party ne jume vari nahi laye?

Ha khure Brahme ne lai see, nahi pata nahi, and sayeed Brahme ne hi laye see".

"Te Maa, uh ki kehnda see ki kehadi galo mare ne?

Put bedose hi marte, mere puttan di gwahi te sara Pind denda va, kade kise nu manda bolh nahi san bole, kise nu ji ton siva bolh de nahi se uh dove bhra, ki pata ki aaye uhana de dil chu mera ghar ujar dita, bedose mar te put Bedose hi..........."

"Son it was around 7.00 pm when suddenly they called at our door. My elder son went to open the door of death; they killed him immediately and encircled us. Soon we all were in their clutches. Then my younger son was targeted by them. They pushed him and pointed guns on him. He sat on the stairs and covered his eyes with hands when they shot him dead. Unfortunately they saw my husband too who was hiding himself inside the room when they killed my elder son.

They did not killed him earlier because they wanted to show him the dead bodies of his sons. Finally, they got him from the room and killed him after showing the dead bodies of my sons. One of them wanted to kill my grandsons also. But we both beseeched them a lot to spare the lives of my grandsons, as they were innocents. The elder one who was of 2 years was crying on the dead body of his uncle, the younger one was just 7 months old at that time. With the grace of Almighty, they spared us and we immediately hid them in the room.

When they were going back, suddenly one of them asked me to come out to see the dead bodies of my sons because he wanted to see the fear and anguish on my face. But one of them stopped him and said that she would see them later and that this would not make any difference to her.

After sometime, I thought that there was no guarantee that they would not come again. Son, I advised my daughter-in-law to take the kids and blankets, so that we could hide ourselves somewhere outside the house. We covered the kids with the blankets and hid in the pound of waste water, which was dry at that time. Although we hid ourselves for the sake of the lives of my grandsons, our eyes were still at the gate of our home where the dead bodies were.

We again shuddered at the sudden enterance of a man in our house. I asked my daughter in-law to take the kids and move further in the pound so that she could run to the other side of the pound if the man approached them. But the man moved here and there in the house and came-out of door. Then he walked around the outskirts of the village. We could not come to know who he was and why he came to our house. He walked into the house and came out without doing anything.

After spending a long and terrible night of winter in the dry pound, we got out of the pound early in the morning. I started crying in the street and people from the neighbouring started coming; soon our court-yard was crowded with people while dead bodies were lying on the ground.

Chowkidar went to inform the police and police came around 9.00 am. They took the dead-bodies for post-mortems. It took around a day to carry out post-mortems as the doctors were to examine the other dead bodies also. Relatives had gathered in our home when we came back with the dead bodies. They had made the arrangements for funerals as the night was approaching and they had to go back. Soon we moved for the funerals. My brother showed the fire to the three piles of wood and the distance relatives left for their places from the cremation ground. Only one or two close relatives who dared stay to fulfil social responsibility were also full of fear and preferred to stay in the neighbouring houses. My daughter-in-law and I with small kids were alone in our house on the same night."

"Son the real aloneness started after the bhog ceremony (a religious ceremony which is held after ten days of death), as the real faces of our relatives and the malevolence of community came into limelight. I had to take care of a family whose members had been killed by the militants.

I was taken aback when the father of my daughter–in-law came to take away her and the kids with him. But she refused to go and told her father that my mother-in-law would die alone and our land and house would be occupied by others and kids would suffer afterwards. Let me be with my mother-in-law to confront the fate.

Not only the relatives but also the people of the village were afraid so much so that no one even wanted to speak to us. We had no one to visit. If by mistake we visited our neighbourhood, we would remain unsolicited as no one would ask to sit so that we would not visit them again. They were so terrorised that they thought that even our visit to their homes could throw them into the pit of problems. Our condition was no better than a street dog because people used to abuse the street dog but we had even lost that right in our own village..."

Now the cathartic tears rolled down from her eyes. And now I started asking some key questions which I needed for my research.

"Mother didn't any relative dared come close to you", no son! No!" "What about the parents of the girl?" What girl are you talking about?" "Your daughter–in law, Mother", no no! Everyone came to take advantage of our situation.

What about the police and government, Mother?

Yes they gave us the compensation; yes! Yes! I remember! SHO Brar of local Police Station once visited our home when he was on evening patrol."

"He came and asked how we were living in the village in those circumstances." "At that time I was having my meal with salt. I showed him that and said, "We don't have any fear of death because we are already half-dead and living just for the kids. If militants had killed us, we would have joined our males." "After listening to this, Brar went back and never came back again.

Mother what about the militants? Didn't they come again?

No son!

"Mother, when did you get the compensation, how long did it take?

It took very long, I think more than six to seven months."

What did you do with that money?

Son my niece who was living in Amritsar came to us and asked to come to Amritsar for the sake of the lives of the kids. We both agreed and went with her. There we took an accommodation on rent near to her place. But we were not aware of her purpose of coming closer to us. She borrowed the money which we had got as reimbursement with a promise that she would return it soon as was she had been in the dire need. We could not understand her motive at that time because my mind was not working properly and my daughter-in-law was too young to understand anything and we were beguiled by her. And she has not returned the money till date.

Mother! What are the kids doing now?

Elder one got a clerical job in Food and Supply Department on priority basis and the younger one has also passed the senior secondary. He is also looking for the government job."

My final question made her a little bit upset, when I asked,

Mother! Haven't you come to know about the killers?"

"No son, nobody would bother about anything then.

Then I plunged into the factual question.

Mother! Did any one take the responsibility of their murders?"

With a little hesitation, she opened her lips, "I think it was Brahma who took the responsibility. No! I don't remember exactly. I suppose Brama took the responsibility."

Then I moved to my next question,

Mother what were they saying when they came to your home and killed them? Did they give any reason before killing them?"

"No son no! The whole village knows how polite and honest my Sons were. They never had any dispute in the village, and they were very generous too.

They killed the innocents! They killed the innocents!

After interviewing Piar Kaur, I went to Gurdwaras to have lunch, where I had an interaction with the elders of the village, who were sitting under the shade of a Banyan Tree. A discussion on the village environment and the activities of the terrorists were exposed, though the village Chowkidar had already given the details of the victim.

After interacting with the villagers and the victims for a while in the evening, we arrived at the Dera (Farm House) of late Shri. Gian Singh whose son was waiting for us because my friend had called him in the morning to inform about my arrival. My interaction with Joginder Singh was very different from the other respondents because he was not only a friend of my friend but also a Graduate of 55 years and a landlord with 40 acres of land. He had an understanding of my objective. He not only strip teased some unknown facts about the killing of his family, but also revealed some of the hidden facts of the "political economy of the "compensation policy" of the government to the victims militants, and the character of the fighters of movement from the near villages.

In the very beginning, he told me that the killing of his family has nothing to do with the movement. In fact, it was the result of a minor feud over a Kacha path with another Jat-Sikh Kulwant Singh who was the owner of neighbouring farmhouse. Kulwant's brother-in-law Gurbachan Singh who was practicing as RMP Doctor in their village had joined the KCF. On the call of her sister's husband, Kulwant arrived with 7-8 militants at the dera of her sister on the evening of that night. They stayed at Kulwant's house and waited till the sleeping time and came in at 11 pm so that no one could see them and that they would kill us and escape in dark. Looking into the opportunity, Kulwant Singh also joined them to kill us as Kulwant had the information that the whole family was at home.

Joginder Singh said that they could kill all of us and escape easily. But fortune favoured us as electricity came up and we both my brother and I went to start the tube wells, younger one escaped by jumping to the backyard fields from the roof of house, they were not to be identified, otherwise...

Through this conversation on the issue over a cup of tea, I found him a stable man and I decided to start the interview. As I proceeded, I came to know that we were sitting in the same place where the whole of his family was killed on that unfortunate night of 20 August, 1989. The man explained that how the members of his family had been laying dead in the pound of blood where we were sitting at that time and how he collected the body and the head of his three years old daughter separately, when he alone entered into the house immediately after the incident. He went to everyone to check if anyone was left alive. But unfortunately he found that the interminable firing had not only killed the family on the spot but also the limbs of the some members got separated. Without wasting any time by waiting for someone, Joginder started searching for his brothers who were not there among the dead-bodies. He hunted them in the near farmhouses and gathered the 7-8 men from near farmhouses. After two and a half hours of search he came back with neighbours. They thought that the terrorists took them and they would kill them elsewhere.

Suddenly, a neighbour came and said that his younger brother was alive and was hiding in a farmhouse of neighbouring village. When terrorists were threatening him to come down from the roof, instead of coming down he jumped from the roof to backards and escaped through the fields where the crops which were grown up to the height of a man. It was around 4.00 am when Chanan Singh (elder brother of Joginder) entered into house suddenly. Chanan Singh said that he escaped because he had seen around 7-8 armed men entering into their house from the backdoor while he was at tube well. In no time he heard the firing and fled to save himself. Joginder asked his friend to call his younger brother and depute some men to call the CRPF, which was stationed at near village Sur Singh. CRPF informed the authorities at above and arrived there at 7.00 am. Soon the whole village was converted into a police cantonment for senior officers like SSP and DIG were also to visit the site. 'After some days, the Governor of Punjab and DGP K.P.S. Gill also visited to console the family,' Joginder Singh said.

Then I came to the second part of my questionnaire corresponding to the government policy of compensation and security of the victims of militancy. I was shocked to learn that they were not satisfied with the security and compensation the government had provided. He exposed the facts of corruption and bureaucratic hassles which came in their way of getting the compensation from government. He said, "*bhai ji meri juti tut gaye Chandigarh gere mar ke, pher ja ke nau jian da compensation milia, ek ji da ajje tak nahi milia, uh we Y.S. Ratra, te S.P. headquarter R.P. Singh di maherbani rahi ehna ne sadi pain laye see.*"

Brother, I had to toil hard to get compensation. I had to visit Chandigarh for innumerable times to before getting compensation of nine members. Yet we have not received the compensation of our Grandmother because of the legal hassles. It was Y. S. Ratra Secretary of the Governor and SP Headquarter R.P. Singh who took pains for me. Without their support, it would have been worse.

Then I asked about the amount of money that they received as compensation and other benefits which the government generally provided to the victims of militancy. He replied "*Nahi sanu pehal de adhr te kujh nahi milia, Bhra ne ve nakuri general che layee see", aasi Sarkar di policy de virudh attvadian de pehchan kiti se te First Information Report (FIR) Chu vi uhna da naam likhaya see", Sarkar di niti see ke aatvadin de pehchan na likhwan di, sayed Sarkar ne uhna nu mur vasun da programme bnaya see", Par mai keha chahe kujh na devo par assi pehchan ta jaroor likhwani wa." Eh compensation we RP Singh te YS Ratra de meharbani ae uhani sadi bauht pain laye see, kujh bande change hunde ne*".

"No we got nothing on priority basis. My younger brother also got his job in general category because we went against the government policy of compensation. Police did not want the names of the culprits in FIR, but we did not agree and asked the police to write the names of culprits without bothering of compensation. I think government was thinking about the rehabilitation of the militants. So their identification could hamper the process.

Then I moved onto the question of security and rehabilitation of family in such circumstances like how they coped up with the situation and defended themselves against the enemies who had joined the KCF and what kind of arrangements were made by the state for security?

"Bhai ji phir zindgi di settlement keve rahi, Sarkar ne tuhadi security vaste koi entzam kita ke nahi?"

"Bahut muskal hoi, ek var ta enjh lag reha see ke Punjab hi chhadna paye ga. Baki tusi sayane ho je Chidi da bot ek vair ahalane chon dig jaye ta uh vapse nahi panda, te ensaan da te keda tana -bana hunda wa. Assi ta ek vari buri tra put dite tine bahi, Na koi aurat Te Na koi bacha bacahya, daso es halt chu ki baki reh gaya see sade kol?"

"Te bahi ji srakar ne bilkul madad nahi kiti, koi police ja hathyar nahi dite tahnu udo ta denday see"

"Ha do ko mehnaya vaste CRPF de 10 ku bande ethe ghar rahe see, uh we Sarkar ne mga laye"

"Te phir Bhai ji keve gujra kita?

"Assi Shaher chale Gaye see, aapne hathyar, see te chhota Police Chu ho gya see, uhnu sarkari gun mil gaye see."

"Vade vaste kureva kar leya see do saal khlo ke, uh ta aaj tak shrab Chu dubya VA, uh te eh pata nahi ke ghar kaun aya ja geya ah samne baitha dekho lo tusi hai koi surat es nu. Eh dhi te put rab nee s aurat jo ujar ke vsi ae de bhaga nu de dite ne, cahlo es di ve jad reh gaye..."ya va ke nahi." Bus oh ta jindgi kad reha nakoi bahin na bhra di khabar hai es nu............." Eh tae k shara hi reh gya jis de asare eh parivar ethe baitha va, mai ta us din to bad kade raat pind nahi reha, shahr hi rtahes wa hun din aa ke kheti dekh mur janda wa."

Brother how did you defend yourselves in such circumstances? Did the government provide any security to you?

"It was very tough to cope with the situation. Once we thought to leave Punjab. Well you are wise enough to understand that once a chick of sparrow falls from the nest, it does not go back to it on its own. And the same is true to human beings. We were uprooted badly. All the kids and the women of the family were killed. I left with a younger who was forced to join the police because of security issues and elder one became alcoholic because he could not cope with the circumstances.

Brother! Are you sure the state did not bother about your security? Didn't they provide you with arms or any security?

"Initially they provided 10 CRPF commandos for about two months but after that government withdrew them and we were left on our own. We moved to city and managed the security with our own weapons. Meanwhile we found a suitable widow for the elder brother and remarried him. We returned to the village after some peace and for some time we used to stay only for a day. Now my elder brother and his family are living here to manage agricultural affairs. 'I also visit here daily in the day time and never spend night after that incident,' said Joginder Singh.

The frantic incidents of violence continued in the village and the arrival of the news of the killing of youths of the village who joined the police, militants and lotus became a routine till the end of militancy. Besides of the routine news village was shocked on 5.5.1990, when three innocent youths from the village became victims to the militant's violence. Three youths of the village, who went to village Ratul on Mang (an old agriculture tradition to help the relatives and village by calling the males for the crop harvesting), along with the elders of villagers suddenly fell prey to the militants. As in the evening and after finishing the work Lakhbir Singh wanted to meet his Masi (Maternal Aunt) who had been married in near village. Chanan Singh and Baljet Singh two other youths from the village also joined him, as the three were close friends. Lakhbir's aunt's village was 5km away from Village Ratual. They decided to go on foot. After walking for some time they decided to take a tractor from a farmhouse and entered in the farmhouse. The owner of the farm house got suspicious as some days ago he had lost his tractor to three miscreants claimed to be militants. Three youths took his tractor with the promise to return it back as they are in need. The owner of the farmhouse got alert and near the farmhouses he caught them and started beating. Unfortunately a group of militants arrived and before anyone could come from the village to help them, they were killed by the militants after a brutal torture. Most unfortunate is that the families of the victims were also denied any help by the state as the militants killed them by terming them *lotus*. The police took the version of militants and did not bother to conduct any further inquiry of the case.

Another mishap happened within the two months when the militants picked the three young women from the Vehra (a dalit lócality of village) and killed them on the charges of moral turpitude in the government school of village.

Militants also killed some of the youths who did not follow the dictates of militants and had a verbal confrontation to challenge the militant dominance. The other victims were the friends of the militants who were killed by the other group of miltnats due to internal rivalries of militant groups.

The other group who became victim to the militants and state violence was the Hindu minority, which had 8 houses and around 100 members. According to the information provided by Mr. Deshraj, the only Hindu who returned back after peace, the Hindu families were living without any fear upto 1988 but in the month of December 1988, all the Hindu families were forced to flee from the village, due to the panic created by the militants atttepted of killing of Ashok Kumar family and killing of Hindus in Bhikhiwind a nearer border town.

The Hindu Families which were Forced to flee from the Village

Name of the Family Head	*Father's Name*
1. Desraj	Kishanchand
2. Baldevraj	Kishorchand
3. Ashok Kumar	Kishorchand
4. Sukhdevraj	Harbhanshlal (returned to the village)
5. Sitaram	Buadas
6. Babbu S.	Pyaralal
7. Chamanlal	Ganpat
8. Kewalkrishan	Ganpat

Militants from Padhari

Sl. No.	Name	Father's Name	Group	Sex	Caste
1.	Jagga Singh	Gian Singh	KCF	M	Jat-Sikh
2.	Risal Singh	Banta Singh	Lotu		Mazhabi
3.	Bira Singh	Banta Singh	Lotu	M	Mazhabi
4.	Dilbag Singh	Najjar Singh	KCF	M	Jat-Sikh
5.	Mohinder Singh *alias* Mamma	Ujjagar Singh	Lieut-Gen of KCF	M	Jat-Sikh
6.	Sukhdev Singh (Hira)	Ujjagar Singh	Babbar Khalsa	M	Jat-Sikh
7.	Sukhchain Singh	Darshan Singh	BTF	M	Jat-Sikh
8.	Buta Singh	Gurmakh Singh	BTF	M	Jat-Sikh
9.	Ranjit Singh	Mukhtiar Singh	BTF	M	Jat-Sikh

Victims of the Militants

Sl. No.	Name of Victim	Father's Name	Age	Sex	Date of Killing	Caste
1.	Harnam Kaur	Mangal Singh	95	F	20-8-1988	Jat-Sikh
2.	Gurcharn Kaur	Gian Singh	60	F	20-8-1988	Jat-Sikh
3.	Swarn Kaur	Chanan Singh	33	F	20-8-1988	Jat-Sikh
4.	Gurmit Kaur	Chanan Singh	15	F	20-8-1988	Jat-Sikh
5.	Karmjit Singh	Chanan Singh	13	M	20-8-1988	Jat-Sikh
6.	Prabhpreet Singh	Chanan Singh	11	M	20-8-1988	Jat-Sikh
7.	Parmjit Kaur	Joginder Singh	28	F	20-8-1988	Jat-Sikh
8.	Amritbir Kaur	Joginder Singh	3	F	20-8-1988	Jat-Sikh
9.	Parmjit Kaur	Gian Singh	20	F	20-8-1988	Jat Sikh
10.	Harbir Singh	Jagtar Singh	15	M	20-8-1988	Jat-Sikh
11.	Arjan Singh	Banta Singh	50	M	27-12- 1987	Jat-Sikh
12.	Bakhsis Singh	Arjan Singh	23	M	27-12- 1987	Jat-Sikh
13.	Anokh Singh	Arjan Singh	22	M	27-12- 1987	Jat-Sikh
14.	Piar Kaur	Massa Singh	32	M	6-3-1989	Jat-Sikh
15.	Sucha Singh	Baghel Singh	32	M	Feb. 1988	Jat-Sikh
16.	Sukhdev Singh	Mangal Singh	40	M	1990	Jat-Sikh
17.	Kewal Singh	Ajaib Singh	42	M	March 1989	Jat-Sikh

18.	Jagtar Singh	Dalbir Singh	22	M	7-8-1992	Mazhabi-Sikh
19.	Kundan Singh *alias* (Kundan Baba)	Outsider	35	M	1990	Mazhabi-Sikh
20.	Baljit Singh	Joginder Singh	20	M	5-5-1991	Jat-Sikh
21.	Chanan Singh	Gulzar Singh	23	M	5-5-1991	Jat-Sikh
22.	Lakhbir Singh	Mukhtiar Singh	22	M	5-5-1991	Mazhabi-Sikh
23.	Bindo	Nirmal Singh	22	F	20-7-1990	Mazhabi-Sikh
24.	Shindo	Mangta Singh	25	F	20-7-1990	Mazhabi-Sikh
25.	Bir kaur	Piara Singh	18	F	20-7-1990	Mazhabi-Sikh

Victims of Militants Violence

BRAHAMPUR

Brahampur holds a vital place in Akali and Congress politics of Punjab. Ranjit Singh Brahmapura who is known as *Jarnail* of Majha regions in Akali Dal belongs to this village. The leading figure in terrorist activities and the chief of Bhindranwale Tiger Force (B.T.F.), Avtar Singh Brahama who is fondly known as the Robinhood was also from the same village.

Although Congress Party does not possess a strong leader against Ranjit Singh Brahampur of Akali Dal Badal but both the parties give tough fight to each other while electing a Sarpanch in the village. In fact, electing a Sarpanch in the village is so significant that it remains an important issue with Chief Minister Office. The selection of a Sarpanch in the village often falls prey to party politics. The undue intervention of the ruling party and the misuse of public machinery results in winning of Sarpanch of the village from ruling party in the village panchayat election in the majority times.

Brahampur which is twenty-six kilometers away from Taran Taran is one of the remote villages near River Beas in Majha region. Doaba region starts from the other side of the River Beas. The village shelters almost three thousand people of different castes in more than seven hundred houses. The village Brahampur presents a very different picture in terms of development as compared to the other villages of Punjab situated on the river. In-spite of the fact that the village is away from city, it is far more developed than other villages of Punjab both economically and educationally.

There are three people who are retired from the post of DSP and there are almost five bank managers, bank clerks, and some school teachers in the village. Apart from these, there are many people who are serving in Indian Army and Punjab Police.

This village has not undergone much tortured as compared to the other villages situated on the bank of the River Beas because there were only seven people who lost their lives during militancy in comparison to the small villages like Bhail where the number is twenty, *Munda Pind* Village where it is ten and in Rahal Chaal and Chohla Sahib. The number of deaths recorded in these villages are more than Brahampur. But the atrocities committed by CRPF on 26 December 1986 left a serious blot on the Government and Security forces in Punjab and which ultimately sowed the seeds of hatred in the hearts of people of Punjab against the government and security forces.

The story of militancy in Brahampur starts with Operation Blue Star and reaches at its heights with the violence committed by CRPF on the people of this village on 26 December, 1986.

It was Captain Hem Singh from Intelligence Bureau who became the first target of violence during militancy. According to Captain Hem Singh's brother, Hem Singh used to halt at Harimandir Sahib and offer prayers every time he would come home and while going back to his duty. In the same way on 2 June 1984, after his usual visit to Golden Temple he came home and he was to join his duty on 4th June. Capt. Hem Singh left his home on 2nd June to join his duty and since then there has been no news of Capt. Hem Singh.

According to Capt. Hem Singh's brother, Hem Singh was killed in Operation Blue Star and his dead body was perhaps cremated by the army with other dead bodies. That is why till day, there has been no clue of Capt. Hem Singh's death.

After that, there had been peace for quite a long time. But after the Operation Blue Star, the whole village was in the grip of tension because the government school of the village was occupied by CRPF. Due to the night patrols of CRPF in and around the village, the villagers had to face difficulties every time they went out to water their fields and came back late night because when any one would want to go out of the village late night or before 6:00 am, the soldiers of CRPF would make him sit at their post for the whole night and he would be released only in the morning. The Panchayat of the village other people went against the CRPF as a result of which there was a tension between people of the village and CRPF.

Avatar Singh Brahma assured protection to the Hindus of the village against militants and he urged them to stay in the village only and at the same time he warned the other militants not to enter his village. But the peace of the village was taken away on the evening of 26 December 1986 when at 7:00 pm in the evening, Avatar Barhma ordered people of the village from the speaker of Gurdwara not to come out of their homes and also warned CRPF to reform their behaviour. After the announcement, Brahma attacked the CRPF post with *Rocket launcher* but it did not land on the post. Then Brahma with the help of his two companions started firing on the camp of CRPF and afterwards three of them went to Doaba after crossing the river. According to the people of the village, Brahma attacked the CRPF camp in his reaction to the growing love relationships among the CRPF men and the school girls.

THE RETALIATION OF CRPF: A REPORT

The soldiers of CRPF did not come out for three hours after the attack of Brahampura. When the CRPF Battalion, situated just 5 miles away from the village, reached there to help their fellows, the soldiers of CRPF scattered in the whole village and encircled it. They started dragging the men of the villages out of their homes by thrashing them. And those who did not open the doors of their houses, their doors were broken. Even the women and children were badly beaten. The cases of ill -treatment with the women also came into limelight but those cases were suppressed by some prominent people of the village because they did not want their village to earn any bad name. However, the ill-treatment given by the soldiers of CRPF to Baljit Kaur w/o Mukhtiar Singh who belonged to a Suniara family and was running the only grossary shop in the village, left deep scars on her body and the worse condition of her body was visible to the media and people of the other villages. In spite of the ruthless beating of Mukhtiar Singh and the ill-treatment given to his wife by the CRPF, he was stopped by the prominent people of the village from file any report against CRPF.

On the same night, CRPF set the village Gurdwara on fire due to which the holy book, i.e. Guru Granth Sahib was also burnt. The Sarpanch and the members of the Panchayat were thrashed naked in the bone chilling cold of December. Many young people of the village were also beaten to the extent that their bones were broken. The members of the panchayat were made to stand in a queue and threatened for the whole night. The people of the village kept sitting naked and helpless for the whole night in the village school in front of CRPF soldiers.

Finally, when the news traveled to near of Sarhali SHO in the morning, he along with the other cops reached Brahampura at 8:00 am. He first of all ordered the villagers to take the injured people at home and also asked the other villagers to go home.

As the day advanced, the news traveled like the jungle fire to the other villages and people of other villages started encircling Brahampura. The current Sarpanch Baldev Singh who is a retired CBI Inspector and who was at CBI Headquarters at the time of incident read a fax about this occurrence in the village. The thick crowd led the police and CRPF cordoned off the village. Any sort of procession was banned in Taran Taran. Therefore, in the cities like Moga and Harike of Malwa region, people marched in procession against the atrocities of CRPF at village Brahampura.

The Governor of Punjab and DIG K.P.S. Gill went to Brahampura to console and calm down the people of the village. They assured the people that they would get the CRPF soldiers suspended and immediately agreed to withdraw CRPF from the village. However, no solid action was taken against the ill-treatment of women because no complaint was lodged by the people of the village. And the only Suniaar family that raised its voice against the ruthlessness of CRPF had to pay the price for it. The family was accused of being disgrace on the village and it was only after twenty days of that incident that militants shot three bullets on Baljit Kaur's husband but fortunately he survived. The family left the village after this grim incident and got settled in Amritsar.

There was peace in the village till 1990 for about four years after that episode. However in 1990, a young Majhabi Sikh who had an illicit relationship with a woman belonging to Jat-Sikh family was got killed from militants by the Jat-Sikh family.

Second tragedy happened when Hemlatta, second wife of Capt. Hem Singh, and her daughter Bittu Kaur were killed by militants. According to the family, they were accused of supplying information to CRPF by the militants. But actually the murders were the part of the conspiracy hatched by Capt. Hem Singh's first family that had acquired the property of Capt. Hem Singh and also got the compensation money in 2008. The prevailed partiality in the village made Akali Dal people suspicious of the murder of two women by the militants and they demanded for enquiry also. But in the times of Congress party headed by Capt. Amrinder Singh, a new list was prepared of the victims' families that were deprived of the compensation due to some partialities in the village. And it was decided that the compensation would be given to those families. The first sons of Capt. Hem Singh with the help of Sarpanch went to police station and again claimed compensation of Hemlata's and Bittu's death and in 2008 the compensation was given to Hem Singh's first family.

The only person who has not yet received any compensation is Majhabi Sikh Kuldeep Singh's mother Bhajan Kaur. Kuldeep Singh who belonged to a Mahjabi Sikh family and who was killed by the militants due to his illicit relationship with a Jat-Sikh girl. When police investigated for the reason of Kuldeep Singh's murder, Jat-Sikh families along with the members of Panchayat misinformed the police by saying that Kuldeep Singh was killed due to some mutual conflict between the militants as a result of which the family of Kuldeep singh has been deprived of compensation from government. Neither this poor family was able to get any reimbursement nor did they bring the real culprits of the murder into limelight to get them punished. Till today, the widow mother of Kuldeep Singh lives in fear and she tells the whole story to the persons coming to her house by making them sit in the house. At the same time, she remains worried about her second son's safety who earns his livelihood by pulling rickshaw.

Victims of Militants

Sl. No.	Name	Father's /Husband Name	Age	Sex	Date of Killing	Caste
1.	Jagjit Singh	Gurdit Singh	52	M	6-4-1990	Jat- Sikh
2.	Hardip Singh	Virsa Singh	18	M	13-8-1991	Jat- Sikh
3.	Mukhtiar Singh	Fauja Singh	25	M	3-5-1991	Mazhabi Sikh
4.	Kuldip Singh	Mukhtiar Singh	23	M	12-5-1990	Jat -Sikh
5.	Captain Hem Singh	Udham Singh	40	M	During operation Blue-Star	Jat -Sikh
6.	Hem Lata	Captain Hem Singh	40	F	1990	Bengolan
7.	Bittu Kaur	Captain Hem Singh	16	F	1990	Jat-Sikh

Victims of State Oppression

Sl. No.	Name	Father's/Husband Name	Age	Sex	Date of Killing	Caste
1.	Gurdit Singh	Eishar Singh	65	M	29-12-1986	Jat-Sikh

KHAIR-DEEN-KE

Khair-Deen-Ke was the third village of our survey. This village is home for about 2800 people and it has got 650 houses in total. Five hundreds of the total houses are of Majhabi Sikhs whereas there are hundred houses of Kamboj Sikhs and 49 houses are of Jat-Sikh Families. However, there is only one Hindu family in the village. It is here noteworthy that before militancy, there was a Hindu landowning family that had 50 acres of land. All the five brothers of the family used to be great landowners. This Hindu family had no enmity with militants and they used to live like Jat-Sikh family. But their massive land became a reason of intimidation for them as two Kamboj Sikhs started getting them frightened from militants and as a result of which the family sold their land at the rate of 25000 per acre to Joginder Singh and Malkit Singh who were uncle and nephew in relationship and were big landowners in the village.

From economic and educational point of view, Khair-Deen-Ke like other villages of border area is underdeveloped. This village is 25 km away from District Taran-Taran and located at the last Tehsil, i.e. Jhabal of District Taran-Taran. District Amritsar starts after this village.

This village like the other villages of Punjab has also lost seven of its members in those black days. In addition to this, the people of this village faced the ruthlessness and brutality of both police and militants numerous times. The cases like burning of a Roadways bus in 1990 by militants on village road, the attack of militants on a private bus, and the following ill-treatment given to the people of the village by police came into limelight in our survey.

In spite of the fact that Jatt Sikhs are lesser in number, the village represents a complete picture of the villages situated in border area from every aspect. Kamboj Sikhs and Majhabi Sikhs are separated in two groups in the village. Kamboj Sikhs possess a big land area in the village and also hold politics of the village due to which many Majhabi Sikh families are with them. The murders committed during militancy were the outcome of old animosity. The reason of mutual enmity between Kamboj Sikhs and Majhabi Sikhs like in the other villages of Punjab situated in border area was the smuggling of narcotics. The fact came out from the village that some Majhabi Sikhs of the village were not only used to do smuggling of narcotics by Kamboj Sikhs but also they were used as a tool to threaten and kill those Majhabi Sikhs who were against Kamboj Sikhs. It is told that the reason of the murder of three minor Majhabi Sikh boys in police encounter was the result of old enmity.

The three of the seven persons killed during militancy were minors. They were Tarsem Singh (14 years), Raju (15 years), and Manjit Singh (15 years) and were killed in a fake police encounter by SHO Bikramjeet of Jhabal Police Station on 06-09-1992. Kulwant Kaur, a Jat-Sikh(45 years), Beer Singh, a Majhabi Sikh (35 years), and Harbans Singh, a Majhabi-Sikh (40 years) were killed by militants in the years 1990-91 under the suspicion of selling illegal liquor and supplying information to CID. Mohan Singh, a Majhabi Sikh (65 years) was a congress worker and he set up a congress booth against Simranjit Singh Maan in the polls held during militancy.

THE KILLING OF THREE INNOCENT DALIT BOYS BY POLICE : A REPORT

According to the mothers of Tarsem Singh (14 years), Raju (15 years), and Manjit Singh (15 years), three of them had qualified till fifth class. The fathers of both Tarsem and Raju had died. In the words of Raju's mother, Raju's father was also killed by a Majhabi Sikh of the village under the aegis of Joginder Singh and the same man got her growing son killed from his friend Bikramjeet, SHO Jhabal. It is believed that the primary reason of murder of the fathers of both Raju and Tarsem was the smuggling of narcotics.

According to the villagers and the mothers of these boys, when they saw Raju, Tarsem, and Manjit roaming aimlessly in the streets of the village, they got them placed in a sweet shop of the village to do some basic tasks. They used to sleep at shop only and all of them were in the habit of smoking.

One day they all felt like smoking but they did not have any cigarettes. However, there was a tube well of Joginder Singh nearby the sweet shop. His servants used to live there. They all planned to snatch cigarettes from them and went to Joginder Singh's tube well. The moment they reached there they started threatening the servants of Joginder Singh like militants and asked them to press their legs. The servants out of sheer fear started doing whatever was told to them. But when these children demanded cigarettes from those servants, they understood that they were not militants because militants did not smoke at all. One of the servants secretly slipped away to call Joginder Singh. Joginder Singh reached his tube well with his armed men. He recognized all of them and took them to his home after tying their hands and legs. His nephew Malkit Singh and his companions beat them for the whole night and their arms and legs were broken.

In the morning when the news traveled to the ears of the families of Raju, Tarsem, and Manjit Singh, they went to Joginder Singh's house to get them released. But Joginder Singh and Malkit Singh did not lend their ears to them, nor did they allow them to meet their children. Meanwhile, SHO Bikramjeet Singh and ASI Tarlochan Singh arrived with their cops.

Though all of the Kamboj Sikhs of the village were at one side, the Mahjabi Sikhs like Sakatar Singh pleaded with SHO Bikramjeet not to take those boys to police station. Even ASI Tarlochan Singh also asked Bikramjeet to leave them as they were poor people. But Bikramjeet did not pay heed to anyone for he was a fast friend to Joginder Singh. In fact, they were much like brothers.

SHO Bikramjeet ordered the cops to throw those boys to the jeep and he went to sit in the jeep. When some villagers went to request him, he told them to prepare for Akhand Path. On the same night, all of the three boys were killed on nearby Canal-side at Noordi village in a fake police encounter and their bodies were cremated at crematorium of Taran-Taran.

The families of the boys were not informed at all. When the villagers used to go to police station to enquire about the boys, they would be told that they had been taken to Taran-Taran in SSP Sh. Ajit Singh Sandhu's chamber for regular investigation. But when the relatives of the boys and the villagers could not extract any information from Taran-Taran also, they staged a *dharna* against SHO Bikramjeet Singh. At this, Bikramjeet put all of them in the lockers of the police station till evening and told the families of the boys that they had been shifted to the hospital of Faridkot jail for treatment. At last, the widow mothers of those boys searched the jails and hospitals of Faridkot, Jalandhar, and Patti but could not get any information. After a month when Tarsem's widow mother alone went to request Joginder Singh's nephew Malkit Singh, he said to her, 'Sister-in-law, whatever was to happen, has happened. It will be better if she will concentrate on her daughters and go home because she is going to get nothing now.'

After some time it became clear from Noordi village that on the same night Jhabal police killed three boys on the canal-side. Tarsem Singh's mother along with some persons of the village went Tarn-Taran crematorium and took the ashes of the boys. But the family could not take any action against police and could not even complain against them. Neither the families of those boys were able to file any FIR of their lost boys, nor did they take any evidence of the fake police encounter from the police.

Finally, when a leaflet about the burning of the dead bodies in Amritsar and Tarn-Taran was published by NHR after a case was filed by Khalra Mission, a *dalit* boy of the village Karam Singh asked the families to go to Khalra Mission to file cases. Karam Singh himself had been the victims of police cruelty several times and he also helped the families in the cases that had been filed NHRC.

The families of Tarsem Singh, Raju, and Manjit Singh also presented witnesses against Jhabal police for killing their sons in a fake police encounter. The charges against police were invalidated by court because after the fake police encounter, SHO Bikramjeet Singh also added the case of illegal weapon on the boys in FIR against them. Besides, Bikramjeet also threatened the main witness of the case, i.e. Sakatar Singh. That is why the families were announced compensations only for the illegal burning of the dead bodies, i.e. only Rs. 175,000 by NHRC. But in other cases, an amount of Rs 250,000 as reimbursement was announced. However, the families even could not get the announced compensation as they were advised by the advocates of Khalra Mission not to take that compensation and they would appeal on their behalf in the court to get the same compensation as was given to Jaswant Khalra. But it was all in vain and their case was transferred to Bhalla Commission. No verdict of the case came till 25-06-2011.

Victims of the Militants

Sl. No.	*Name of Victim*	*Father's Name*	*Age*	*Sex*	*Date of Killing*	*Caste*
1.	Kulwant Kaur	Sardool Singh	45	F	8-7-1990	Jat -Sikh
2.	Bir Singh	Santa Singh	35	M	20-2-1991	Mazhabi Sikh
3.	Harbhajan Singh	Piara Singh	40	M	31-1-1990	Mazhabi Sikh
4.	Sohan Singh	Veer Singh	65	M	10-1-1990	Mazhabi Sikh

Victims of State Oppression

Sl. No.	*Name of Victim*	*Father's Name*	*Age*	*Sex*	*Date of Killing*	*Caste*
1.	Tarsem Singh	Mukhtiar Singh	14	M	29-9-1990	Mazhabi Sikh
2.	Raju	Gurnam Singh	14	M	29-9-1990	Mazhabi Sikh
3.	Manjit Singh (Ladu)	Shingara Singh	15	M	29-9-1990	Mazhabi Sikh

Victims of Violence during the Militancy

AMRITSAR

Amritsar is also colloquially known as ambarsar is situated in northern Punjab state of northwestern India lies about 15 miles (25 km) east of the border with Pakistan. Amritsar is an important city in Punjab and is a major commercial, cultural, and transportation centre.[14] This city was founded by Guru Ram Das in 1574 on land bought by him for 700 rupees from the owners of the village of Tung. It is also the centre of Sikhism and the site of the Sikh's principal place of worship.[15]

It is home to the Harmandir Sahib, known as the Golden Temple/Darbar Sahib, the spiritual and cultural center of the Sikh religion. This important Sikh shrine attracts more visitors than the Taj Mahal in Agra as it has more than 100,000 visitors on week days alone and is the number one destination for non-resident-Indians

Amritsar

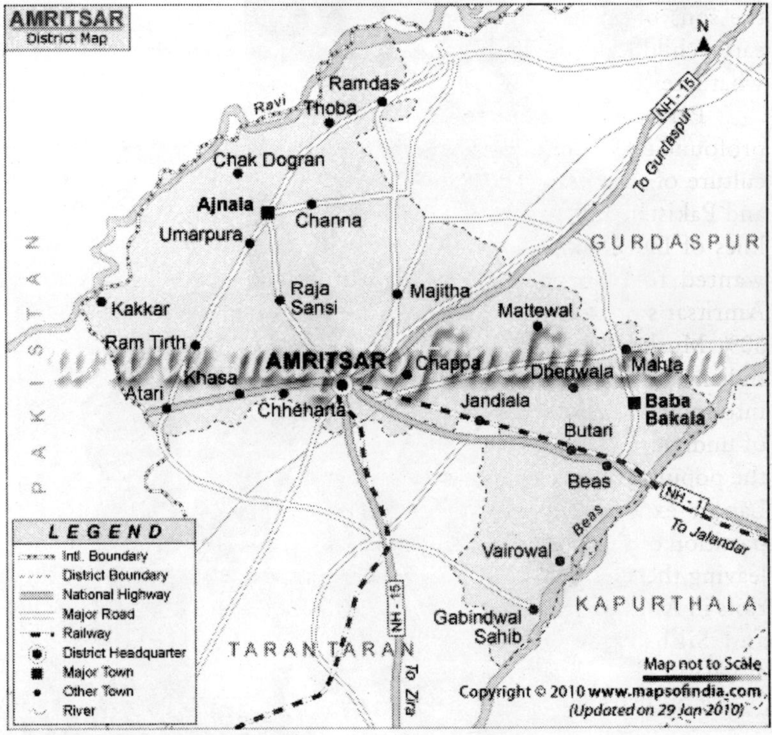

(NRI) in the whole of India.The city boasts of being the main centre of Sikhs' cultural, religious and political history.[16]

Amritsar is also known for the incidents of Jallianwala Bagh Massacre in 1919 under British Rule.[17] The most infamous operation of the India Army on the Sikh highst religious shrine to get the Bhindranwale and his band of terrorist was also happened in the city of Amritsar. It is to note that Operation Blue Star was not only criticised by the Sikh but also by the intellectual cross the globe for its calculated political benefits by the ruling party in centre at that time.[18]

Amritsar is dominated by the history of Hindus and Sikhs and many of their sacred shrines are found in and around the city. The city has highest temporal seat of Sikhs, "The Harmandir Sahib" popularly known as Golden Temple. The sacred city of the Amritsar has come to assume a special significance in Hindu cosmology because of various mythical and historical connections. Amritsar is particularly important to Hindus as it is believed that Luv and Kush, the sons of Rama, along with their mother Mata Sita, spent their early childhood in the ashram of Bhagwan Maharishi Valmiki in what later became Amritsar.[19]

Partition of British India into India and Pakistan had the most profound effect on the demographics, economics, social structure and culture of Amritsar. The state of Punjab was divided between India and Pakistan and Amritsar became a border city, often on the front lines of India-Pakistan wars. Prior to partition, the Muslim League wanted to incorporate Amritsar into Pakistan because of the Amritsar's proximity to Lahore (a distance of 30 miles) and a nearly 50% Muslim population, but the city became part of India. The Indian National Congress had similar aims of incorporating Lahore into India as Lahore was the cultural, economic, and political capital of undivided Punjab of Hindus and Sikhs constituted nearly 50% of the population, but Lahore became a part of Pakistan. Amritsar and Lahore experienced some of the worst communal riots during the partition of India. Muslim residents of Amritsar left the city en-masse leaving their homes and property behind due to violent anti-Muslim riots in Amritsar. Similar scenes of communal carnage against Hindus and Sikhs were witnessed in Lahore and led to their mass evacuation.[20]

Demography

2001

Total population	Religion	Population	Total Rural	Total Urban	Religion-wise Urban population		Reliogion-wise Rural population	
(1)	(2)	(3)	(4)	(5)	(6)	(7)	(8)	(9)
2105720	Hindu	561461	1046209	1110811	Hindu	517914	Hindu	43547
	Sikh	1505123			Sikh	570415	Sikh	980549
	Muslim	5295			Muslim	3351	Muslim	1944
	Charistian	34973			Charistian	15471	Charistian	19501

Statistical Abstract of Punjab, 2001, Economic Advisor to Government of Punjab, 2010 p. 42.

1991

Total population	Religion	Population	Total Rural	Total Urban	Religion-wise Urban population		Reliogion-wise Rural population	
2504560	Hindu	466540	1650729	853531	Hindu	428355	Hindu	63187
	Sikh	1969332			Sikh	418451	Sikh	15501881
	Muslim	4121			Muslim	2258	Muslim	1863
	Charistian	42528			Charistian	7997	Charistian	3451

Statistical Abstract of Punjab, 1981, Economic Advisor to Government of Punjab, 1991, p. 72-73

1981

Total population	Religion	Population	Total Rural	Total Urban	Religion-wise Urban population		Reliogion-wise Rural population	
2188490	Hindu	728362	1466861	721629	Hindu	205831	Hindu	476531
	Sikh	1655205			Sikh	314947	Sikh	1340258
	Muslim	2643			Muslim	940	Muslim	1703
	Charistian	35927			Charistian		7997	34531

Source : Statistical Abstract of Punjab, 1991, Statistical Abstract of Punjab, 2002, Economic Advisor to Government Punjab, p. 72.

MANDIALA

With the population of twenty five hundred people, Mandiala is located at Amritsar-Jhabal G.T. Road. Neither this village produced any famous terrorist nor any case of fake police encounter nor did police arrest of any village youth come into limelight. The village has yet sacrificed seven of its members to that violent phase.

Though the village includes five to ten houses of all the sub-castes of Sikh community such as Kamboj Sikh, Mehra Sikh, Nai Sikh, Ghumiaar, etc. yet Majhabi Sikhs constitute the majority of the population. And like other villages of Punjab, the political and economic strength of the village has been in the hands of Jatt Sikh. Even today also, the Jatt Sikhs exercise a great influence and no caste dares go against them.

Though had no direct link with terrorism, Gursahib Singh, a student of Baba Budha College, was a source of terror in the village. He was the president of Sikh Student Federation and he used to carry pistol. He was the son of Ajit Singh, a landlord of the village and he would never listen to any one which became the reason of his death.

He was famous for incivility and ill-treatment in the village. Once in 1990 when the wheat was being sown, there was a scarcity of diesel and people were purchasing diesel in queue at Kisan Petrol Pump which was 2 km away from the village. Gursahib Singh also went there to purchase diesel for his crop. As per his disposition, he threatened the employees at the petrol pump and engaged in queue-jumping to take diesel first and he was opposed by the youths standing in queue. He had just frightened to kill them that they killed him in return with AK 47 and went away after taking diesel.

The biggest tragedy of the village happened on the night of 2-3-1990, when the untouchables of the village sacrificed their 6 members to the violence of terrorism. Neither from these untouchables was government employee nor was from police or Criminal Investigation Department (CID). Their only fault was that they used to buy animals from the village and they would sell them to butchers in the city. Though this business was not much profitable, they used to earn this much that they never had to work in the fields of landlords. So they refused to work in the fields of landlords. This made the landlords suspicious that these untouchables would become their rivals and this ultimately lead to their murders and rests of the untouchables were also suppressed forever. Though the government took a hard step against that incident and established a police station and also gave 100,000 rupees as reimbursement to the families of victims, the wounds of that incident have not been cured by the economic help of government and the security of police. The younger brother of Baldev Singh and the only son of Makhan Singh have lost their mental balance. These families have spent all of their money that they received as compensation from the government on their medical expenditures. Their imbalanced mental states have deprived them from availing government job.

Victims of Miltants

Sl. No.	*Name of Victim*	*Father's Name*	*Age*	*Sex*	*Date of Killing*	*Caste*
1.	Ghula Singh	Niranjan Singh	26	M	2-3-1990	Majhabi Sikh
2.	Baldev Singh	Niranjan Singh	19	M	2-3-1990	Majhabi Sikh
3.	Rajpal Singh	Ajit Singh	25	M	2-3-1990	Majhabi Sikh
4.	Baldev Singh	Chanan Singh	22	M	2-3-1990	Majhabi Sikh
5.	Amar Singh	Baldev Singh	35	M	2-3-1990	Majhabi Sikh
6.	Makhan Singh	Sunder Singh	50	M	2-3-1990	Majhabi Sikh

IBAN KALAN

Iban Kaḷan, almost 6 km away from Amritsar, is located at the Amritsar-Khemkaran highway. It is one of the largest and most developed villages of Punjab with the populaton of 5000. Today the village is famous for growing vegetables and the vegetable seeds. But the same remained notorious in the times of militancy for perilous terrorists' activities. The most terrifying militants of K.F.C., Kulwant Singh Tyre, ((BTF) Area Commander), Kashmir Singh (Area Commander), and the other four militants, are from the same village.

The Kamboj Sikhs provide a focal point to the local communities and vegetables are also grown by them only. If we divide the population of the village in terms of castes, the population of Majhabi Sikhs is at the top with 2300 followed by Kamboj Sikhs with 2000 while the remaining castes in which Jat Sikhs stands at third position with the population of 300 followed by Nai Sikhs and,

Mehra Sikhs, and Ghumiaar Sikhs with small number. It is here noteworthy that only the Majhabi Sikhs and Kamboj Sikhs became the victims of government and militant violence. No one from the other castes joined any terrorist group, nor did anyone become the sufferer of the violence.

Iban Kalan remained the epicenter of terrorists' activities and the violence of the police. There were 6 terrorists from this village due to which they used to stay at tube wells and farm houses in large numbers. Anyone found guilty of expressing opposition to militants, used to be killed by militants in public places by dragging him from his home.

Five men of the village who were Majhabi Sikhs had been accused of being police touts or selling liquor illegally and ultimately killed by the terrorists. It is here worth mentioning that out of the five men killed Bitta Singh (22 years) was abducted and then strangled to death by Kulwant Singh Tyre in day time. He had also been given a lot of thrash beating before he was killed. Bitta Singh used to go to Amritsar everyday to work on daily wages. But on 22-03-1991, there was a *band* in the city because the former Prime Minister Rajiv Gandhi had been killed in a Bomb explosion and Bitta Singh came back home. On seeing Bitta Singh passing through street, Kulwant Singh Tyre gave him shout and with the help of his companion he took Bitta Singh on Bohdu Canal of adjacent village. He was beaten to death and was accused of being police tout. Similarly, Kulwant Singh Tyre killed another Majhabi Sikh, Bira Singh (35 years) by accusing him of being the police tout. But the primary reason of these murders by Kulwant Singh Tyre was that those persons had made fun of Kulwant Singh Tyre in front of some people of the village. It here worth mentioning that Kulwant Singh who had already become the Area Commander of BTF and who had also gained notoriety through his activities had been working at his brother's shop where he used to fix punctured tyres. Kulwant Singh's parents had died and he from a very small age got totally dependent on his brother for his living. From his childhood, people had started teasing him by calling him Kanta Tyre instead of Kulwant Singh. And after becoming a terrorist, he used to be known as the uncrowned-king of his village that could kill any one on anything. The only fault of Birra Singh and Bitta Singh was that they addressed Kulwant Singh who had acquired the name of Baba Kulwant Singh after becoming a terrorist with the name of Kanta Tyre in front of some villagers which he could not bear.

The terrorist also killed 2 members of a Mahjabi Sikh family that had been a source of terror for the villagers because the family had got seven young members. According to the family and the villagers, the family used to sell liquor. But they had given up their business after the announcement of militants against the drug sellers. But on the evening of 10-05-1991, the militants suddenly encircled their house and started gathering the males of the family at one place. Meanwhile, the 4 men of the family managed to escape. But the women and the three men of the family viz. Mela Singh (70 years), his son Balwinder Singh (35 years), and his grandson Nirmal singh (22 years) were captured by the militants. They all tried to assure them that they had already stopped selling liquor but all in vain. The militants made the three men stand against wall and started shooting bullets at them due to which Mela Singh and Nirmal Singh died on the spot but Balwinder got seriously injured but he survived.

The phase of murders in the village was started by militants to spread terror and to suppress the voice of some youngsters of the village and it started with the killing of a Mahjabi Sikh Shinda Singh (22 year) and ended by taking the lives of 6 other Majhabi Sikhs of the village. All the murders of Majhabi Sikhs that were committed by accusing them of selling liquor illegally and being police tout were committed either by Kamboj Sikhs themselves or were committed at their beck and call.

Only the Kamboj Sikhs of the village became the target of the ruthlessness of police. Police also in their proceedings and investigations bothered Kamboj Sikhs only as the terrorists used to stay at their places only.

In the cases of cremating the unclaimed dead bodies by police at the Durgiana Mandir of Amritsar, two families of the village also have received compensation of Rs. 175,000 each. It is important to note here that out of the two families that received reimbursement for unclaimed dead bodies, one of them was the family of Kulwant Singh Tyre whose dead body was cremated by police after his killing whereas the second case is of Hardeep Singh s/o Ajit Singh who was in Punjab Homeguard.

This young man was first dismissed in the case of snatching of weapons by militants at the police station of Sultanwindi which is adjacent to Amritsar and then he along with his two other colleagues who were on duty with him in Sultanwindi when militants snatched the weapons was arrested. After police detained this Youngman, he was kept at BVN Model School for seven days for interrogation where his father Ajit Singh used to give him food and clothes. But after seven days, police took Hardeep Singh to Majitha and there he was killed in a fake police encounter with some other young men. While giving the news of encounter to a newspaper, poliçe presented Hardeep Singh as an unrecognized militant. The family of Hardeep Singh searched for him in every jail as he had been missing from BVN School. But after a week, the colleagues of Hardeep Singh revealed Hardeep's father that Hardeep had been killed by SHO with some other boys in Majitha and his dead body had also been cremated. It is therefore futile to search Hardeep now.

Village Iban Kalan

Victims of the Militants Violence

Sl. No.	*Name of Victim*	*Father's Name*	*Age*	*Sex*	*Date of Killing*	*Caste*
1.	Balwinder Singh	Mukhtiar Singh	35	M	1990	Majhabi-Sikh
2.	Mela Singh	Phula Singh	70	M	10-5-1991	Majhabi-Sikh
3.	Bitta Singh	Mangal Singh	22	M	22-3-1991	Majhabi-Sikh
4.	Bira Singh	Santa Singh	35	M	7-7- 1991	Majhabi-Sikh
5.	Nirmal Singh	Baldev Singh	22	M	10-5- 1991	Majhabi-Sikh
6.	Shinda Singh	Santokh Singh	22	M	22-10-1989	Majhabi-Sikh

Victim of State Oppression

Sl. No.	*Name of Victim*	*Father's Name*	*Age*	*Sex*	*Date of Killing*	*Caste*
1.	Hardeep Singh	Ajit Singh	25	M	29-8-1990	Kamboj

Miltants from the Village

Sl. No.	*Name*	*Father's Name*	*Age*	*Sex*	*Killed/ Surrendered*	*Caste*
1.	Kashmir Singh	Ajit Singh	25	M	Killed	Kamboj
2.	Kulwant Singh (Tyre)	Bachan Singh	24	M	Killed	Kamboj

MELA SINGH BITU SINGH

NIRMAL SINGH SHINDA SINGH

MUHAWA

The last village on Indo-Pak border, Muhawa is 35 kilometers away from Amritsar with the population of 3500. To do agricultural work, the farmers of this village need to cross the thorny wires that have been used for security purposes on the border by the government. However, they have to abide by the rules of the B.S.F. So they are only allowed to do their agricultural work within the time limit set by B.S.F., i.e. from 8:00 am to 6:00 pm and at the same time they have to undergo a security check every time as they cross the thorny defence wire. According to the people of the village, they came to realize the pangs of being at border in the time of militancy. Earlier like every other farmers of Punjab, they used to do their agricultural work without any interference of state forces. In fact, they had many advantages of living at border. For instance, the things like almonds, raisins, *paan da patta*, etc. were very cheap in Pakistan whereas the things like sugar, etc. were cheaper in India. So they used to exchange these things with the farmers of their neighbouring country, i.e. Pakistan. They would even lend their animals to each other for agricultural purposes. Their love relationships had not been affected by the partition. It was the partition of Delhi and Lahore and not of their hearts.

A discussion with the elderly people of the village revealed that the police headquarters on the both sides of the International Border (IB) are the result of some greedy people and the militancy. According to the people of the village, the sternness of the government and the patrolling by B.S.F. on the border had started to bring to a halt the smuggling of drugs and weapons. The smuggling of weapons and the militants of Punjab who crossed border to join training camps lead the government to seal the border permanently.

Further the conversation with the villagers exposed that despite being the last village at the border of Punjab and the militants crossed border from this village frequently, Muhawa did not become the victim of much violence as compared to other villages of Punjab. The village no doubt produced the three militants of KFC like Gurpal Singh Padda who was considered as the master mind of KFC, Lakhwinder Singh Lakha, and the son of Gurpal Singh Padda's uncle Sukhwinder Singh Lalli who was only 16-17 years old and was studying in 12th class, when he was killed by the police in a fake encounter. They all had relations with militants and all of them were killed in a fake police encounter before they could do any heinous crime.

In spite of the fact that the village was used as a tool to cross border by the militants during 1986-88 and the help that was rendered to the militants by some of the villagers, Muhawa faced a little violence. The main reasons for this were that in 1988, the government of India establish the permanent defence posts of the B.S.F, in the village along with the other border village to seal the border and it was fully sealed in 1990 with thorny wire. It is noteworthy that the use of violence as a tool was started in 1988 by the government and the militants. Hitherto the cases related to militancy had been treated carefully by law abiding police and security forces before 1990. Simultaneously the militants had also not used the people of Punjab for their personal gains and had not made issues out of any activity of security proceedings that included violence against common man and especially against Sikhs.

The phase of murders in Muhawa begins with the killing of Angrez Singh and his two years old son by the militants on 31 January 1990 and ends with the fake police encounter of Sukhwinder Singh Lalli, the son of the notorious militant Gurpal Singh Padda's uncle. Sukhwinder was 17 years old and he was studying in 12th class. He had links with militants because of his cousin and he had already been interrogated by the police. But in November 1990 when he was returning home in an auto from Amritsar, he was caught by the in charge of Islamabad Police Chowki who brought him to the police station. The family of Sukhwinder was informed by a woman from the village. Although the members of Sukhwinder's family reached at police station on the same evening yet Sukhwinder was shot dead in a fake police encounter with two other youths.

According to Angrez Singh's brother, the militants accused Angrez Singh of robberies in the village and killed him. This is why the government did not give any compensation of his murder and the family only received compensation of two years old child Gurwinder Singh.

But as per the views of the villagers, Angrez Singh was not killed by the militants rather he was murdered by his own companions. He had been indulged in smuggling before the border was sealed. But the growing strictness at the border and the ruined environment lead him engaged in the activities like robbery with his companions in the near villages. A row between Angrez Singh and his companions over the distribution of robbed material became the reason of the murder of Angrez Singh and his Son. Angrez Singh was a tall and dangerous man and he used to place weapon by his pillow side at night. Therefore, when his companions came to kill him at the night of 31-01-1990, they started firing at Angrez Singh from the roof of his neighbour and in this firing the two year old son of Angrez Singh was also shot dead who was sleeping with him at that time.

In the August of the same year, the militants attacked Mohinder Singh, the Sarpanch of the village and who was one of the CPI workers and who also safeguarded the Hindus of the village against militants; and at the same time made them protest against the militancy. Both Mohinder Singh and his son in law who was from army combated with the militants bravely but Mohinder Singh's son in law had to pay a heavy price in the form of his two years old son Lovely, who at the time of militants' attack was sleeping in courtyard. While the other members of the family ran towards the rooms to save them, he became the victims of firing.

Another youth of the village, i.e., Rewail Singh who was a constable in Central Industrial Security Force (CISF) was killed by the militants as a result of the mutual disgust. According to Rewail

Victims of Militants Violence

Sl. No.	*Name of Victim*	*Father's Name*	*Age*	*Sex*	*Date of Killing*	*Caste*
1.	Rewail Singh	Ajit Singh	27	M	10-10-1990	Jat Sikh
2.	Angrej Singh	Tara Singh	35	M	May 1990	Jat Sikh
3.	Lovely Singh	Comrade Charn Singh	2	M	Aug 1990	Jat Sikh

Miltants from the Village

Sl. No.	*Name of Victim*	*Father's Name*	*Age*	*Sex*	*Killed/live*	*Caste*
1.	Gurpal Singh (Pada)	Bachan Singh	25	M	Killed	Jat Sikh
2.	Lakhwinder Singh (Lakha)	Dilbag Singh	23	M	Killed	Jat Sikh

Victims of State Oppression

Sl. No.	*Name of Victim*	*Father's Name*	*Age*	*Sex*	*Killed/live*	*Caste*
1.	Sukhwinder Singh	Dial Singh	18	M	Killed	Jat Sikh

Singh's mother and the villagers, Rewail Singh had nothing to do with militancy and militants. Like other people of the village, he was also earning his livelihood by serving the Central Industrial Security Force (CISF). Before getting a job in Rewail Singh had been doing the job of a Punjab Homeguard. And one day when a militant was caught by the police in the village and later was taken to the police station, Rewail Singh was also present in the police station and he did not request the police to free the caught militant who were from his village. He even did not talk to them. This scared him a lot and he left the job of Homeguard and started working in CISF. But the militants took this as the result of revenge as the cousin of Rewail Singh had been killed by the uncle of these militants. That is why when Rewail Singh reached home after taking leave for his marriage, those militants waited for the day of his marriage to come near and just before 4 days of Rewail's marriage, they killed him at his home.

GURDASPUR

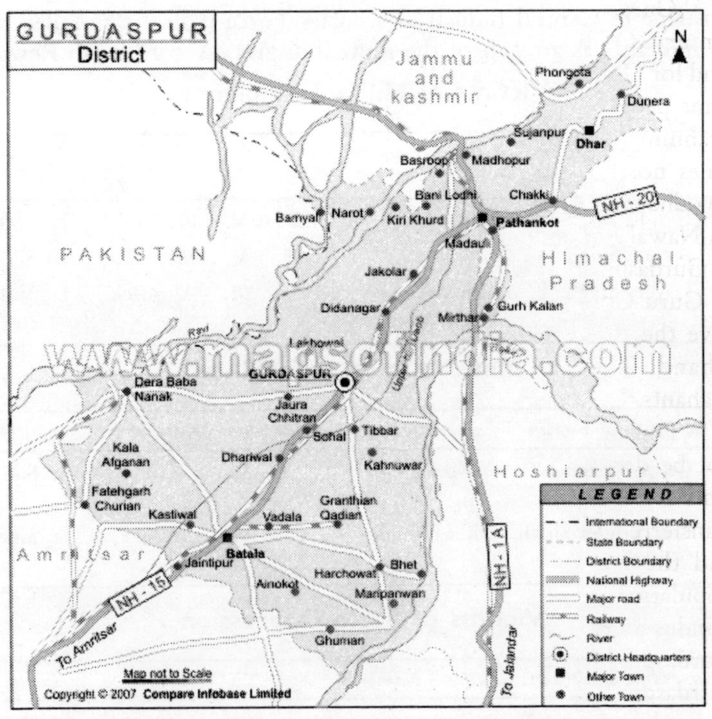

The Gurdaspur district is the northern most district of Punjab state. Total area of the district is 3562 Sq. km. It falls in the Jalandhar division and is sandwiched between river Ravi and Beas. The district lies between north-latitude 31^0-36' and 32^0-34' and east longitude 74^0-56' and 75^0-24' and shares common boundaries with Kathua district of Jammu and Kashmir state in the north, Chamba and Kangra districts of Himachal Pradesh in the north-east, Hoshiarpur district in the south-east, Kapurthala district in the south, Amritsar district in the south west and Pakistan in the north west.[21]

Three Tehsils of the district namely Gurdaspur, Batala and Dera Baba Nanak are plain and similar to the rest of the Punjab plains in structure, genesis lithology and surface configuration out the northern most part of the district, i.e. Dhar and Pathankot tehsils are in the foot of Shivalik hills. The landscape of the Gurdaspur district has varied topography comprising the hilly tract, undulating plan, the flood plains of the Ravi and the Beas and the up land plain.[22]

Gurdaspur was founded by Guriya Ji in the beginning of 17th century. On his name, this city was named as Gurdaspur. He bought land for Gurdaspur from Jats of Sangi Gotra. It is also established that some people used to live in huts in the old city. Guriya Ji a Sanwal Brahmin of Kaushal Gotra belonged to a village Paniar situated 5 miles north of Gurdaspur. The ancestors of Guriya Ji came from Ayodhaya long time ago and settled in Paniar. Guriya Ji had two sons Sh.Nawal Rai and Sh. Pala Ji. The descendants of Nawal Rai settled in Gurdaspur Nawal Rai's son Baba Deep Chand was a contemporary of Guru Gobind Singh Ji. It is believed that Guru Gobind Singh Ji gave the title of Ganj Bakhsh (Owner of Treasure) to Baba Deep Chand. The descendants of Baba Deep Chand are known as Mahants.[23]

During partition of India in 1947 the future of Gurdaspur could not be decided for many days. As majority of population of this district was Muslim, but the "REDCLIFF" awards of Boundary transferred only Shakargarh Tehsil of Gurdaspur district to Pakistan, and the rest of the district was transferred to India. Muslim population of the district migrated to Pakistan and refugees, the Hindus and the Sikhs of Sialkot and Tehsil Shakargarh migrated to Gurdaspur after crossing the Ravi Bridge. They settled and spread in Gurdaspur district.[24]

Demography

2001

Total population	Religion	Population	Total Rural	Total Urban	Religion-wise Urban population		Reliogion-wise Rural population	
(1)	(2)	(3)	(4)	(5)	(6)	(7)	(8)	(9)
2104000	Hindu	561461	1046209	1110811	Hindu	517914	Hindu	43547
	Sikh	1505123			Sikh	570415	Sikh	980549

1991

Total population	Religion	Population	Total Rural	Total Urban	Religion-wise Urban population		Reliogion-wise Rural population	
1756732	Hindu	821365	1370320	386412	Hindu	283120	Hindu	529245
	Sikh	811134			Sikh	86781	Sikh	724353
	Muslim	10649			Muslim	1819	Muslim	8830
	Charistian	120470			Charistian	13296	Charistian	107174

Source : Statical Abstract, 1991, Economic Advisor Government Punjab, 2002, p. 72.

1981

Total population	Religion	Population	Total Rural	Total Urban	Religion-wise Urban population		Reliogion-wise Rural population	
1513435	Hindu	728362	1185167	328268	Hindu	251831	Hindu	476531s
	Sikh	675400			Sikh	66020	Sikh	609380
	Muslim	9362			Muslim	1540	Muslim	7822
	Charistian	99637			Charistian	8713	Charistian	90924

Source: Statical Abstract, 1981, Economic Advisor Government of Punjab, 1991, p. 72.

Victims of Violence During Militancy

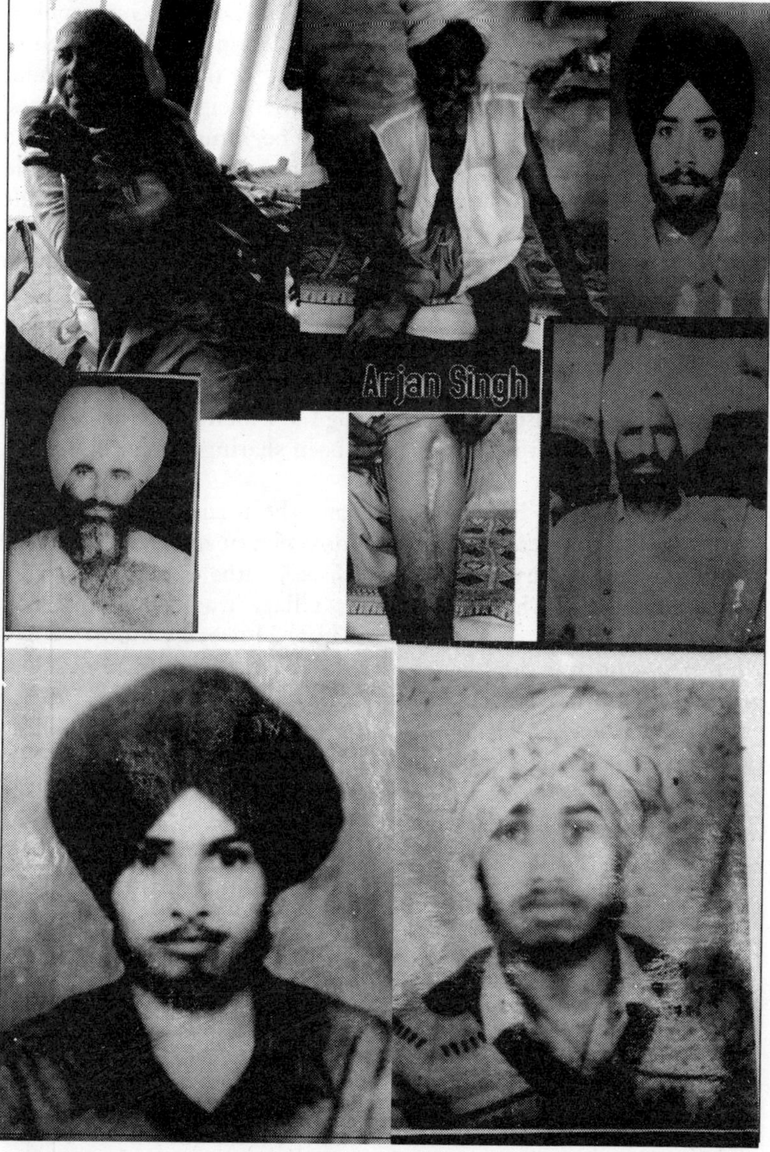

SHAHPUR JAZAN

Shahpur Jazan, situated 4 kilometers away from the Indo-Pak border, falls in the Tehsil Dera Baba Nanak of District Gurdaspur. It is one of the biggest villages with the population of 5000. It used to be called Shahpur Poorbiya before militancy as the number Hindus in the village had been much more than other neighbouring villages. It is noteworthy here that right from the beginning of militancy in 1978 till the end in 1993, Sh Rajinder Kumar who was from Hindu Community remained the Sarpanch of this village. Though like the other villages of Punjab Shahpur Jazan had got more population of Jat Sikhs than the other castes and Jat Sikhs also possessed the maximum land area, they were not able to hold the post of Sarpanch because of the fairly good relations of the Khatris and Brahmins with other castes like Christians and other marginal castes such as Khumaar, Jullaha, Ravidass, Sansi, etc. Besides this, the population of Majhabi Sikhs had also been very negligible which made the Jat Sikhs less influential as both the castes had been sharing agricultural work since ages.

Shahpur Jazan has also undergone the torments of militancy like the other villages of Punjab. Almost eleven members of village persons were killed by militants and three youths were killed in fake police encounter. The youth of this village was less involved in militancy as compared to other villages. However, Gurbaj Singh *Alias* Baja who was the Lieutenant General of KFC was a source of great terror in the village.

The violence in Shahpur Jazan started in 1986 with the killing of three Hindus named Parshan Dev, Shiv Kumar, and Thakur Kuldeep Singh who had been accused of burning the effigy of Bhindranwale by Gurbaj Singh Baja and ends with the death of Gurbaj Singh Baja in 1992.

According to Sh. Rajinder Kumar, the former Sarpanch of the village, these three Hindus (Parshan Dev, Shiv Kumar, and Thakur Kuldeep Singh) were innocent and the complaint against them was out of sheer revenge. In reality, they had collected the street garbage at one place and burnt it up. But some anti-social elements spread the rumor that they had burnt the effigy of Bhindranwale. To settle his old scores, Baja complained against them to the militants.

Rajinder Kumar and the other people of the village believe that the reason of the murders committed by the militants on the complaints of Baja was mutual jealousy and this is why, since

Bhindrawale's time, a number of complaints have been made against the Hindus. According to the former Sarpanch Rajinder Kumar, the downfall of the Hindus in the village started before 1984 as they had been accused of being the police touts. Bhindranwale sent his messenger to call us to Amritsar to justify our part. Rajinder Kumar went to Bhindrawale to defend himself against the charges and Bhindranwale released him. But at the same time he ordered him to send a group of people from his village for their programmes. The moment he came back to his village he immediately sent his family to Amritsar and he himself purchased some land at Sitapur in U.P. but he refused to take a group of people for Bhindranwale from the village.

The Hindus of the village got firmer to live in the village against the militancy in 1984 and due to anti-Sikh riots of 1984, the family of Rajinder Kumar had to come back to the village from U.P. According to Rajinder Kumar, in Sitapur village where he used to live they were mistaken as Sikhs by the villagers and the assassination of Indira Gandhi made it very difficult for them to survive in that village. Besides, the establishment of B.S.F. station in 1984 in the village gave courage to the villagers.

The complete downfall of the Hindus in the village began in 1986. The people of the village gathered against the three killings in the village and B.S.F. was also ready to provide security to them. Yet the killing of the Hindus outside the village by the militants infused a terror in the Hindus living in the village. And the murders of the other Hindus of the village like Piare Lal s/o Raghu Nandan who was a government teacher and who was killed by the militants on his way back to home from his duty and Ashok Kumar s/o Tej Chand, who was a veterinary doctor, and who was also killed in the same manner by the militants did a lot to permeate fear in the village. As a result, the Hindus of the village left the village and got settled wherever they found place. No one except the former Sarpanch of the village was left in the village and who used to spend his nights at B.S.F. post.

Furthermore, the other small families of the village also became the victims of the violence of militancy. Firstly the small farmer of the village Parkash Singh who used to earn his living by selling liquor apart from his agricultural work was killed by the militants. He was accused of being a police tout and was killed on the night of First August, 1990 by the militants. The militants had got suspicious about Parkash Singh because police use to come at his home. But in reality Parkash Singh being a small farmer used to sell liquor to make his both ends meet and police was aware of this. The police used to come at his home for *hafta vasuli* and sometimes like other customers to take alcohol.

Although the family of Parkash Singh was given Rs. 1 lakh as reimbursement and his younger son was also given a job yet their misfortunes did not end with the murder of Parkash Singh. His son Major Singh also fell prey to the violence of the black days. In 1992, Major Singh was caught for a small feud by police. After keeping at Dera Baba Nanak police station for nine days, he was killed in fake police encounter and his dead body was cremated at crematorium of Butala. But the wife of Parkash Singh is keeping mum over the death of his son in a fake police encounter. Moreover, she does not even discuss about the same with any government official, journalist, or Human Rights representatives coming to his home and only tells them about the death of her husband.

Even when I met Lakhbir Kaur (wife of Parkash Singh) for the first time, she only discussed about her husband. Though I had already supplied her complete information about me and had also shown my university identity card to her son, she was still suspicious of me. She was mistaking me for government official. She feared to tell me the truth about her son because she thought that her pension which government had started as compensation after Parkash Singh was killed by the militants would be stopped because her son was killed in a fake police encounter. I again met Lakhbir Kaur after two days. After interacting with her for some time when I asked her about her elder son, her eyes were filled and she poignantly uttered that her son was innocent. I already gathered some information about Major Singh that he had been arrested from the adjacent village Mallowal by the police. I assured Lakhbir Kaur that I had come after meeting the parents of two other youths Hardeep Singh and Manjit Singh who were killed by police and I would not tell the government nor was I having any intentions of a journalist.

The younger son of Lakhbir Kaur also insisted her mother to tell the truth. According to Lakhbir Kaur and the other villagers, Major Singh had no connections with the terrorists. Actually he had a friend Bittu in the adjacent village Mallowal who was running a dairy and he was also running a electronics shop at Shahpur Jazan where he used to repair Radio and would also sell music cassettes. Bittu had a clash with somebody in the village who one day threw away Bittu's milk on the bridge. Major was fond of listening to music so he would keep sitting at Bittu's shop and their friendship had grown stronger. Bittu wanted to settle his scores and he asked Major top help him. And Major agreed for that and went along with Bittu to Mallowal. Bittu and Major attacked that person's home who had thrown Bittu's milk. But they both were caught by him and he immediately called up the police. Police arrested both of them and sent them to Dera Baba Nanak police station. The very next day Major's mother came to know about all that and she went to the police station and met Major.

According to Lakhbir Kaur, police had not thrashed Major. After two days, Bittu's parents got him out of jail by giving bribe. But Major had no one to stand by his side and police did not release him. I asked Lakbir Kaur if they had not informed any of their relatives about the detention of Major. She replied that they were unfortunate and they had thought that their relatives would have been busy in sowing wheat. Also they were under this impression that Major had not committed any heinous crime so police would not do anything to him and would release Major after four to five days. 'I had no money to give to the police because the money that I had received as compensation after the death of my husband had already been spent on the education of my two sons and the marriage of my daughter,' Lakhbir Kaur said. She also added that they had no land to sell which could be used for that purpose. 'I left no stone unturned to get Major out of jail. I requested SDM and also went to SSP in Butala but nobody paid heed to me. So I thought that they themselves would release him. But when I went to the police station on the tenth day, they did not allow me to go to the cell and told me that your son is not in the cell now. And I informed the relatives about it. They enquired about Major and came to know that police had taken him to Butala and there they killed him in fake police encounters with other youths and the ashes of Major are lying in the crematorium of Butala.' Lakhbir Kaur also added that she could not even collect the ashes of her son. Though the employees of the crematorium had informed her about the cremation of Major but they refused to hand over the ashes of Major to her on the grounds that they had been prohibited by police.

I asked them if they have preserved any document or a copy of written request. The younger brother of Major replied in negative by saying that he burnt all the documents because his mother used to cry after seeing them. Major Singh's brother said that there was no use of conducting any investigation as the government was to pay only for those who had been cremated in Amritsar's crematorium and not for those who were cremated in Butala. It is therefore no use of striving for that.

Similarly, there was Baldev Singh's family who had merely two acres of land. Baldev Singh had four sons and his two elder sons were illiterate. However, the two younger sons Manjit Singh and Hardeep Singh had done 10+2. After doing his tenth class, Manjit Singh started working at a T.V. shop in Butala and he used to live there. All his family knew about him was that he was working at a T.V. shop. One day the police suddenly came to their house and asked Baldev Singh about Manjit. Baldev Singh told the police that his son must have been at T.V. shop and he only came home on Sundays. But when Manjit did not turn up on next Sunday, Baldev singh enquired about him at his working place. There he came to know that Manjit had gone for home four-five days ago. After some days, Baldev Singh came to know that a few days ago, Manjit Singh had been shot dead in a police encounter near Butala on 04 October 1987. Police had come to see whether or not Manjit singh's family had come to know about his death. This 75 years old man suffered another jolt after four years when on 22 March, 1991, his youngest son went to the market to buy some medicine and never returned home. Even his dead body was not found. According to Baldev Singh, he had scolded Hardeep by saying that he did not do any work at home before he went out to buy medicine. When he did not turn up after taking medicine, the family thought that he would have gone to some relatives. But when he did not return home after four-five days, his family began to investigate about him at their relatives but failed to find Hardeep. One day they came to know that police had been moving in the village with the dead body of Hardeep and his body was also placed at Dera Baba Nanak police station for identification. But nobody identified his dead body and did not inform the family. When Baldev Singh came to know about this, he went to the Sarpanch and requested him to go to the police station and get the information. Sarpanch informed Baldev Singh that it was the dead body of Hardeep and there was no point of going to the police station because if the police came to know that Hardeep was the son of Baldev, they would detain the whole family for his elder brother had already been killed with militants. This family has not gone to the police station to know the reason of their son's death and whether or not he was killed by the police. They only know that police carried Hardeep's dead body in the village and after that his body was cremated at Butala's crematorium.

A little away from this house, there is another unfortunate house of big landlords. This family used to be known as *Naggan Wale*. The three bread winners of the family suddenly became the target of militants' bullets on the night of 16 March 1991. The only fault of this family was that their land was near to the land of militant Gurbaaj Singh Baja. In a movement against the terrorists after 1990, police arrested the families of militants and their houses were ruined. And when the police arrested the members of Baja's family, the police used the tractor of these *Naggan Wale* to destroy their fields of wheat. This family had not known that they had to pay heavy price for this. On the very next night, Shingara Singh Naggan wala and his two sons Surinder Singh and Baldev Singh were killed by the militants at their home.

After loosing everything in the storm of terrorism, the remaining sons of the family uplifted the agricultural work of the family who were kids at the time of their grandfather's and their father's deaths. But the remaining families of the village are still in a pathetic state. These families have not been able to raise both economically and psychologically.

Some Hindu families of Shahpur Jazan which was once known as Shahpur East have come back to the village. These families are also suffering economically because they had to sell their lands at the lowest prices and their businesses were also closed.

GURDASPUR VILLAGE SHAHPURJAZAN

Victims of Militant Violence

Sl. No.	*Name of Victim*	*Father's Name*	*Age*	*Sex*	*Date of Killing*	*Caste*
1.	Parkash Singh	Hemant Singh	40	M	1-8-1990	Jat-Sikh
2.	Baldev Singh	Shingara Singh	38	M	10-11-1991	Jat-Sikh
3.	Swinder Singh	Shingara Singh	40	M	10-11-1991	Jat-Sikh
4.	Shingara Singh	Sohan Singh	60	M	10-12-1991	Jat-Sikh
5.	Parshan Dev	Puranchand	50	M	Aug 1989	Brhamin
6.	Shiv Kumar	Parshanchand	35	M	Aug 1989	Prahmin
7.	Thakur Kuldeep Singh	Randhir Singh	55	M	Aug 1989	Rajput
8.	Piaralal	Ragunathmal	30	M	1990	Hindu-Khatri
9.	Ashok Kumar	Tejchnad	36	M	1990	Hindu-Khatri

Victims of State Oppression

Sl. No.	Name of Victim	Father's Name	Age	Sex	Date of Killing	Caste
1.	Hardip Singh	Baldev Singh	23	M	22-3-1991	Jat Sikh
2.	Major Singh	Parkash Singh	16	M	Oct. or Nov. 1992	Jat Sikh

Militants from the Village

Sl. No.	Name of Militant	Father's Name	Age	Sex	Killed/Lives	Caste
1.	Gurbaj Singh Baja	Bawa Singh	25	M	Killed	Jat Sikh
2.	Manjit Singh	Baldev Singh	22	M	Killed	Jat Sikh

Hindu Families Forced to Leave the Village

Sl. No.	Name of the Head of Family	Father Name
1.	Parhan Dev	Puranchand
2.	Shiv Kumar	Parshanchand
3.	Thakur Kuldeep Singh	Randhir Singh
4.	Piaralal	Ragunathmal
5.	Ashok Kumar	Tejchnad
6.	Kaluram	Mohinderpal
7.	Rajinder Kumar	Mohinderpal
8.	Kulwantram	Sunderdass
9.	Mangatram	Gianchand
10.	Balkrishan	Gianchand
11.	Satish Kumar	Chananlal
12.	Subashchander	Mangatram
13.	Satpal	Piaralal
14.	Ghugga	Brahmdutt
15.	Thakur Sardool Singh	Raghbir Singh
16.	Buttamalh	Gianchands

SHIKAR MACHHIAN

With the population of 2800, Shikar Machhian is located about 8 km. away from Dera Baba Nanak. Like other villages of Punjab, Jat-Sikhs exercise a great sway on the economic and political force of the village. But religiously, *Dalits* are attached with Christians and Hindus. However, religiously, the partition between Hindus and Sikhs or Sikhs and Christians is almost negligible. This village, like other villages of Punjab, has sacrificed five of its members during terrorist upheaval without any strong political, social, or economic reasons. Like other villages, three youths from this village, viz. Niranjan Singh Alias Mathra, Labh Singh *Alias* Labh, and Ajit Singh joined Khalistan Liberation Force.

It is believed that the grim murders by the militants in the village were the outcome of tiny rancours.

The violence of militancy in Shikar Machhian starts with the murder of a retired Army Subedar by militants on 18 March 1988 and ends with the murder of a village militant Labha by police in 1991. And the phase of torture by the police and the government on masses also ends after the peace in Punjab in 1993. It is a notable fact that after capturing all the three militants from the different places, police shot them dead on the defense drain of the village in a fake encounter.

Alhough people of Shikar Machhian got aware of the violence of militancy in 1984 and the militants frequently crossing border used to stay in the village yet Hindu-Sikh brotherhood of the village was in no way affected by militancy and Khalistan Movement and the Hindu families of the village were living safely like before. Even the closest friend of Labh Singh *Alias* Labha, the most notorious militant of the village was Bunty, a Brahmin boy of the village. It is worth mentioning here that in 1991 when police arrested Labh Singh from the village, Bunty was also with him. Police took both of them in custody and according to the people of the village, Bunty was equally involved in the murders committed by Labh Singh in the village. Police killed Labh Singh in a fake encounter on the defense drain after the interrogation of ten days. But Bunty was released on the recommendation of the former speaker of Vidhan sabha Sri Brij Bhushan. After the end of militancy and the releasing of Bunty, his family shifted to Amritsar with bag and baggage.

Joginder Singh Fauji was the first one to be killed in the village. The underlying reason of Joginder Singh's murder was told by his own wife Charan Kaur was the unwanted advice given by Joginder Singh to Labh Singh, a member of KLF that he should concentrate on his family. Actually, the fields of Joginder Singh's family were adjacent to the fields of Labh Singh's family and at the same time the father of Labh Singh was a good friend of Joginder Singh. On the request of Labh Singh's father, Joginder Singh on the morning of 8

March 1988, made him understand the family reponsibility and Labh Singh in return showed no sign of retaliation. However on the same night, Labh Singh along with Bunty (the Brahmin boy) killed Joginder Singh. Similarly, Labh Singh killed another youth from the village Tasif Masiah just for the sake of a bottle of liquor.

Other farmers of the village Balkar Singh and Ajit Singh also became the victims of the violence of militancy on 22 July 1991. According to Ajit Singh, the companion of Balkar Singh who was killed in the violence of militancy, on the evening of 22 July, he was sitting on his tube well at about 7:00 pm, when he saw Balkar Singh coming with some militants. The militants also gave shout to Ajit Singh and asked him to drop them on the other side of the defense drain, i.e. they wanted him to help them in crossing the Pak border. Both Ajit Singh and Balkar Singh helped the militants to cross the drain. And, when they were coming back, the militants suddenly attacked on them in which Balkar Singh got killed on the spot whereas Ajit Singh was badly injured. Ajit Singh was though saved by the B.S.F. soldiers on the spot; one of his legs got paralysed. He did not get any kind of help from the government as a result of which he sank in debt from head to toe.

The impact of that violence and the economic downfall of Ajit Singh are very much conspicuous on his body and house. In the same way, another woman of the village Sawarnjit Kaur was accused of being characterless and ultimately killed by the militant Shingara Singh. But the main reason of Sawarnjit Kaur's murder was that she had refused to make any illicit relationship with Shingara Singh. Sawarnjit Kaur's husband Ajit Singh was working with Border Road Organisation and her wife was living alone with her children at home. To make the most of it, Shingara Singh used to come forcefully at her place.

Although the people of the village abus militancy and the militant Labh yet they praise two other militants of the village Niranjan Singh (Mathura) and Ajit Singh. According to them, after joining militants Ajit Singh never came back to the village, nor did he do any injustice to any one in the village. When he was caught by police, he did not name any one and ultimately was killed in a fake police encounter.

Similarly, Niranjan Singh Mathura, Lieutenant General KLF, is also praised by people of the village. Mathura belonged to a poor family and after his photograph was discovered in the pocket of a militant by police that he escaped from his home in fear of police. He was otherwise learning how to drive a truck for he could not get a job in military. Mathura was 6 feet 4 inches tall and he could run faster than a horse. After joining militancy, he came to his village only twice. Once he came to the village only to tell the Hindus of the village that as long as he was alive they should not leave the village in any fear. Secondly, he came to the village in opposition of the murder of Sawarnjit Kaur committed by Shingara Singh only to warn Shingara Singh that he should not enter the village. But he did not go to his home, nor did he render any help to his poor family. Finally he was brought to the village by the police to kill him on the defense drain. According to the people of the village, police arrested Mathura in Haryana and brought him in his own village and killed him in an encounter.

Village Shikar Machhian

Sl. No.	*Name of Victim*	*Father's Name*	*Age*	*Sex*	*Date of Killing*	*Caste*
1.	Tafel Mesiah	Rehmat Mesiah	18	M	1-10-1988	Christian
2.	Joginder Singh	Bal Singh	50	M	18-3-1989	Jat-Sikh
3.	Swarnjit Kaur	Ajit Singh	25	F	1990	Jat-Sikh
4.	Balkar Singh	Rewail Singh	20	M	22 July 1991	Jat-Sikh

Militants from the Village

Sl. No.	*Name of Militant*	*Father's Name*	*Age*	*Sex*	*Killed/Lives*	*Caste*
1.	Niranjan Singh (Mathura)	Pal Singh	25	M	Killed	Jat-Sikh
2.	Labh Singh	Darshan Singh	22	M	Killed	Jat-Sikh

Hindu Families Forced to Leave the Village

Sl. No.	*Name of the Head of Family*	*Father Name*
1.	Ashwani Kumar	Gurdasdas
2.	Jaspal	Beantram
3.	Swinder Kumar	Beantram
4.	Dharmpal	Beantram
5.	Audhaya Nath	Sadhoram

TIBBER

Tibber is one of the biggest and developed villages of Punjab and it is located around 6-7 km away from Gurdaspur. It shelters almost 12,000 people. The political scenario of the village is quite different from the other villages of Punjab because of less population of the Sikhs which is only to the tune of 26% in which 25% of them are Jat Sikhs and 10% are Nai Sikh and Mehra Sikh (OBC). Economically, Jat Sikhs are richer than anyone else in the village and 90% of the whole land area is also owned by them. However, the politics of the village especially the post of Sarpanch is in the hands of Bhatt Biradari, popularly known as Bhatt Brahmin. No Jat Sikh has been able to be the Sarpanch of the village since independence. If one analyses the village from religious and caste point of view, the Bhatt Brahmin holds the firm position with 50% of the total population followed by Hindu Khatri Brahmin 5% and Dalit Christians and Mahasha Biradari 10% each. The population of the village, on the basis of religion and caste, is directly related to the political and economical strength of the village. Like the Jat Sikhs of the village, Akali-BJP alliance has been the favorite for the Bhatt Bramins and other upper Hindu after militancy. However, the Dalits of the village whether they belong to Hindus or Christians caste their votes to Congress. The most interesting fact about this religious and castist association is that neither Akali-BJP alliance nor Congress remains at the centre during the Sarpanch elections rather there is a direct fight between Jats and Bhatts. Due to the economic force of the village, the Jat Sikhs of the village are able to attract the Dalits both Hindu and Christians during elections.

On the other hand, Bhatts who neither have much land area nor any big businesses always manage to win the Sarpanch election because of their unity. The economic strength of Jat Sikhs has not been able to diminish the distance between 45 and 55. Right from the beginning, the Bhatts had not been in any way dependent upon Jat Sikhs. They did have some land area which they used to give to Jat Sikhs for farming on rent. But eventually they sold that land to Jats due to their growing needs and business requirements.

The Bhatts though do not have any shops or big businesses in Gurdaspur or Punjab; they earn their livelihood by purchasing fabrics and other domestic goods and by selling them not only in Punjab region but also in the villages of Himachal and Jammu and Kashmir.

The village has not only faced the violence of government and militancy but it has also been the target of Hindu-Sikh communalism. All the murders in the village were committed by Surjan Singh and Pinder Singh, the followers of Bhindranwale at the early stage of terrorism.

Although the violence of militancy had broken out in the times of Bhindranwala, this violence could not gather much moss in villages and cities of Punjab on religious grounds and the Hindu-Sikh brotherhood remained intact in the same way. Like Hindus, many Sikhs of Punjab were not against the staunch ideology and religious doctrines of Bhindranwale. But the attack of Indian Army on 03 June, 1984 at the Golden Temple complex to kill Bhindranwale and his companions sowed the seeds of hatred in the hearts of Sikhs against the government. On the other hand, the Hindus of Punjab who were thinking this attack to be a mission to kill Bhindranwale ignored Sikh sentiments. The people of this village also became the target of the anguish that was spread in 1984. Several people of the village expressed their happiness when they heard the news of attack on Golden Temple Complex and the subsequent killing of Bhindranwale. The Bhatts distributed sweets and burnt crackers at the death of Bhindranwale on 07-05-1984. However, the Sikhs of the village were very disappointed with the gesture shown by the Bhatts on Bhinranwale's death. This is because their holy and pious place was desecrated by the army and at the same time, they were also alive to the deaths of thousands of innocents Sikhs that included children and women also.

The Sikhs of the village though did not directly put any question mark on the expression of happiness shown by the Bhatts, they refused to accept the sweets and at the same time no Sikh from the village joined the Bhatts.

Surjan Singh and Pinder Singh, the followers of Bhindranwale, gained from these deteriorating conditions of the village on the same evening. Pinder Singh and Surjan Singh had been very close to Bhindranwale and they had weapons too. They started firing in the common place against the happiness shown on the death of Bhindranwale on the evening of 07-05-1984 in which Sunil Kumar, Mohan Lal, and Chunni Lal died. The sound of the bullets led every one escaped to their homes. But Pinder Singh and Surjan Singh were searching even the streets to kill the Bhatts. And when they were going towards the fields from the streets, they saw Shimla Devi who was studying in 10th class and was running to her home from the neighbouring house after the firing stopped and she was also shot dead by them.

The event completely threatened the Bhatts. The village police post was failed to catch the militants and infuse faith in the Bhatts. There was no protest of that event by the Sikhs of the village, which ultimately led Surjan Singh and Pinder Singh to formulate new plans against the Bhatts. They dropped a bomb on the house of Jai Kishan, one of the most successful Bhatt Brahmins of the village, on 25-06-1984.

The bomb missed its intended target, i.e. Jai Kishan who had already gone to Kashmir on that evening. The wife of Jai Kishan and her two daughters Aruna (6 months) and the eldest Anchal (3 years) were sleeping in the courtyard and the rest of the family were sleeping in their respective rooms. The bomb was mistakenly dropped in a jug of water that lessened its harmfulness. But in the blast, the 6 months old daughter of Jai Kishan was blown to pieces as the jug of water was on her side and his wife and other daughter got critically injured. Jai Kishan got the compensation of Rs 50,000 for the death of his younger daughter. An army barrack was permanently placed in the village on the request of the Bhatt community and there was no subsequent militant activity.

The moment the army got into action, they captured Surjan Singh and Pinder Singh was arrested on the third day. Darshan Singh, a friend to Jai Kishan, immediately went to give treatment to Jai Kishan's wife and daughter after the bomb blast, spent two days at Gurdaspur hospital with them. And when Jai Kishan's wife was to be shifted for treatment because of her serious injury, he arranged an ambulance for her and paid for that. When Darshan Singh was returning village after sending Jai Kishan's family to Amritsar, he was captured by the army on the bus stand only and he was not able to reach home. According to Jai Kishan's wife, Dr. Darshyan Singh explained his part to the army and he also gave details of the help he had rendered to the family of Jai Kishan and at the same time told them about his friendship with Jai Kishan. He also requested them to seek explanation from Jai Kishan's family. The army informed Jai Kishan about the whole incident but Jai Kishan refused to give any explanations and asked the army people to proceed with their investigation.

Darshan Singh along with Surjan Singh and Pinder Singh was sent to Jail under TADA by the army. These two people Surjan Singh and Pinder Singh took Darshan Singh in their confidence and told him that they were innocents. And Darshan Singh believed them for he himself was innocent and had no idea of the bomb blast. But one day when Pinder Singh and Surjan Singh had a small tiff over something, Darshan Singh came to know about the underlying truth that they both were the culprits of the bomb blast case and he had been hook bated by them because he was from a well to do family and at the same time he was a friend to Jai Kishan. These factors could help them to get out from the jail.

The moment Dr. Darshan Singh was released from the jail; he reported their misdeeds to the whole village. But he has been cross with Jai Kishan since then. Jai Kishan though has been repenting for his mistake and his one mistake and suspicion made his friend suffer a lot and he had to spend 4 years in jail, he consoles himself that it was a bad time then.

Gurdaspur Village Tibbar

Sl. No.	Name of Victim	Father's Name	Age	Sex	Date of Killing	Caste
1.	Aroma	Jaiparkash	3	F	25-5-1984	Bhatt, Brahmin
2.	Prempal (Police Constable)	Daulat Ram	22	M	31-1-1990	Bhatt, Brahmin
3.	Sunil Kumar	Motiram	18	M	7-5-1984	Bhatt, Brahmin
4.	Mohanlal	Mohinderpal	18	M	7-5-1984	Bhatt, Brahmin
5.	Chunilal	Tulsidas	18		7-5-1984	Bhatt, Brahmin
6.	Shimla Devi	Daleep Kumar	18	F	7-5-1984	Bhatt, Brahmin

SUMMING UP

The village level reality on the violation of human rights is qualitatively distinct from that of the macro-level discourse of both the state as well as the adherents of the autonomist movement. The villages where we have conducted our field survey have presented a very confusing picture of the autonomist movement as well as the action and strategy of the India State, which it adopted to 'deal' with the autonomist movement in the strife-torn decades 1980's and 1990's in Punjab. The actions of both the terrorists are viewd as being

driven by their personal agenda rather than based on any idelogical agenda. The terrorist actions got interwoven with the social and political dynamics of the local character. In this regard the local societal set-up and the vested interests of the dominant families and groups played an instrumental role in the killings and the displacement of people belongs to both communities. In terms of caste dynamics it is obvious that Jat-Sikhs landed peasantry became the main targets, but their becoming so had non-ideological reasons. Inter-family rivalry and dispute over land were the two major non – idelogical factor which contributed to terrorists violence. The disappearances, torture and preventive detetion of the youths by the state armed agents were connected with the fueds and disputes over the land of powerful families. An another important factor which we noticed during our field survey in all the villages causing the abuse of power and the violation of human rights by the state forces was the greed for promotion and rewards.

Notes and References

1. "Tarn Taran Sahib—Wikipedia, the free encyclopedia," en.wikipedia.org/wiki/Tarn Taran Sah, 1-10-2011.
2. "Bhangi Misl-SikhiWiki, free Sikh encyclopedia." www.sikhiwiki.org/index.php/Bhangi Mi, 1-10-20111, Punjab—Jatland Wiki, www.jatland.com/home/Punjab, 1-10-20111.
3. *Ibid.*
4. http://tarntaran.nic.in/
5. "Punjab Development Statistics 2010," www.scribd.com/doc38050614, 21-8- 2010.
6. "Tarn Taran (Punjab) City: Welcome to City Tarn Taran (Punjab), citytarntaran.com/2-10-2011.
7. Statical Abstract of Punjab, 2010, *op. cit.*, No. 1, p. 42.
8. *Ibid.*, p. 42. see also : Gurdwara Sri Tarn Taran Sahib—Wikipedia, the free encyclopedia, en.wikipedia.org/wiki/Gurdwara Sri T, 3-10-2011, Krishan Gopal Lamba, 1999, *Dynamics of Punjabi Suba Movement*, Deep & Deep Publications, New Delhi, pp. 6-8.
9. *Ibid.*
10. Satyapal Dang, *et. al*, 2000, *Terrorism in Punjab*, Gyan Publishing House, New Delhi, pp. 152-53.
11. It is to be noted that despite of the loss of the eight members of the village, I did not heared the word Indain Army as it is presented by the some scholars in the sense of making the other, the word Fauj (Army) and Fauji Raj was used by my respondents and village folk in commonly to explain the misbehave and atrocities which were commited by the army immediately after the Operation Blue Star.
12. The use of villagers as the human shield is confirmed by all respondents from all villages.
13. Mal Mandi is a government land on the outskirts of the Tarn Taran that was earlier used for monthly as a cattle market, but during the militancy this place was converted into a Interrogation Centre by Police.

14. Census, 2001, *District Cesus Handbook,* Amritsar District, p. 1.
15. *Ibid.*, p. 7.
16. "Amtirsar—Wikipedia, the free encyclopedia," en.wikipedia.org/wiki/, 21-7-2011.
17. Harish Jain, 2003, *The Making of Punjab*, Unistar Books Pvt. Ltd., Chandigarh, pp. 226-27.
18. Harminder Kaur, 1990, *Blue Star Over Amritsar*, Ajanta Publications, New Delhi, p. 52, See also: Ram Naryan Kumar *et. al.*, 2003, *Reduced to Ashes: The Insurgency and Human Rights in Punjab, Final Report,* Vol. 1, Published by South Asia Forum for Human Rights, p. 52, Sangat Singh, 1996, *The Sikh History*, Greater Kailash, New Delhi, pp. 201-02, Mark Tully and Satish Jacob, 1987, *Amritsar: Mrs. Gandhi's Last Battle*, Jonathcape, London, p. 50
19. "History and Culture—District Amritsar," amritsar.nic.in/html/history culture.html, 21-7-2011.
20. Satya, M. Rai, 1965, *Partition of Punjab: Study of its Effects of the Politics and Administration of Punjab,* Asia Publishing House, New Delhi, pp. 130-40.
21. Census 2001, *District Census Handbook*, Gurdaspur Dsitrict, Director of Census Operation, Punjab, p. 1.
22. *Ibid.*
23. Districts of Punjab, Gurdaspur district catched, www. Indianetzone.com results, 10-9-2011.
24. "History—District Gurdaspur," gurudaspur.nic.in/html/profile.html, 10-9-2011.

In Lieu of Conclusion

The notion of human rights is founded on the core democratic values of freedom, equality and justice. It insists on equality of treatment in legal, socio-economic and political terms and disapproves of any form of discrimination against any human beings. Human rights are basic guarantees of entitlements and freedoms that every human being must enjoy in order to live a life of dignity and pursue opportunities to realise one's full potential. The human rights discourse has been gaining in terms of significance day-by-day in the present world order as there has been great insistence on the processes of democratization in the wake of first the velvet Revolution and now the celebrated Arab Spring.[1] The post-soviet world has been witness to civil society-led insistence on democratic governance and people's resistance against despotism, authoritarianism and barbarity perpetrated by the state. Insistence on realization of social democracy has meant that the age-old values and practices promoting forms of social and cultural discriminations are being questioned and disapproved at the global level.

As a result of the near universal acceptance of the western liberal values, the democratic regimes are becoming more and more inclusive in nature in terms of the socio-economic, political and legal governance. The state's entities are either developing new laws or amending their earlier legal frame-work to include human rights to promote socio-economic, political and legal governance. The interaction and networks of the human rights groups from local to global level have further enhanced the capacity of human rights groups to make a global pressure on the national governments for implementing the human rights laws Linder their territorial jurisdictions.

In a significant development, the human rights discourse has been extended to private domain. Major societal issues like gender justice, domestic violence and child rights are no longer being considered a matter of individual prerogatives as argued earlier. The violence of human rights within and outside the private domains of households is being much debated upon in recent times and the socio-economic and political initiatives have also been taken to curb the menace of violence against women and children both at the state as well as at the global level. The global campaigns for the women rights, child rights and the other deprived sections of the society have become the matter of great concerns for contemporary political theory.[2]

The massive scale of human rights violation during the Second World War and the rise of the former colonies as independent countries witnessed the development of human rights mechanism at regional and international levels. The establishment of Inter-American Human Rights System, European Human Rights System, African Human Rights System and the Arab Human Rights System with their own regional mechanism of implementing and monitoring of Human Rights proved far more effective with the establishment of United Nations Human Rights Commission by the General Assembly of United Nations. The establishment of the National Human Rights Commissions by the national governments with their autonomous status following the Paris Principles was an important step in strengthening the mechanism to protect human rights.[3] These have been important developments during the last decade of the twentieth century. More recently, the long demand of the developing countries for more democratic functioning and to decrease influence of "super-power" on the functioning of Human rights bodies of all has been fulfilled by the creation or United Nations Human Rights Council (UNHRC) in 2006.[4] These remarkable developments in the last half of the twentieth century look place in the history of Human rights. That is why the then Secretary General of UN, Boutros Boutros-Ghali, while making his inaugural remarks at Vienna Conference of Human Rights in 1993 called the Twentieth century as the "Age of Rights".[5]

The Human Rights theorists and activists have a very different view regarding the development or human laws and protecting mechanism at the global level for the protection or Human Rights. They have argued that human rights as an idea and value have not been able to acquire an independent entity and space despite the passing of immunerable laws and establishment of the institutional mechanisms. The argument goes that the violation of human rights can not be effectively controlled until and unless the state prerogatives against the human rights are not stopped. States continue to be overbearing sovereign entities. As a subject of national level governance, human rights come under the state prerogative across the globe, which creates contradiction in the theory and practice of human rights across the world. The international mechanism for the protection of human rights and human rights laws have often been found helpless as the national states have refused to follow the human standards under the pretexts of their right to preserve national security and integrity. More importantly, the instrumental use of the human rights by the powerful nation against the poor nations in their international trade diplomacy has further politicized and defamed the human rights discourse. The rich economies of west are using the human rights as diplomatic instrument to impose the trade sanctions and more tariffs on the trade in the name of child labour and human rights violations on the developing and poor economies.

It is to be mentioned that the states arc not all against the human rights protection as they are increasingly recognizing the international efforts and law to protect the human rights. One may refer to the constitutional provisions and the signing of International Treatises and Human Rights Convention by the states, under which the states are committed to protect the human rights. In fact, some states made special provision, passed laws and amend their constitutions to implement the International Human Rights standards in their territories. It is to be recorded that the Universal Declaration or Human Rights was passed by the United Nations General Assembly without a single dissenting vote.

It would thus be fair to argue that the states have both love and hate relationship with human at different historical disjuncture. The human rights discourse of the state is always determined by its relationship with the human rights groups and the ideology of the human rights movement at a wider level. We can refer to the voices or cultural relativism against the western understanding of human rights by some countries. The questions regarding the inclusion or the rights of women and children under the theocratic Islamic regimes are still being protested upon under the carpet of cultural-relativism underlining the cultural diversity and cultural values across the territorial regions. Simultaneously, a great degree of women rights has become the part of legal rights in majority of developing democracies.

We can take India as an example of the current trend marking the "new democracies new found concern for the protection of Human Rights. India has not only signed long back the two international Covenants on Human Rights as mentioned in the preceding chapters but has also approved the international mechanisms to protect the Women Rights. A comprehensive legal mechanism at domestic level has been adopted. Many laws like Domestic Violence Act, 2005, Maternity Benefits Act and Equal Remuneration Act have been passed by Indian Parliament to protect the gender rights, national Human Rights Commission (NHRC) as well as State Human Rights Commission has been set-up. At the same time state has been unable to check effectively the community-based violence like *honour killings. Khap Panchayats* and the denial of the equal rights or Maintenance and Divorce to the Muslim Women.

The most challenging task to which the Human Rights protection and promotion mechanism in todays world is facing is the assertion of the ethnic groups for their right to self-determination. Newly mobilized ethno-regional groups have been asking for their collective rights often in contradiction with imagined nation of the dominant/majority ethnic groups. State apparatuses have often been dominated by these groups and all used with impunity against the minority groups asking for their collective rights for democratic justice and equality. So while the process of democratization continues, millions of people continue to be forced across the world to cross the border and nee from the conflict areas for safer places to save their lives, ironically, not due to the external threats but threats from their own governments and from armed indigenous ethnic, secessionist groups. The state practice of adopting the extraordinary laws to empower the state security agencies to tackle the insurgency and secessionism has resulted into gross violation of human rights in the conflict areas.[6] The concept of "positive peace" and the democratic solution to the human rights problems is still lacking as the political protest and the demand of autonomy by the minorities across the globe is often identified as secessionism and terrorism by the states even under the democratic set-up. The conflict with the minorities and the deprived sections over the distribution of resources and political power sharing is taken as a challenge to the state's sovereignty and integrity which has to be solved by 'minimizing the other party' and not by 'minimizing the conflict or by solving it through the democratic means of negotiation and confidence-building measures.

The vaunted territorial integrity and sovereignty of the states, enshrined in the Charter of United Nations increasingly confronts the doctrine of the self-determination of people. The national agenda often is carried to the extreme of secessionist rebellions (self-determination, of course needs not imply secession). Self-conscious 'ethnics', proud of their distinctive culture and history of late been demanding political voice, economic access and cultural autonomy. National states, at the same time, continue to make efforts to impose a common identity upon resisting peoples. One can refer to some of the cases to illustrate the point: Kurds in Turkey and in Iraq; Basques in Spain; Turks in Bulgaria; Islamic authoritarian government in Sudan; Tibet in China; Kashmir valley in India: Blauchistan and Sindh in Pakistan.

Insistence on assimilation as against integration and mutual accommodation has helped to reduce ethnic conflicts in western democracies, even as power sharing and cultural pluralism have become favoured policies in countries as different as Canada. Belgium and South Africa. Efforts to manage or resolve dangerous cleavage by adhering to multi-culturalism have included the measures like proportional electoral systems, federalism and devolution of authority and many other "structural" devices.[7]

STATE AND THE MODERN MINORITY PROBLEM IN SOUTH ASIA

The colonial and post-colonial historical and cultural contingency of multi-religious and multi-ethnic South Asia Region has made up for a landscape of inequality. As elsewhere globally, the modern triumvirate of the state, nation and liberal democracy has produced the problem of minority rights in modern set-up. As Andreas Wimmer has argued that 'nationalist and ethnic politics are not just a by-product of modern state-formation' (built on democracy, citizenship and popular sovereignty), but that modern principles and institutions of inclusion (or belonging to the "true nation") are tried to ethnic and national forms of exclusion.[8]

Nation states produce minorities as an essential part of their construction process, since the majority, in producing the state, also produces the 'other' or the minorities.[9] Minority is posited as a political category, understood in contradistinction to nation-state. Ashis Nandy, a psycho-sociologist, draws attention to the significance of the modern state's praxis of statistical enumeration of population in fixing the fluid identities of communities into neat and precise categories *via* census operation.[10]

Other scholars from the multiculturalism stream have fondly hoped that the modern liberal states with their shared (at least state inculcated) basic values of popular sovereignty, equal rights and respect for individual human dignity and above all the practice of representative politics would depoliticise the politics of numbers in an expanding common civic culture and identity. The practice of democracy has always been expected to universalize equal rights. However, the reduction of democracy to largely procedural democracy, structured around electoral politics has ended up producing permanent majorities and minorities based on primordial identities.

Today more than ever, 'identity' politics has emerged as the dominant motif of political articulation. The struggle for recognition and redistribution is fast becoming the basis of the political conflict. The political challenge for liberal democracy and post-socialism discourse is how to democratise the 'nation' so that 'minority' as a category of subordination and oppression vanish.[11] The challenge is also to negotiate and meet the collective claims and demands.

To the varying degrees, the states of the region have shown up the inability of a hegemonic collectivity to deal with the subordinated and oppressed ones. The modern structure of governance of these states has proven to be centralising, coercive, hegemonic and exclusionary in nature. Moreover, minority assertion for 'recognition' of cultural rights and 'redistribution' of power and resources has conjured up in the majoritarian national imagination, anxieties about the integrity of the nation-state and true 'belonging'. In these majoritarian state and societies of South Asia, the minorities problem has splintered into question of nationalism *versus* separatism, of 'who is a true citizen' and who is a 'proxy citizen', of communalism *versus* secularism, of 'special rights' *versus* 'equal rights' and' insider *versus* 'outsider'.[12]

The threat to human rights from the state laws and practices has increased after the 9-11 terrorist attack on the World Trade Centre.

Human rights came under the serious threats due to USA-led 'global war' against what has been dubbed as pan-Islamic, anti-democratic terrorism. UN Secretary-General Kofi Annan, in his address to the UN Security Council gathered to evaluate the results of counter-terrorist measures three months after 2nd September stated, "We should all be clear that there is no trade-off between effective action against terrorism and protection of human rights. On the contrary. I believe that in long-term, we shall find that human rights, along with democracy and social justice are one or the best prophylactics against terrorism. It will be self-defeating if we sacrifice other key priorities-such as human rights in the process of preventing terrorism.[13]

Human Rights groups had warned in 2001 itself that some authoritarian regimes were likely to use the Security Council mandate for smearing campaign against the political opponents. Human Rights Watch in its annual report said in 2001 that some states, including US allies in its war in Afghanistan such as Saudi Arabia, Egypt, Russia and Uzbekistan were using the anti-terrorism campaign for illegitimate ends. The advocacy groups also criticised the United States for not following international humanitarian law in its treatment of prisoners captured in Afghanistan.[14]

In an open letter to the Council Amnesty International reported: "it had already studied several national reports and notes that governments are simply describing the actions are taking, without indicating whether these actions are in conformity with their international human rights obligations". In the same vein, Asian Human Rights Commission said, in its message on 10 December 2001, " ... the war on terrorism in Asia can easily become a war on human rights in the region ..."[15]

HUMAN RIGHTS AND INDIAN STATE

The human rights activism and discourse in India has emerged during the freedom struggle and evolved into the written guarantee of the rights of the Indian citizen under the constitution of free India. The goals which were established by the *"Karachi Resolution"* passed by the Congress and the urge of Congress to implement the civil liberties and fundamental freedom in an independent India to which it was showed by the repealing emergency powers of the provincial government provided by the *Public Safety Act* and by lifting the ban from on the illegal political organization such as *Hindustan Sewa Dal* during its twenty month rule in the different provinces under the colonial India.

The notion of freedom and human rights in India was celebrated with the adoption of Constitution of Independent India. A fairly elaborate accommodative framework for the protection of the rights of the marginal social groups and the minorities was done under the Fundamental Rights and the Directive Principles of the State Policy under the Part 3rd and 4th of Indian Constitution respectively. The demands for social justice and effective implementation of thc human rights of the weaker section were further strengthened by the new legislative measures like, Protection of Civil Liberties Act, 1955, Dowry Prohibition Act, 1961, Commission of Sati (Prevention) Act, 1987, Schedule Castes and Scheduled Tribes (Prevention of Atrocities) Act, 1989. Employment of manual Scavengers and Construction of Dry Latrines (prohibition) Act, 1993, Protection of Human Rights 1993, National Commission for Women Act, 1998, National Commission for Children, National Commission for Scheduled Castes and Tribes and National Commission for Minorities etc.

The state sponsored notion or the human rights was first criticised by the human rights activism during the emergency period. Absence of the democratic rights during these eighteen months of emergency rule galvanized students, political activists, intellectual trade unionists and artists into action. The educated middle class of India had thrived upon an uninterrupted flow of democracy in its national life since it gained independence in 1947. The emergency period was marked by detention without trial of large number of people, students youths, political leaders and news censorship trespassing.[16]

The excesses committed by the government coercive agencies against the civil liberties and human rights activists has been on rise in India. Hundreds and thousands of people have joined the massive rallies to protest against the anti-democratic acts of the government and to mobilise public opinion to save the Indian democracy. Organisation such as Citizen for Democracy, People's Union for Civil Liberties and Democratic Rights, Chhatra Yuva Sangharsh Vahini have been at the forefront of human rights struggle at national level. Many state-level and city based-groups have also been formed during the period. For example, Committee for Protection of Democratic Rights (Mumbai), Association for Protection of Democratic Rights (APDR) and Andhra Pradesh Civil Liberties Committee (APCLC).

The focus or the recent social movements in general and the human rights groups in particular tend to be sharply critical of the state as serving the interest of the dominant groups of the society in India. At the same time, the human rights activism and social movements hold that within the forms of democracy, state can be forced to deliver basic rights. Whether seeking to protect the civil liberties of citizens as enshrined in the Constitution but which are not maintained by the state or fighting for broader social economic rights of the citizens, presence of democracy in India of help.[17]

The legal and constitutional notion of human rights in India can also be traced in the human rights activism emerging through the collective wisdom from the tribal movement, dalit movement, women liberation movement, child rights movement and struggle of differently abled persons in the post-emergency era. While this understanding and political practice it inspired has certainly served in the last seven decades since independence to empower citizens, we have reached a point when such a strategy is no longer fruitful. Some trends can be outlined which point to the necessity to rethink the emancipatory potential of rights as it is conceived by contemporary social movements.[18]

Now days, the democratic rights assured by the Constitution are claimed by the communal forces. The political set-up and the calculated electoral political gains by the political parties have always influenced the human rights movements and state discourse over the protection and violation of human rights in India. Particularly the protection of minority rights has become a matter of serious concern in designed politics of 1980's and 1990's. The anti-Sikh riots in 1984, following Indira Gandhi's assassination was a ghastly reminder that communalism could well just beneath the surface. The Baghalpur massacre in 1989 represented another extreme manifestation of communal forces. The demolition of Babri Masjid on 6th December 1992 may be acknowledged as turning point in majoritarian communalism and impunity. The killing of Graham Stains and his sons in Orissa was another gruesome aspect of the communalism in addition to Godhra violence. Constitution provisions for thc minorities have been communalized to an extent that any question on the special status of the minority governed states and minority rights like implementation of Article 370 or Constitution regarding the Kashmir and the Anandpur Sahib Resolution passed by Akali Dal to demand more autonomy for the state are taken as part of the secessionist communal agenda by the minorities. The political discourse under which the future of human rights has to be determined in India is being communalized to an extent that any dissent with the mainstream discourse can be taken as the anti-national.

The vacuum of charismatic leadership and decline of party politics in 1960's has been tilled with the sinister designing of communalising the social relation in the late 1970's and early 1980's by the new class of political elite in India. In this context, the notion of nation and national identity are hegemonically dependent on the idea of the 'enemy within'. Randhir Singh in his Five Lectures in Marxist Mode argued that the failure of the State owned model of the development, the administrative corruption and the failure or plan and plan holidays not only has enhanced the distance between the political leadership and people, however, it also has alienated them from the nation-building project or the ideals of the freedom struggle. Further the communalisation of politics and chauvinist nationalism or the ruling class has divided the social fabrics of India. The electoral politics has been dominated by bigotry slogan like "are you for National Unity or *Anti-Nationalist, for Nation or (United Liberation Front of Assam (ULFA)* and for Reservation or Anti-Reservation etc.? We can say that, the decline of politics and the division of people have not only helped the political elite to deny the basic rights to the people but it also strengthen the state repression.

The ruling class has been allegedly in alliance with the bourgeoisies for negating of issues of development and welfare by converting the development issues into the communal politics. The demand of the people for the democratic rights, like right to health, education and livelihood has been always converted into the divisive politics of caste and religion. The basic demand and the struggle for the basic rights of the people have been dealt as the law and order problem. The vitiation of the social environment and chauvinistic nationalism has always helped political elite to oppress the political opposition and to convert the democratic struggles into law and order problem.[20]

The communalization of state machinery and connivance of the administration into the communal 'violence against the Minorities' in India in the last 60 years further enrooted the crisis to the minority rights. The vitiation of social environment and political use of the "chauvinistic nationalism" and the communal use of the state forces not only threatened the minority rights but it also resulted into the crisis of governance. The armed secessionist movements for the socio-economic and political justice can be seen as the result of the crisis of the political governance in India.[21]

The other important issue of analysis related the human rights standards and culture in India is the government responses and measures which are being adopted by the Indian government to handle the ethnic-movements for the self-determination same holds for naxal movement for socio-economic justice. Definitely state measures against the militancy have provoked various extra-ordinary measures which have, in turn, promoted human rights groups into protests and challenge as the provision made under these extraordinary laws are in contradiction to the provisions of the protection of human rights made under the international human rights standards. The Terrorism and Disruptive Activities (Prevention) Act (TADA) was one such instance. The Armed Forces Special Powers Act (AFSPA) continues Encounter killings, forced disappearances and ineffectiveness or judicial system in places where extraordinary situation prevail, characterise the human rights related scenario.

There has been another aspect to the whole scenario. The militants who claim to fight for the rights to self-determination for the communities and socio-economic justice have been also violating the human rights. The nexus between the militants and the drugs smugglers was well exposed by the security forces in Punjab. The killings of the innocent civilians to take personal revenge have been also a dangerous trend for the violation of human rights during the militancy. The mass violence which has been reported to be adopted by the Sikh militants in Punjab has also become serious of human rights groups, mainstream media and academicians. We can refer to the criticism of the mass-violence of and the killing of some academicians by the Sikh secessionists in Punjab by the Amnesty International, academicians and journalists. The forced migration of Kashmiri Pundits and the killings of the minorities by the Bodos in the other secessionist states of India and Union Territories are also the matter of serious concerns for the human rights groups.[22]

The use and abuse of power both by the state as well as by the anti-state forces has been a matter of serious concern for the human activists and academicians, since the inception of secessionism and the state responses to the secessionists in India. The state responses to the secessionist movement in India can only be analysis from its legislative and security measure as till the date no movement for socio-economic justice and right to self-determination has been resolved through the democratic method, political concessions and dialogue.

It is pertinent to mention that the Punjab is the only state where the Union government is claiming to curb the Naxalite and well as the secessionist movement successfully. But the legislative and the security measures, which had been adopted by the state while dealing with the Naxalite and Sikh Secessionist have been bitterly criticized by the human rights groups' journalists and researchers across the globe. Simultaneously a section of Academia and human rights groups are also criticizing the violence and the methods to which were used by the Sikh secessionist against the civilians during the autonomy movement in Punjab.

Punjab is also the only state where the Supreme Court has handed over the cases of forced disappearance and illegal cremation of more than 2097 youths only in the three cremation grounds of Amritsar district to the National Human Rights Commission (NHRC). It is also the exceptional state where the relative of the victims of human rights has adopted the human rights jurisprudence to demand justice from the state at large.

Although the violence of the state and the militants has been ended with the suppressing or autonomist movement, however, the wounds which it left behind have a long-term effects on the psyche, health and economy of victims and their relatives. The legislative measures like TADA has come to an end in 1995 and the absolute majority of the persons who were arrested under the extraordinary provisions of TADA had been also released by the government from the various jails of Punjab without any conviction after spending many years in the different jails.[23] They have been starting their lives again: with physical and economic deficit due to the excess which was adopted by the police during their investigation and the bribe to which their families had given to the security forces to save their lives.

The worst is the position of the parents of innocent youths who were killed by the security forces and then illegally cremated in the two cremations of Amritsar and one at Tarn Taran. They had waited for years to come-out with the Central Bureau Investigation (CBI) investigation for recognisation of the dead bodies of their sons among the illegally cremated dead bodies by the security forces during the militancy. Their wait could bear any fruit if the C.B.I. had recognised that their sons were among the dead and illegally cremated, however, the C.B.I. denied the possibility or the recoganisation of majority of the illegally cremated dead-bodies and limited its inquiry only to the 582 illegally cremated dead bodies for investigation and compensation claim initially.

The worst outcome was the politicisation and communalisation of the human rights violation during the militancy. The human rights discourse has been communalised and challenged to an extent by the security forces in Punjab that the groups and activists who were working against the excess of the security forces are labeled as anti-nationalist and terrorists, even the personals of high reputation like the retire Justice Ajit Singh Bains who dared to speak against the police excesses was falsely fabricated in a case of Khalistan conspiracy registered at Anandpur Sahib. Although Justice Bains got his release after the partial inquiry appointed by Punjab and Haryana High Court but he was badly humiliated by the police during the time of his custody." [24]

On the other hand, those who voiced for humanism and true Sikhism and voiced against the brutal violence of the Sikh militants were also labeled as traitors and killed by the militants. The democratic voices could not get any space as the violence started; the whole period of militancy in Punjab had witness the rule of gun. The order of the state forces can shut mouths of the people and make them to stay under the sun in summer and in the field during the winter on the name of search operations and establishing the rule of the law. Simultaneously it can be the order of militants to shut the mouth and not to come out from the houses in nights and not to water the crops as the war for freedom was going on. The movement of people in the night can result into the killing as they can be taken as 'enemy' or security forces by the militants.

The various studies conducted on the militants and the state strategy to counter the militancy including our own field survey established the grim situation of human rights in Punjab. The common man or Punjab was denied of all his democratic and constitutional rights by the armed forces during the insurgency operations. Villagers were used as human shields and the brutal torture on the villagers occurred if any terrorists challenge comes to the security forces from the village.

To illustrate the above argument, one can refer to the excesses of the armed forces can be measured from the murder of well known human rights activist Jaswant Singh Khalra, who dared to file a petition in court against the violation of human rights by the security forces, even after the establishment of peace. All the legal measures like *habeas corpus* and campaign against the illegal picking of Khalra from the front of his house were adopted by the Khalra family but proved to be of no action by the state to correct its illegal act. Khalra was murdered by the police and his dead-body was disposed-off in the *Hari-Ke-Canal* head works after the brutal torture in the different police posts of Tarn Taran without recognizing his arrest.[25] The arrest and killing of Khalra was reported by the special police officer Kuldip Singh who later on became witness in court.[26]

The most unexpected was the organized and systematic campaign against the violation of human rights charges by the state coercive agencies during the insurgency operation in Punjab enjoying patronage from the political high and ups. The concerns of Home Ministry over the violation human rights and the protection of security forces against the human rights litigation particularly in Punjab and other states, where states are facing with the secessionists and naxal problems were expressed by Home Minister Mr. L.K. Advani then at a conference in Jalandhar showed the government attitude towards the human rights concerns in the conflicted states.[27] The other argument on prosecution of the security forces on the violation of human rights in Punjab is that the prosecution of the security forces in Punjab can demoralise the security forces in other states where they are fighting the same kind of militancy and violence for the national integration.

The much waited decisions of the National Human Rights Commission (NHRC) on the alleged forced disappearances and illegal cremations by the security forces particularly in Amritsar has also not helped to assuage the wounded psyche of the victims and their families. While deliberating over the issue, the NHRC has limited its decision over the illegal cremation and the critical matter of forced disappearance has been left upon while announcing the compensation. The total amount of Rs. 250 lakhs is announced as compensation to the relatives of those youths whose custody was recognised by the police before their killing, and the majority which was not recognised by the police before the killings and just their cremation by them as unidentified dead bodies is recognised have received the ashes of 1,75,000 thousands only.

The shock received by the parents of the victims of human rights violation and the human rights groups from the nationalist perspective and the lacking of support from the secular forces have made them alien and anti-nationalist in their own country. The suffering and the cold-blooded murder of large number of youths by the security forces for rewards and personal gains were and even now continue to be covered under the unique carpet of 'national integration'. The impunity to the members of the security forces against the alleged violation or human rights is against the "international human rights laws" and the sole of the "Indian constitution" and also damages the social fabric of the multinational state like India.

The closing of the investigation and rewarding of compensation to the next of kin raised the serious doubts on the government intention on the administration of criminal justice system and the rule of law in the state. Simultaneously the refusal of NHRC to investigate the cases of fake encounters and illegally cremation of dead bodies by the police during the terrorism outside the three crematorium of the Amritsar also creates doubts on autonomy and honesty of the investigating agencies of the state.

The state, of course can become oppressive tyrannical or dictatorial. But this sort of behaviour may lead to rebellion and revolution. In both cases, the rule of law is the causality. Human rights organizations are most concerned that in order to preserve an open society everybody observe the law. A state functionary has much duty to obey the laws as private citizen. Hence, it is imperative that a, government itself never violates laws if it is of retain that ultimate power of administering justice and maintaining law and order. For there is nothing more injurious of law and order than feeling that the guardian of law and order themselves are not orderly and little better than those whom the terms criminals and little better than those whom the law terms criminals and who are to be dealt with in accordance with the law by these very people.

The delicate task of human rights groups to monitor government agencies for wrongdoing is never appreciated by any government. Men, when clothed with statutory power and authority, behave like god-tyrannical gods at that. History proves that people in power behave arbitrary and whoever exposes them runs the risk of state power being used against him.

The major criticism against human rights organizations is that they are more concerned about the right of the prisoners and the rights of the suspects than the rights of their fellow citizen who are endangered by the acts of these suspects. The dominant powers and the government are able to mislead the people that these human rights groups are nothing more than front organizations for terrorists and extremists should be given a chance to prove that they arc suspected to be.

In fact, preservation of human rights standards is the only way to ensure that the nation-states or multi-national states like India remain stable and retain the loyalty of the citizens. Violation of the human rights either by the state or non-state agents undermines the legitimacy of the nation state and creates alienation among the victims. In the present post-Soviet world where there has been such an emphasis on democratization and concerns for human rights protection, a key component of 'good governance agenda' has been to ensure greater transparency and accountability from the political regimes. It has become imperative that a line of demarcation is drawn between the state and non-state coercive acts of violence/terrorism.

It is the basic argument that the non-state actors who are perpetrators of violence and infringement of the human rights must be punished by the state but strictly in accordance with law and human rights standards. The use of politics of fear for narrow electoral and short-term political gains serves to undermine the legitimacy and willingness of the state agencies to follow the cannons of human rights and work within the criminal justice system as mandated by the legal-constitutional order.

Notes and References

1. Editorial, 2011, "Republic Killing it own Children" and "Islam and Arab Spring", *Economic and Political Weekly*, December 10, pp. 8-9.
2. It is also argued that the decline of the communist rule and the falls of the dictatorship have paved the way or a resurgence of democracy human rights under the globalised capitalist economy. The recent assertion of the people of Libya against Colonel Gadaffi and Muhammad Hosni Sayyid-Mubark in Egypt can be seen as the triumph or democracy and human against the dictatorial regimes, which were the by-product of the Super-powers rivalries during the cold war. On the other hand, the demise of communism and welfare state is also taken as serious threat to the social security of weaker section and the working across the globe.
3. David P. Forsthy, 2000, *op. cit.* No. 6, p. 13. See also J.K. Chopra, 2010, *Human Rights and The Modern World,* D.P.S. Publishing House, New Delhi. pp. 38-68, 69-89. Margot E. Salomon, 2007, *Global Responsibility for Human Rights : World Poverty and the Development of International Law,* Oxford University Press, New York. The Resource : Part III, The Regional Human Rights System 4/6, www.un.org/socdev/enable/comp303.htm, 23-7-2010, African Commission on Human and Peoples' Rights Commission... www.achpro.org/ 23-7-2010, The African Human Rights System a critical evaluation...Hdr.undp. org/ en/reports/global/hdr2000/papers/MUTUA pdf. 24-8-2010. Regional human rights system

in other parts of the world. OHCR...Bangkok.thehr.org. 24-8-2010, Protection of Minority Rights in the Inter-American. www.ohehr.org/ documents Publications/Guide Minorities5en pdf, 24-8-2010. Inter-American Human Rights system, www1.umn edu/humanrts/inter-americansystem htm, 25-8-2010. Inter American Commission on Human Rights. Wikipedia the free...en.wikipedia org/Inter-american commission on Human rights 25-8-2010. The Inter-american Human Rights System-HREA. www hrea org. 25-8-2010. The League of Arab States and the Arab Charter on Human Rights. Wwwacthl orgarticles htm?article id 6, 25-8-2010. Human rights in Africa-wikipedia, the free encyclopedia. En Wikipedia org/wiki/Human rights in Africa, 25-8-2011. Human rights in the Arab world, www at bab com/arab/human htm, 26-8-2010. Document, The Casablanca Declaration. www.al-bab.com/arab/docs/ international/hr/1999.htm, 26-8-2010.

4. Human Rights Council, www.ohchr.org/english/bodies/hrcouncil, 5-4-2007.
5. Upendra Baxi, 2002, The Future of Human Rights, Oxford University Press, New Delhi, pp. 1-2.
6. R.J. Rummel while narrating the violation of human rights by the states has argued that the state of modern world are killer of the own people than the armies of the enemy countries. According to the data compiled by Rummel about 170 million persons were killed the state in democides and genocides from 1900 to 1987, about four times the total deaths in battles. R.J. Rummel, 1994, *Death by Government : Geocide and Mass Murder Since 1900*, N.J. Transaction Publishers, Brunswick, U.S.A., pp. 51-67.
7. Robin M. Williams Jr. 2004. *The Wars Within: Peoples and States in Conflict*, See chapter 10. "Termination, Accommodation and Resolution". And chapter II, "Peace at last? Reflection on the Paths towards Reconciliation and Reconstruction", Manas Publications, New Delhi, pp. 236-63 to pp. 288-91.
8. Andreas Wimmer, 2002. *Nationalist Exclusion and Ethnic Conflict: Shadow of Modernity*, Cambridge University Press, Cambridge, pp 4-5.
9. Rita Manchanda 2010, "Ethnic Kin Slates", Rita Manchanda (ed). *States in Conflict with their Minorities,' Challenges to Minority Rights in South Asia*, Sage Publications, New Delhi, pp. 5-6.
10. Ashis Nandy, 2010, "Violence Culture Diversity and the Fantasies of a Monolithic Nation State", Rita Manchanda (ed.). *op. cit.*, 10, pp. 313-39.
11. Andreas Wimmer, 2002. *op. cit.*, No. 7, pp. 13-14.
12. Randhir Singh, Five Lectures in Marxist Mode, Ajanta Publication, New Deihi, pp. 39-40, 61-72.
13. Human Rights Speeches, Nhrc.nic.in/speeches.htm, 4-1-2012.
14. Security with Human Rights Amnesty International, www.Amnesty. org/en/campaigns/security-with-human-rightscached, 4-1-2011.
15. Terrorism, counter terrorism and international law, www.hrschool.org/ doc/manifile.php/lesson22/83/cached, 4-1-2012.
16. Ashwani Ray, 2003, Human Rights Movement in India; A Historical Perspective, *Economic and Political Weekly*, Vol. XXXIII No. 31, August 15, pp. 3409-341.

17. We can refer to use of PIL, by the Civil Liberties and Human Rights groups against the excess which is adopted by the state agencies during the extraordinary situation. The women activism and demand for the fast trial and special provision for the victims of rape including the providing of advocate on the state expenses at the time of registration of F.I.R and the hearing of case in the special have all been the result of PIL. The long legal battle of the people from the river valley or Narmada under the *Narmada Bachao Andolan* for the basic rights and protest against the armada Hydel Project to which they lost in the Supreme Court and latter on their campaign for suitable compensation and rehabilitation through the democratic protest in the national Capital can be connected with the above argument.
18. Gurpreet Mahajan and Srinder Singh Jodhka, 2012, Religion Democracy and Governance: Space for the Marginalised in Contemporary India, *Economic and Political Weekly,* Vol. XLVII, No. 1, pp. 45-52.
19. Randhir Singh, 1993, *op. cit.*, No. 12, New Delhi, pp. 39-40, 61-72.
20. *Ibid.*, p. 27, see also, Ashgar Ali Engineer, 2002, "State and Civil Society", Somen Chakraborty and R.M. Pal, *op. cit.*, pp. 1-18. See also Asghar Ali Engineer, 1991, "Is India for Hindus only", A.R. Desai, *op. cit.*, No. 29, p. 6, Gobind Mukhoty and Rajani Kothari, 1991. "Who are the Guilty", 'Punjab, The Delhi Riots and Parliament Power Politics—Main Culpability of Congress-I'. A.R. Desai, *op. cit.*, No. 29, pp. 33-60. Special correspondent, 1984, "Who are Guilty", *Economic and Political Weekly,* Vol. XIX, No. 47, November, 24, pp. 1979-85. Romesh Thapar, 1984, "The So-Called Indira" *Economic and Political Weekly,* Vol. XIX, No. 47, November, 24, p. 1975, Romesh Thapar, 1984, "The Truth is Savage", *Economic and Political Weekly,* Vol. XIX, No. 48, December 1, p. 2017, Sumantra Banerjee, 1984, "Contradiction With a Purpose". *Economic and Political Weekly,* Vol. XIX, No. 48, December 1, pp. 2028-31, Bharat Dogra, 1984, "Rehabilitation of Riot Victims", *Economic and Political Weekly,* Vol. XIX, No. 50, December 15, p. 2111-12, Romesh Thapar, 1984. "The Rajiv Party and Hindu", *Economic and Political Weekly,* Vol. XIX, No. 50, December 15, pp. 2105-06, Special Correspondence. 1986. "Delhi. Terror in the walled City: A Report", *Economic and Political Weekly,* Vol. XXI, No. 17, April 26, pp. 728-32.
21. Asghar Ali Engineer, 2002, "State and Civil Rights", Somen Chakraborty and R.M. Pal, (eds.), *State and Civil Society: Revisiting Contemporary India*, Indian Social Institute, New Delhi, pp. 9-19. See also Gobind Mukhoty and Rajani Kothari, 1991, "Who are Guity?, "Punjab, Delhi and Parliament Power Politics—main Culpability of Congress-I". A.R. Desai, *op. cit.*, No. 29, pp. 33-59, 60-79.
22. Dang, Satpal, *et. al.* 2000, *Terrorism in Punjab,* Gyan Publishing House, New Delhi. See also: TNS, 2006, "Protest against killing of student: Harkat militant killed", *The Tribune,* August, 10. TNS, 2006, "12 students hurt in police action", *The Tribune.* August 11, H.T. News Service, 2006, "Justice Y.K. Sabharwal, Human Rights: State commissions need teeth", *Hindustan Times,* August 13.
23. It is to note that the statistics concerning TADA are quite startling. As of June 1994 total persons arrested under TADA had crossed 76,000 people of these 25 per cent of cases were dropped by the police itself

without of any charges being framed. Trials were completed in about 35 per cent of cases that were actually brought to trials, of these 95 per cent ended in acquittals. So that finally 1 percent of those arrested were actually convicted. It is to note that absolute majority among these cases was from Punjab. Ujjwal Kumar Singh, 2003, Democratic Dilemmas: Can Democracy do without Extraordinary Laws, *Economic and Political Weekly*, February 1, p. 439.

24. Ajit Singh Bains, 1992, State Terrorism and Human Rights, *Seminar*, Vol. 398, October, pp. 36-41.
25. Although the identification of the police persons who abducted Mr. Khalra was done by Mandip Singh, a journalist with Indian Express and Mr. Rajiv Singh Randhawa who were with Mr. Khalra for a interview at the time of abduction of Mr. Khalra by the police. Ram Naryan Kumar, 2003, *Reduced to Ashes: The Insurgency and Human Rights in Punjab*, South Asia Forum for Human Rights, Kathmandu.
26. *Ibid.*, p. 9.
27. A Judicial Blackout: Judicial Impunity for Disappearances in Punjab. www.law.harvaed.edu/studorgs/iss15/kaur/shtml, 3-1-2012.

Index